CLASSICAL INFLUENCES ON
EUROPEAN CULTURE
A.D. 500–1500

CLASSICAL INFLUENCES ON EUROPEAN CULTURE A.D. 500–1500

❧

PROCEEDINGS OF AN
INTERNATIONAL CONFERENCE
HELD AT KING'S COLLEGE, CAMBRIDGE
APRIL 1969

❧

EDITED BY R. R. BOLGAR

❧

CAMBRIDGE
AT THE UNIVERSITY PRESS
1971

Published by the Syndics of the Cambridge University Press
Bentley House, 200 Euston Road, London N.W.1
American Branch: 32 East 57th Street, New York, N.Y.10022

© Cambridge University Press 1971

Library of Congress Catalogue Card Number: 77–113599

ISBN: 0 521 07842 3

Printed in Great Britain
at the University Printing House, Cambridge
(Brooke Crutchley, University Printer)

PREFACE:
THE KING'S COLLEGE CONFERENCE

In 1963 Lord Annan proposed to the governing body of King's College, Cambridge, of which he was then Provost, a modest enlargement of the traditional rôle of a Cambridge or Oxford college. By a tradition which dates from the monastic institutions of the Middle Ages, these colleges have been places of residence and education. Research, along with laboratories, lectures and examinations for degrees, has been the province of the University. Provost Annan's proposal was that King's College should establish a research centre of its own where its Fellows could further projects in which they were interested. He had in mind both long-term group activities, for which the College would provide facilities (including Fellowships where appropriate) but not finance, and short conferences, for which it would be wholly responsible. The governing body agreed that the new buildings it was planning should include a research centre. These buildings, associated with the name of Lord Keynes, formerly Bursar of the College, were completed in 1967.

As soon as Lord Annan's proposal was accepted, Dr Bolgar and I applied for help with a conference on classical influences, a subject in which we were both interested. Having taken this step, our first thought was to ask for advice and assistance from the Warburg Institute, and these were generously given by its Director, Professor E. H. Gombrich and its Librarian, Mr J. B. Trapp. Of the limited number of periods which could be offered to us, we chose 8–12 April 1969. Unfortunately, this proved to clash with the annual conference of medievalists at Spoleto and lost us some speakers we should have welcomed.

Our next task was to decide what form the conference should take. The field of classical influence has been very unequally explored. Some parts of it are known in great detail. Other parts remain virtually uninvestigated, their very existence hidden from all but a few specialists. It seemed therefore that the most useful function a conference could perform would be to bring to light the avenues which, given the present state of our knowledge, research could most usefully follow. We hoped that if we brought together a body of scholars with varied but overlapping interests, all concerned with the survival of antiquity their discussions would draw the map of what has been discovered and indicate the obvious gaps which remain to be filled. To help with planning and running the Conference we needed a Cambridge committee and were fortunate to secure as colleagues Professor J. A. W. Bennett, Dr P. Boyde, Mr E. P. M. Dronke, Professor L. S. Forster and Mr E. J. Kenney. We decided after some heart-searching to restrict our field to the influence of Roman antiquity. It is true that Greece and Rome cannot be effectively separated, as can be seen from the numerous references to Greek authors which will be found in this volume. But to bring in Greek studies during the Middle Ages is to bring in Byzantium; and that is a huge subject, which would have needed a much longer conference to do it justice.

Our freedom of action was circumscribed by practical considerations. The capacity of the College's private dining-room limited the number of invited guests to between thirty and forty. We had about that number coming from outside Cambridge; and if the majority of them were to be given a chance to speak, then it was obvious that the amount of time allotted to each would have to be severely curtailed. Some authorities, chosen as representative, were asked to speak for half an hour. Others, often no less distinguished, were invited to make shorter ten- to fifteen-minute communications if they chose. No suggestion was made as to topics, and the field was so wide that in the event there proved to be hardly any instance where one encroached upon another.[1] In addition to those specially invited, other scholars from Cambridge and elsewhere were encouraged to attend. We had decided to save valuable time by omitting complimentary speeches of introduction and thanks and by having no formal discussion. This was in the belief that the time saved would be more fruitfully employed in private conversation, both among the guests themselves and between them and the outside visitors who came for particular sessions. They came as it turned out in large numbers, attendance at the sessions varying between forty and seventy-five, and the contacts which were made proved to be a most useful aspect of the Conference.

[1] We are acutely aware that through ignorance or oversight we must have overlooked some scholars who had a good claim to be invited, had there been room. We were also very sorry that Professors T. Kardos, C. Leonardi, C. Mohrmann and A. Perosa, Dr R. Walzer and Mlle M.-Th. d'Alverny, having originally accepted, were eventually prevented from coming. Mlle d'Alverny's paper was however read by her collaborator, Mme Garand, while an English summary of Professor Kardos's contribution was read by Dr Bolgar. Both are printed in this volume, Professor Kardos's in its original form.

It remains to say that the Cambridge University Press paid us the compliment of agreeing to publish these Proceedings; and we are particularly indebted to the Syndics and their officers. But the Conference Committee would like also to record their appreciation of Professor Schalk's kindness who, approached by Professor Forster on our behalf, consented to see that the Proceedings were published in the series *Wege der Forschung*, if the Cambridge Press proved unable to undertake the work.

Since this Preface was written we have had the sad news of the death of Professor Weiss. The final draft of the paper included in this volume must have been one of the last things he wrote. Its quality shows the measure of his scholarship and the extent of our loss, which are brought to mind also by the recent publication of his book *The Renaissance Discovery of Classical Antiquity*, the first full study of the beginnings of classical archaeology. But the memory of his unfailing kindliness and charm, seen last in the pleasant surroundings of a friendly gathering, will remain part of everyone's recollections of the King's Conference.

L. P. WILKINSON

EDITOR'S NOTE

The papers do not follow here the order in which they were delivered at the Conference. They have been arranged in six groups according to subject and then chronologically in each group so as to provide a more connected story. It is a rough and arbitrary arrangement for which no great claims can be made. Many speakers discussed a wide range of topics, and their papers could figure with equal justice in some other group. This is particularly true of Professor Bischoff, Professor Courcelle and Professor IJsewijn. The chronological order is equally uncertain. Many papers cover large periods of time and overlap their predecessors and successors, and what is perhaps a more serious blemish, some adventure well beyond the fifteenth century, so that the retention of our original title with the date 1500 is not easy to justify. It was felt however that this title was still the one which best reflected the central purpose of the conference, and justifiably or not, it has been kept for that reason.

Authors were asked to correct their contributions, and in some cases substantial notes have been added.

Since the original purpose of the Conference was to call attention to the gaps in our knowledge of the survival and revival of Antiquity, it seems appropriate to call attention here to the item 'Research Opportunities' in the Index which lists the pages where some obvious gaps are specifically indicated.

Finally, the editor would like to take this opportunity to offer his personal thanks to the Syndics and Staff of the Cambridge University Press; and also to Mrs Julie Bird, Administrative Secretary of the King's College Research Centre, without whose constant help neither the Conference, nor this book would have got off the ground.

CONTENTS

CONTENTS

ILLUSTRATIONS

PLATES

(between pp. 272 and 273)

ILLUSTRATIONS

FIGURES

ACKNOWLEDGEMENTS

Acknowledgement is due to the following for their permission to reproduce the plates listed: Alinari Fratelli, Florence, for Plates 5*a*, 6*b*, 7*a* and *b*, 9*b*, 10*b*, 11*b*; The Biblioteca Comunale, Siena, for Plate 8*c*; The Biblioteca Reale, Turin, for Plates 3*c* and 8*d*; The Courtauld Institute, University of London, for Plates 6*c* and 12*b*; The National Gallery, London, for Plate 10*d*; Opera della Primaziale Pisana, for Plate 2; Soprintendza alle Gallerie, Florence, for Plates 5*b*, 8*a* and *b*, 9*a* and 12*a*; The Galleria degli Uffizi, Florence, for Plates 3*a* and *b* and 4; The University Library, Cambridge, for Plate 1; The Royal Library, Copenhagen, for Plate 11*a*; The Vatican Library, Rome, for Plate 12*c*.

CONTRIBUTORS

Professor A. H. ARMSTRONG is Gladstone Professor of Greek in the University of Liverpool. He is editor and part-author of the *Cambridge History of Later Greek and Early Medieval Philosophy* (1967).

Professor Dr L. BIELER is Professor of Palaeography and Late Latin, University College, Dublin. He is the author of *Das Bild des göttlichen Menschen in Spätantike und Frühchristentum* (1935–6); *The Life and Legend of St Patrick* (1949); *Ireland: Harbinger of the Middle Ages* (1963); *History of Roman Literature* (1966); and the editor of *Libri Epistolarum S. Patricii* (1952) and *Boethius: Philosophiae Consolatio* (1957).

Professor G. BILLANOVICH is Professor of Medieval and Humanistic Philology in the Catholic University of the Sacred Heart, Milan, and editor of *Italia medioevale e umanistica*.

Professor B. BISCHOFF, Hon. D.Litt. (Dublin), Hon. D.Litt. (Oxford) is Professor Ordinarius of Medieval Latin Philology in the University of Munich. He is the author of *Die südostdeutschen Schreibschulen und Bibliotheken in der Karolingerzeit*, I (1940) and *Mittelalterliche Studien*, I and II (1966/7).

Dr R. R. BOLGAR is Fellow of King's College, Cambridge. He is the author of *The Classical Heritage and its Beneficiaries* (1954).

Professor T. BUDDENSIEG is Professor of Art History, Free University of Berlin.

Mr H. BURNS is a lecturer at the Courtauld Institute of Art, University of London.

Professor P. COURCELLE is Member of the Institut de France, Professor of Latin literature in the Collège de France and Directeur d'Études at the École Pratique des Hautes Études. He is the author of *Les Lettres grecques en Occident de Macrobe à Cassiodore* (1948, Eng. tr. 1969).

Dr M.-TH. D'ALVERNY is Directeur de Recherche at the Centre National de la Recherche Scientifique and lecturer at the Centre d'Études médiévales at Poitiers. She was editor in chief of the *Catalogue général des manuscrits latins de la Bibliothèque Nationale*, 1946 to 1963 and is the author of *Avicenna latinus* (8 fasc. publ. 1960–8).

Mr P. DRONKE is Fellow of Clare Hall and Lecturer in Medieval Latin in the University of Cambridge. He is the author of *Medieval Latin and the Rise of the European Love-Lyric* (2nd ed. 2 vols. 1968), *The Medieval Lyric* (1968) and *Poetic Individuality in the Middle Ages* (1970).

CONTRIBUTORS

Mrs U. DRONKE is Fellow of Clare Hall, Cambridge and the editor of *Þorgils Saga ok Hafliða* (1952) and *The Poetic Edda*, I (1969).

Mme M. GARAND-ZOBEL is Chef de la Section de paléographie at the Institut de Recherche et d'Histoire des Textes.

Dr L. GARGAN is Deputy Head Librarian and Lecturer in Palaeography and Diplomatic in the Catholic University of Milan. He is the author of 'Giovanni Conversini e la cultura letteraria a Treviso nella seconda metà del Trecento', *Italia medioevale e umanistica*, VIII (1965) and *Lo Studio teologico e la biblioteca dei domenicani a Padova nel Tre e Quattrocento* (Padua, 1970).

Dr A. GERLO is Rector of the Vrije Universiteit Brussel and Director there of the Institut pour l'Étude de la Renaissance et de l'Humanisme. He is the editor of *Tertullianus, de Pallio* (2 vols. 1940) and *La correspondance de Juste Lipse conservée au Musée Plantin-Moretus* (with H. D. L. Vervliet and I. Vertessen, 1967); and the author of *Inventaire de la correspondance de Juste Lipse 1564–1606* (with H. D. L. Vervliet, 1968) and *Erasme et ses portraitistes* (1969).

Professor E. H. GOMBRICH is Director of the Warburg Institute and Professor of the History of the Classical Tradition in the University of London. He is the author of *The Story of Art* (1950), *Art and Illusion* (1960), *Meditations on a Hobby Horse* (1963) and *Norm and Form* (1966).

Dr R. W. HUNT, F.B.A. is Fellow of Balliol College, and Keeper of Western Manuscripts in the Bodleian Library, Oxford. He has been the editor (with R. Klibansky) of *Medieval and Renaissance Studies*.

Professor J. A. M. K. IJSEWIJN is Professor Ordinarius and Director of the Seminarium Philologiae Humanisticae in the University of Louvain. He is the editor of *Humanistica Lovaniensia* and the European editor of *Neo-Latin News*.

Dr E. JEAUNEAU is Maître de Recherche at the Centre National de la Recherche Scientifique in Paris. He is the editor of *Guillaume de Conches: Glosae super Platonem* (1965) and *Jean Scot: Homélie sur le prologue de Jean* (1969).

Professor T. KARDOS is Professor of Italian Language and Literature in the Eötvös Loránd University, Budapest and a Corresponding Member of the Hungarian Academy of Sciences. He is author of (titles translated from the Hungarian) *Medieval Culture, Medieval Poetry* (1941), *Antique Traditions of the Hungarian People* (1942), *The Age of Humanism in Hungary* (1955), *The Romance of Árgirus* (1967).

CONTRIBUTORS

Mr E. J. KENNEY is Fellow of Peterhouse and Lecturer in Classics in the University of Cambridge. He is the editor of *P. Ouidi Nasonis Amores, Medicamina Faciei Femineae, Ars Amatoria, Remedia Amoris* (1966) and part-editor of *Ouidiana Graeca* (1965) and *Appendix Vergiliana* (1966).

Dr C. N. J. MANN is Lecturer in French in the University of Warwick.

Professor F. SCHALK is Professor of Romance Philology and Director of the Romanisches Seminar and Petrarca-Institut in the University of Cologne. He is the author of *Moralisti italiani del rinascimento* (1940), and *Das Publikum im italienischen Humanismus* (1954) and the editor of *Die Celestina* (1959) and *Alberti: vom Hauswesen* (1962).

Professor D. SCHALLER is the Director of the *Mittellateinisches Seminar* in the University of Bonn.

Dr B. SMALLEY, Emeritus Fellow, St Hilda's College, Oxford is the author of *English Friars and Antiquity in the Early Fourteenth Century* (1960).

Professor R. D. SWEENEY is Associate Professor of Classics in the Vanderbilt University, Nashville, Tennessee. He is the editor of the *Catalogus Codicum Classicorum Latinorum* (in progress).

Mr J. B. TRAPP is the Librarian of the Warburg Institute, University of London.

Professor S. VIARRE is Professor of Latin in the University of Lille. She is the author of *L'Image et la pensée dans les Métamorphoses d'Ovide* (1964) and *La Survie d'Ovide dans la littérature scientifique des XIIe et XIIIe siècles* (1966).

Professor R. WEISS was Professor of Italian in the University of London, and the author of *Humanism in England during the Fifteenth Century* (3rd ed. 1968) and *The Renaissance Discovery of Classical Antiquity* (1969).

Professor J. H. WHITFIELD is Serena Professor of Italian Language and Literature in the University of Birmingham. He is the author of *Petrarch and the Renascence* (1943), *Machiavelli* (1947), *Dante and Virgil* (1949), *Giacomo Leopardi* (1954), *A Short History of Italian Literature* (1960), *Leopardi's Canti Translated into English Verse* (1962), *Discourses on Machiavelli* (1969), etc.

Mr L. P. WILKINSON is Brereton Reader in Classics, Orator and Fellow of King's College in the University of Cambridge. He is the author of *Horace and his Lyric Poetry* (1945), *Letters of Cicero* (1949), *Ovid Recalled* (1955), *Golden Latin Artistry* (1962) and *The Georgics of Virgil* (1969).

INTRODUCTION:
A WAY AHEAD?

R. R. BOLGAR

Was bedeutet das Nachleben der Antike? What we know about our debt to
Greece and Rome would fill a sizeable library, and yet Aby Warburg's question always catches us off balance so that we have to grope
for an answer. We have to admit that we are not in a position to
assess the full extent or the precise nature of our indebtedness to the
ancient world. After centuries of effort—fifteen centuries as a matter
of fact—we see ourselves still at the primitive stage of discovery,
where the unexplored ground before us is so vast that we can do no
more than just probe it at random. Like early travellers in Africa, we
are familiar with a stretch of coastline here, a river there, but the
overall plan of our continent is hidden from us.

The aim of the King's College Conference, as first conceived, was
simply further reconnaissance, further probing in the unsystematic
manner that has so long characterised our field of study. We wanted
to pinpoint some ready openings for research. We made no arrange-
ments for covering the whole span of existing knowledge, so that
speakers were left free to select their own topics with only the proviso
that they chose something consistent with our exploratory intentions.
All the same, when one comes to examine the papers which were
read, one finds that nearly all the major divisions of our subject were
represented. Luck, it must be supposed, was on our side; and with its
aid, one can glimpse something of the way ahead.

My task is to construct a general picture, showing how the papers
printed here dovetail and supplement each other; and in doing this,
I shall call upon what I can remember of the talk that went on among
the participants. That informal talk was not uninformative. We shall
find Professor Billanovich referring in his paper to the *Italia medioevale
e umanistica* as his *kibbutz*, a co-operative of scholars. To have been
just such a co-operative is a claim which could be made at a more
modest level for the King's College Conference. As the days passed,
there grew up a feeling that a concerted effort was being mounted to
solve problems in which all were interested. What I shall have to say,
in so far as it is of value, will derive from this common inspiration.
Only the mistakes, the false assessments are my own: instances of

erroneous reporting. It often happens—and has happened here—that a shared enterprise of moment is delivered into the hands of a single fallible scribe.

What comes first of all into clear focus when we read the proceedings of the Conference is an urgent need of a most basic sort. Efficient work is impossible, if one has not ready access to the tools one requires. Our principal tools are the MSS in which the writings of the ancients have been preserved; and the facts about them provide the natural starting point for all our research. We want to know their contents, their location, their age, what has been discovered about the relations between them and the history of each. But as things stand at present our need for this information is hard to satisfy.

Professor Sweeney describes what must be a very common experience:

The classicist or textual critic who desires to know what the evidence for a given text might be immediately finds that there are very few definitive lists of MSS of individual works or authors. If he suspects that the lists which he does find are incomplete and feels compelled to do something about this, he rapidly finds himself involved in the singularly complex and unpleasant field of manuscript cataloguing.

We do not possess a comprehensive list of all available classical MSS; and even lists which would give every example of a particular text or of the works of a particular author are in very short supply. It is significant of the present state of our knowledge that a recent excellent bibliography of the printed editions of Lucretius which was published in 1962 should have relegated the manuscript tradition to an appendix with the remark that a full description would demand a volume to itself,[1] and that now after another seven years the required volume still has not appeared.

Having drawn his gloomy picture of existing conditions, Professor Sweeney puts forward a plan for a comprehensive catalogue which is to cover everything written in Latin before A.D. 600, while its indexes will offer a ready guide to the manuscript tradition of every text and will enable scholars to trace not only the history of particular works, but also which works were in circulation in a given area at a given time. That such a catalogue would transform the study of classical influences goes without question. It would save individual research workers weeks, sometimes months, of labour, With it, the New World

[1] C. A. Gordon, *A Bibliography of Lucretius* (London, 1962), p. 279.

would redress in a most decisive manner the procrastinations of the Old.

Later however we listened to another paper which is bound to cast some doubt on the feasibility of Professor Sweeney's project. This concept of a comprehensive catalogue had been in the mind of Félix Grat when in 1937 he founded the *Institut de Recherche et d'Histoire des Textes*; and the communication which bears the names of Mlle d'Alverny and Mme Garand, giving an account of the work of this Institute, tells us that after a third of a century of steady effort its research teams have not yet completed the inventory of the MSS of Latin texts written before A.D. 400, of which Grat had dreamt. Much has been done, but not all. A list of authors and works has been compiled with tables of *incipits* and *explicits*. The relevant Latin MSS in the *Bibliothèque Nationale* as well as a number located outside France have been rigorously surveyed. A complete inventory of those in French provincial libraries is being prepared, and a similar inventory for the Vatican Library is almost ready for publication. But it is plain that these very considerable achievements still leave ground to be covered.

It is normal for work which demands expertise and a meticulous attention to detail to proceed at a slow pace; and one is bound to ask oneself if Professor Sweeney and his collaborators will be able to make the speedy progress they anticipate. But surely there is a chance that they will. It would be invidious to credit them with more energy or a larger measure of technical inventiveness than their predecessors in the field. But there are, it would seem, some considerations which tell in their favour. First, the labours of the Institute, interrupted anyway by a major war, have not been exclusively directed to the preparation of a Latin catalogue. Secondly, a new enterprise launched today is bound to benefit from what has been already achieved. Thanks in great part to the labours of the Institute, we do not stand where we stood in 1937. Finally—and this is perhaps the most important factor—the catalogue which Professor Sweeney has planned will be more concise in its descriptions than has been the practice in the past. Information about the physical make-up of MSS will be cut to a minimum. This is a case where less may easily mean more.

A *Catalogus Codicum Classicorum Latinorum* may well appear in our lifetime. But one is tempted to ask—what of the rest? We are not concerned in this volume with studies outside the field of classical Latin, but it would be absurd to avoid mentioning that Professor

Sweeney's project ought to be followed, if not accompanied, by similar projects to cover ancient Greek and patristic texts. Something of the sort was mooted for Greek more than ten years ago by A. Juilier at the eleventh international congress of Byzantine studies;[1] and it is interesting to note that here again, the suggestion was for an inventory of a more summary kind than usual, designed primarily, as Professor Sweeney's will be, to serve the purposes of literary scholarship.

Alongside this question of the cataloguing of MSS, to which these two papers are dedicated, we have to place the putting into order of another important source of information which we find mentioned by Professor Sweeney and Dr Hunt. The study of classical influences has been greatly indebted to surviving accounts of medieval and renaissance libraries, lists of books purchased, lists of *desiderata*, references in letters to what a man read, bought or borrowed. From the time of Gustav Becker, efforts have been made to consolidate this material without definitive success. Paul Lehmann's noble edition of the medieval catalogues of Germany and Switzerland covered substantial ground, but remained unfinished after his death, and its completion is now likely to be on a less elaborate scale. Renaissance catalogues have been individually edited, but no one has tried to bring them together in a single conveniently comprehensive work.

The difficulties which would face an editor of this material are admittedly formidable. To start with, new lists are constantly being discovered. Professor Billanovich mentions the forthcoming publication by T. Foffano of a memorandum which Niccoli composed for Cosimo de' Medici, listing for him MSS which were believed to be available in the libraries of Northern France; and Dr Gargan discusses in this volume an inventory which describes the collection of a fourteenth-century bibliophile, Oliviero Forzetta. Where these two young scholars have harvested, others will no doubt harvest in their turn; and an end to the process is not yet in sight. Moreover the information which inventories and lists provide cannot be dissociated from kindred details which the study of a MS can bring to light. It is by combining facts from a variety of sources that scholars have been able to reconstitute some of the important book collections of the

[1] A. Dain, *Les Manuscrits*, 2nd ed. (Paris, 1964), p. 80: 'En 1958, lors de la session à Munich du XIe Congrès international des Etudes Byzantines, A. Juilier, qui ne manque pas de courage, a présenté un système simplifié de catalogage des manuscrits grecs, qui permettrait un inventaire général de tous nos fonds. L'idée est à suivre. Conçu en effet sous forme d'inventaire sommaire, ce travail sera peut-être un jour réalisable.' I owe this reference to Professor Dale Sweeney.

Renaissance; and their hard-won conclusions ought to figure in any general survey, a requirement which raises Heaven knows how many problems of copyright.

Nevertheless it is evident that here too we need a vast project, as bold as Professor Sweeney's, to bring order into chaos. A comprehensive catalogue of classical MSS and an equally comprehensive survey of medieval and renaissance libraries emerge as our most urgent requirements. But they are not the only ones. We have still another set of tools to consider. There is not a paper in this volume which does not rest some part of its argument on writings composed during the Middle Ages or the Renaissance. If we want to establish what the classical heritage meant to later generations, we cannot avoid using the records which these generations left behind them; and we need to have these records readily available, not only to experienced scholars in favoured libraries, but to young research workers everywhere.

This is a *desideratum* which was not stressed in the formal part of the conference except by Professor Bischoff, who mentioned it in connection with twelfth-century commentaries, and by Professor IJsewijn, who called for up-to-date editions of the first Netherlands humanists. But the need is more general and so ought perhaps to be given emphasis here. When we try to familiarise ourselves with the literature of the Middle Ages and the Renaissance, we find ourselves well enough served so long as we stick to the vernaculars. Let us turn however to the more important field of Latin writing, and we come across some distressing *lacunae*. The urgency of the problem is to some extent blurred by the existence of Migne's huge collection. But the *Patrologia* is less useful than we generally imagine. Its possession is restricted to a relatively small number of libraries; and huge as it is, it omits a great deal and is often inaccurate. Nor does it contain those aids to learning, the critical apparatus, the historical and philological commentaries, the indispensable cross-references that a modern scholar faced, say, with a classical text regards as his due. Even for the works it covers new critical editions are often needed.

It is time someone edited William of Conches's *Dragmaticon* and *Philosophia Mundi*. Hildegarde of Bingen clamours for attention. And what about Walter of Chatillon's *Alexandreis*, Joseph of Exeter's *de Bello Troiano*, Bernard Silvestris's *de Mundi Universitate* and Alan of Lille's *de Planctu Naturae*? The invaluable volumes of the *Monumenta Germaniae Historica* help us with the Carolingian poets. What Raby called sacred Latin poetry is available in extensive, if not always very scholarly, collections of hymns. But post-Carolingian secular verse is in many cases difficult to come by. There are some excellent editions of individual works, but many more are needed, if we want to discover how the poetic art of antiquity came to be absorbed into our poetic tradition.

In no other field of literary study is the apprentice scholar so straitened for good and easily accessible texts on which to work. And if the situation is bad where philosophy and poetry are concerned, we find it even worse when we come to look at educational works. Here the material which has been properly edited is very thin on the ground. Alberic de Monte Cassino's highly influential treatise, the *Rationes Dictandi* or *Breviarium de Dictamine*, which Professor Gerlo regards as the source of the medieval tradition in letter-writing, remains unpublished though an edition of it has been announced.[1] Much of Buoncampagno's work is similarly still in manuscript. But above all we need full critical editions of the medieval commentaries on classical authors. We have reason to be grateful to the scholars working on the *Catalogus Commentariorum*, but it is plain that their labours cannot stand alone. Several of our speakers (Professor Bischoff, Professor Courcelle, Dr Jeauneau) have mentioned particular texts which require editing. Even with an author as important as William of Conches, we find several commentaries, on Juvenal, Priscian and Boethius for example, which still await publication; and Petrus Helias's *Summa Prisciani* is another paradoxically neglected work.[2]

For the humanist period the picture is equally unsatisfactory. Much of the material we need to consult is still in manuscript, or we must hunt for it in rare printed texts. Only fragments have been edited of Bersuire's great moralisation of Ovid. Among the classicising friars whom Dr Smalley brought into prominence was the industrious and for his age curiously original Trevet. His commentaries have still to capture an editor's attention. Professor IJsewijn's paper tells us of the numerous gaps which must be filled before the study of early Netherlands humanism can be placed on a firm footing; and every reader of Professor Weiss's *Humanism in England in the Fifteenth Century* will call to mind a whole series of major texts—Whethamstede's works for example—which he would like to see published.

[1] By H. H. Davis in *Medieval Studies* (1966).
[2] I am indebted to Mr E. P. M. Dronke for much of the material in the preceding two paragraphs.

Italy, the family seat of humanism, does no better. If you want a copy of Petrarch's complete works—to take the most telling example —you have to go back to the Basel printing of 1581, and this in spite of half a century of ardent labour by the scholars in charge of the *Edizione Nazionale*. It is true that this famous enterprise has covered a good deal of ground, and that several of Petrarch's major works have been independently edited during the last twenty years. But even so, the *de Remediis* has still to see its final ordering; and it is in Fracasetti's Italian translation that the *Seniles* are easiest to procure.[1] The Latin Petrarch remains difficult of access where a vernacular writer of equal stature, a Machiavelli or a Rabelais, can be bought without trouble by every student. And the handicaps which thwart us in the case of Petrarch thwart us (as might be expected) even more oppressively in the case of the lesser humanists: Boccaccio, Filelfo, Traversari, and a host of others.

We have been altogether too slow to recognise that our study of classical influences (and therefore our understanding of what antiquity means to us) is directly dependent on our knowledge of later Latin literature; and as a result, medieval and renaissance writers of Latin have for the most part been shockingly neglected. Place the work done on them alongside that which has been done on their vernacular contemporaries or on the classical authors, and its insufficiency will become obvious. Their further exploration and critical analysis must be the modern Latinist's first task.

Catalogues and editions, the infrastructure of scholarship, have to be provided, but the business of providing them is not easy to talk about, so that most of the speakers at the conference preferred to discuss the more colourful achievements and possibilities of research, and it is to this field we must now turn. The papers we are to consider can be divided for convenience into two categories. We have, on the one hand, those which deal with the problem of *what* classical texts or classical remains were studied, when, where and by whom; and on the other hand, we have those which deal with the allied problem of *how* these studies were conducted, how the influence of antiquity made itself felt.

The first of these categories is represented by the contributions from Professor Bieler, Dr Hunt, Professor Billanovich, the late Professor Weiss and Dr Gargan, by parts of Professor Courcelle's many-sided account of Augustine and Boethius and parts of the two

---

[1] I am indebted to Dr C. N. J. Mann for this material on Petrarch.

architectural surveys by Professor Buddensieg and Mr Burns. As we can see from the last three papers mentioned, the categories we have postulated—*what?* and *how?*—are not mutually exclusive. Every analysis of how a classical text or monument was used presupposes the assumption that it was known to the user. The distinction between the two approaches is one of emphasis.

Our attempt to discover openings for research had the incidental effect of throwing light on problems of method; and one can see in retrospect that it was bound to do just this. Facts derive their significance from the way they are selected and analysed. The quest for facts presupposes a survey of the techniques we use to learn about them. Read in conjunction, the papers we have listed above illustrate most of the techniques employed in tracing what was known about ancient literature at different times and places. Until recently, scholars were generally content to note obvious mentions of a classical work or obvious quotations and to treat these as proof that the work in question was familiar to a medieval or renaissance author. This naïve procedure dominates the argument not only in Sandys's *History of Classical Scholarship*, a product of the first decade of our century, but also in Max Manitius's monumental survey of medieval Latin literature, which belongs to its next twenty years. But since then we have seen the development of more sophisticated methods. These are characterised by a readiness to bring together information drawn from a number of different sources and by a much higher degree of critical rigour. Professor Bieler and Dr Hunt both direct our attention to the fact that quotations cannot be accepted at their face value as proofs of a direct acquaintance with a classical text. Such quotations often come from secondary sources—grammars or *florilegia*—whose possible use requires to be carefully checked. Dr Hunt also stresses the need to match quotations—and with even greater reason, apparent echoes—against our knowledge of which MSS were currently in circulation. If there was a *lacuna* in the only MS of a classical work known to have been around at a particular time, then a contemporary quotation derived, as it would seem, from the missing part would have to be scrutinised with unusual suspicion.

To some extent with Professor Bieler, and more decisively with Dr Hunt, we are introduced to the modern study of the interrelations, wanderings and ownership of MSS. This line of research had its roots in nineteenth-century textual criticism and in the problems created by the formula *recentiores non deteriores*. Its first foundations were laid by Sabbadini, but Professor Billanovich is the man who has made it so very much his own. It would be pointless for me to summarise his lucid account of forthcoming publications in his *Italia medioevale e umanistica*, which readers can turn to on a later page. The section on the Querinian *ad Lucilium* is the most interesting from the point of view of method, showing how palaeographical evidence, data from inventories and letters and the identification of particular annotators are woven into a conclusive argument. Close analysis of annotations is the main feature of this line of study and justifies the efforts made by the *Institut de Recherche et d'Histoire des Textes* to assemble samples of the handwriting of the best-known humanists. Reading Professor Billanovich's paper, we come to see why that collection fills a manifest need and could be usefully reproduced elsewhere.

Professor Weiss and Dr Gargan give us further examples of how the method which we have been discussing operates when applied to particular problems. Like proconsuls on the march they conquer fresh provinces for a growing empire. It is important to note that they do not claim the same degree of validity for all their findings. The name of a grammarian, a list of students, identifiable as belonging to Treviso, establish a Horace MS as present in that city during the thirteenth century. A marginal note by a fourteenth-century Veronese humanist shows him to have known the titles of many of Ausonius's works. What he says about the poet shows that he had read at least some of them. These are certainties; and they help us to form a new picture of the beginnings of humanism. But there are arguments alongside these findings which range from the almost certain to the probable, from the probable to the possible. That the Veronese humanist who listed the works of Ausonius had access to a MS containing them must be regarded as almost certain. That this MS should have been the one which Benzo d'Alessandria had seen in the Verona chapter library a few years before is only a little less probable. But the possibility that an Ausonius fragment sent to Politian in 1493 was part of the MS which Benzo saw is, let us face it, no more than a possibility. It has not the same likelihood as the instances mentioned earlier. The evidence is clearly stated; and to see a web of persuasion woven out of such varying elements is one of the seductions of this form of scholarship; but it is a scholarship that calls for attentive readers, if they are to avoid confusing conjecture and fact.

All these papers have however in addition that other interest which is more directly connected with the advertised aims of the Conference.

9

They call attention to possibilities which research could exploit straightaway. The motifs that Irish vernacular literature shares with the authors of antiquity may have something to tell us about the classical studies of the early Irish schools. The work of B. L. Ullman on the medieval *florilegia* ought to be continued.[1] The teaching of rhetoric in Ducento and Trecento Italy needs to be scrutinised centre by centre. The notebooks of renaissance architects—a mine of information about their attitude to Roman buildings—deserve meticulous examination. And it is worth noting that all these suggestions for research have an element in common. We have here fields of study which have already been probed to good effect; and the next step forward involves a systematic filling in of gaps. As with the cataloguing of MSS, we have reached a point where consolidation is the prime essential.

Studies of the '*what?*' type seem often to take it for granted that any information we acquire about the fortunes of the classical heritage is intrinsically worth having. That is an assumption which we all readily make; but in our more guarded moments we are all aware that it cannot stand. Our interest is not—and should not appear to be—an arbitrary enthusiasm. The truth is that the Greco-Roman past fascinates us because it has shaped our culture and therefore our lives; and a rational desire to know the manner of that shaping is what finally justifies our work.

It is not surprising therefore that the majority of the papers read at the Conference should have been concerned with the use which has been made of the classical inheritance, with cultural rather than purely historical or antiquarian issues.

How Roman civilisation transformed the thinking of later ages is such an enormous subject that we must divide it up somehow, if we are to keep control of our material even within the narrow range of topics that a single conference could cover. The most convenient divisions will be those which we normally establish between the different products of man's cultural activity. Language, creative literature, scientific knowledge and thought, architecture and the fine arts provide four obvious headings. To these four we must however add a fifth which will be of a rather different kind. In sculpture or architecture a classical work could make a direct impact on a medieval or renaissance imitator. But in language, literature and to some

[1] B. L. Ullman, 'Classical Authors in Medieval Florilegia', *Classical Philology*, XXIII (1928)–XXVII (1932).

extent thought, the impact was always moulded by the teaching given at school. Education therefore—the character of that teaching —is a topic all on its own and being in a way prior to many others requires to be considered first.

The history of education is a big subject, and it is known to offer a great number of opportunities for research. The medieval curriculum has not been adequately studied. Was there a fixed canon of authors? If so, when was this established? And what changes did it undergo?[1] Another problem concerns the teaching of verse composition. Where did it originate? Poetry was certainly read in the schools of Imperial Rome, and some teachers of grammar and rhetoric gained distinction as poets. Ausonius is an obvious example. But the writing of verse does not seem to have been systematically taught in antiquity, so that its emergence in the Carolingian schools requires explanation. And above all we need that detailed study of rhetorical teaching in the thirteenth and fourteenth centuries which Professor Billanovich calls for. It would do more than inform us about the classical reading of the age. It might demonstrate how that reading managed to exercise such a decisive influence when boys passed from rhetoric to logic at such an early age.

But what can tell us most about the methods of medieval teachers are probably the commentaries which they compiled, and it was this aspect of educational history which speakers at the Conference were most concerned to stress. A commentary is at once a record of its author's teaching and a guide which his successors would use. The ancient tradition of such writings survived in a number of examples, of which Servius on Virgil, Donatus on Terence and Macrobius on the *Somnium Scipionis* were perhaps the most popular; and by the Carolingian age the practices of biblical exegesis were there to provide a further model. (The interrelations of classical and biblical scholarship would, incidentally, furnish a most attractive subject for a thesis: they revolutionised each other in turn.)[2] Medieval commentaries on secular authors made their appearance at the end of the ninth century, and from that date onwards they were produced in large numbers. The need for modern editions of them has been

---

[1] Professor B. Bischoff mentioned that a pupil of his was working on this problem.

[2] Professor Bischoff's paper mentions the influence of biblical commentaries on the twelfth-century commentators on classical texts. The impact of classical scholarship on New Testament studies during the Renaissance is a commonplace of cultural history. For a later link between the two fields: L. D. Reynolds and N. G. Wilson, *Scribes and Scholars* (Oxford, 1968), pp. 138–9.

already mentioned. But there exists also an equal or even greater
need for an analytical study of the teaching aims and methods
which they embody.

Professor Bischoff's paper deals with scholia on the Satirists, dating
for the most part from the early twelfth century. Their debt to the
classical tradition of Servius was evident; but at the same time they
attempted to make the past comprehensible by likening it to the
present. This strikes the reader immediately as an interesting development, but its importance does not become fully evident until we have
read Dr Jeauneau's parallel paper on William of Conches. One
would not expect a commentator on Macrobius to illustrate his
material by references to the life of his times, and William does not
do so. But he does attempt to introduce an element of commonsense
explanation into Macrobius's mysticism. He brings Neoplatonism
down to earth, much as Professor Bischoff's commentators reduced the
strangeness of the classical world to the familiar detail of their own
when they called a Vestal Virgin an abbess. Taking the two accounts
together we glimpse what may have been a common rationalising
element in twelfth-century teaching. This is the kind of broad perspective that we want, not only for the twelfth-century commentators,
but also for their numerous successors in the later Middle Ages and
the Renaissance, about whom we know even less—at any rate as
educators. It is true that particular scholars like Trevet and Bersuire
are now being studied in detail,[1] and that allegorical interpretations
of classical works have aroused a measure of interest, but these are
isolated exceptions, and the field remains largely unexplored.

Another aspect of educational activity, the character of textbooks
in common use, is mentioned by Professor Gerlo and Professor
IJsewijn. Instruction in letter-writing formed in theory part of the
medieval rhetoric course, but the subject came to be studied independently and at certain periods and in certain places seems to have
replaced rhetoric altogether. Professor Gerlo surveys the textbooks
which the *dictatores*, as the instructors in letter-writing were called,
composed for their pupils. Many of these still await analysis and, since
the examples in them mirror the habits of the time, will have an
interest for social historians as well as for historians of education.
Professor IJsewijn's excellently informative paper covers some of the

---

[1] According to Dr Smalley, *English Friars and Antiquity in the Early Fourteenth Century*
(Oxford, 1960), Miss J. R. Dean has a study of Trevet's life and works in preparation.
Bersuire is being investigated in detail by Dr J. Engels.

same ground, but brings in works on rhetoric and poetics as well. We are left with the impression that the comparative study of text-books, like the study of commentaries, offers almost limitless opportunities for research. Which were the most popular? How do they differ one from another? Does their development parallel in any way the development we observe in the commentaries? Everything is still to be done.

We now come to a paper which seems to belong to the category we have been discussing, but whose inclusion in it must be justified on the grounds of probability alone, since nothing in the shape of hard evidence is available to us. Mr Kenney writes on the history of textual criticism—he is the only contributor to do so—in the brilliant tradition of Housman and Wilamowitz. The production of accurate texts has been for centuries the most respected branch of classical learning and has provoked its greatest intellectual triumphs, matching the finest achievements of chess and formal logic in complexity and imaginative depth. Textual critics, like teachers or commentators, can be said to have prepared the heritage of antiquity for public consumption; and it appears overwhelmingly probable that the changes they introduced into their texts did alter the ideas and the modes of expression which these texts transmitted. But paradoxically enough, these alterations have never been collected and analysed, so that we are in no position to assess their importance. For want of this evidence, which it would be easy to obtain, we cannot tell what it is precisely that the labours of scholarly correctors have added to our understanding of the ancient world.

On the allied problem of how much this added understanding contributed to classical influences on European culture, we are better informed. Mr Kenney brings facts to our notice which seem almost to settle the issue. He takes as his subject the development of textual scholarship between 1350 and 1550, and he demonstrates that up to the end of that period the critical techniques which we now associate with that scholarship were hardly used at all. Attempts were made at recension. A genius like Politian could hit upon the elimination principle; but the golden age of expertise lay still in the future. In short, the medieval and renaissance centuries, when the classical heritage played a predominant role in the dissemination of ideas and literary skills, were the very centuries when accurate texts were hardest to come by, while the achievements of a Bentley, a Lachmann, a Wilamowitz belong to an age when classical writings had ceased to make a really important direct contribution to man's intellectual growth. Even if (as is probably the case) textual criticism can be shown to have contributed notably to our understanding of classical writings, that contribution would seem to have come too late. Mr Kenney's salutary iconoclasm forces us to revise our views on the merits of medieval and renaissance scholarship and shatters a legend.

Our next category takes us from these propaedeutic labours of teachers and scholars to the use creative authors made of their classical models. And here again we find that a striking change has made itself felt during the last thirty years, a change parallel to the one which we noted when we were considering the study of what classical works were read, and which distinguishes the scholarship of Sandys from the scholarship of the *Italia medioevale e umanistica*. Up to the nineteen-forties it had been the practice to equate the use later authors made of classical texts with borrowings of an identifiable kind; and listing borrowed elements was the prime concern of every scholar who occupied himself with the relationship between the classical and the modern traditions.

The elements listed were almost infinitely various. We find among them, on the factual side, data about the physical and natural sciences, history, geography, ethics and politics, together with categories of explanation and theories about the nature of things. On the literary, and what it is convenient to label the imaginative, side, we have metres, stylistic devices, the formal characteristics of literary genres, imaginative concepts such as the earthly paradise (which fascinated John the Scot) or the personifications discussed by Professor Gombrich; and also stereotypes of emotional response, sentiment and sensitivity. These great accumulations of data, collected for the most part author by author, are very impressive; and no one is going to pretend that they are without value. One must always begin by taking a look at one's material, and in this case, since the material was not there to be inspected it had to be assembled. But in all branches of study the stage is reached sooner or later when we see— inevitably—that accumulation is not enough. Tracking down facts has a compulsive fascination; and it is possible to collect them for their own sake. But once they are collected, we weary of the sport. The mind demands something better.

Having discovered what was borrowed, even if one is far from knowing all that was borrowed, one is driven to ask what difference the borrowing made. It is the measure of this difference which justifies or fails to justify the whole laborious business of fact-collecting. What emerges from the papers here is that we have reached the point in the study of the classical heritage where the question of significance has become insistent. Interest has been shifting from the actual borrowings to the influence exerted by the borrowed material. Professor Whitfield makes this new orientation very clear:

> For to me it seems that the strength of the classical tradition is that it remained fertile for so long, over so wide an arc; and that the weakness of classical scholars is that they limit themselves to tracing the pure element like an electric current passing through a conduit, with here a point and there a point, but always the same current waiting to be tapped. Instead of watching the family grow, you are content to guard the parent stem.

It is foolish, he says, to be satisfied with looking for father's lineaments in the son. What is worth knowing is the function which inherited traits have in a new organism. Professor Whitfield sees the classical heritage as a creative force which inspired each person who came in contact with it according to his ability. This is undoubtedly the correct view; and if our study of classical influences is to develop, we must learn to handle our material in its dynamic aspects.

That task will not be easy. Mrs Dronke draws attention to some of its more obvious problems. Writing about the possible influence of Sallust on the historian, Snorri Sturluson, she asks:

> Was this influence only the initial stimulus to writing history at all, with the occasional copying of a mannerism of style—or was it a more subtle thing, an external influence that held up a mirror to the native traditions, stimulated self-recognition and developed in the native creative genius a power of coherence and of carrying through themes of imagination on a scale greater than oral tradition was capable of maintaining?

We have to choose between two alternatives. Did the study of Sallust impart just the idea of writing history, or did it impart the conception of history as a specific form of narrative built on an attempt to discover what had actually occurred? The difference is a subtle one. But it is all-important. And making lists of borrowings will not help us to decide the issue. What is needed is a perceptive analysis of the Norse historical tradition before and after Snorri which cannot be carried through without some knowledge of historiography and some critical acumen.

Moreover, difficult as it appears at first sight, the problem which Mrs Dronke poses can be seen on reflection to be a relatively simple one of its kind. A research worker who wanted to analyse some other major topic, such as the influence of Neoplatonism or that of classical mythology, along the lines she advocates would need to cover a more extensive field and master even subtler forms of expertise. While the patent borrowings which interested earlier generations of scholars could be substantiated piecemeal, creative influence must always be studied within a broad context that calls for great learning and effort. But the day is plainly coming when we shall have to take familiarity with broad contexts for granted as a necessary precondition for research in our field. What concerns us in the last analysis is not a series of mechanical echoes but, as Professor Whitfield points out, the dynamic relationship between the borrowed elements and the work which the borrower created.

This principle applies of course as much to language as to literature; and it is unfortunate that the Conference had no chance to discuss this point in connection with the development of Latin style. Professor Mohrmann was invited, but as matters turned out she could not come. The lack of a paper on linguistic problems is the result of an absence we had every reason to regret since there is no limit to the questions which suggest themselves. The general postulate that language shapes thought is easy to accept. But what significance must one attach to the replacement of an 'incorrect' idiom by a 'correct'—that is classical—one? What are the purposes served by harmony and rhythm, by the choice of a simple or a complex form of statement? What was the function of the norm which educated usage provided for French and English in the seventeenth century? Can it be said that classical Latin had this same function for the humanists? While some work has been done on patristic Latin— principally by Professor Mohrmann—the *florida verborum venustas* of the later Middle Ages and the classical usages of the humanists have not yet been submitted to close analysis. We have still to discover what criteria we ought to use when we compare the style of Petrarch with the style of Erasmus.

Such problems appear very daunting in the context of a dead language, and it seems safe to say that the critic who chooses literary topics has a more manageable task, but even so, his problems are considerable. We have here seven papers which deal with creative literature. They could not possibly cover the output of a millennium; and it would be useless to try to extract from them a picture of what has been done or what remains to do. The information they hold for us is again on the subject of method. We are still at the stage of having to decide how to handle our material, and they provide examples of formidably different techniques.

Tracing the whole history of Augustine's *Confessions* and the *de Consolatione Philosophiae* and touching upon every aspect of their survival, Professor Courcelle's paper plainly transcends the crude categories we have been using. He covers art, as well as literature and thought. But in so far as he deals with the question of literary influence, he can be said to take the ancient works as his starting point and then to list imitations and derivatives without analysing them in detail. What he produces is a summary guide that takes us actually over fifteen centuries. Professor Schaller and Professor Whitfield stand, as far as method is concerned, at the opposite end of the scale from Professor Courcelle. Professor Schaller's squabbling poets bring Charlemagne's court alive for us; and we enjoy the experience. But the emphasis is all on the medieval scene. We are left to guess at the part played by classical influences. Would Theodulf's irony have found such successful expression, if he had not read Ovid and Horace? Professor Whitfield is not quite so drastic in his disregard of antiquity. He mentions Lucian as his author's classical source. But the concession remains largely meaningless. His real concern is with Alberti and with characterising Alberti's work. Lucian just hovers as a presence off-stage.

These three scholars offer us a choice between a cause-oriented and an effect-oriented treatment. Mr Dronke and Professor Kardos achieve a synthesis which gives cause and effect, the classical model and the later imitation, almost equal weight. But to do this they have had to restrict themselves to the examination of what are essentially short passages of verse. Completeness has been gained at the sacrifice of scope.

Professor Kardos's genial sketch of Janus Pannonius shows that unlucky bishop using material from the *Tristia* to depict his own misfortunes. Since Janus's troubles did not correspond exactly to Ovid's —being compelled to leave Italy for less civilised, less comfortable surroundings was about all they had in common—this use of Ovidian themes results in a certain measure of exaggeration. The Hungary of Corvinus's golden age is painted in the bleak colours of Sarmatian Tomi. Professor Kardos protests at the unfairness of this, but clings to his conviction that Janus was genuinely concerned to identify himself with Ovid. The reader who may be unwilling on the evidence to credit Janus with an excessive capacity for self-deception is left puzzled and comes to suspect that this kind of analysis, if attempted, should be carried beyond a *simpliste* stage.

How that can be done, we learn from Mr Dronke. Having made honourable mention of scholars like Max Manitius and Paul Lehmann who assembled the details relevant to classical borrowing, he continues:

the next and equally important stage of enquiry [is] the evaluation of this evidence, the detailed literary study of the classical elements in medieval Latin verse, distinguishing their various functions and assessing for each poet what the classical elements contribute to his poetic intentions, to his artistry, to the fabric of his verse.

Convinced that the starting point for any study of classical influences must be a full critical understanding of later literature, he gives us an example of his method in a brilliant analysis of a passage from the *Waltharius*. What distinguishes his approach from the traditional one exemplified by Professor Kardos is the attention which he pays to the fabric of the verse and the possibilities of irony. He sees the classical references as existing at two levels in the reader's mind—the old and the new simultaneously—with the result that each illuminates the other. Medieval poetry is treated as the sophisticated product of a literary—perhaps an over-literary—culture; and it stands up to the test remarkably well. Mr Dronke's method is a most fruitful one. It could be applied to the work of any poet steeped in the ancient classics. Its only shortcoming, which derives from its very excellence, is that its findings depend on such detailed evidence. They are in fact for the most part constituted by the evidence itself, which cannot be generalised; and the method cannot therefore be applied successfully to a broad topic such as the one discussed by Professor Courcelle.

The remaining two papers in this category have an interest which is all their own. Mrs Dronke, writing on Norse literature, has a topic which covers developments over a large area during a long period of time. Consequently, she employs what I described earlier as a cause-oriented method of presentation. The evidence she gives us is conventional in character—with some notable exceptions. But the imaginative grasp which these exceptions display lifts her account right out of the conventional rut. She breaks new ground. She hammers home a truth implicit in Professor Whitfield's Alberti sketch, but which is here stated explicitly: that the influence exercised by classical reading is often on a scale that *Quellenforschung* of the 'A quotes B' type cannot expect to measure. The form given to a work of art, a writer's attitude to human behaviour and even something so intangible as the very idea of history can come to us from the Greco-Roman past and are among our greatest debts. The vague is more dynamic than the precise.

Dr Smalley's contribution is interesting because it represents a compromise between the techniques outlined above. She writes about the influence of Sallust, but she does not attempt to treat that influence in its totality. Working within the confines of a relatively short period of time, she selects certain themes and contents herself with analysing the response to her author as a moralist, a stylistic model and an historian. By these means, she produces a survey which is broad enough to touch on large issues, but which has enough detail to make it more than just a summary. Her approach is cause-oriented. She moves outwards from Sallust, but she has time to spare for his imitators, whom she characterises in some detail with reference to her chosen themes. To some extent therefore she satisfies Professor Whitfield's injunction that the study of classical influences should be based on a critical assessment of post-classical writings. And finally while she makes some use of evidence from quotations and obvious references, she leaves us in no doubt that the mainstream of Sallustian influence was general rather than specific, the product of inspiration rather than mechanical borrowing. What medieval historians derived from their reading of this Roman predecessor was an attitude to mankind, a cynical view of human motive, an interest in geographical, economic and social conditions, all traits capable of development, dynamic rather than static.

Dr Smalley demonstrates that a compromise between the old and the new methods is possible and may keep the advantages of both. But she had chosen her subject cleverly. Not every subject would lend itself easily to this kind of treatment, and not every mean is golden. Some formidable problems of method still remain to be solved.

We must now turn to the transmission of ideas. Unlike the literary field, where great efforts have been made to trace imitations of ancient writers or genres, the history of thought has little to show us by way of systematic explorations of classical influences. Some work has been done on Neoplatonism, on concepts like Caesarism or civility, but these enquiries have tended to be limited in their scope. The study of Plato and Aristotle in the Middle Ages and Renaissance has attracted a good deal of attention, but this has been more for the purpose of labelling particular thinkers as Platonists or Aristotelians than of portraying the transmission of a body of classical doctrine.

This lack of enterprise has plainly been due to the extreme complexity of the subject. Classical thought had reached medieval Europe through Christian sources long before the classical authors came to be widely read; and its Christianised interpretation continued to play an important part in European culture throughout our period. We cannot hope to form a clear picture of the influence which classical ideas exerted on medieval—or even renaissance—thinking without first having at our disposal an adequate analysis of the pagan element in patristic literature. But this analysis does not exist. So far only the groundwork for it has been laid, notably by Professor Courcelle.

Another difficulty, not generally emphasised, is that we have to watch not one, but two lines of transmission. We must consider, on the one hand, the metamorphoses of classical theories at the hands of professional philosophers, the scholastic use of Aristotle for example; and on the other hand we want to trace the influence which these theories had when they were distorted and popularised, as happened to Neoplatonism in the Renaissance. These lines of development call for different techniques of study, and any failure to distinguish between them can lead to a great waste of effort.

This is why the group of papers which we are coming to now appears more disconnected than those we considered earlier. They are probings valuable in themselves and full of hints for future research, but they do not give us a view of the field as a whole. In this case, an overall view is not yet possible.

Professor Armstrong reiterates a lesson implicit in the new *Cambridge History of Later Greek and Early Medieval Philosophy* which he edited. He impresses on us that the different forms of later Platonism cannot be lumped together into an amorphous whole, and that within Neoplatonism itself the teachings of Plotinus, Porphyry, Proclus and the Cappadocians represent separate lines of influence. If he is correct (and I see no reason to doubt this), then much of what has been written about the Neoplatonists of the Italian and French Renaissance will have to be done again. He has placed a bomb under a thriving academic industry and has blown it sky high. And he makes incidentally a couple of suggestions for research that are certain to provoke attention: a rigorous analysis of concepts of hierarchy in medieval Platonism and a study of the influence exercised by the belief that in the last analysis theology ought to have a rational basis. This is a short but outstandingly useful paper.

Professor Viarre (to take the paper which comes next in the chronological order of its subject) is interested in the systems of classification used by medieval encyclopedists and the debt they owed in this respect to the older Pliny. She was the only speaker to touch upon a scientific or near-scientific topic. We felt that the use made of Pliny's *Historia Naturalis* and of the Roman writers on agriculture and medicine belongs to the history of science as well as to the general study of classical influences, and by reason of the specialised knowledge it requires is better explored in the former context, and so made little effort to invite historians of science. But Mlle Viarre did more than just function as the distinguished representative of an absent army. She drew attention to the fact that the principle which applies in literature applies also in science. The works of the Middle Ages and the Renaissance must be studied in their own right before we can estimate their indebtedness to the past. So long as we regard the encyclopedists as mere repositories of borrowed knowledge, they have nothing to tell us, as Hraban's *de Universo* had nothing to tell Manitius.[1] They become interesting when we look at the classifications they employed which reflect the mind of their age.

As has been pointed out, popularisations present the historian of thought with some very awkward problems; and we have reason to be grateful for any insight we can obtain about them. Dr Mann takes the fortunes of Petrarch's *de Remediis* as his subject and shows us how it was distorted by its readers and epitomists. Men borrowed from Petrarch what was in harmony with their own thinking. Where he offered them an amalgam of Christian and Stoic, medieval and classical lore, they treasured the former and overlooked the latter. The importance of this finding cannot be sufficiently stressed.

What Dr Mann describes is a case of self-imposed censorship, the unconscious or perhaps conscious rejection of classical ideas which did not fit into a traditionally Christian outlook. In the studies by Professor Schalk and Mr Trapp we have a variant of this process, not a rejection of humanism, but the men of the Renaissance using classical or humanist values to justify their actual attitudes and actions. Professor Schalk takes as his starting point the conflicting claims of *negotium* and *otium*, which Petrarch according to his usual practice interpreted simultaneously in classical terms (as we may find them set out by a Velleius Paterculus) and in Christian terms as the opposition of the world and the spirit. This antithesis then be-

---

[1] See the attack on him by Paul Lehmann, *Erforschung des Mittelalters*, Band III (Stuttgart, 1960), 198 ff.

came linked with humanist activity in the political field, for which it provided a symbolic framework. Where there were opportunities for political action, and such action met with success, we find a glorification of *negotium*, the Petrarchan concept being enriched by a fuller ideal of civic duty derived from Cicero. Where opportunities were lacking, or action ended in failure, men came to put their trust in *otium*; and here again the original concept was enriched, this time by associating it with the Platonic contemplation of the Ideal. Professor Schalk demonstrates how discussion of these opposed values led eventually to a compromise which we find stated in Bodin's theory of the three ascending levels of experience: science or knowledge of facts, prudence or knowledge of men and true religion. This theory in its turn simply rationalises the choices open to Bodin's contemporaries.[1] Active participation in public service was felt to be desirable, but had to be subordinate to established values.

The problems raised by this survey are exceptionally important. Would the idea of *negotium* as civic duty have developed without the help of classical models? What significance are we to attribute to the change of tone which occurred when *otium* came to be viewed as philosophical contemplation rather than as the peace of a monastery? What, in short, is the role of ideas in human existence? What real difference did the coming of humanism make?

That intellectual activity is a growth *on* life, which can remain largely independent of practical considerations, is suggested by the contents of Mr Trapp's paper. The theory that French had some special affinity with Greek was a product of the desire common among renaissance Frenchmen to give their language a higher status, and the attention it received from a number of respectable scholars has long been regarded as one of the curiosities of literary history. But putting this paper alongside its two predecessors, one notices an interesting parallel. The same kind of general sentiment which could determine the rejection of ideas (Dr Mann) or their adoption (Professor Schalk) could also, it appears, lead to their elaboration. We are given further light here on the mechanics that governed the spread of classical modes of thought.

The fine arts and architecture form the subject of our final section. Professor Gombrich's brilliantly conceived paper on *Personification*,

---

[1] The idea that Bodin's view is a rationalisation is mine, not Professor Schalk's. For a parallel case see my paper 'Humanism as a Value System' in A. Levi (ed.) *Humanism in France* (Manchester, 1970).

which actually opened the Conference, provides a convenient bridge between the world of ideas and the world of art. The field he explores is one whose importance is often ignored. Concepts fit into philosophical systems and have their importance at that level; but they are also, at a different level, the modes which shape our responses to experience, and as such they have a power over us whose extent is hard to estimate. Professor Gombrich examines the forms taken by personification in literature and art and hazards some guesses at the nature of their influence. Since the habit of personification was manifestly a prominent characteristic of Greco-Roman thought, we have here an important and very little known facet of classical influence and one which can offer many opportunities for future research.

Professor Courcelle reminds us, in connection with the *de Consolatione Philosophiae*, that classical authors supplied artists with subjects from the beginning of the Middle Ages. The strongly visualized descriptions which Dr Smalley noted in Ridewall and Holcot, and which Dr Yates would attribute to the influence of the mnemotechnicians,[1] provide another link between art and literature as does the work of Panofsky and Wind which has brought to light connections of a subtler and more detailed kind. It is to be regretted that these lines of investigation are not more fully represented here. But at any rate there can be no doubt that in all these forms of classical influence personification played a leading part.

The two papers on architecture which complete the volume have the interest of bringing to our notice parallels to the developments we have observed in the literary field. Professor Buddensieg's account of the Pantheon shows later critics of that building blind to the obvious and ready to transform classical elements to fit contemporary tastes in a way which calls to mind Dr Mann's description of the readers of Petrarch. Mr Burns's various observations also strike a familiar note. The element of confusion introduced into naïve attempts to trace the antique element in Quattrocento architecture by the presence of antique survivals in Trecento work reminds one of the confusions that result from classical concepts present in the patristic tradition. Similarly, the fact that buildings conceived in an undeniably antique spirit often contained later motifs from Romanesque or Gothic calls to mind the many medieval elements we discover in humanist thought. There is a surprising uniformity about the processes which governed the transmission of classical material.

---

[1] Smalley, *English Friars*, pp. 110 ff. and 165 ff.; F. Yates, *The Art of Memory* (London, 1966).

What emerges from the volume as a whole will be evident after this discussion of its component parts. The study of classical influences has reached a point where charges are imposing themselves and must impose themselves further if progress is to be made. A long era of casual exploration and the gradual accumulation of detail is giving way to a new age of large-scale, systematic effort. This change is manifesting itself differently in different parts of the field. At the most basic level, where we are concerned with making the material we work upon readily available, it will lead sooner rather than later to the production of that comprehensive *Catalogus Codicum Classicorum Latinorum* which Félix Grat envisaged, and to which Professor Sweeney is devoting his energies. Our methods of studying the fortunes of MSS have altered already. This is the department in which our knowledge is greatest and our technique most perfect. Here the primary need is for co-ordination, and this is being provided by Professor Billano-vich's *kibbutz*. The history of scholarship and classical teaching is on the other hand an almost virgin field for the research worker, where the importance of detailed investigation has only just been realised. All the same, it is when we come to the creative literature and thought of antiquity and to estimating the impact they made, that we see change striking most deeply. We see that the painstaking labours of the past—the collecting of quotations, references, common motifs and other parallels—have laid a foundation, but that this is no more than a foundation, valueless until it is built upon. The inspiration men drew from their classical reading was dynamic in its effects, and our task is to trace the workings of this living force. Some at least of the papers in this volume make it plain that attention is shifting from the borrowed material taken from classical authors to a perceptive critical analysis of the works in which that material was used. And what is true of literature and thought is true also of art. There too we must examine in their own right the statues, paintings, buildings which were produced and look for the contribution that antiquity made to their growth.

The survival of antiquity did not consist of the conveyance of inanimate treasures, like fragments of a mosaic; it was the seminal cause of organic developments.

One further problem remains. When we have learnt to see the influence of antiquity as a dynamic process, we shall still have far to go. Even then we shall still be at the stage of viewing our material like exhibits in a museum—all on a level. Some of the exhibits will be larger than the rest with a multitude of interrelated parts—huge machines instead of isolated flints. But the essential question of which counts for more, the machine or the flint, the complex influence or the simple will (if we disregard mere size) continue to baffle us.

Eventually we shall have to learn to grade different forms of influence in some sort of hierarchy. Some, we may presume, mattered more than others. But which? Some prepared the way for successful action. The transmission of scientific ideas comes in here. Some inspired action, which may have been successful or disastrous, by mobilising human energies round values or symbols. Some aroused emotions or widened men's sensitivity. Action, emotion, the ability to respond to one's environment—which was the most important? Many influences moreover were transmitted through literature. Imaginative literature with its offer of alternative possibilities for existence (located usually within an arbitrarily restricted framework of circumstances) overlaps life. But is its importance limited to the area of this overlapping, or can it be said to possess some autonomous value?

The resolution of these problems is a task for historians of culture. And it would be more correct to say 'future historians'. At the present moment cultural history has not the resources for an enterprise of this magnitude; and the student of classical influences, dependent upon the findings of the larger discipline, would seem to have little choice but to wait. It is interesting to note however—if only incidentally—that for this hammering out of criteria, for assessing what is more and what is less important for the flowering of human life, the history of the classical tradition with its well-documented material, circumscribed in bulk but catholic in its scope, could afford an exceptionally useful testing ground. Even if we choose to look into the distant future and consider very broad issues, our subject appears to have possibilities which should not perhaps be neglected.

Having come this far I may perhaps be allowed a personal comment. If the Conference was (as I believe) felt to be a success by most of those who attended it, and largely because of the opportunities it provided for informal discussion, the credit must go uniquely to Mr Wilkinson. It was his liberal awareness of change ruling in the midst of tradition that provided the motive force for the whole enterprise. He planned its organisation and his benevolent presence made its wheels run smoothly. Certainly, his nominal aide, myself, was a mere passenger. The Conference was his from first to last.

PART I

LATIN MANUSCRIPTS AND
THEIR CATALOGUES

1

VANISHING AND UNAVAILABLE EVIDENCE: LATIN MANUSCRIPTS IN THE MIDDLE AGES AND TODAY

R. D. SWEENEY

It is not my intention here to reveal the results of any new research, but rather to spread on the record of this Conference what I see as certain clear needs for future work in the Classics and in the study of the survival and influence of classical literature in later times, and to suggest certain steps which might be taken to fill these needs.

There are several approaches which one can make to the question of the extent to which the classical Latin authors were known in the Middle Ages; it will be the task of this Conference to define and evaluate these approaches to the study of the classical remnant, and I shall here forbear to discuss the various subtle and indirect methods by which this influence has been or may be isolated and studied in the various aspects of life and literature in this period. My own interest is in the direct evidence for the survival of classical texts in the Middle Ages and Renaissance: to be specific, in the evidence found in manuscript catalogues, which provide a direct record of the books available to scholars, writers, or more general readers at various times and places. I wish to stress this—at various times and places—for it has become increasingly clear to me that library holdings and the availability of books must be studied synchronically as well as dia-chronically in order to appreciate the full literary heritage of the past.

The classicist and textual critic who desires to know what the evidence for a given test might be immediately finds that there are very few definitive lists of MSS of individual works or authors. If he suspects that the lists which he does find are incomplete and feels compelled to do something about this, he rapidly finds himself involved in the singularly complex and unpleasant field of manu-script cataloguing.

It was to introduce some order into the chaos of this field that I recently proposed the preparation of a *Catalogus Codicum Classicorum Latinorum*, a summary catalogue of all the manuscripts of Latin classical authors and works now existing. 'Classical' authors have been defined rather arbitrarily to include those authors writing before A.D. 600 whose works were not specifically Christian in content, and the same definition applies to anonymous or pseudonymous works of this period. Certain authors and works are of uncertain age or, while of definitely later age, are of relevance to the nature of pagan literature and antiquity—need I mention here the first and second Vatican Mythographers?—so that a classicist might desire a list of their manuscripts as much as one of more ancient texts—in all of these cases I have had to make rather arbitrary decisions. Whether or not such a catalogue should include the MSS of Boethius, for example, is not so important as the certainty that some parts of the catalogue will not include them while others will—an absolute essential for such a catalogue, far more important than the consistency or even palaeographical accuracy of its descriptions, is consistency in the application of the criteria for inclusion.

It is here that the first major problem of this work arose. It is ironic that the study of classical philology, blessed with so many monuments of Herculean labour, should not possess, indeed should hardly even have contemplated possessing, a catalogue of Latin classical MSS: this is, however, at least intelligible, for in the golden age of our discipline when such great projects were being conceived and initiated the tide of hyper-Lachmannianism was at its height, and the lesson that *recentiores, non deteriores* is often true came after this age had waned, as did apparently the appreciation of MSS, not merely as sources for a text, but also as carriers of culture, whose presence and number is a fact of some importance; it is even more ironic that the field of classical studies should not even possess a full and useful list of all known Latin classical authors and works.

Such a list would require—and a similar list is a necessity, as I see it, for any similar catalogue of, shall we say, the Latin fathers or Greek classical authors and works—a full listing of all known authors and anonymous works, with a full list of the works of the various authors, all variant MS identifications of these authors and works, extensively cross-listed, and the relevant bibliographical information, giving current textual editions, studies of the MS tradition, and the *editio princeps* for each work. Linked with this, for firm identification of these works, there would have to be a full list of *incipits*, and a separate list of *incipits* alphabetically arranged would be useful and indeed necessary for some purposes. The researchers who are to work on this *Catalogus* will often find themselves in libraries where a full collection of texts and other aids is not readily available, and the confusions and uncertainties which often arise from identifying even relatively common texts could be readily avoided by having such a guide-book in hand.

It should be clear that such a list would have to be founded on two sources, the list of abbreviations in the *Thesaurus Linguae Latinae*[1] and the lists of *corpora, anonyma,* and authors in the *Catalogus Translationum et Commentariorum,*[2] neither of which is sufficient for the present purpose: a fuller discussion of the relationship between these lists and the one which I am preparing, as well as a fuller presentation of the scope and contents of the *Catalogus Codicum Classicorum Latinorum,* is to be found in the revised prospectus of this work, which Professor Giuseppe Billanovich has now published in *Italia medioevale e umanistica,* XL (1968), 339–44. I hope to have a preliminary draft of this list of authors and works ready to circulate to various scholars for additions and corrections in about two years.

There is one point which I should like to make now about the *Catalogus,* one which I think is applicable to similar proposals in general. A scholarly work must be as accurate and thorough as possible, but there must be a certain realism in the scope and contents of a scholarly proposal if the work proposed is ever actually to be accomplished or, if accomplished, to be usable, and this can only be attained by a clear appreciation of the scholarly audience to whom it is addressed and by subjecting each detail of the proposed contents of such a work to a thorough scrutiny to decide its usefulness and relevance.

It is to such a scrutiny that I have subjected the proposed descriptions in the *Catalogus,* with the invaluable help of numerous scholars to whom I have circulated my preliminary prospectus or whom I have visited for the purpose of discussing this matter. As presently constituted, the information given for each manuscript containing the text of a classical author or work would consist solely of the collection and number,[3] author or putative author, individual work, the

---

[1] *Thesaurus Linguae Latinae: Index Librorum Scriptorum ex Quibus Exempla Adferuntur,* ed. Fr. Vollmer (Leipzig, 1904) and *Supplementum* (Leipzig, 1958).

[2] *Catalogus Translationum et Commentariorum: Mediaeval and Renaissance Latin Translations and Commentaries: Annotated Lists and Guides,* ed. Paul Oskar Kristeller, 1 (Washington, 1960), 38–76.

[3] The arrangement of the MSS in this catalogue would be geographical, by city and library. An additional feature of this work would be a capsule history of each library, indicating the origin of and major accessions to the MS collection, so as to give an indication of the nature of the collections as presently constituted.

century or date of the MS, the folia on which the text is found, an indication of the state of completeness of the text, a note on special features of possible relevance to the text, such as Beneventan or some other unusual script or the presence of scholia—here I realise there is a wide opening for uncertainty, but one must trust in the principle of *solvitur ambulando* and settle the questions of what should be included as they arise—an indication of scribe, provenance and previous owners, where known, and bibliographical references when these are either the source from which the information given was derived or when they do, in fact, contribute something real to the discussion of the MS either as a MS or as a source for the text. These should be kept sparse: the scholar really interested in a MS which is a significant textual witness will hardly be sufficiently aided, for example, by a full bibliography to warrant the expenditure of the compiler's time and the publisher's paper; a reference to the *last* significant discussion, from which previous discussions can be identified, should usually suffice. Here once again the desire to be informative must be tempered by discretion, and completeness and accuracy by parsimony.

The omissions from this description are obvious. Is the manuscript on paper or parchment?[1] *Quid ad rem?* What is its size? How many lines are there to a page? How is it pricked? What are the gatherings? Once again, *quid ad rem?* Unless such information enables the scholar to date the manuscript or ascribe a provenance to it, it is, *for the present purpose*, irrelevant, and if and only if it does should it be noted. This information can be of value to the student studying the practices of particular scriptoria or areas or ages, without doubt, or to one studying a group of MSS of a certain type united by certain physical features, but what could be the value of full palaeographical descriptions of a group of MSS brought together in one volume solely on account of their texts? I suspect, indeed, that a reconsideration might be in order of the content of the MS descriptions in catalogues of collections whose sole unity is that their MSS were all swept together by some librarian or private collector, or series of librarians and collectors, in the Renaissance or even later. Is it possible that by reconsidering the necessity for these details catalogues equally useful might appear with more speed, catalogues produced *in usum scholarum* rather than *sub specie aeternitatis*?

[1] It has been suggested that the fact that a MS is on paper is worthy of mention as indicating the possible use to which the MS was to be put, and that the size of a MS is of interest to the scholar who wishes to procure photographs of it. Both of these suggestions are now under consideration.

All this has led me not only into scholarly heresy but also, apparently, rather far away from the original topic of the value of catalogues for the study of the extent of classical influences in the years A.D. 500–1500. Yet for such a study the indices of the *Catalogus*, with their lists of provenances and previous owners, can provide in themselves a tool for research of great value. In the preparation of indices lavishness of design and magnificence of execution are merely sensible practice, and with modern methods of indexing it is an extremely simple matter to prepare any number of different indices arranged by authors and works or whatever other geographical, chronological, or other criteria might seem desirable, once the text has been typed into machine-readable form and properly proof-read.[1]

This diachronic and synchronic view of the availability of individual classical texts at various times and places will thus provide concrete evidence for possible classical influences. This information must be supplemented, however, by evidence from other sources, of which I shall name only a few. Citations and reminiscences of classical authors in various medieval and renaissance texts can be of great value, always providing that caution is exercised in ensuring that the quotation is actually derived from the author directly. References to the actual possession of books in various texts, such as the letters of Lupus of Ferrières and Alcuin's *de Sanctis Euboricensis Ecclesiae*,[2] may provide valuable information. Special works on great libraries, such as that of San Marco in Florence or the library of Matthias Corvinus,[3] may be consulted, and their production should be encouraged. The evidence for the movements of *codices descripti* should be more carefully analysed (and here I should like to point out how useful it would be

---

[1] The saving in time and work which computers can lead to in indexing has not yet been properly appreciated by most classicists. Here most of the relevant work so far has been in the field of concordance making, of which the most notable example so far is David Packard's *A Concordance to Livy* (4 vols. Cambridge, Mass., 1968), containing some 500,000 entries: to the computer, a concordance and an index are the same thing. The amount of work involved should be reduced again by a considerable amount when, within a decade or so, the optical scanner is perfected, rendering all our laboriously compiled concordances so much waste-paper.

[2] These have been partly collected in Gustav Becker's *Catalogi bibliothecarum antiqui* (Bonn, 1885), but much probably still remains to be done.

[3] On the library of Matthias Corvinus cf. G. Fraknói, G. Fógel, P. Gulyás, and E. Hoffmann, *Bibliotheca Corvina: La Biblioteca di Mattia Corvino Re d'Ungheria* (Italian tr. by L. Zambra, Budapest, 1927). A full study of the library of San Marco at Florence, begun by the late Professor B. L. Ullman and continued and completed by Professor Philip A. Stadter of the University of North Carolina (*The Public Library of Renaissance Florence: Cosimo de' Medici, Niccolò Niccoli, and the Library of San Marco*) is now in the press.

to have a list of these manuscripts made conveniently available for the codicologist, the textual critic, and the palaeographer).

There is one further source that I must mention here briefly. The catalogues of libraries dating from the Middle Ages and Renaissance are extremely numerous and very badly collected, except for a few such works as the great, but unfortunately incomplete, compilation of the *Mittelalterliche Bibliothekskataloge Deutschlands und der Schweiz*.[1] A major need here is a guide to the location of these catalogues, city by city and library by library, a work comparable in arrangement to Professor Kristeller's *Latin Manuscript Books before 1600*,[2] and one almost certainly more difficult to compile. Only then can the scope of this problem become clear.

The picture of the past which we can thus compile is of necessity incomplete, but the methods of approach are so different that the *lacunae* which remain from the use of one method can often be filled in by another. A true picture of the availability of classical texts at various times and places can thus be formulated, or at least one in which the flaws are those of the inevitable attrition of time, and not flaws arising from inaccuracy of restoration or inability to perceive the necessity of using all our evidence in this restoration. Yet very much remains to be done.

I have entitled this paper 'Vanishing and Unavailable Evidence: Latin Manuscripts in the Middle Ages and Today'. We know that the losses of MSS in the Middle Ages were very extensive: fire, war, and neglect were all great enemies, neglect perhaps the greatest, and the isolation and inaccessibility of texts in various monasteries and cathedral libraries is hard for us to imagine and even harder to estimate precisely. Yet MSS and texts survived in considerable numbers. The major cultural watershed between antiquity and the Middle Ages, in one sense, was the change from the perishable papyrus roll to the durable codex, when what was not recopied perished, and relatively little classical literature seems to have survived this crucial stage and been later lost: it would be valuable to have a compilation of all the evidence for such works, from palimpsests (the final volume of the *Codices Latini Antiquiores* should be

[1] Ed. Paul Ruf and Paul Lehmann (Munich, 1918 ff.). The last catalogue volume to appear was III, 3 in 1939 (III, 4, an index to volume III, preface signed by Paul Lehmann, appeared in 1962). Work on this great project has now been resumed, as I understand, on a less elaborate scale.
[2] Paul Oskar Kristeller, *Latin Manuscript Books before 1600: A List of the Printed Catalogues and Unpublished Inventories of Extant Collections*, 3rd ed. (New York, 1965).

invaluable for this), fragmentary MSS, and the sources I have indicated above. In and after the Renaissance, despite the passion for finding new texts which characterised so many humanists, the losses continued: witness the sack of Fleury in 1562 and the mysterious fate of the *de Bello Germanico* of Pliny the Elder.[1]

Yet even today we are not free from losses. The destruction of the libraries of Strasbourg and Turin and the extensive devastation of the two World Wars come to mind immediately, while the great Italian floods of 1966 could easily have been far more destructive of MS materials than they were. It is not impossible that some classical texts may have perished unpublished in some of these disasters; certainly many MSS which could have been used as evidence for classical texts were among those destroyed. The progress of micro-filming and photographic reproduction, that useful but unsatisfactory substitute for autoptical investigation of the MS itself, can help somewhat to prevent further losses from being totally irremediable, but it is by making knowledge of the MSS currently existing more widely available, that we can best remove the remnants of the medieval inconveniences and insularities which continually confront the scholar who works in the field of Latin manuscript studies. I have, accordingly, proposed and undertaken a *Catalogus Codicum Classi-corum Latinorum*; there are other areas in which much more work,

---

[1] Cf. M. Lehnerdt, 'Ein verschollenes Werk des älteren Plinius', *Hermes*, XLVIII (1913), 274–82. Nicolaus Cusanus told Poggio Bracciolini in 1427 that he had seen a MS of this work, and there were apparently independent later reports of its existence. Remigio Sabbadini's explanation (in *Le scoperte dei codici latini e greci ne' secoli XIV e XV* (new ed. prepared by Eugenio Garin, Florence, 1967; original ed. Florence, 1905), p. 111), 'Si capisce che in capo al codice da lui veduto della *Natur. Histor.* stava, come spesso occorre, il cenno biografico di Svetonio, dove lesse le parole: "bella omnia quae umquam cum Germanis gesta sunt XX voluminibus comprehendit; item naturalis historiae XXXVII libros absolvit"; e i 37 libri della *Natur. Histor.* furono trasformati dal suo cervello nei 20 libri della *Historia bellorum Germaniae*', seems very improbable, especially (as Lehnert noted, p. 278) in the face of Nicolaus Cusanus's explicit statement that he had read the *Naturalis Historia* as well, and that this was not the same work. Some sort of mistake is of course very possible but, as Lehnert points out (p. 279), we know of at least two other ancient works which were known at that period but have since been lost, a *Carmen de Bello Nautico Augusti cum Antonio et Cleopatra*, the MS of which belonged to Angelo Decembrio, and a *Liber Epigrammatum et Epistolarum* of Augustus, which once came into the hands of Petrarch. Sabbadini (*Le scoperte dei codici latini e greci ne' secoli XIV e XV*, pp. 138–9) is once more sceptical of the first work, and (in his *Le scoperte dei codici latini e greci ne' secoli XIV e XV: Nuove ricerche* (new ed. prepared by Eugenio Garin, Florence, 1967; original ed. Florence, 1914), p. 201 n. 3) states firmly of the latter, 'Fu un'illusione del Petrarca'. Since many authors were preserved into the Renaissance in only one copy (Sabbadini gives a partial list in his earlier work, pp. 211–12), and some authors, such as Terentianus Maurus and Velleius Paterculus, were printed from a *codex unicus* since lost, such scepticism seems excessive.

painstaking and often tedious, must be done before we can judge with any accuracy what MSS and what texts were available for the use and perusal of the men of the past; and the gathering of all this evidence, available only as the result of long devotion by scholars to the accumulation of facts often meaningless or worthless in themselves, can contribute notably to the study of classical influences in this thousand-year period, which in turn is but part of the great effort in which we are all engaged, and which is our only real justification as scholars, the investigation, the demonstration, and the preservation of the continuity of culture.

2

L'INSTITUT DE RECHERCHE ET D'HISTOIRE DES TEXTES ET L'ÉTUDE DES MANUSCRITS DES AUTEURS CLASSIQUES

M.-TH. D'ALVERNY ET M.-C. GARAND

L'Institut de Recherche et d'Histoire des Textes a été fondé en 1937 par un ancien élève de l'École des Chartes et de l'École de Rome, Félix Grat. Au cours de son séjour à Rome, il avait porté un intérêt croissant aux manuscrits des auteurs classiques latins; il avait constaté qu'en ce domaine une exploration systématique permettait de faire parfois des découvertes et en tous cas d'arriver à une meilleure connaissance de la transmission des textes pendant le Moyen Âge et la Renaissance. C'est surtout dans ce but qu'il voulut organiser un Institut consacré à la recherche et à la description des manuscrits, et destiné à devenir un centre de documentation pour les érudits. On devait y conserver les notices de manuscrits rédigées par des collaborateurs qualifiés, constituer une photothèque, et élaborer des instruments de travail pour permettre aux historiens, aux philologues, aux paléographes d'exploiter au mieux les ressources offertes.

La direction de l'Institut fut confiée à l'une des collègues de Félix Grat, comme lui élève de l'École des Chartes et de l'École de Rome, Mlle J. Vielliard. L'activité de ce nouvel organisme fut dédiée primordialement à la littérature classique; peu à peu, en se développant, elle se porta vers l'étude des manuscrits des auteurs médiévaux, en latin et en langues romanes, à celle des manuscrits grecs, des manuscrits arabes et hébreux, plus tard des cartulaires, et les sections se multiplièrent, mais le programme primitif fixé par le fondateur resta l'un des objectifs primordiaux.

Félix Grat avait projeté un inventaire complet des manuscrits des classiques latins répertoriés méthodiquement. La première étape du travail consista en un recensement des bibliothèques publiques et privées, en dépouillant des catalogues imprimés et en commençant les investigations sur place. Une liste des auteurs latins et des textes anonymes de l'antiquité fut dressée jusqu'à l'an 400. On fit une table complète des *incipits* et *explicits*, en relevant pour les œuvres importantes le début et la fin de chaque livre. On établit d'abord des notices succinctes, puis des notices détaillées, en relevant tous les renseignements d'ordre codicologique: type d'écriture, date approximative d'après les critères paléographiques, si possible localisation; copistes, scriptoria, possesseurs. Des microfilms furent exécutés pour les manuscrits ou parties de manuscrits qui paraissaient présenter un intérêt particulier. La collection de microfilms, régulièrement accrue, doit être maintenant l'une des plus riches du monde.

Dès le début, les membres de l'Institut des Textes commencèrent à explorer les bibliothèques en province et à l'étranger, tandis qu'un groupe italien entreprenait l'étude des manuscrits de la Bibliothèque Vaticane. A cette époque déjà lointaine, les 'missionnaires' devaient être à la fois codicologues, philologues et...photographes, transportant leur Leica pour prendre des microfilms sur place, avec des moyens de fortune. Inutile de dire que les premières collections ainsi constituées étaient de valeur fort inégale !

Le résultat de ces missions fut fructueux.[1] Dans une communication présentée à l'Académie des Inscriptions en décembre 1938, Félix Grat signalait plusieurs manuscrits qui avaient jusque-là échappé aux érudits.[2] Notons un manuscrit du IXe siècle contenant l'*Épitome Rei Militaris* de Végèce (Pal. lat. 1572); un manuscrit du IXe siècle, commentaire du *de Inventione* de Cicéron par Marius Victorinus (Vat. lat. 3862); un ms. Ottob. lat. 1660, en partie du IXe siècle, renfermait un texte d'Horace analogue à celui du *Blandianus vetustissimus* aujourd'hui perdu. A Venise (Musée Correr), fut découverte une pièce de vers de Sulpicia, connue seulement jusque-là par une édition incunable; on trouva un Juvénal du Xe siècle au Musée de Split (Spalato). La mission accomplie en juin 1939 à Louvain par Mme Boucrel-Vernet, qui fut pendant de longues années le chef et l'animateur de la Section latine, lui permit de publier après la guerre la description de quatorze manuscrits d'auteurs classiques disparus dans l'incendie de 1940, et de donner quelques indications sur les autres.[3]

---

[1] Au sujet des travaux exécutés pendant les premières années de l'existence de l'Institut d'histoire des textes, cf. un exposé de J. Vielliard, et M. Th. Boucrel-Vernet: 'La recherche des manuscrits latins', dans *Mémorial des études latines* (1943).

[2] Cf. F. Grat, 'Manuscrits inconnus d'auteurs latins découverts par l'Institut de recherche et d'histoire des textes', dans *Bibliothèque de l'École des Chartes*, XCIX (1938), 433-4.

[3] Cf. M. Th. Boucrel-Vernet, 'Quelques manuscrits de classiques latins à la Bibliothèque universitaire de Louvain', dans *Mélanges Félix Grat*, II (1949), 351-86.

La guerre interrompit les voyages, mais non les travaux. Félix Grat, officier de réserve, avait été tué en mai 1940, mais sa première collaboratrice, Mlle J. Vielliard, continua l'œuvre entreprise et la développa autant que le permettaient les circonstances. L'Institut avait commencé à décrire les manuscrits classiques de la Bibliothèque nationale; les notices concernant l'ancien fonds latin (no 5757–6000) ont été rédigées. Un peu plus tard furent décrits quelques manuscrits du fonds de Saint-Victor, du Supplément latin et des nouvelles acquisitions latines, ainsi qu'un certain nombre de manuscrits de la Bibliothèque Mazarine. En province, l'on étudia avec une particulière attention les riches fonds de Montpellier, Orléans (manuscrits provenant de Fleury), Troyes et Tours. Dès qu'il fut possible de reprendre les missions à l'étranger, les collaborateurs de la Section latine continuèrent leurs explorations. Des techniciens photographes, munis d'un matériel approprié, furent envoyés à leur suite pour faire les prises de vues nécessaires. La liste qui nous a été communiquée par Mlle Pellegrin, chef actuel de la Section, et qui est reproduite ici indique les pays et les villes dans lesquels a été effectuée une enquête systématique au sujet des manuscrits classiques: *Belgique*; *Suisse* où, en principe, tous les manuscrits ont été vus; *Autriche* (Bibl. nat., Couvent des Écossais et Bibl. Lichtenstein à Vienne, Bibl. de Klosterneubourg); *Hongrie* (Musée national et Université de Budapest); *Balkans*; *Turquie* (Vieux Sérail); *Roumanie*; *Bulgarie*; *Grande-Bretagne* (quelques fonds du British Museum, Bibl. d'Édimbourg, Glasgow, Bodl. Library à Oxford); *Irlande* (Dublin); *Espagne* (Bibl. nat., Academia de la Historia à Madrid, et quelques fonds du Palais-Royal); *Allemagne* (Augsbourg, Beuren, Brême, Darmstadt, Dillingen, Düsseldorf, Hambourg, Memmingen, Lindau, Lübeck, Lunebourg, Munich, Nuremberg, etc.); *Pays-Bas* (Leyde, La Haye, Amsterdam, Utrecht); *Pays-Scandinaves* (Copenhague, Göteborg, Stockholm, Upsal, Linköping); *Italie* (Bibl. Braidense, Trivulziana, Ambrosienne de Milan); *Vatican* où, comme nous l'avons dit plus haut, une équipe italienne travaille pour l'Institut des Textes depuis 1938.

Le résultat de quelques-unes des missions a été publié dans le *Bulletin d'information de l'Institut de Recherche et d'Histoire des Textes*. Dans le fascicule II (1953) Mlle Pellegrin a donné une description sommaire des manuscrits de classiques latins à Madrid (Bibliothèque nationale, Palais royal (ces derniers transférés pour la plupart à Salamanque), Université, Real Academia de la Historia), Tolède (Bibliothèque capitulaire); dans les t. III (1954) et IV (1955) 'Manuscrits d'auteurs latins de l'époque classique des bibliothèques publiques de Suède'; dans le t. VII (1958) 'Notes sur divers manuscrits latins des bibliothèques de Milan', Mlle Pellegrin a relevé dans les trente-trois volumes de l'inventaire manuscrit de l'Ambrosienne plus l'inventaire du fonds Trotti et celui de l'appendice, tous les manuscrits contenant des textes classiques; il y en a environ 550, la plupart du XVe siècle. Enfin, le fascicule XIII (1964–5) du *Bulletin de l'I.R.H.T.* contient un rapport de Mme Françoise Bichelonne-Hudry intitulé 'Notes sur divers manuscrits latins conservés en Allemagne du Sud' (Augsbourg, Harbourg, Memmingen), en relevant particulièrement les manuscrits classiques.

Ces publications ne représentent qu'une faible partie des travaux et des trouvailles des collaborateurs de la Section latine de l'Institut. Nous indiquerons simplement que Mme Vernet avait entrepris un répertoire des manuscrits des commentaires de Valère Maxime; que Mlle Pellegrin s'est attachée à retrouver les *membra disjecta* des manuscrits de l'abbaye de Saint-Victor à Berne et à la Vaticane et de ceux de Saint-Benoît-sur-Loire à Orléans, Berne, Leyde et dans le fonds de la Reine à la Bibliothèque Vaticane; que Mlle Colette Jeudy, qui s'intéresse surtout aux grammairiens latins, a dressé un inventaire de soixante-dix manuscrits de Phocas; que Mlle Pellegrin a étudié les manuscrits classiques annotés par Pétrarque, et en a retrouvé deux au British Museum.

Le programme actuel de la Section a deux objets principaux. Le premier est l'inventaire complet, accompagné de notices détaillées, des manuscrits classiques dans les bibliothèques de province en France. Le travail de la Section latine sur les fonds de province s'effectue de deux façons: en faisant venir des manuscrits à Paris pour les étudier et les photographier; en allant voir sur place les manuscrits dont le déplacement n'est pas autorisé (dans ce cas, il n'est pas toujours possible d'en avoir le microfilm).

Le second est la publication du catalogue des manuscrits des classiques latins conservés dans les fonds de la Bibliothèque Vaticane, travail demandé à l'Institut de Recherche et d'Histoire des Textes par le Préfet de la Bibliothèque, et pour lequel l'équipe italienne reçoit maintenant l'appui de missions venues de France. L'on sait que certains fonds: Ottoboni, Chapitre de Saint-Pierre, Reginenses (à partir du no 500), une partie des *Vaticani latini* sont fort mal connus, car il n'existe que des inventaires manuscrits très sommaires. Si les manuscrits du XVe siècle sont en majorité, le relevé que nous avons

pu consulter indique un certain nombre de témoins anciens (VIIIe–
Xe siècle), en particulier dans le fonds Ottoboni et le fonds de la
Reine. De plus, l'Institut de Recherche et d'Histoire des Textes
continue, comme il le fait depuis des années, à acquérir par achat,
prêt ou échange des microfilms dans les grandes bibliothèques du
monde.

La documentation accumulée depuis trente ans à l'Institut, sous
forme de notices rédigées selon les normes minutieuses prescrites par
les fondateurs, et sous forme de microfilms, est à la disposition des
érudits, et en particulier des éditeurs de textes. La collaboration est
constante avec les éditions Teubner et l'association Guillaume Budé,
et les chercheurs individuels peuvent avoir recours, non seulement au
prêt des documents, mais à la science et à la complaisance des
membres de la Section latine. Ceux-ci se chargent fréquemment
d'établir des listes de manuscrits pour un auteur donné. Les visiteurs
qui font une enquête sur place peuvent profiter du fichier biblio-
graphique des classiques, comportant pour les auteurs et les anonymes une série de manuscrits des œuvres, d'après les catalogues et
les travaux de l'Institut. Ils peuvent aussi avoir recours pour compléter leurs recherches aux services des sections de codicologie, de
paléographie, d'histoire de l'humanisme. Outre les renseignements
fournis par ses fichiers sur les anciennes bibliothèques, les scribes et
les possesseurs de manuscrits, la section de codicologie prépare la
publication des inventaires encore inédits des bibliothèques anciennes
de France et de celles du haut clergé français; elle dépouille les
papiers des Bénédictins de Saint-Maur et des érudits du XVII–
XVIIIe siècle, tels que Chifflet ou Peiresc, pour y retrouver tous
renseignements concernant le sort des bibliothèques médiévales à
cette époque. La section de paléographie, qui prépare et publie le
catalogue des manuscrits datés conservés en France, en tire un
fichier de manuscrits datés classés par auteurs où figurent de nombreux textes classiques; elle étudie également l'évolution des abré-
viations aux XIIIe, XIVe et XVe siècles, selon les disciplines. Quant
à la section d'histoire de l'humanisme, elle rassemble les éléments
d'un album paléographique des écritures d'humanistes (ont été
étudiés, notamment, à Berne, la correspondance de Pierre Daniel et
de ses amis, à Vienne celles de Kepler et de Tycho Brahé, au Vatican
celle du cardinal Bembo); ce travail permettra d'améliorer l'étude de
la tradition des textes, d'identifier certaines gloses et annotations.

C'est ainsi que cet Institut de recherche scientifique contribue à établir la 'Bibliothèque idéale' dans laquelle sont conservés les trésors de la littérature latine, surtout à en faciliter l'accès.

Nous devons spécifier que l'orientation des travaux de la section est surtout de type codicologique: la description du texte, très détaillée, et comprenant celle des gloses et commentaires marginaux, est faite de manière objective. Les membres de l'Institut tiennent à offrir aux éditeurs un instrument de travail; ils considèrent qu'il appartient à ceux-ci de faire des remarques philologiques et d'établir des stemmata.

En terminant, nous devons dire un mot de la Section grecque. Ses travaux sont surtout consacrés aux manuscrits de patristique et d'auteurs byzantins; cependant, la très riche collection de microfilms contient des manuscrits de classiques grecs. Le chef de la Section, M. Richard, spécialiste courageux des missions au Mont Athos, a découvert dans plusieurs monastères des témoins inconnus des auteurs anciens profanes. Le fichier de références signale les manuscrits classiques analysés par la section et les microfilms exécutés. Ces microfilms sont communiqués et prêtés aussi libéralement que ceux de la Section latine et les savants collaborateurs sont prêts, eux aussi, à aider les éditeurs de textes à dresser la liste des manuscrits de leur auteur.

PART II

THE READERS AND FORTUNES OF
CLASSICAL MANUSCRIPTS

3

THE CLASSICS IN CELTIC IRELAND

L. BIELER

My communication poses a problem. On the one hand, the wandering Irish (*Scotti peregrini*) were praised for their superior learning by the writers of the countries where they went, praised sometimes grudgingly, but more often with genuine enthusiasm. On the other hand, among surviving classical manuscripts (grammatical works excepted) there is not a single one that was demonstrably written in early Ireland, and even the evidence of quotations and echoes from the classics in the writings of Irishmen is furnished mainly by the works of those who went abroad. As a result, such well-known writers as Mario Esposito, Dom Cappuyns and more recently E. Coccia[1] have drawn the conclusion that the learning of the Irish schools and the literary production of the Irish monasteries were almost exclusively religious in character, with Latin grammar as an indispensable preliminary, and that even within those limits they were not of the highest order. According to this school of thought a Columbanus, a Sedulius Scottus, an Eriugena acquired his familiarity with classical literature on the continent of Europe; and the achievements of these men in the world of ideas and letters owed little or nothing to their cultural background at home.

This contention, though difficult to answer on its own terms, does less than justice to the known facts because it fails to relate them to the context of which they were a part. It is within this context that we need to establish (*a*) what direct evidence there is of learning in Ireland itself, and (*b*) how far it is legitimate to attribute the learning of the *peregrini* to an Irish source.

Let me start with a frank admission. The knowledge in Celtic Ireland of Latin, let alone Greek, literature even during the golden age of Irish learning from the sixth to the ninth century would appear to have been far more restricted than it was in continental literary circles from the ninth century onwards. Classical studies in early Ireland should be viewed against the literary scene, or more pre-

---

[1] E. Coccia, 'La cultura irlandese precarolina—miracolo o mito?' *Studi Medievali*, 3rd ser. VIII (1967), 257-420.

45

cisely against the virtual absence of literary interests, in most of
sixth- and seventh-century Europe and particularly in Merovingian
Gaul and Lombard Italy. Very little first-hand information is available about schools and learning in Ireland itself during the sixth
century. At the turn of that century however we encounter the outstanding literary achievement of St Columbanus, who was as famous
for his writings as for the revival he brought about in the religious
field. Granted that his knowledge of the classics may be in part
derivative[1]—an assertion which still awaits proof—it has been
thoroughly assimilated, and in at least one of his poems (*ad Fedolium*)
he is felicitous in its display. Admittedly, most if not all of his
writings date from the time after he left Ireland (A.D. 591–615). But
must this mean, as has been so often maintained, that he acquired his
classical learning on the continent? I do not think so. The founder of
Luxeuil and Bobbio was a man of mature years when he arrived in
Gaul; and as has been emphasised, among others, by P. Riché,[2] his
main preoccupations after his arrival were religious. They were not
literary; and the troubled life that awaited him upon the continent
was likely to have left him little time for study. Moreover, according
to his biographer Jonas, Columbanus had devoted his youth and
early manhood, prior to his *conversio*, to *liberalium artium doctrinis et
grammaticorum studiis*. This may be no more than a *topos*. It does
however fit into the picture which we have of Irish education at a
slightly later date; and we cannot disregard the possibility that such
an education may have flourished here and there in Ireland already
before the end of the sixth century. Reading Columbanus, we certainly have the impression that his classical reminiscences, especially
those which we find in his letters, are not 'purple patches', like the
'Hisperic' words which he occasionally uses, but are the fruit of a
long-standing familiarity. Besides, as has been pointed out by Professor Christine Mohrmann,[3] his Latin style is not that of sixth-century
Gaul. It is modelled on the sort of late Patristic Latin that would
have come to Ireland with the introduction of Christianity.

The debt of Columbanus to Irish culture is admittedly open to
question. But then during the seventh century the Irish homeland
produced some Latin writers of distinction, among whom are the
anonymous author of the *de Duodecim Abusivis Seculi*, Adamnán of

[1] P. Riché, *Education et culture dans l'Occident barbare* (1963), p. 358.
[2] *Ibid.* p. 376.
[3] C. Mohrmann, 'The earliest continental Irish Latin', *Vigiliae Christianae*, XVI (1962), 216 ff.

Iona and Muirchú, the biographer of St Patrick. It is perhaps not without interest to note that at a time when Virgil was comparatively neglected, to judge from the lack of surviving manuscripts of his poems from the sixth to the eighth century,[1] he was known to both Adamnán and Muirchú and also to Cellanus, the abbot of Perrona Scottorum in Picardy. Adamnán furthermore may have been the compiler of a commentary, based partly on Junius Philargyrius, on Virgil's *Eclogues* and *Georgics*. Cellanus was, it is true, one of the *peregrini*; but as far as we know neither Adamnán nor Muirchú ever set foot on the continent of Europe.

To assess the range of authors known *at first hand* to the Irish in Ireland or abroad is a most difficult task. As Dr Bolgar justly remarks,[2] a quotation merely proves knowledge of the passage in question, but not necessarily of the work in which it occurs. Quoting at second- or third-hand and giving the impression of a first-hand acquaintance with the ultimate source of the quotation has at all times been common practice. Latin grammarians illustrate their teaching from a wide range of writers, and the Irish had some grammatical texts which were more complete than those current on the continent.[3] The possibility that many of the quotations we find in the works of Irish writers have come to them second-hand cannot be discounted. It seems probable therefore that once the stage of grammatical instruction was past, the Irish for the most part concentrated on the study of the Bible and the Fathers. Only exceptional individuals took an interest in ancient literature. There is no trace of a general humanistic attitude.

The rôle of the Irish in the text tradition of Latin authors is again not easy to establish. The number of classical texts which have come down to us in copies made by Irish scribes is exceedingly small, and these few copies were made on the continent where Irish script was practised widely during the seventh and eighth centuries. As for the influence exerted by this Irish work, insular symptoms in continental manuscripts (misreadings of insular letter-forms, ligatures or abbreviations) are insufficient for deciding between an Irish or an Anglo-Saxon exemplar without some such supporting criteria as localisation. Certain types of spelling are admittedly less ambiguous; and it is

---

[1] E. A. Lowe, 'Virgil in South Italy', in *Studi Medievali*, n.s. v (1933), 44.

[2] R. R. Bolgar, *The Classical Heritage and its Beneficiaries* (Cambridge, 1954), p. 9.

[3] See the anonymous commentary on the *Ars maior* of Donatus in the eighth-century MS of St Paul in Carinthia 25.2.16: B. Bischoff in *Archives d'histoire doctrinale et littéraire du moyen âge, 1958* (1959), p. 14, reprinted in *Mittelalterliche Studien*, 1 (1966), 182.

mainly on these grounds that an Irish text tradition has been postulated for Petronius by Professor Díaz y Díaz of Santiago.[1] But even so, it does not follow that Petronius was read in Ireland; nor does this follow for the text of Caesar from the single fact of its connection with Bobbio. The case of Horace is different. In the transmission of Horace's poems the Irish do seem to have played a leading part during the eighth and ninth centuries. A substantial portion of Horace's *œuvre* is contained in a ninth-century codex in Irish script (Berne 363) which is connected with the circle of Sedulius Scottus; and the fact that Horace was known also to Columbanus is possibly suggestive of a tradition of Horatian studies in Ireland from the sixth century onwards.

Any attempt to appraise the Irish contribution to the Carolingian revival will reveal a similar state of confusion. Again, we find tributes to Irish learning. There is the well-known story in the *Gesta Karoli Magni* about the two Irish monks who were called to the court of Charlemagne and given a prominent part in his educational reforms. But we also find sharp and occasionally hostile criticism.[2] And again we have the same problem which troubled us before. How much of their scholarly and literary education did the Irish bring with them from their own country? Dicuil had apparently received some training in the arts at home; but his obvious struggle with Pliny's figures for longitude and latitude would seem to result from the fact that this author was new to him when he came to compose his *Liber de Mensura Orbis Terrae*. The poem in which Sedulius Scottus tells how he and two fellow priests became members of Bishop Hartgar's household at Liège (II. 3) would seem to imply that it was their learning that primarily impressed their host. Sedulius had a limited knowledge of Greek of a kind also found in the Irish circle at Laon. But that knowledge did not go beyond a familiarity with biblical bilinguals. It was the interest in these bilinguals that provided the focus in most cases for the Irish study of Greek and, on however small a scale, must have existed in Ireland itself as early as Adamnán who refers for the correct spelling of *Thabor* to *libri graecitatis*.[3] Where John Scottus (Eriugena) learnt his Greek we do not know. His success in trans-

---

[1] Díaz y Díaz, 'La tradición textual de Petronio', *Euphrosyne*, n.s. I (1967), 71–106.

[2] A revealing incident of this kind is discussed by B. Bischoff, 'Theodulf und der Ire Cadac-Andreas', *Historisches Jahrbuch*, LXXIV (1955), 92–8, reprinted in *Mittelalterliche Studien*, II (1967), 19–25.

[3] Adamnán of Iona, *de Locis Sanctis*, Sec. 27 (ed. L. Bieler, *Scriptores Latini Hiberniae*, III, 96 = *Corpus Christianorum*, CLXXV, 220).

lating from that language and rethinking works of Christian Neo-platonism is above all a manifestation of his own genius.

One last question: did the Latin scholars of early Ireland have an artistic appreciation of classical literature? Sedulius Scottus certainly had, but then he was a poet by nature. Pre-Carolingian writers of Latin in the Irish homeland do not give the impression of responding artistically to their classical reading. They are not exceptional in this, since the same is true of their counterparts on the continent down to the time of Alcuin. But it is also worth noting that if Celtic Ireland failed to establish a tradition of *belles lettres* in Latin, the reason may have been that a highly developed literature, both prose and verse, existed already in the vernacular. The question of classical influences on Irish sagas in their known literary form was raised first of all by James Carney; and some of his interpretations—for example that of the 'watchman device' as a development of the *teichoskopia*, perhaps via the *Thebaid* of Statius[1]—opens an approach to our problem which might lead further than many that have been tried in the past.

---

[1] J. Carney, *Studies in Irish Literature and History* (1955), pp. 305 ff.

4

THE DEPOSIT OF
LATIN CLASSICS IN THE
TWELFTH-CENTURY RENAISSANCE

R. W. HUNT

Much is known about the history of the transmission of Latin classical texts, and a good deal of work has been done in identifying quotations from Latin classical literature in medieval authors. But still too often scholars in suggesting sources for quotations neglect to inform themselves about what is known of the history of a given text. To take an extreme instance, a serious scholar who has done excellent work writing on St Bernard has professed to find echoes of Cicero's *Letters to Atticus*, Tacitus's *Histories* and Catullus. I need hardly take up the time of this audience to demonstrate that none of these works would have been available to St Bernard.

To attempt to cover the whole period from A.D. 500 to 1500 and the whole of Europe in half an hour would be an impossibility, and even the period suggested by my title and its geographical range require a gloss. I shall concentrate on the twelfth century. The beginnings of this renaissance are still too little known to be properly dealt with. And I shall concentrate on France and England, giving only occasional illustrations from Germany and Italy. A further limitation: an enumeration of the authors known in the twelfth century in France and Italy would be intolerably dull. I shall try therefore to concentrate on some of the problems involved.

In some respects the range of authors in general circulation had shrunk from that available in the Carolingian period. Take for instance Lucretius. His poem had never been widely disseminated. Given his philosophy, it is surprising that it survived at all. But there are enough traces to show that it was being used in parts of Germany more than one would have expected, and lines from it were used as illustrations in works of prosody. In the eleventh century there are possibly a few echoes in the *Encomium Emmae*, written by a chaplain of Queen Emma who had close connections with St Bertin where we know that there was a manuscript. By the twelfth century he has vanished. The only quotation from his poem in common circulation is the verse:

ex insensilibus ne credas sensile nasci

which M. l'Abbé Jeauneau has shown to have been a favourite with William of Conches. It comes not directly from Lucretius, but from an illustrative quotation in the *Institutiones Grammaticae* of Priscian. The writers of the twelfth century may have had fewer texts, but they exploited those they had very thoroughly.

Again take Cicero.

Orbis nil habuit maius Cicerone Latinus

wrote John of Salisbury. But he did not set out to collect all the works of Cicero which he could have found. He was content to read those which were readily available. It is true however that he makes far more extensive use of the works in the philosophical corpus than any other writer of this period. He himself possessed copies of the *de Oratore* and of the *de Officiis*, which he bequeathed to Chartres. He had of course studied the *de Inventione Rhetorica*. But of the letters, his quotations (there are only four) come from books IX, XV and XVI of the *Epistolae ad Familiares*. Now there is a family of the MSS containing these letters which contains books IX to XVI, and it circulated in France. We may be reasonably sure that it was a manuscript of this class that John of Salisbury used. His other references to Cicero's letters can be traced to Quintilian and Macrobius. The speeches of Cicero, John of Salisbury seems to have ignored. In this he is at one with his contemporaries in France and England. We can find some knowledge of the *Orationes in Catilinam*, which may perhaps be connected with the wide use made of Sallust and of the pseudonymous *Invectivi*. We also find traces of some of the Caesarean speeches and of the *Philippics*. The position in Germany was quite different. A contemporary of John's at Corvey put together the largest collection of Cicero's speeches extant in any manuscript, the MS now in Berlin known to the editors of Cicero as E.

John of Salisbury's reading cannot be taken as typical. The works of Cicero in common circulation apart from the *de Inventione* were the *de Amicitia*, of which profound use was made by St Bernard and by Ailred of Rievaulx in working out their doctrines of Christian friendship, the *de Senectute*, the *de Officiis* and rather surprisingly the *Paradoxa*.

I have referred to John of Salisbury's use of a mutilated MS of

Cicero's *Epistolae ad Familiares*. The phenomenon of such mutilated MSS is a commonplace to editors of classical texts, and work has been done on its application to quotations in medieval authors. A notable example is the Quintilian available to John of Salisbury. He had a type of text which contained the 'great *lacunae*', and this particular type can be identified in extant manuscripts. Quintilian happens to be an author who was relatively seldom used in the twelfth century, and the question of determining the type of text used does not arise. But in the case of Seneca's *Letters*, where the two halves of the collection circulated separately, it is a matter of consequence. Seneca was an author widely read and studied. Peter Abailard calls him *summus inter universos philosophos morum aedificator*. His deep influence on the Golden Letter of Guillaume de St Thierry has been convincingly demonstrated by Père Dechanet. The part of the *Letters* known to these writers was the first, containing letters 1–88. It was this part and this part only which commonly circulated in France. It was this part only that was known to John of Salisbury and later to Vincent of Beauvais. It is therefore very rash of Dom Leclercq to state that letter 95 is the certain source of a passage in St Bernard, even though he qualifies his statement with the phrase 'known perhaps through a *florilegium* or some other intermediary'. The two certain quotations of the *Letters* by St Bernard are from letters 22 and 28, i.e. from the part from which we should expect to find quotations.

I have spoken thus confidently about Seneca's *Letters* because we have now a masterly exposition both of the transmission of these *Letters* and of the use made of them by medieval writers from Mr Leighton Reynolds. He has not only set out the facts about the circulation of letters 1–88, but he has also shown that in certain parts of southern England the whole collection of letters was known; and he has been able to demonstrate this by the convergent evidence of extant manuscripts and of quotations from writers working in these parts. Recently, I came across a quotation of a letter from the second part in a work of Giraldus Cambrensis which has escaped notice, and it was very satisfactory because it fits neatly into the picture drawn by Mr Reynolds.

At this point it is necessary to enter a *caveat*. The evidence about Seneca's *Letters* is clear and abundant, but we must never expect all the loose ends to be tied up. There are always puzzles. The *Verbum Abbreviatum* of Petrus Cantor who taught at Paris in the latter part of the twelfth century contains quotations from both parts of the *Letters*.

So far I have spoken almost entirely of prose writers. When one turns to the poets some fresh considerations arise. There are hundreds of tags of classical verses in twelfth-century writers, whether they are historians or chroniclers or biblical commentators, not to mention the echoes in the poets. Let me pick out one example.

In letter 342 of St Bernard, addressed to Jocelyn bishop of Soissons in 1140, he exhorts the bishop to use his influence to dissuade the king of France from bringing the archbishop of Bordeaux into a court of law. After a series of rhetorical questions designed to show the injustice of the charge, he ends:

Attendite vobis, episcopi, vestra enim res agitur, paries cum proximus ardet.

Mabillon duly gave the reference to Horace, *Ep.* 1.18.84:

nam tua res agitur, paries cum proximus ardet.

Bernard's biographer, Geoffrey of Auxerre, relates (*Vita* v. 15) how later Abailard used the same quotation with telling effect to Gilbert de la Porrée at the Council of Sens. In the *Exordium Magnum Cisterciense* the line is quoted as a warning to Cistercians to keep in mind the decline of fervour at Cluny. Alan of Lille in the *Anticlaudianus* most daringly puts it in the mouth of Phronesis addressing the Almighty. It is perhaps idle to ask how many of these were conscious at the time that they were quoting Horace. Horace's *Epistles* and *Satires* were very widely read, and one can only weigh the probabilities in each individual case. Of those that I have given, I feel quite sure that Alan of Lille knew what he was doing. He was writing as a conscious artist. It is usually only when one finds a quotation deformed that one can be reasonably sure that it was not direct. To take an example from St Bernard again, he once runs two halves of two lines of the *Metamorphoses* together. The same misquotation is found in other writers and in at least one *florilegium*, as Dom Leclercq has pointed out.

The history of *florilegia* of classical writers is still very imperfectly known. The only two of the twelfth century that have been seriously studied are the so-called *Florilegium Gallicum* and the work known as the *Moralium Dogma Philosophorum*. I forbear to put an author's name to it. Both contain prose as well as verse excerpts. Gagner, I think, made out a convincing case for the use of the *Florilegium Gallicum* by the author of the *Moralium Dogma Philosophorum*, but the only other proved instance of its use that I know is by Vincent of Beauvais. The *Moralium Dogma Philosophorum* probably had a rapid and certainly a wide circulation. It was used by the Italian canon lawyer, Simon of

Bidiniano before the end of the century. It was drawn upon by Giraldus Cambrensis in his *de Instructione Principis*.

There is one late Carolingian *florilegium* that had some circulation in the twelfth century, that is the excerpts of Heiric of Auxerre, of which we have at last a full edition from an Italian scholar. It has been shown that John of Salisbury used it for Suetonius and for an excerpt of Orosius that Heiric has put at the end of his excerpts from Suetonius.

It may reasonably be asked whether one should not expect to find that John depended on other *florilegia* than this. It may be so, and I think that this is more likely to apply to prose writers than to the poets. Works like the *Memorabilia* of Valerius Maximus, Pliny's *Natural History*, Aulus Gellius's *Noctes Atticae*, Macrobius's *Saturnalia* were certainly available in France and England in the period, and were no less certainly read and consulted; but to judge from the evidence of extant MSS and from references in library catalogues, they were not to be found everywhere; and it is more likely in such cases—I am thinking especially of Pliny's *Natural History*—that the references to it were often made at second hand. If we except what we may call the textbooks—Priscian, Donatus, the *vetus logica* with Boethius the *Timaeus*, Boethius *de Arithmetica* and *de Musica*, Macrobius\] *in Somnium Scipionis*, Boethius *de Consolatione Philosophiae*—the poets, Virgil, Horace, Ovid, Statius (but *not* the *Silvae*), Juvenal, Persius and Claudian were more often read in the schools than prose-writers and became part of the furniture of the minds of educated men in the twelfth century.

To sum up the burden of my discourse. It is, that we can find a firm basis for a knowledge of the classical texts, at any rate in certain regions and at certain times, by putting together and comparing the evidence of extant MSS supported by references to library catalogues and the use made of the work by writers. It is an essential preliminary clearing of the ground.

5

I PRIMI UMANISTI E
L'ANTICHITÀ CLASSICA

G. BILLANOVICH

IL KIBBUZ D' 'ITALIA MEDIOEVALE E UMANISTICA'

Da dieci anni non sono più un operaio autonomo, ma il lavoratore di un kibbuz. Il mio kibbuz è l'annuario *Italia medioevale e umanistica*. In questo kibbuz la scelta degli argomenti e la discussione sui dattiloscritti, la revisione delle bozze e la compilazione degli indici avvengono tra tanti scambi, orali ed epistolari, che alla fine si perde abbondantemente il significato dei pronomi possessivi: mio, tuo, suo. Ma solo così può operare una squadra animosa e concorde; e questa è la strada più corta e più buona per insegnare il mestiere ai giovani. Naturalmente chi sta al centro di questa impresa apprende con forte anticipo molte novità e vede mutare velocemente i metodi delle ricerche e gli orizzonti delle discipline.

Approfitto dunque di questa condizione, che in parte è di fatica e pena e in parte di privilegio, per la solenne occasione in cui si tenta di delineare un bilancio delle influenze esercitate dalle letterature classiche nei mille anni tra il 500 e il 1500; e, restando nel tema che più mi è familiare, del primo Umanesimo, anticipo in un rapido racconto episodi che saranno lentamente narrati e analiticamente documentati nei prossimi volumi d'*Italia medioevale e umanistica*.

LA TRADIZIONE DELLE 'AD LUCILIUM',
BRESCIA CAROLINA E BRESCIA GOTICA

Quando cominciò l'Umanesimo? O almeno quando cominciò nelle zone allora più avanzate d'Italia? La decifrazione del lineare B della scrittura cretese-micenea ha anticipato di parecchi secoli la storia della lingua greca. E così sembra che anche gli studi sull'Umanesimo ora si siano allungati con l'aggiunta, all'inizio, di un secolo. Cioè negli ultimi vent'anni si è visto sempre più chiaramente che i vecchi retori italiani — notai o giudici o tutt'al più preti secolari — entrarono molto più presto di quanto credevamo nelle

57

biblioteche di cattedrali o di monasteri, studiarono i codici lì conservati e spesso ne asportarono i testi, nell'originale o in copia, e così resero piano piano queste opere ricchezza viva per i lettori e per le scuole. Quindi se dovessimo riscrivere le *Scoperte* del maestro indimenticabile Remigio Sabbadini, la parte più antica risulterebbe molto più precoce e molto più ampia. Rinunciamo alla questione fastidiosa, e in parte cavillosa, se già questi retori meritino del tutto o no il nome di umanisti. *Rem tene, verba sequentur.* Piuttosto quando quei vecchi retori incominciarono ad agire in queste loro avventure? Ci era parso molto dire che essi imbastirono le loro prime imprese filologiche verso la fine del Duecento. Ma ecco qui un episodio ancora più antico: che ci mantiene nella solita zona fortunata dell'Italia nord-est e ci fa risalire addirittura al principio del Duecento; e che insieme ci mostra come riordinando avventure di cultura dell'età umanistica o dell'età gotica spesso si scoprono e si sistemano anche episodi di cultura dell'età carolina.

Certamente una delle tradizioni più impressionanti, per la qualità altissima del testo e per i movimentati passaggi, è quella delle *ad Lucilium* di Seneca. Più di mezzo secolo fa, nel 1906, il bresciano Achille Beltrami presentò il censimento dei codici di classici latini conservati nella biblioteca italiana che per i suoi manoscritti resta fino ad oggi tra le meno esplorate, la Queriniana di Brescia, e elencò anche un esemplare delle *ad Lucilium*: che presentò come una copia tarda, del s. XIV; e che perciò, quale volgare *deterior*, non fu nemmeno considerata da chi poco dopo, nel 1914, preparò per la Teubner il testo di queste epistole. Invece in seguito il Beltrami annunciò che il Queriniano era molto e molto più vecchio: addirittura del s. X. La segnalazione era tanto fruttuosa che si perdonò che chi attendeva a comporre censimenti di codici potesse avere confuso le forme più arcaiche della carolina con le piene forme della gotica. Così il Queriniano si rivelava uno dei codici più antichi delle *ad Lucilium*; e insieme l'unico tra i vecchi codici che non contenesse solo la prima o la seconda metà, ma intero il *corpus* di queste epistole: e perciò giustamente prima il Beltrami, nelle sue due edizioni, del 1927 e del 1937, e poi gli editori successivi usarono il Queriniano come testimonio fondamentale.

Dove fu formato questo grande codice di un grande classico? Il Beltrami propose: nel monastero più insigne dell'Italia del nord, a Bobbio; ed ebbe l'approvazione del migliore conoscitore allora dei codici e delle carte di Bobbio, il Cipolla. Però poi il saldissimo card.

Mercati, ricostruendo la biblioteca di Bobbio, respinse questa proposta, con argomenti rapidi, ma decisivi. E solo per forza d'inerzia si continuò qua e là a ripetere che il Queriniano proviene da Bobbio. Ora le *ad Lucilium* hanno avuto la fortuna che ne rinnovasse l'edizione, e che anzi descrivesse in un suo libro la tradizione che esse ebbero nel Medioevo, uno dei filologi classici che credo abbia più meritato di essere ammirato negli ultimi anni: Leighton Reynolds, del Brasenose College di Oxford. Cosa propone questo nuovo editore per l'origine del Queriniano? Egli propone, ma con prudente incertezza, che esso sia il codice con le *Epistolae Senecae ad Lucium* registrato nell'inventario che fu formato nel s. XI dei libri del monastero di Pomposa, situato presso il delta del Po.

Reynolds è tanto discreto, che non mi chiama in causa; ma temo di avere un po' di colpa in questa attribuzione: perchè proprio io ho attirato l'attenzione sul monastero di Pomposa, spiegando che lì il caposcuola dei vecchi retori padovani, Lovato Lovati, compì mirabili imprese, ancora prima che finisse il s. XIII: specialmente perchè vi conquistò la lezione isolata delle tragedie di Seneca contenuta nel codice che i filologi classici chiamarono Etrusco e che invece ora che ne scopriamo l'origine chiameremo Pomposiano. E perciò sono obbligato ad intervenire. Nella biblioteca di Pomposa certamente figurarono le *ad Lucilium*, come chiaramente testimonia il vecchio inventario, e quindi dovremo sforzarci di riconoscere le tracce che questo codice può avere lasciato nella tradizone. Ma il codice di Pomposa con le *ad Lucilium* non è affatto il Queriniano. E infatti il blocco più forte dei codici di Pomposa fu formato molto più tardi: nel s. XI sotto il governo felice dell'abate Girolamo, come ricorda la lettera famosa del monaco Enrico che accompagna quell'inventario. Proprio allora fu formato il Pomposiano con le tragedie di Seneca.

Per uscire dal labirinto tentiamo di applicare la regola cara al maestro Lowe: la *home* di un antico codice è, salvo prove contrarie, l'ambiente stesso in cui esso riappare. Già da una diecina d'anni Bernhard Bischoff, la cui generosità è grande quanto la sua esperienza, mi ha aiutato a riunire un gruppetto di codici costruiti nel s. IX in uno stesso scrittoio: con al centro appunto il Seneca Queriniano. E il Seneca e questi altri codici furono formati a Brescia. Per il monastero di S. Faustino, fondato appunto nel s. IX, o per la cattedrale? Credo per la cattedrale.

Reynolds avvertì che il Seneca Queriniano fu postillato da un attento lettore del s. XIII; e formulò la proposta che questo lettore possa essere stato il causidico e retore Albertano da Brescia, i cui trattati morali ebbero intensa fortuna per alcuni secoli. La realtà è sempre tanto vivace e talora tanto poco razionale, che su dieci ipotesi di lavoro di un ricercatore intelligente e cauto nove rischiano di essere sbagliate. Invece ora questa proposta di Reynolds appare pienamente confermata dalla nuova situazione. Lo stesso lettore commentò con costanti postille, e anche con estrosi disegni tanto il Seneca quanto un altro dei grandi codici bresciani del s. IX. Non solo il confronto tra tutte queste postille e le opere di Albertano ci rende perfettamente sicuri che Albertano studiò e annotò qualche codice imponente di un'antica biblioteca bresciana — cioè, ripeto, della biblioteca della cattedrale — ma anche ci rivela che Albertano trovò e studiò, almeno un altro testo illustre e allora presso che ignoto: gli *Epigrammi* di Marziale; e li lesse attentissimamente.

La conquista è molteplice: Seneca, Marziale e anche gli altri testi nobili connessi col Seneca Queriniano; e insieme Brescia carolina e gotica e Albertano. Finora non si è mai parlato con risolutezza della cultura e delle biblioteche a Brescia durante l'alto Medioevo. E invece Brescia fu una delle più robuste città d'Italia nell'età tra i Longobardi e i Franchi. Basti pensare al monastero di S. Salvatore e S. Giulia, sede dapprima di principesse longobarde e franche, e poi appannaggio costante delle regine italiche; e magari anche al museo di arte medioevale che adesso lì è ospitato. Infatti ora intravvediamo nella Brescia del s. IX un grande scrittoio e una grande biblioteca: connessi in scambi frequenti con forti centri transalpini, specialmente, per ovvie ragioni geografiche, della Germania meridionale. Poi, con la nuova civiltà comunale, fiorì Albertano: che si preparò a comporre i suoi fortunatissimi trattati morali studiando con costanza e con profitto gli antichi codici di classici e di Padri nella sua Brescia.

I RETORI PADOVANI, SENECA E LIVIO

Da Albertano si discende naturalmente ai vecchi retori padovani: che, perchè vennero parecchi decenni dopo, furono tanto più colti e tanto più esperti. Padova fu distrutta nel 602 dagli invasori Longobardi; e cominciò a risorgere solo un secolo dopo; e così la nuova Padova non dispose di vecchi tesori librari. Ma, tra l'ultimo Duecento e il primo Trecento, i suoi retori ebbero la forza di andar a conquistare i testi classici che essi tanto amarono, muovendosi da un'estremità all'altra della loro regione: da Pomposa a Verona. Per quanto vedo, due sono le strade attraverso cui meglio si scenderà a scoprire le virtù filologiche che, con un'intensità finora quasi incredibile, ornarono i capofila padovani Lovato Lovati e Albertino Mussato. Una è la tradizione di Seneca, sopra tutto delle tragedie: e qui taccio, perchè non voglio togliere niente al piacere di chi sta per esporre le vicende fondamentali di questa storia in un lungo e articolato racconto per *Italia medioevale e umanistica*. L'altra è la tradizione di Tito Livio. Quasi vent'anni fa presentai nel *Journal of the Warburg and Courtauld Institutes* un nuovo panorama della tradizione degli *ab Urbe Condita*; e in una pagina dell'appendice avvertii che mi restava da esporre come i primi umanisti padovani, una o due generazioni prima del Petrarca, già avevano rinnovato la tradizione delle Decadi. Uno dei recensori di quella memoria, l'amico Alessandro Perosa, avvertì la minaccia di questa proposta e cominciò a domandarsi come questa impresa dei padovani si sarebbe accordata con ciò che conoscevamo della tradizione di Livio. Ora rispondo apertamente che il racconto di questa impresa rivelerà molte virtù recondite di quei vecchi retori e insieme sarà quasi dinamite sotto alcuni degli stemmi, e quindi alcuni degli apparati, proposti dagli editori degli *ab Urbe Condita*. Calcolo di fornire, finalmente, dentro il 1970 questo racconto: il più lungo e il più complicato che mai mi sia toccato di ricostruire.

BENZO D'ALESSANDRIA: VERONA, AVIGNONE E PARIGI

Il più forte vicino e corrispondente di Albertino Mussato fu Benzo: che, come cancelliere, si trovò al centro della politica e della cultura della Verona scaligera; e che esplorò con un ardore pari a quello dei suoi contemporanei padovani i tesori di vecchie biblioteche della Lombardia e del Veneto. Respingiamo subito la proposta, avanzata recentemente, d'identificare il nostro bravissimo Benzo col minimo grammatico del contado veronese maestro Penzo da Ilasi, figlio del notaio Aiolfo. Invece Benzo Cona venne certamente da Alessandria; quindi passò a Milano e a Como; e in fine si fissò a Verona, cancelliere di Cangrande e poi dei suoi nipoti. Ma aggiungiamo un'appendice del tutto nuova: Benzo ebbe un figlio, che visse prima ad Avignone, capitale della repubblica cristiana, dove si alleò col maestro del secolo, Francesco Petrarca, e poi visse a Parigi nella cancelleria del re di Francia. E così scopriamo un collegamento immediato tra Verona e il Petrarca, e persino tra Verona e Parigi.

Padova nella sua ultima età comunale fu rinvigorita dal grande

fortilizio dell'Università e dispose di guide eccezionalmente ener-
giche: nella retorica e nella filologia Lovato e Mussato, nella scienza
e nella filosofia Pietro d'Abano, nel diritto Marsilio da Padova.
Verona godè di una fortuna diversa: ebbe nel suo cuore la miniera
inesauribile della biblioteca della cattedrale. E perciò almeno per
altri cinquant'anni continueremo a scoprire nuove vicende che le
tradizioni di testi classici e sacri incontrarono nella Verona del Trecento. Ne conosco già qualcuna; e solo la strettezza del tempo mi
vieta di raccontarla.

Accanto a Padova e a Verona ebbero forza anche alcuni centri
minori. Già in questa stessa riunione il mio amico Gargan provvederà
a descrivere gli affetti che per i testi classici si ebbero durante il
Trecento a Treviso. Ed è da augurare che, a completare la carta
animosa del Veneto tra l'età di Dante e quella del Petrarca, presto si
ottengano descrizioni simili per Venezia e per Vicenza.

LA LINGUA GRECA E I TESTI GRECI

E la lingua greca e i testi greci? Fino a poco fa questa sarebbe apparsa
una domanda assurda per un'età del tutto cruda: come cercare
nell'orto le ciliege a gennaio. Ma oramai il buon riordinatore di
questo territorio, il collega e amico Agostino Pertusi, ci ha rivelato
come a metà del Trecento un giurista padovano già si presentava al
giudice tenendo sottobraccio il testo greco dell'*Iliade* e, per rafforzare
la sua arringa, ne traduceva in latino qualche brano. Ora un giovane
amico americano sta per narrarci che un maestro che insegnò a
Padova grammatica latina mentre vi operava il Mussato possedette
lì un codice di grande classico greco formato pochi decenni prima in
una forte scuola bizantina. E un altro studioso, tanto bravo quanto
modesto, ci racconta come all'amico del Petrarca e del Boccaccio
Leonzio Pilato fu concesso di studiare e postillare a Pisa l'archetipo
preziosissimo delle *Pandette*. Cioè anche le attenzioni per il greco e lo
studio del greco cominciarono a svilupparsi tra il Veneto e la Toscana
molto più presto e con più forza di quanto pochi anni fa potevamo
immaginare.

UN FALSO ANNUNCIO: LUCREZIO

Naturalmente alle felici rivelazioni qualche volta si mescola un falso
annuncio: che occorre subito reprimere per evitare che si sprechino
tempo e forze in una campagna ricca di messi e povera di mietitori.

Così ora ci viene detto e ripetuto che il Petrarca e il Boccaccio avrebbero letto e imitato Lucrezio; e addirittura nel testo che nel s. IX era conservato a Bobbio. Proprio perchè le nuove ricchezze autentiche sono molte, non ci lasceremo illudere da vane lusinghe: il Petrarca e il Boccaccio non conobbero Lucrezio, nè naturalmente ebbero alcun sospetto delle ricchezze mirabili sepolte a Bobbio. Se essi avessero potuto studiare il *de Rerum Natura*, ne avrebbero riportato richiami e echi massicci nelle loro opere e nelle postille sui loro libri; e dai grandi bacini delle loro biblioteche il poema di Lucrezio sarebbe subito defluito a molti lettori al di qua e anche al di là delle Alpi.

POGGIO BRACCIOLINI E NICCOLÒ NICCOLI

Mi permetto di uscire dal secolo che più amo e di affacciarmi alle porte del Quattrocento. Nella prima metà del Quattrocento l'estrosissimo Poggio Bracciolini operò più fortemente di ogni altro sia nel provocare il passaggio dalla scrittura gotica alla nuova scrittura umanistica, sia nell'accelerare il ricupero glorioso dei testi classici dimenticati. Una fortunata scoperta, annunciata per la via traversa di un catalogo d'antiquariato, rivelò mezzo secolo fa, il *Commentarium Nicolai Nicoli in Peregrinatione Germaniae*: cioè l'elenco di *desiderata* che il Niccoli consegnò ai cardinali Giuliano Cesarini e Niccolò Albergati quando nel 1431 erano in partenza per la Germania. Dieci anni fa Nicolai Rubinstein ritrovò, e pubblicò nel primo volume d'*Italia medioevale e umanistica*, una lettera che il figlio di Poggio, Iacopo, formò sugli appunti del padre, per indicare quali scoperte erano state recentemente operate e quali si potevano ancora operare.

Ora ci arriva sul tavolo la terza grande carta di questo gioco. Il nostro giovane amico Tino Foffano pubblica e illustra un promemoria che il Niccoli, basandosi ancora sulle confidenze di Poggio, compose per Cosimo de' Medici e per i suoi agenti in Francia, sui nuovi testi che si potevano trovare nelle biblioteche di alcuni monasteri di Parigi e della Normandia: S. Vittore, Fécamp, Le Bec-Hellouin. Insieme Foffano presenta i fascimili della scrittura corsiva del Niccoli nelle sue lettere in volgare: facsimili fondamentali, se proprio al Niccoli deve essere attribuita, come l'Ullman propose, l'iniziativa del passaggio dalla corsiva gotica alla nuova cancelleresca all'antica.

EPIGRAFIA E ARCHEOLOGIA

Torno all'ultimo Duecento e al primo Trecento: per affacciarmi lì su un altro versante. Non solo allora i precoci grammatici veneti, e specialmente i padovani, perseguirono con una caccia vigorosa i testi dei classici e dei Padri dentro le vecchie biblioteche. Essi cominciarono anche ad ammirare le antichità: cioè accanto alla filologia cominciarono a sviluppare, sia pure embrionalmente, l'epigrafia e l'archeologia.

Nel 1283, presso le due chiese padovane di S. Stefano e di S. Lorenzo, ricche di memorie remote, fu scavato un antico sarcofago cristiano. Subito accorse l'esperto Lovato Lovati; e dichiarò che quello era il sepolcro del fondatore di Padova, il troiano Antenore. E perciò quel sepolcro fu rapidamente sistemato dentro un'edicola e ornato con un'epigrafe composta dallo stesso Lovato. Non sorridiamo per tanto ingenua fiducia. Invece pensiamo che, mentre l'Europa feudale continuava a essere ornata solo di tombe di prelati e di cavalieri, Bologna alzava le tombe ai glossatori maestri del suo Studio e a Padova Lovato, ispirato appunto dalla tomba di Antenore, si apprestò un nobile sepolcro e suo nipote Rolando da Piazzola, anch'egli letterato, adattò per sè e per i suoi addirittura un sarcofago classico. Insieme pensiamo che la tomba che un secolo dopo accolse il corpo del grandissimo Francesco Petrarca davanti alla chiesa parrocchiale del villaggio padovano di Arquà fu costruita sul modello della presunta tomba di Antenore.

Intanto, pure prima della fine del Duecento, non come tutti ancora dicono già avanti nel Trecento, si ritrovò a Padova presso l'abbazia di S. Giustina una lapide che presentava il nome del più illustre tra gli antichi padovani: di Tito Livio (*CIL*, v, 2865). Naturalmente fu subito creduta l'epigrafe della tomba del grande storico e fu murata nell'atrio della basilica di S. Giustina; e questa epigrafe animò Lovato e il Mussato a ricercare e a restaurare le Decadi superstiti degli *ab Urbe Condita* e poi il Petrarca a comporre la sua lettera a Livio: la *Familiare*, xxiv, 8. Più tardi, credo già nel Quattrocento, riemerse a Padova la lapide della tomba dei Livi: *CIL*, v, 2975. E nel 1413 il cancelliere Sicco Polenton e le autorità padovane vollero illudersi di avere ritrovato, sempre scavando nel l'abbazia di S. Giustina, addirittura il sarcofago di Tito Livio.

Intanto già Albertino Mussato propalava che al posto della basilica di S. Giustina vi fosse stato in antico un tempio dedicato alla dea

Concordia. E Sicco Polenton docilmente, come sempre, lo ripeteva; e i successori accettavano e allargavano la leggenda: quel tempio sarebbe stato costruito dallo stesso Antenore, dopo che aveva accordato i due popoli, i suoi Troiani e i Veneti.

Naturalmente questo scenario archeologico, in piccola parte vero e in gran parte presunto, che gli umanisti padovani intravvedevano nella loro città, prima fondata dagli esuli troiani e poi madre del più grande storico di Roma, eccitò questi letterati a perseguire con zelo intenso la ricerca e lo studio dei testi classici; specialmente dei testi storici, sopra tutto delle storie del loro grande compaesano Tito Livio.

FABULA DOCET

Tentiamo di ricavare da questo mazzo di episodi, vari ma concordi, le conclusioni più tempestive e più utili. Prima di tutto dichiariamo che la carta geografica della cultura italiana tra il Duecento e il Trecento dovrà essere ricomposta per molti tratti con le vicende subite dalle tradizioni dei testi dei classici e anche dei Padri durante questi secoli e con le postille con cui allora furono ricoperti i codici dei classici e dei Padri. Poi aggiungiamo che proprio mentre la specializzazione sta diventando sempre più esclusiva e ciascuno di noi si sente chiuso in un campo sempre più ristretto, si rende sempre più necessario che l'esplorazione e la ricostruzione delle tradizioni dei classici e dei Padri siano svolte in scambi costanti, d'informazioni e di metodi, tra cultori di varie discipline: dalla filologia classica alla filologia medioevale e umanistica e alla paleografia; e alle letterature nelle lingue nazionali, specialmente alla letteratura italiana, che fu connessa più presto e più fortemente con il nuovo stile umanistico; e anche alla storia dell'arte, all'epigrafia e all'archeologia; alla storia della filosofia e alla storia del diritto. Infatti gli umanisti furono essenzialmente grammatici e retori, ma essi agitarono e rinnovarono, tra il Trecento e il Cinquecento, i programmi e i metodi delle altre discipline. E d'altronde le scoperte migliori si fanno, non nelle acque calme al centro di ogni disciplina, ma nelle zone tanto rischiose, quanto fruttuose al confine tra diverse discipline.

NOTA BIBLIOGRAFICA

Nei prossimi volumi d'*Italia medioevale e umanistica* Claudia Villa racconterà la storia del Seneca Queriniano e delle letture di Albertano da Brescia; Guido Billanovich narrerà come i primi umanisti padovani affrontarono le tragedie di

Seneca; Anna Maria Gadda presenterà insieme Benzo d'Alessandria e suo figlio; Philip Stadter illustrerà il grande codice greco appartenuto al vecchio grammatico padovano e Filippo Di Benedetto dirà degli studi di Leonzio Pilato sull'archetipo delle *Pandette*; Tino Foffano pubblicherà il promemoria di Niccolò Niccoli sui codici di autori classici nelle biblioteche francesi; e anche vi si discorrerà della passione che i grammatici padovani ebbero per le antichità. Che il Petrarca e il Boccaccio abbiano conosciuto Lucrezio è stato appena affermato da G. Gasparotto, 'Il Petrarca conosceva direttamente Lucrezio, Le fonti dell'egloga IX, *Querulus* del *Bucolicum Carmen*' e 'Lucrezio fonte diretta del Boccaccio?', *Memorie della Accademia Patavina, Cl. di sc. mor., lett. ed arti*, LXXX (1967–8), 309–55, e LXXXI (1968–9), 5–34; e da B. Hemmerdinger, 'Le Boccaccianus perdu de Lucrèce', *Belfagor*, XXIII (1968), 741.

6

AUSONIUS IN THE
FOURTEENTH CENTURY

R. WEISS

Extant medieval library catalogues reveal only three copies of the poems of Ausonius, two at Bobbio in the late ninth[1] (but no longer there in 1461),[2] and one at St Oyan in the late eleventh century.[3] To these one can add the now lost 'Veronensis' and a certain number of still extant medieval manuscripts,[4] which show how the poetic production of Ausonius had never been entirely forgotten. Little surprise then, that the beginnings of humanism in Italy brought a wave of interest in his poems which, on the other hand, had never been altogether forgotten, if only because some of them occurred in MSS of Bede[5] and Suetonius.[6]

The humanist study of Ausonius began during the first decade of the Trecento, when Benzo d'Alessandria discovered the Veronensis in *archivo ecclesie Veronensis*, that is to say in the Verona Chapter Library, at some date before 1310.[7] Sabbadini, who published the quotations from Ausonius given in Benzo's chronicle,[8] suggested that

---

[1] G. Becker, *Catalogi Bibliothecarum Antiqui* (Bonnae, 1885), pp. 69, 72.

[2] G. Mercati, *De Fatis Bibliothecae Monasterii S. Columbani Bobiensis et de Codice ipso Vat. lat. 5757* (in *Codices e Vaticanis selecti*, XXIII, Biblioteca Vaticana, 1934), p. 61.

[3] L. Delisle, *Le Cabinet des Manuscrits de la Bibliothèque Nationale*, III (Paris, 1881), 386.

[4] On which see, among recent studies, S. Prete, *Ricerche sulla storia del testo di Ausonio* (Roma, 1960), A. Pastorino, 'A proposito della tradizione del testo di Ausonio', *Maia*, XIV (1962), 41–68, F. Sirna, 'Ausonio, Paolino e il problema del testo ausoniano', *Aevum*, XXXVII (1963), 124–35, D. Nardo, 'Varianti e tradizione manoscritta in Ausonio', *Atti dell'Istituto Veneto di scienze, lettere ed arti*, CXXV (1966–7), 321–82.

[5] See G. G. Meersseman & E. Adda, *Manuale di computo con ritmo mnemotecnico dell'arcidiacono Pacifico di Verona* (1844) (Padova, 1966), pp. 25, 29–30, 41, 43, 132 and R. Avesani's review of this book in *Studi Medievali*, ser. 3, VIII (1967), 918–20.

[6] Ausonius's *Caesares* occasionally occur in MSS of Suetonius, cf. Bibliothèque Nationale, Paris, MS Lat. 5802, f. 68v, E. Pellegrin, 'Bibliothèques d'humanistes lombards de la cour des Visconti-Sforza', *Bibliothèque d'Humanisme et Renaissance*, XVII (1955), 224–5, 233.

[7] R. Sabbadini, *Le scoperte dei codici latini e greci ne' secoli XIV e XV*, II (Firenze, 1914), 145–6. On Benzo see the bibliography in R. Weiss, 'La cultura preumanistica veronese e vicentina del tempo di Dante', *Dante e la cultura Veneta...a cura di V. Branca e G. Padoan* (Firenze, 1966), pp. 271–2.

[8] First in R. Sabbadini, 'Bencius Alexandrinus und der cod. Veronensis des Ausonius', *Rheinisches Museum*, n.s. LXIII (1908), 230–3 and again in Sabbadini, *Le scoperte dei codici*, II, 146–9.

he had removed the Veronensis, his suspicion being strengthened by the fact that neither the Veronese author of the 1329 *florilegium* nor Guglielmo da Pastrengo appears to have mentioned Ausonius.[1] The presence of the Veronensis in Verona at some date after 1320 forces one, however, to reach a different conclusion, i.e. that either Benzo did not remove the MS, but transcribed instead from it those poems which had particularly aroused his interest; or, if he had removed it, he returned it when he settled in Verona about 1328, on becoming a notary in the chancery of the lord of the town, Cangrande della Scala.[2]

The presence of the Veronensis in its original home after 1320 is actually revealed to us by an early humanist from Verona, Giovanni de Matociis, generally known as Giovanni Mansionario from his office of sacrist in the Cathedral.[3] It is true that neither in his *Historia Imperialis*,[4] nor in his *de Gestis Pontificum Romanorum*,[5] nor in the tract where he first established the existence of two and not only one Pliny,[6] as was commonly believed during the Middle Ages, does he show any acquaintance with the poems of Ausonius. But following on the completion of the *Historia Imperialis* in 1320 (or very shortly after),[7] he continued for some time to insert additions on the margins of his own fair copy of this treatise.[8] Thus at the end of his account of the Emperor Theodosius, he added on the left-hand margin an account of Ausonius, consisting almost entirely of a list of his writings.[9] Now, that Giovanni gave here a list of the contents of the Veronensis seems more than likely, not only because we know that he relied entirely upon the resources of the Verona Chapter Library for his knowledge of classical texts,[10] but also because some features in the

---

[1] *Ibid.* II, 148.
[2] *Dante e Verona per il VII centenario della nascita* (Verona, 1965), pp. 36–7.
[3] On Giovanni see the bibliography in Weiss, 'La cultura preumanistica', p. 271.
[4] In Vatican Library, MS Chig. I–VII. 259, Biblioteca Capitolare, Verona, MS CCIV, and Biblioteca Vallicelliana, Rome, MS D. 13, 1r–210v. Giovanni's *Descriptio Italie Provincie* in Biblioteca Universitaria, Genova, MS F.I.14, 114v–116v (cf. P. O. Kristeller, *Iter Italicum*, I (London–Leiden, 1963), 245) is merely a section of the *Historia Imperialis*.
[5] Biblioteca Vallicelliana, Rome, MS D.13, 211r–230v.
[6] Cf. Sabbadini, *Le scoperte dei codici*, II, 90 n. 10.
[7] He was still writing the *Historia Imperialis* in 1320, cf. Vatican Library, MS Chig. I. VII. 259, f. 223v.
[8] This being the Vatican MS, which was first identified as the author's own copy by Prof. A. Campana, who attracted my attention to it. An examination of the copy now at Verona has driven me to conclude that this also is an author's working copy.
[9] See below, p. 71. The fact that the additions do not occur in the Vallicelliana MS indicates that they were written after the text of the *Historia Imperialis* had been released by the author.
[10] Cf. Sabbadini, *Le scoperte dei codici*, I, 2–3, II, 88–90.

68

list of works which he provides (he often indicated here the actual metre of some of the verses) point to his having direct access to a very substantial collection of Ausonian poems, while the few bio-graphical data given in it also indicate a reading of at least some of them; all this besides the fact that the list includes some writings which we know for certain to have been in the Veronensis.[1]

The later history of the Veronensis is uncertain. It was no longer in the Chapter Library in 1625, when it was not included in the catalogue of the MSS of the Verona Chapter compiled by the canon Agostino Rezzani,[2] just before these volumes disappeared for about ninety years. All that we know for certain is that the text of the *Cathalogus Urbium Nobilium* in the fifteenth-century codex Tilianus now at Leiden[3] and that in the MS found in the library of Sant' Eustorgio, Milan, by Giorgio Merula, which is now lost but was reproduced in Ferrari's edition of 1490,[4] appear to derive directly or indirectly from the Veronensis.[5] Just as at the same time one cannot dismiss the possibility that the fragment sent to Politian from Verona in 1493 by Matteo Bossi, and not returned to its owner,[6] was actually part of the Veronensis.

A feature of this fragment, which was in a pre-Caroline script,[7] was its inclusion of some items by Prudentius.[8] Now this is not without interest, since some poems by this author also occur in the MS of

---

[1] Below, pp. 71–2.

[2] Printed in G. Turrini, *Indice dei codici capitolari di Verona redatto nel 1625 dal canonico Agostino Rezzani* (Verona, 1965).

[3] University Library, Leiden, MS Voss. Lat. Q. 107, 60r–62r. This section of the MS is generally described as written in a hand endeavouring to reproduce an earlier script, cf. *D. Magni Ausonii Opuscula*, ed. C. Schenkl (Berolini, 1884), p. xx, Sabbadini, *Le scoperte dei codici*, II, 148. This makes one wonder whether any of these scholars ever glanced at the Tilianus, as the folios in question are in fact written in a typically fifteenth-century humanist hand, showing no attempt whatever of reproducing an earlier script.

[4] Ausonius, *Opera* (Mediolani, 1490). No trace of the MS may be found in the 1494 catalogue of the library printed in T. Kaeppeli, 'La bibliothèque de Saint-Eustorge à Milan à la fin du XVe siècle', *Archivum Fratrum Praedicatorum*, XXV (1955), 21–69.

[5] Sabbadini, *Le scoperte dei codici*, II, 148–9. I am not prepared, on the other hand, to accept Sabbadini's identification of the 'Eustorgianus' with part of the Veronensis, particularly as his two main arguments in support of this view, i.e. that the Veronensis had already left Verona during the first half of the fourteenth century and that fos. 60r–62r of the Tilianus show an effort at reproducing an earlier script, can no longer be accepted.

[6] M. Bossus, *Familiares et secundae epistolae* (Mantuae, 1498), fo. 48v, C. Dionisotti, 'Calderini, Poliziano e altri', *Italia medioevale e umanistica* XI (1968, 151–85).

[7] This we know from Bossi, who described the fragment as 'Langobardoque charactere conscriptum', cf. Bossus, *Familiares et secundae epistolae*, fo. 48v, 'scriptura langobardica' then meaning an early script difficult to read, and therefore neither Caroline nor Gothic, cf. S. Maffei, *Verona Illustrata*, pt. I (Verona, 1732), 321, G. Battelli, *Lezioni di paleografia* (Città del Vaticano, 1949), p. 12.

[8] Bossus, *Familiares*, fo. 48v.

Ausonius known as *P* now in Paris and once belonging to Petrarch,[1] which of course suggests some possible relationship between *P* and Veronensis, just as the fact that the Ausonius section in *P* is preceded by the *Mythologicon* of Fulgentius necessarily reminds us that one of the two Bobbio MSS of Ausonius also included this treatise.[2]

When Petrarch acquired *P* is uncertain.[3] Its script and illuminations point to the second rather than the first half of the fourteenth century, while Petrarch's extremely rare annotations are in the hand commonly associated with his old age.[4] In view of this, one is forced to assume that he had another copy of the *Ludus Septem Sapientum* at his disposal in 1343–5 when he was writing the *Rerum Memorandarum Libri*.[5] The Ausonius section of *P* combines texts from different traditions. Thus it is certain that while the *Ludus Septem Sapientum* (and perhaps the pseudo-Ausonian *Periochae Homeri* as well as other poems and the Prudentius items) derive from the Veronensis,[6] this is definitely not the case with the *Cathalogus Urbium Nobilium*.[7]

Apart from the *Rerum Memorandarum Libri*, where he made an extensive use of the *Ludus Septem Sapientum*, Petrarch did not refer very often to Ausonius, although he had access to a MS of his poems long before he acquired *P*,[8] nor did he quote him very often.[9] Boccaccio was also well acquainted with Ausonius's writings. It is true that he seems to have quoted him only twice, both times from

[1] Bibliothèque Nationale, Paris, MS Lat. 8500, fos. 27r–29r.

[2] Becker, *Catalogi Bibliothecarum Antiqui*, p. 72.

[3] On *P* see now A. Petrucci, *La scrittura di Francesco Petrarca* (Città del Vaticano, 1967), p. 128, E. Pellegrin, *La Bibliothèque des Visconti et des Sforza—Supplement* (Florence–Paris, 1969), p. 7, pl. 51.

[4] Petrucci, *La scrittura di Francesco Petrarca*, p. 128.

[5] Where he found it invaluable for his account of the 'septem sapientes' cf. F. Petrarca, *Rerum Memorandarum Libri*, ed. G. Billanovich (Firenze, 1943), pp. 147–53.

[6] The dependence of the *P* text of the *Ludus* from the 'Veronensis' is established in Sabbadini, *Le scoperte dei codici*, II, 149. The fact that the *Periochae Homeri* were in the Veronensis (cf. below, p. 71) certainly suggests that their text in *P* was derived from it. It may be noted here that the *Periochae Homeri* also occur in Bibliotheca Malatestiana, Cesena, MS Plut. XII, cod. 6, on which see P. De Nolhac, *Pétrarque et l'humanisme*, I (Paris, 1907), 207, n. 2, Biblioteca Nazionale, Napoli, MS V.E.29, fos. 1r–9r (only the *Periocha Iliados*).

[7] This is guaranteed to us by the textual differences between *P* and Benzo d'Alessandria's quotations from the *Cathalogus*.

[8] Cf. R. Sabbadini, 'Il primo nucleo della biblioteca del Petrarca', *Rendiconti del R. Istituto Lombardo di scienze e lettere*, XXXIX (1906), 384–5, De Nolhac, *Pétrarque et l'humanisme*, I, 208, F. Petrarca, *Laurea occidens-Bucolicum Carmen X...a cura di G. Martellotti* (Roma, 1968), pp. 81–2.

[9] Cf. De Nolhac, *Pétrarque et l'humanisme*, I, 208, 246, II, 80, to which add *de Remediis Utriusque Fortunae*, II, 125, *Bucolicum Carmen*, X, 338–41, *Rerum Familiarium Libri*, XXII.1, R. Weiss, *Un inedito petrarchesco* (Roma, 1950), p. 60.

Eclogue 6, in the *Genealogia Deorum*.[1] On the other hand, he was also the scribe of a copy of Ausonius's poems, which perished with his library in the Santo Spirito fire,[2] and which had the same beginning and ending as the *editio princeps* of 1472.[3]

Boccaccio's copy meant the introduction of Ausonius into the humanist world of Florence. Thus either Boccaccio's MS or a copy of it was available to Domenico Bandini when he was engaged on his huge encyclopedia,[4] where he also found room for Ausonius in the biographical section.[5] Nor was Ausonius entirely overlooked by Coluccio Salutati who, besides owning the MS now known as *M*,[6] mentioned him more than once in his letters,[7] echoed him once in the *de Seculo et Religione*,[8] and quoted several times from *Eclogue* 25 in the *de Laboribus Herculis*.[9]

The efforts of fourteenth-century humanism proved quite invaluable for the divulgation of the works of Ausonius. It is true that during the first half of the fifteenth century Sicco Polenton did not mention him in his *de Scriptoribus Latinis*. On the other hand, the number of fifteenth-century editions, 1472, 1490, 1494, 1496, and 1499, speaks for itself.

APPENDIX

Vatican Library, MS Chig. I. VII. 259, fo. 119 v.

Decius magnus ausonius uir illustrissimus plura et preclara opera metrico stilo composuit. Scripsit enim paschales uersus stilo heroico. Item ad poncium paulinum primo beati ambrosij notarium, postea nolanum episcopum epistolas metro heroico tres. Item librum de ludo septem sapientum uersu trimetro iambico ad repanium proconsulem. Item epistolas prosaicas ad theodosium imperatorem et ad symachum patricium. Item periochas homerice yliados et homerice odyssie. Item de gripo numeri ternarij uersu heroico librum unum. Item ad hesperium filium suum et ad deoforium ausonium nepotem eodem genere metro. Item eglogam de ambiguitate uite eligende eodem metro. Item ad hesperium filium suum de ordine imperatorum.

---

[1] Boccaccio, *Genealogia Deorum*, IX, 4, XV.7, cf. also A. Hortis, *Studi sulle opere latine del Boccaccio* (Trieste, 1879), p. 410.

[2] O. Hecker, *Boccaccio-Funde* (Braunschweig, 1902), p. 42, P. Gutierrez, 'La biblioteca di S. Spirito in Firenze nella metà del secolo XV', *Analecta Augustiniana*, XXV (1962), 84.

[3] Sabbadini, *Le scoperte dei codici*, I, 30.

[4] *Ibid.* II, 185.

[5] Cf. for instance Vatican Library, MS Urb. Lat. 300, fo. 51 v. The biographical account mostly consists of the text of the *Epicedion in patrem*.

[6] Now in the Biblioteca Nazionale Centrale, Florence, MS Conv. Soppr. I.vi.29, cf. B. L. Ullman, *The Humanism of Coluccio Salutati* (Padova, 1963), p. 173.

[7] *Epistolario di Coluccio Salutati*, ed. F. Novati, II (Roma, 1893), 409, III, 87, 483.

[8] C. Salutati, *de Seculo et Religione*, ed. B. L. Ullman (Florentiae, 1957), p. 61.

[9] C. Salutati, *de Laboribus Herculis*, ed. B. L. Ullman (Turici, 1951), pp. 191, 228, 231, 271, 275, 284, 327, 362.

Item ad eundem de imperatoribus res nouas molitis a decio usque ad dioclecianum uersu iambico trimetro iuxta libros eusebij nannetici ystorici. Item monasticon de erumpnis herculis. Item de institucione uiri boni. Item de etatibus animantum secundum hesiodum. Item de pitagoricis diffinitionibus. Item de cathalogo urbium illustrium singulos libros omnes uersu heroico. Item eodem genere metri de regibus qui regnauerunt in Ytalia inter bellum troianum et principium romani imperij librum unum. Item ad hesperium filium concordie libri fastorum cum libris consularibus librum unum. Item cronicam ab initio mundi usque ad tempus suum. Item libellum de nominibus mensium hebreorum et atheniensium. Item de eruditionibus hebreorum et interpretationibus hebraicorum nominum librum unum. Scripsit et alia plurima et fuit natione burdegalensis et ob ingenii gloriam a theodosio augusto magnis dotatus honoribus et consul est ordinatus.

As was already stated, the above list of Ausonian writings is in all likelihood but an account of the contents of the now lost Veronensis. Besides the reasons already given in support of this view, there are also the following: it includes two works which, thanks to Benzo's quotations, we know for certain to have been in that MS, these being the *Ludus Septem Sapientum* and the *Cathalogus Urbium Nobilium*. Furthermore the fact that the latter is given as *Cathalogus Urbium Illustrium*,[1] is quite significant, since such a title appears only in Benzo's quotations, and must therefore have been in the Veronensis.

A few of the mistakes in the list, such as *deoforium* and *repanium* for *Drepanium*, and *monasticon* for *monostica*, might perhaps suggest that the Veronensis was written in an early minuscule hand, but I would also like to add here that it would be very rash to infer from these very few instances the actual script of the lost MS or its archetype.

The writings given in the list show that the MS seen by Giovanni Mansionario included a number of poems not found together in MSS of one family. And unless I am mistaken, such works as 'Ad eundem (i.e. Hesperium) de imperatoribus res nouas molitis a Decio usque ad Dioclecianum versu iambico trimetro juxta libros Eusebij nanneteci ystorici', the 'Item eodem genere (i.e. heroico) metrum de regibus qui regnaverunt in Italia inter bellum Troianum et principium romani imperii librum unum', the 'Cronicam ab initio mundi ad tempus suum' or the 'De traditionibus hebreorum et interpretationibus hebraicorum nominum librum unum' are not known to occur in any of the extant MSS.

---

[1] One should also note that although in the 1490 edition the *Cathalogus* has the title 'Decius Magnus Ausonius in Cathalogo urbium nobiliu', at fo. A ii v the editor states that 'adiecimus que ex catalogo illustrium urbium nonnulla excerpta epigrammata quae Georgius Merula polyhistor praeceptor noster et primarius dicendi artifex in bibliotheca divi Eustorgii primus indagavit'. As was stated above, p. 69, the *Cathalogus* in this edition shows the text of the Veronensis.

7

OLIVIERO FORZETTA E LA DIFFUSIONE DEI TESTI CLASSICI NEL VENETO AL TEMPO DEL PETRARCA

L. GARGAN

Tra le figure di bibliofili e amatori d'arte del Trecento italiano quella del trevigiano Oliviero Forzetta è senza dubbio una della più singolari. Figlio di un notaio che si era accumulato una notevole sostanza prestando denari ad usura, Oliviero fu usuraio di professione e accrebbe a dismisura il già cospicuo patrimonio paterno fino a diventare uno dei cittadini più ricchi di Treviso e forse della Marca trevigiana. Dopo due infelici esperienze matrimoniali giovanili, nel 1323 gli veniva data in sposa Elisabetta, figlia di Enrico conte di Gorizia e del Tirolo e signore di Treviso, la quale morì nel 1337 senza avergli lasciato prole; altrettanto infecondi furono i due successivi matrimoni con Belladonna, figlia del medico Bettino da Brescia, capostipite della nobile famiglia trevigiana dei Bettignoli, e con una gentildonna padovana, Adeleita da Vigonza, vedova del nobile Enrico da Onigo. Tuttavia queste e altre notizie che il Biscaro potè raccogliere all'inizio del secolo dagli archivi trevigiani,[1] se ci permettono di valutare l'alto grado di riputazione raggiunto dal Forzetta grazie alle proprie ricchezze, sono insufficienti a spiegare in un uomo d'affari del primo Trecento dedito all'usura, una passione per i codici antichi e gli oggetti d'arte che trova riscontro tra i contemporanei solo nel Petrarca e in alcuni suoi seguaci. La celebre nota, più volte pubblicata, dove egli segnò gli acquisti che si proponeva di fare a Venezia nel 1335, è stata giustamente considerata il primo documento a noi giunto di una collezione d'arte e archeologia in senso moderno: tra i manoscritti prevalgono quelli di autori classici e gli oggetti artistici sono rappresentati da lavori di oreficeria, bronzi, medaglie, monete, disegni, pitture, sculture di autori antichi e moderni. Egli non disperava neppure di far entrare nella propria collezione quattro dei celebri putti marmorei del Trono di Saturno di S. Vitale in Ravenna ('quatuor pueri de Ravenna lapidei, qui sunt

---

[1] G. Biscaro, *L'Ospedale (di Treviso) e i suoi benefattori* (Treviso, 1903), pp. 49–69.

taglati Ravenne in Sancto Vitale'), che in seguito furono conosciuti e imitati dal Mantegna, dai Lombardo e dal Sansovino, prima di diventare proprietà della chiesa veneziana di S. Maria dei Miracoli, e che oggi si possono ammirare al Museo Archeologico di Venezia.[1]

Anche dopo il 1335 il Forzetta continuò a ricercare con singolare intraprendenza manoscritti e opere d'arte, riuscendo a mettere insieme, in poco più di trent'anni, una raccolta che poteva certamente competere con più di una collezione rinascimentale sia per il numero che per la qualità dei pezzi. Nel suo testamento, dettato il 16 luglio 1368, mentre era ancora *corpore sanus* (sarebbe morto soltanto cinque anni più tardi), dopo aver nominato sua erede universale la confraternita di S. Maria dei Battuti, dispose che dopo la sua morte gli oggetti artistici fossero venduti poco per volta e il ricavato fosse erogato nel dotare ragazze povere, e volle che i libri venissero divisi tra le biblioteche di due conventi trevigiani: S. Margherita degli eremitani di S. Agostino e S. Francesco dei frati minori. Purtroppo non è stato finora ritrovato nessun catalogo della collezione artistica, posteriore alla nota del 1335; mentre ci è giunto l'inventario dei manoscritti (complessivamente 138 volumi), redatto il 29 novembre 1374, quando gli esecutori testamentari, a un anno dalla morte del Forzetta, spartirono la raccolta tra i due conventi trevigiani; per i codici assegnati a S. Margherita possiamo inoltre disporre di una descrizione più particolareggiata, contenuta nell'inventario della biblioteca di questo convento, compilato nel 1378.

I due inventari, segnalati quasi settant'anni or sono dal Biscaro ma tuttora inediti,[2] si rivelano di estremo interesse per chi voglia studiare la diffusione dei testi classici nel Veneto nell'età del Petrarca e più

---

[1] La nota fu edita per la prima volta da R. Azzoni Avogaro, *Trattato della zecca e delle altre monete che ebbero corso in Trevigi fin tutto il secolo XIV* (Bologna, 1785), p. 51 e in seguito riprodotta da E. Müntz, *Les arts à la cour des papes pendant le XVe et le XVIe siècle*, II (Paris, 1879), 163–5, da I. Schlosser, 'Die ältesten Medaillen und die Antike', *Jahrbuch der kunsthistorischen Sammlungen der allerhöchsten Kaiserhauses*, XVIII (1897), 104 e da A. Serena, *La cultura umanistica a Treviso nel secolo decimoquinto* (Venezia, 1912), pp. 321–2. Vedi inoltre: Müntz, *Precursori e propugnatori del Rinascimento* (Firenze, 1920), pp. 28–9; F. Saxl, 'Iacopo Bellini and Mantegna as antiquarians', nelle sue *Lectures*, I (London, 1957), 150–1, e II, fig. 90; R. Weiss, 'Lineamenti per una storia degli studi antiquari in Italia dal dodicesimo secolo al Sacco di Roma nel 1527', *Rinascimento*, IX (1958), 154. In particolare per i *quattuor pueri* vedi: L. Planiscig, *Venezianische Bildhauer der Renaissance* (Wien, 1921), pp. 325–7; A. Moschetti, 'Le fonti classiche di una celebre opera di Andrea Mantegna', *Atti dell'Istituto veneto...*, LXXIX (1929–30), P. II, 725–9 e fig. 2 e cf. F. Colonna, *Hypnerotomachia Poliphili*, ed. G. Pozzi e L. A. Ciapponi (Padova, 1964), I, 44 e II, 81.

[2] Conto di pubblicarli presto, insieme a un altro catalogo della biblioteca di S. Margherita del 1362.

precisamente la fortuna che essi ebbero in questo tempo nelle città di Venezia e Treviso, dove verosimilmente il Forzetta si procurò la maggior parte dei manoscritti della propria collezione. La *nota* che abbiamo appena ricordato ci fa sapere che nel 1335 il Forzetta cercava manoscritti di autori classici nelle scuole di grammatica e nei conventi veneziani:

Item querere fratrem Symonem de Parma ordinis predicatorum in conventu Veneto pro Seneca completo...Item a fratre Titiano ordinis predicatorum conventus Veneti querere de libro Orosii. Item querere a bidellis de maiore Ovidio et omnibus aliis Ovidiis, Sallustio, Marco Tullio, Rhetorica nova et antiqua Tulli, Servio, Tito Livio, Valerio Maximo, Moralibus super Iob Sancti Gregori, Historiis Romanis, Tullio opere completo.[1]

Oltre che a Venezia, negli anni seguenti egli trovò certamente testi antichi anche nella sua Treviso, dove ora sappiamo che esistevano in gran numero scuole di grammatica e retorica[2] e non mancavano neppure, fin dal primo Trecento, copisti di professione.[3]

Accanto agli autori e ai testi classici più noti, che ricorderemo tra breve, nella collezione figurava qualche opera che nel primo Trecento aveva ancora una diffusione limitata, come le *Odi* e gli *Epodi* di Orazio, di cui il Forzetta possedeva addirittura più esemplari, alcune opere non identificabili di Apuleio, gli *Stratagemata* di Frontino, il *Breviarium* di Rufo Festo, le *Mitologie* di Fulgenzio e forse anche gli *Epigrammi* di Marziale; ma vi mancavano i testi più rari che i preumanisti veronesi e lo stesso Petrarca andavano allora riscoprendo nella Biblioteca Capitolare di Verona e che in parte i padovani avevano conosciuto fin dal secolo precedente.[4]

La presenza nella collezione delle opere liriche di Orazio è probabilmente da mettere in rapporto con un esemplare della *Odi* del s. X–XI, oggi conservato alla Biblioteca Ambrosiana di Milano (MS Q 75 sup.), che verso la metà del Duecento fu letto e studiato in una scuola di grammatica di Treviso (come mostrano le scritture dei fogli di guardia finali e, tra queste, specialmente un elenco di scolari

---

[1] Serena, *La cultura*, p. 321. Dei classici qui ricordati mancano negli inventari soltanto Orosio, Livio e Servio. Le *Historiae Romanae* potranno essere identificate con il *Breviarium* di Rufo Festo.

[2] L. Gargan, 'Giovanni Conversini e la cultura letteraria a Treviso nella seconda metà del Trecento', *Italia medioevale e umanistica*, viii (1965), 86–111.

[3] Come risulta da alcuni documenti ancora inediti, conservati negli archivi trevigiani.

[4] Per il preumanesimo veronese basterà qui rinviare a Weiss, 'La cultura preumanistica veronese e vicentina del tempo di Dante', in *Dante e la cultura veneta. Atti del convegno di studi organizzato dalla fondazione 'Giorgio Cini' per il VII centenario della nascita di Dante* (Firenze, 1966), pp. 263–72; e per quello padovano a Guido Billanovich, '*Veterum vestigia vatum* nei carmi dei preumanisti padovani', *Italia medioevale e umanistica*, i (1958), 155–243.

sicuramenti trevigiani *qui solverunt* o *qui non dederunt* al maestro una certa tassa per l'insegnamento ricevuto) e in seguito divenne proprietà del notaio trevigiano Marco di Michele Adelmario (†1345), che vi aggiunse un suo atto del 24 settembre 1291. Un'altra mano ducentesca aveva in precedenza trascritto nell'ultimo foglio di guardia una canzone provenzaleggiante in volgare settentrionale, riconducibile all'area trevigiana, pubblicata recentemente da Ignazio Baldelli.[1]

Gli *Epigrammi* di Marziale, poco divulgati nel Medioevo, furono noti nel Veneto ai preumanisti padovani e veronesi molto tempo prima che il Boccaccio li riscoprisse a Montecassino nel 1362–3; ma è impossibile stabilire con certezza se anche il Forzetta sia riuscito a procurarsene una copia, perchè il 'Marcialis (MS: Marcianus) Cocus' che in uno dei suoi manoscritti figurava vicino al *de Planctu Naturae* di Alano da Lilla, all'*Apocalypsis Goliae* attribuita al medesimo autore, al *de Nuptiis* di Marziano Capella e a un commento all'*Etica* di Aristotele, poteva anche essere il poeta medioevale inglese Goffredo di Winchester, con il quale Marziale veniva spesso confuso.[2]

Sconosciuto ai preumanisti padovani e veronesi sembra invece Apuleio, di cui il Petrarca possedette quasi tutte le opere, almeno dal 1343, nel Vaticano lat. 2193.[3] Poco dopo la metà del secolo Zanobi da Strada scopriva a Montecassino il famoso Mediceo II comprendente le *Metamorfosi*, il *de Magia* e i *Florida* che il Boccaccio si copiò nel Laurenziano 54, 32 aggiungendovi il *de Deo Socratis*.[4] Il codice che

[1] Baldelli, 'Una canzone veneta provenzaleggiante del Duecento', *Studi di filologia italiana*, XVIII (1960), 19–28 e v. in particolare le note di pp. 19–22, dove sono riportati ampi brani tratti dai fogli di guardia del manoscritto. Il Baldelli tuttavia, pur riferendo nomi come *Odoricus de Sancto Bartholomeo qui legit de Donato, Bonus puer, Cabriellus filioçus magistri*, non sembra accorgersi che ai ff. 123v e 125r vengono elencati scolari di grammatica (e l'esame dei vari nomi e cognomi ci assicura che si tratta di trevigiani) e trascrive erroneamente, non riconoscendolo, il nome del notaio trevigiano Marco di Michele Adelmario: sul quale vedi A. Marchesan, *Gaia da Camino nei documenti trevisani* (Treviso, 1904), pp. 170–3 e *Treviso medievale* (Treviso, 1923), I, 93, 218, 402 e II, 128, 255, 265,453.

[2] R. Sabbadini, *Le scoperte dei codici latini e greci ne' secoli XIV e XV*, II (Firenze, 1914), 227 e 235; M. Manitius, *Handschriften antiker Autoren in mittelalterlichen Bibliothekskatalogen* (Leipzig, 1935) (Beihefte zum Zentralblatt für Bibliothekswesen, 67), pp. 130–1; Gius. Billanovich, *Petrarca letterato*, I. *Lo scrittoio del Petrarca* (Roma, 1947), pp. 263–4; G. Martellotti, 'Petrarca e Marziale', *Rivista di cultura classica e medioevale*, II (1960), 388–93; A. Mazza, 'L'inventario della "parva libraria", di Santo Spirito e la biblioteca del Boccaccio', *Italia medioevale e umanisticae* IX (1966), 16, 49.

[3] F. Petrarca, *Rerum Memorandarum Libri*, ed. Gius. Billanovich (Firenze, 1943), CXXVI e 29. Per una tavola del codice vedi M. Vattasso, *I codici petrarcheschi della Biblioteca Vaticana* (Roma, 1908), pp. 161–2.

[4] Gius. Billanovich, *I primi umanisti e le tradizioni dei classici latini* (Friburgo (Sv.), 1953), pp. 30–2; Mazza, *L'inventario*, pp. 42, 47, 62, 66–7, 72.

ora ritroviamo nella collezione Forzetta sembra essere la prima testimonianza di una tradizione veneta di Apuleio e dovrà essere accostato all'esemplare delle *Metamorfosi* posseduto a Venezia da Paolo de Bernardo almeno dal 1380[1] e al *de Magia* trascritto verso la fine del Trecento dall'umanista feltrino Antonio da Romagno nel Marciano zl 469, insieme al *Timeo* di Platone nella traduzione di Calcidio, al *de Natura Deorum* di Cicerone e ai *Saturnalia* di Macrobio.[2] Dalla descrizione che ne dà l'inventario del 1378 non possiamo tuttavia precisare quali opere di Apuleio fossero comprese nel codice del Forzetta, che conteneva anche il *Timeo*, come il Marciano, e altre opere platoniche.

Gli *Stratagemata* di Frontino, il *Breviarium* di Rufo Festo e le *Mitologie* di Fulgenzio erano testi conosciuti nel primo Trecento a Verona,[3] ma dovevano essere abbastanza diffusi anche in altre città venete.[4] Nella raccolta del Forzetta Frontino e Rufo Festo erano tramandati insieme a un'*Ars Rhetorica* medioevale e a un *Opusculum de Vitiis et Virtutibus* e Fulgenzio figurava vicino ad alcuni trattati anonimi.

Gli altri classici latini della collezione Forzetta furono quasi tutti molto noti nel Medioevo. Di Cicerone il bibliofilo trevigiano possedette due copie dei *Paradoxa*, il *de Officiis*, il *de Amicitia*, il *de Senectute*, tre copie del *de Inventione* e due della pseudociceroniana *Rhetorica ad Herennium*; di Sallustio il *Bellum Catilinae* in ben quattro esemplari; di Virgilio un'opera non identificabile (probabilmente l'*Eneide*); di Orazio, oltre alle *Odi* e agli *Epodi*, che abbiamo già ricordato, le *Satire* e l'*Ars Poetica*; di Ovidio due copie delle *Epistulae*, l'*Ars Amatoria*, i *Remedia Amoris*, le *Metamorfosi*, i *Fasti*, i *Tristia*, due copie delle *Epistulae ex Ponto* e un florilegio di varie opere. Nella collezione figuravano inoltre l'*Epitome* di Giustino delle *Historiae Philippicae* di Pompeo Trogo, le *Satire* di Persio e quelle di Giovenale, la *Farsaglia* di Lucano, uno dei due poemi di Stazio e l'opera di Valerio Massimo. Di Seneca il Forzetta riuscì a procurarsi quasi tutte le opere, alcune

---

[1] L. Lazzarini, *Paolo de Bernardo e i primordi dell'Umanesimo in Venezia* (Genève, 1930), pp. 87 e 133.

[2] Sabbadini, 'Antonio da Romagno e Pietro Marcello', *Nuovo archivio veneto*, n.s. xxx (1915), P. 1, 211; Plato, *Timaeus a Calcidio translatus commentarioque instructus*, ed. J. A. Waszink (Londinii et Leidae, 1962), pp. cxvii–cxviii.

[3] Sabbadini, *Le scoperte*, ii, 224–5 e 249. Un codice del *Breviarium* di Festo (Bergamo, Biblioteca Civica, ms. Δ v 18) venne scritto nel maggio del 1378 *dum in Veronensi agro domini Bernabovis immanis exercitus permoraretur*: cf. P. O. Kristeller, *Iter italicum*, i (London–Leiden, 1963), 8.

[4] Per un codice di Fulgenzio posseduto nel 1372 dal veneziano Ludovico Gradenigo vedi Manitius, *Handschriften*, p. 304.

delle quali in più copie: dai *Dialoghi*, al *de Clementia*, al *de Beneficiis*, alle *Naturales Quaestiones*, alle *Epistole* alle *Tragedie*: comprese il *de Formula Honestae Vitae*, altre opere spurie e le cosiddette *Declamationes* di Seneca retore. Gli inventari ricordano inoltre le *Declamationes Maiores* dello pseudo Quintiliano, il *Liber in Rufinum* di Claudiano, le *Institutiones Grammaticae* di Prisciano in più esemplari, il *de Nuptiis Philologiae et Mercurii* di Marziano Capella, e una trascrizione medioevale in versi della medesima opera (*Liber Marciani Capelle per versus*),[1] il *de Differentiis Topicis* e il *de Consolatione Philosophiae* di Boezio.

Di autori greci la collezione comprendeva la *Geometria* di Euclide nella traduzione di Gerardo da Cremona, la versione medioevale del Πρὸς Δημόνικον di Isocrate, numerose traduzioni di opere aristoteliche e due copie del *Timeo* di Platone nella versione di Calcidio.

Gli autori cristiani erano rappresentati da S. Ambrogio (estratti dal *de Ieiunio*), S. Agostino (*de Civitate Dei*, *Soliloquia*, commento all'*Epistula ad Parthos* e altri trattati spuri), S. Crisostomo (*Homiliae de Laudibus Pauli*), l'epistola *Cogitis me* dello pseudo S. Gerolamo e altre opere patristiche, S. Gregorio (*Moralia in Iob*, *Homiliae in Hezechielem*, *Dialoghi* e *Pastorale*), Cassiodoro (*Variae* e *de Anima*) e Isidoro di Siviglia (*Synonyma*).

Un cenno particolare meritano i commenti medioevali a classici latini presenti in numero considerevole nella collezione, anche se non tutti facilmente identificabili. Tra questi ultimi sono un 'Commentum super Rhetorica Tullii. Principium: "Materia"; finis: "Aristotelis"'; uno 'Scriptum Oracii'; un 'Commentum super Prisciano minori' e una 'Sententia Johannis Theotonici sive Commentum super Prisciano minori.' Si possono invece riconoscere il commento di Arnolfo d'Orléans ai *Fasti* di Ovidio, che ci è giunto completo soltanto in tre manoscritti,[2] quelli, più diffusi, di Roberto Kilwardby a Prisciano[3] e di Nicola Treveth al *de Consolatione* di Boezio[4] e le *Glosse*

---

[1] Cf. Cl. Leonardi, 'I codici di Marziano Capella', *Aevum*, XXXIII (1959), 478.

[2] F. Ghisalberti, 'Arnolfo d'Orléans, un cultore di Ovidio nel secolo XII', *Memorie del R. Istituto Lombardo di scienze e lettere*, XXIV (1932), 161–6.

[3] Su questo commento (al 'Priscianus maior' e al 'Priscianus minor') vedi da ultimo J. Pinborg, *Die Entwicklung der Sprachtheorie im Mittelalter* (Münster, 1967) (Beiträge zur Geschichte der Philosophie und Theologie des Mittelalters, XLII, 2), p. 355 s.v. e in particolare p. 225.

[4] P. Courcelle, 'Étude critique sur les Commentaires de la *Consolation* de Boèce (IXe–XVe siècle)', *Archives d'histoire doctrinale et littéraire du Moyen âge*, XIV (1939), 97–100 e 133–4 e *La Consolation de philosophie dans la tradition littéraire. Antécédents et postérité de Boèce* (Paris, 1967), pp. 318–19 e 412–13.

anonime a Lucano di cui sono stati pubblicati ampi estratti dal Weber nel secolo scorso.[1]

La raccolta era anche singolarmente ricca di opere grammaticali, di *summae dictaminis* e di testi poetici minori di autori medioevali che venivano letti nelle scuole di grammatica dagli scolari che dovevano ancora intraprendere lo studio dei classici. Non mancavano numerose opere di filosofi e trattatisti medioevali: delle quali qui ricorderemo, come più significative, il *de Mundi Universitate* di Bernardo Silvestre, il *Moralium Dogma Philosophorum* attribuito a Guglielmo di Conches, l'*Epistolario* e il *de Amicitia Christiana* di Pietro di Blois, il *de Amore* di Andrea Capellano, la *Clavis Physicae* di Honorius Augustodunensis, il *de Puritate Artis Logicae* di Walther Burley e la *Monarchia* di Dante.

Nel suo testamento il Forzetta faceva obbligo ai due conventi trevigiani ai quali legava la propria collezione libraria di conservare i volumi nelle rispettive biblioteche

et ibidem concatenari et firmari, ita quod nunquam possint inde auferi nec alienari, sed semper ad usum dictorum fratrum in dictis armariis remaneant catenati, ut inde dicti fratres possint vias intelligere rectas et mentes eorum ad celestia sublimare, ac etiam ad seculares homines per ipsorum doctrinam procedatur effectus seu possit hostendi.

Nonostante questa clausola la collezione andò presto dispersa e alla fine del Cinquecento sembra se ne fosse perduto persino il ricordo.[2] Dalla biblioteca degli eremitani alcuni volumi uscirono probabilmente fra il Tre e il Quattrocento se, come sembra, da un Seneca con estratti dell'*Etica* di Aristotele, assegnato nel 1374 al convento di S. Margherita, venne tratto l'attuale codice lat. 3134 della Biblioteca Nazionale di Vienna, scritto da due o tre mani francesi del primo Quattrocento. Nell'inventario del 1378 il codice del Forzetta è così descritto:

Liber Senece in quo sunt eius opuscula, videlicet octo Epistole quas misit ad Paulum; Epistole morales ad Lucillum centum XXV quas redegit in libros XXII; item De clementia ad Neronem libri II; De remediis fortuitorum; De septem liberalibus artibus; De quatuor virtutibus; Declamationum libri IX; De questionibus naturalibus libri sex; Proverbia; De moribus; De beneficiis libri VII; De providentia dei libri duo; De beata vita; De tranquillitate animi; De brevitate vite; De ira libri tres et De consolatione ad Marciam, Elbiam et Pollionem. Principium: 'Lucius Alneus'. Finis: 'omnibus seculis'. Item in eodem volumine continentur

[1] M. A. Lucani *Pharsalia*, ed. C. F. Weber, III (Lipsiae, 1831); cf. B. M. Marti, 'Literary criticism in the mediaeval commentaries on Lucan,' *Transactions and Proceedings of the American Philological Association*, LXXII (1941), 245–6.

[2] Biscaro, *L'Ospedale*, pp. 67–9.

excepta de libro Ethicorum Aristotelis secundum translationem de arabico in latinum. Principium: 'Unusquisque'. Finis: 'commixti sunt'; cum tabulis et corio viridi.

Le medesime opere di Seneca, in successione pressochè identica, troviamo nel codice di Vienna, con la sola esclusione della *Consolatio ad Pollionem*, assente probabilmente anche dal codice del Forzetta che finiva, come il Viennese, con la *Consolatio ad Helviam Matrem*. Corrispondono inoltre perfettamente nel titolo, nell'*incipit* e nell'*explicit* gli estratti dell'*Etica* di Aristotele, che nel codice di Vienna si trovano tra le *Quaestiones naturales* e i *Proverbia* e non sono stati finora rinvenuti in altri manoscritti.[1]

[1] Per una descrizione sommaria del codice di Vienna vedi S. Endlicher, *Catalogus codicum philologicorum latinorum Bibliothecae Palatinae Vindobonensis* (Vindobonae, 1836), pp. 97–100; *Tabulae codicum manuscriptorum in Bibliotheca Palatina Vindobonensi asservatorum*, II (Vindobonae, 1878), 211–12. In particolare per gli estratti di Aristotele: G. Lacombe, *Aristoteles latinus*, I (Romae, 1939), 294.

PART III

METHODS OF TEACHING
AND SCHOLARSHIP

8

LIVING WITH THE SATIRISTS

B. BISCHOFF

The subject which I should like to treat concerns a group of poets belonging to that canon of Roman and early Christian authors that was read in the medieval schools of the pre-Scholastic period. In the selection of these authors as well as in the development of the type of commentary made on them an important part was played by the generation of Irish scholars who worked on the Continent in the middle of the ninth century and by Lupus of Ferrières, as well as by the two Auxerre masters, Heiric and Remigius, who stood on their shoulders. These men were aware that a fruitful study of ancient authors required more than mere verbal glossing and were eager to provide the necessary apparatus. It is in the context of the development of this kind of classical scholarship that we must set the examples I shall mention.

If we take the commentaries which were composed during the early Middle Ages, we find that some of them are obviously dependent on ancient scholia. Their approach is largely impersonal. But there are also cases where a medieval commentator modernises the basic material he has borrowed from his predecessors. He makes allusions for example to the legal usage of his day;[1] and where no ancient commentary existed, as happened with the work of Martianus Capella, we find these medieval scholars taking endless trouble to collect learned explanations; and they even invent some more or less fanciful ones of their own.

The desire to produce new explanations became more insistent as the cathedral schools rose to prominence towards the end of the tenth century, since their growing fame was accompanied by jealous rivalries between their teachers. But compared to what we know about textbooks for the teaching of the liberal arts, including the *quadrivium*, our knowledge about the commentaries which were produced is very meagre. Only a small number of them have been studied so far. We have the commentary on the *Metamorphoses* by that

---

[1] E. M. Sandford in P. O. Kristeller (ed.), *Catalogus translationum et commentariorum: Medieval and Renaissance Commentaries* (Washington, 1960), I, 177.

6-2

once famous teacher, Manegold of Lautenbach[1] who glossed also Cicero's *de Inventione*, Priscian and several books of the Bible. Excerpts from his work on Ovid are available in print.[2] But the glosses to Virgil by his contemporary Magister Ansellus or Anselmus still await careful examination. This commentator is probably to be identified with Anselm of Laon, and it is likely that glosses to Lucan and to Statius can also be ascribed to him.[3]

A medieval Latin scholar looked upon the Roman writers and especially upon the authors of school texts, the *auctores*, as teachers from whom he could acquire a standard of writing, who presented him with the rules of literary technique and awoke his creative imagination. But they were also close to his heart, and he lived with them as with friends. The separation caused by the centuries that had passed was forgotten, and the barrier between the Christian and the pagan became negligible. Such an attitude was accentuated by the idea that there had been pagan prophets and by the invention of pure fables.[4]

Already in the eleventh century the Christianisation of Ovid was begun: Manegold of Lautenbach maintained that the learned poet had outwardly professed faith in the heathen gods because he feared the emperors, but that in reality he had hidden Christian truth in his works. The *melior natura* in *Metamorphoses* I, 21 is explained as *voluntas dei*,[5] or even as *filius dei*.

In a commentary on Horace—about which I shall speak in more detail later—the homage paid to Mercury–Augustus (*Odes* I, 2, 41 ff.) is explained in the following way:

Hoc hic intelligitur dictum de Augusto, sed in veritate quamquam nescienter loquebantur et quasi prophetabant de Christo, qui in tempore Augusti natus fuit et Vergilius: 'Iam nova progenies caelo demittitur alto'. (*Ecl.* IV, 7).[6]

---

[1] Mary Dickey, 'Some Commentaries on the *de Inventione* and *ad Herennium* of the eleventh and early twelfth centuries', *Medieval and Renaissance Studies*, VI (1968), 9–13.

[2] C. Meiser, 'Ein Commentar zu den Metamorphosen des Ovid' in *Sitzungsberichte der Königl. Bayerischen Akademie der Wissenschaften: Philosophisch-philologische und historische Classe* (1885), pp. 47 ff. For the commentary on Cicero, *de Inventione*, see MS XVIM 7, saec. XII of York Cathedral Library.

[3] V. Rose, *Verzeichniss der lateinischen Handschriften der Königlichen Bibliothek zu Berlin*, 2, 3, 1306 for the Virgil commentary in Berlin MS Lat. fol. 34, saec. XII which also contains the glosses on Lucan and Statius.

[4] E.g. Ps.-Ovidius, *de Vetula* and the legend of Ovid's conversion at the hands of St John the Apostle; B. Bischoff, *Mittelalterliche Studien* (Stuttgart, 1966), I, 144 ff.

[5] Meiser, 'Ein Commentar', pp. 51 ff.

[6] H. Botschuyver, *Scholia in Horatium* (Amstelodami, 1942), IV, 8.

Research which seeks to evaluate the medieval commentaries according to the amount of material they contain from lost scholia, will be disappointed by works which propagate views of this nature. However, it is precisely from such works that we can gain interesting insights into the relation between the medieval teachers and students and their ancient friends, the *auctores*. It is astonishing to see to what extent the *auctores* could be assimilated, if not wholly absorbed. I do not wish to speak here about the well-known problem of the allegorisation of Homer, Virgil or Ovid. Rather, I want to illustrate this process of assimilation from some commentaries on the satirists taken from the late eleventh and the first half of the twelfth century, which are either unknown or to which little attention has been given so far. It is the content of such popular-philosophic poetry as we find in Roman satire which could appeal most directly to the medieval mind.

The first text is a fragmentary commentary of Persius which extends from the middle of the first satire to verse 11 of the fourth satire. This commentary is found in a late eleventh-century manuscript from the monastery of St Gall.[1] As far as I know it has not been identified and has not received attention apart from the vague reference in the catalogue with no author indicated.[2] Nevertheless it does deserve special notice, not only because it can be dated with precision, but also because it can be assigned to a famous school.

Let us look at the exposition of verse 95 of the first satire in which after *Berecyntius Attis* and *qui caeruleum dirimebat Nerea delphin* a third sample of the poetry in the now fashionable style is given:

Sic: costam longo subduximus Appenino

In this passage Persius rebukes those who with enormous exertions begin a great undertaking from which they will derive no benefit once it is finished. It is just as if the king would command the people from Liège to help him in the war against the Saxons. Then they would all assemble and choose a peasant [*rusticum*] whom they would send to the king. But the peasant would say, 'I shall certainly not go [*Ego certo non ibo*], because I have no horses nor any of the other necessary things.' And then they would give him all that he needed. Now he would start out, but would cover only one mile a day. At long last he would reach the king, but no one would pay any attention to him because he was only an ordinary person. If they, the people, would say after his return, 'What did you do?' and he would answer, 'I saw the king', then this would be just as useless as when someone went to the Apennines with a great cart and many people in order to make the mountains longer by one rib etc.

[1] MS. 868, pp. 194–201.
[2] G. Scherrer, *Verzeichniss der Handschriften der Stiftsbibliothek von St. Gallen* (Halle, 1875), p. 300.

From what follows I want to mention only the explanation of the word *subduximus*: '*sub, idest parum* (that is to say one mile per day), *duximus*...' Now let us consider another sample from the second satire, the gloss on verses 6–7:

> Haut cuius promptum est murmurque humilesque susurros
> Tollere de templis et aperto vivere voto

which are a part of the polemic addressed to Macrinus (*Hunc Macrine diem*...) against the foolish and sinful prayers which the people offer to the gods. Starting from the very first verse of the poem, the commentator has horribly misunderstood the intended meaning: according to him it is a satire against a *leccator* who is trying to persuade a pious man to take up *leccatura*. But the pious man whom the *leccator* addresses is by no means Macrinus, as we should expect from *Macrine* in the vocative case. Instead the commentator makes the following paraphrase of '*macrine*': 'Shall we pass this feast-day with an empty stomach?'

Verse 7 is then interpreted in such a way that the bad counsellor, whose main argument seems to be that the gods do not grant prayers anyhow, is made to give the following advice:

> There is one more reason why you should not strive for a holy way of life: even a man who was capable of building many temples in God's honour, who can daily sing the psalms in church, who, what is more, can raise ten dead to new life again, even such a man cannot be raised (*tollere*) to a higher way of life by such works, yes, even if he should accomplish the reconciliation of two kings.

A few lines further the meaning is made quite clear:

> *Tollere* means to let someone attain to a high office, particularly that person who can reconcile two kings with each other, such as Rudolf and Henry when they want to engage in battle (*congredi*), which is a bad thing.

The kings in question are Henry IV and Rudolf of Swabia. The latter had been elected as rival monarch on 15 March 1077 and he died on 15 October 1080, after he had lost one hand in the battle. The Saxons were Henry's enemies with whom he had been fighting since 1074. They were also the strongest supporters of his rival. There is no question that the above words of the commentary must be dated between 1077 and 1080. But it is not certain that the word *congredi* must refer to the first encounter between the two royal armies. Should this be the case however, then the time-span can be narrowed down to the time between the election of Rudolf and the battle of Mellrichstadt which took place on 7 August 1078.

Moreover it is not by chance that the commentator chose the people of Liège as an example. Further allusions do indicate that the commentary must have been composed by a scholar from that city. For the author names two fellow teachers, a Magister Lambert whom he esteems greatly and a Magister Nizo who had been chased away by the citizens of Liège. He also mentions a certain Hugo who 'est garrulus sicut ille pessimus leccator qui est in Leodio', and he is acquainted with the fair in the near-by city of Maastricht: 'illud forum quo multi conveniunt in anno sicut Traiectum ad missam Sancti Johannis'. There can be no doubt then that this exposition is a product of the school of Liège which attracted a great number of students from the end of the tenth to the beginning of the twelfth century.

The commentary, which curiously enough does not seem to have made use of ancient scholia, displays a consistency of method that has a flavour of pedantry. As in the case of *subduximus* the author explains almost regularly composite words according to his own definite rules:

> each *de* means *deorsum* (*id est parum*), hence *deceptus*, i.e. *deorsum captus*
> each *di* means *diverso modo*, hence *dirigat*, i.e. *diverso modo regat*
> each *ex* means *extra*, hence *edictum*, i.e. *dictum extra omnia*
> each *in* means *intus* or *interius*, hence *ignovisse*, i.e. *intus* (*bene*) *novisse*

and so forth.

It is obvious that such explanations will lead him in many cases to wrong interpretations which will often postulate a meaning that is the opposite of what the poet had intended.

The commentator also makes copious use of etymologies, e.g. *magister: maior in statione*. He defines pronouns with great precision: *hic: demonstrabilis; ille: a longe demonstrabilis;* and has a certain predilection for periphrastic constructions using the participle *ens*, e.g.

Et quale est illud dedecus? Certe in quo ens id est cogitans secum. Trossulus id est ille qui parum est Troes id est qui parum est curialis quia Troes erant multum curiales, ille qui ita parum curialis est ens in decore etc.

Should further glosses with these characteristics be found in the future, it will be possible to establish identity of authorship or at least of the school from which the work proceeded.

A half or three-quarters of a century later several commentaries to Horace were written which show some points of similarity with those just cited. One of them has been edited by H. J. Botschuyver in volume IV of his *Scholia in Horatium*. The edition is based on two manuscripts from Paris, one of which is from the first half of the twelfth century. Botschuyver did not give any conclusive proof for his assumption that this particular commentary should be ascribed to Heiric of Auxerre.[1] Nor did he make any attempt to disprove the theory of Paul Wessner who had attributed a different one of the commentaries in Botschuyver's volumes to the Carolingian school of Auxerre.[2] The commentary edited in volume IV seems to be the work of a single author who wrote glosses on the entire works of Horace. For material explanations, especially of proper names, he borrows a great deal from earlier scholia. But in spite of his indebtedness to tradition, it is from his commentary that I have been able to cite the *nescienter prophetantes*.

Of quite another vein is a commentary included in the same miscellaneous volume of the St Gall monastic library which contains the commentary on Persius. It has been put together from several parts of unequal size all of which originated in the middle of the twelfth century or slightly earlier. With the exception of part of the odes all the books of Horace are explained, the *Ars Poetica* in no fewer than three series of glosses.[3] In contrast to the texts mentioned above, some parts of this commentary are interspersed with French or German words which in places occur actually side by side. When explaining the word *coactor* in *Serm.* I, 6 the author mentions the town of Zürich: he says *coactor* is either a merchant who sells all kinds of wares or he is a man who gathers clients for the merchant who is offering his goods with the word *chouf*—as they do in Zürich. But the commentator is also familiar with conditions in France. The poor Thracians employed by the Romans for public services remind him of the Bretons who have to perform the same ugly chores in Laon.

It is certain that the commentary to the satires (I, 5) was written after 1066: for the dedication of a chain *ex voto* to the Lares is compared with the custom of captives offering their chains to St Theobaldus, a great helper in all kinds of trouble, and the saint died in that year. Likewise in the explanation to *Epistles* I, i reference is made to an unfavourable rumour about a certain Gregorius who must be Gregory VII, who became Pope in 1073. It follows therefore that

[1] Botschuyver, *Scholia in Horatium*, IV, ix.
[2] P. Wessner in (*Bursians*) *Jahresbericht über die Fortschritte der klassischen Altertumswissenschaft*, CLXXXVIII (1921), 216.
[3] S. Gallen MS 868, pp. 13–193.

this commentary too must have been composed about the same time as the commentary to Persius. But as I said before, we cannot be sure that all the texts on Horace contained in the manuscript proceeded from only one source, that is from one classroom, as it includes the three series of glosses on the *Ars Poetica*.

Mention should also be made in this connection of a commentary to Juvenal[1] which shows certain similarities in vocabulary and mentality to the above-mentioned commentary on Persius. The older of the two manuscripts in which it is contained, a twelfth- or possibly eleventh-century codex of the cathedral library of Cologne, also has glosses on Lucan in which the mention of the *Bardi* (1, 449) reminds the author of the poets of the city of Liège. But there is no definite proof for a Liège origin of the commentary on Juvenal.

The talents and temperaments of these commentators vary, but what binds them together is that they are not afraid to make frequent references to the Christian and medieval world, its ideas and its reality. Now more now less successfully they make use of comparisons, and in the hope of bringing home the meaning of a text more surely to their readers, they often employ medieval terms to describe people and things mentioned by the author although the medieval term and the original classical one are not exactly synonymous. This is a naïve way of simplifying the understanding of the past by appealing to the present. Antiquity is presented in the costumes of one's own days. Here are some examples: the commentator of Juvenal who is rather sober and reserved calls the vestal virgins and the priestesses of Isis simply *moniales* even when their moral lapses are mentioned. In a similar way, there is no strict boundary between *sacerdotes*, i.e. pagan priests, and *presbyteri*. The rather simple-minded commentator of Horace whose work has been published by Botschuyver substitutes for the 'Attic virgin who is carrying sacred things dedicated to Ceres' (*Serm.* II, 8, 10) an *abbatissa* who solemnly moves along with relics of the goddess Ceres. The same author also speaks of the missal and the collects which Numa Pompilius had ordered to be recited; according to him the Roman people sang a *Te Dominum*

---

[1] Sandford, *Catalogus translationum et commentarium*, pp. 196 ff.; Ph. Jaffé–G. Wattenbach, *Ecclesiae Metropolitanae Coloniensis codices manuscripti* (Berlin, 1874), pp. 142–50; for Lucan, *ibid.* p. 140. As to the meaning and value of the much-discussed passage on the *bardi* of Liège, see J. F. Gessler, 'Nihilistenwerk op historico-philologisch gebied', *Philologische Studien*, XI/XII (1939–41), 198 f. and B. M. Marti in 'Arnolfi Aurelianensis Glosule super Lucanum', Papers and Monographs of the American Academy in Rome, XVIII, p. xxxvi (Rome, 1958).

laudamus for the health of Maecenas (*Odes* II, 17). In his gloss to *Odes* III, 3 he even manages to maintain that the gods had granted Romulus release from the *peccatum originale*.

The commentary to Persius is also full of vivid comparisons with things pertaining to the life of the medieval Church.

There are so many common traits in these different works that I should like to regard them as representing one trend or mode of interpretation of classical authors and to see this as flourishing in the late eleventh and the early twelfth century, a mode which is more appropriate to the satirists than to any other group of authors.[1] Whether this type of commentary had established itself originally in the heart of France, or was more at home in the old schools of Lorraine so that its influence spread primarily to German schools, is a question which can be answered in all probability only if more commentaries of this type come to light.

As far as we can see at present the three authors, Horace, Persius and Juvenal, were all looked upon as censors and preachers of morality. Now this is in full agreement with the intentions of Persius and Juvenal, even though the naïve commentator on them exaggerates wildly at times—as is shown by the example of the rib and the Apennines. But where Horace is concerned, treating him invariably as a moralist was bound to have serious consequences. The Odes are misinterpreted in a most incredible manner in order to make them fit this medieval concept. Time and again we find in the commentary such remarks as: 'in this ode Horace writes as if he were someone (who acted in such and such a way)', or again 'Horace is said to write *ex persona* of those who think in this way'.

An example will illustrate what can result from such a procedure. The commentary now in St Gall makes the following observation on *Odes* I, 36, *Et ture et fidibus iuvat*, the gay table-song for the return of Numida:

A friend of Horace called Numida used to go abroad quite often. Perhaps Horace even invented (*fingere*) the name of his friend, because Numida means *instabilis*. And when he, Numida, returned, he used to invite his *meretrices* and *amasii* in order to engage in all sorts of disgraceful shamelessness. Therefore Horace reprimands him and feigns that he would take part in this luxurious and excessive feast— *promittens se illam luxuriam explere cum eo*. But this was not his real intention. Rather

[1] One might compare with this mode an analogous tendency in late eleventh and twelfth century biblical exegesis in which figures and events of contemporary history serve to illustrate the contemporary relevance of the text: B. Bischoff, *Lebenskräfte in der abendländischen Geistesgeschichte* (*Festschrift Walter Goetz*), Marburg, 1948, pp. 22 ff.

he wanted to point out that Numida was actually engaging in these practices. Just as we oftentimes say: 'Thank Heaven, the mistress of Rupert has come back! Now we shall drink again at night on the market square.' This we do not say with reference to ourselves but as a criticism for Rupert who does such things. *Reversa est amica Ruperti, deo gratias, nunc iterum bibimus nocte per plateas.*

Such is the spoken Latin of the Middle Ages, of its students and of its clerics, as we find it quite often in this commentary.

At this time—the eleventh to the twelfth century—medieval Latin had already made its contribution to the vocabulary used for reproof. In all texts of this kind one often finds with various meanings the word *leccator*. Thus it is applied to the parasite, the gossip, the glutton, to the adulterer and fornicator, to the pander and to various other categories of shameless people. If one day this word will receive the distinction of being included in the *Thesaurus Linguae Latinae*, it will be thanks to the *Glossae Scaligeri*, which are a very haphazard collection and contain among other things medieval words.[1] *Leccator* is derived from the Germanic *likkon*, German *lecken*, and appears for the first time in medieval Latin literature in the late eleventh century. We find it in the work of Amarcius who wrote satires against the corruption of his time. There is also a *leccatrix* and there are further derivatives from this word: *leccaria* for fastidiousness and daintiness; *leccatura* for gluttony; *leccacitas* for moral defectiveness, questionable ethical behaviour; *lecare* for the doings of prostitutes. To designate the glutton, however, the word *nebulo* is also employed. Along with these, there appear in the commentaries of Horace such undefined but pithy words as *bilfardi, busnardi, amusnardones* and so forth.

In the exposition of Persius we find again and again the discussion of this or that sin (for which often the students, but not only the students, are blamed):

> comedere carnes in quadragesima
> tota die bibere in taberna
> ire ad meretrices
> occidere hominem

Against these are placed the good works such as:

> orare—cantare psalmos
> ire ad ecclesiam
> ieiunare
> dare elemosynam

Some light is thrown on the school milieu in which the life of the student as a cleric begins. Laziness and lack of education are drasti-

[1] G. Goetz (ed.), *Corpus Glossariorum Latinorum*, v (1894), 602, 51: cf. also i (1922), 250 ff.

cally reproved. In the commentary to Persius the teacher recommends himself by pointing to his unscrupulous colleagues who have to instruct the sons of nobles whom they encourage to raid neighbouring farms:

ante primam docent eos diligenter, post prandium hortantur eos ut eant occidere porcos et anseres dicentes: vos estis nobiles et ideo nemo faciet vobis malum.

The one domain from which the commentaries have drawn particularly many lively features is the world of the *clerici*. The word *clerici* does not only designate ecclesiastical persons, but includes all those who have learned and can speak Latin. Now and then this word is used in connection with Horace and his friends in the commentary edited by Botschuyver. The commentary from St Gall says of Iccius, the addressee of *Odes* I, 29 that he, Iccius, *dimisso clericatu*, having quit his studies, has become *miles*, a soldier. This again shows that the Roman *litteratus* and the medieval *clericus* are looked upon in the same light.

Several times in this commentary it is taken for granted that it must be the desire of the young *clericus* to become eventually if not a bishop, an abbot or a patriarch, at least a *capellanus* to a bishop or to some great lord. He could then fancy himself as having attained something comparable to the position of Horace, since *capellanus* is also applied in the same way to the suite of Maecenas who himself is called the *cancellarius* of Augustus in three texts.

The venality and corruption which often accompanied the grant of clerical positions by nobles or monarchs are brought to mind when the relationship founded on personal respect between the aristocrat Maecenas and Horace, the son of a freedman (*Sat.* I, 6) is glossed with the remark: 'Horace did not give Maecenas ten pounds for the *capellania*.'

The impression we have at first sight is one of ridiculous misinterpretation and wrong perspectives; but I am inclined to attribute to the authors of these commentaries on the satirists a positive value and real merit for the period in which they were writing. Their merit is perhaps greatest when they are most obviously in error. In making equations between ancient and medieval terms and in projecting their milieu on to the background of antiquity, these *magistri* showed that they had a sharp eye for the characters and situations of their own time. To the types already mentioned such as the Zürich *coactores*, the captives trusting in St Theobald's help, the poor Bretons in Laon and the unscrupulous teachers, we can add lords who instead of listening to their priests let them be beaten by their servants, simple peasants who in a church think that the relics covered in gold are more efficient than those without and a host of other rogues and fools.

Material for comment is also provided by the peculiarities of other countries and other nations: what we call the *proprietates gentium*. Horace's invective against garlic (or was it against an excess of garlic?) in *Epodes* 3 makes the commentator say: 'the Lombards do not believe that garlic is noxious'. And in connection with the *leges insanae bibendi* (*Sat.* II, 6), reference is made to the immoderate drinking habits of the Saxons and the Danes. Such allusions and those which I mentioned earlier are not easy to find in the literary works of the time. At most they occur here and there, in chronicles, in letters, in satirical or comic verse, such as the *Sermones* of Amarcius or the poem on *Unibos*. I think that the close study of the Roman satirists must have helped people to observe the everyday life of their time and encouraged those realistic tendencies which we encounter for the first time in the Ruodlieb epic—for the first time, that is, in medieval Latin and maybe even in the vernacular.

If I have dared to mention the vernacular like this at the end of my contribution, it is because the author of the St Gall commentary on Horace shows a remarkable liking for colloquial phrases in French, which he uses as parallels for Horatian expressions in order to achieve a more exact characterisation of the poet's irony. They are phrases of which this is much the earliest written record, so far as I have been able to discover. Two or more generations before Rutebeuf,[1] we find here a summary rejection of such outmoded authorities as Ennius and Roscius in the following rude phrase: '*Ennius non valuit* un strunt de schin, *id est canis*', and again *doctus Roscius* is described as one of '*isti veteres qui non valuerunt* un strunt de schin'. In modern French the phrase would read *un étron de chien*. Of a *doctissimus rhetor* it is said that '*il sat trop*' (*il sait trop*) and the Latin '*Esto*' *concedatur* is rendered *ironice*: '*zu put bin estre*' (*ça peut bien être*). Finally, as my trump card, I can produce an unknown medieval equivalent of lavender water, if not of eau de Cologne. Speaking of the spring of the ancient Italian goddess Feronia (*Sat.* I, 5, 24 in the *iter Brundisinum*), the commentator says: '*O Feronia civitas. Nos lavimus* dolant *tam bene ora quam manus. Non habuimus* gutta di Liun. *Nota deliciosum*', where *gutta di Liun* is readily identifiable as *goutte de Lyon*.

[1] A. Tobler–E. Lommatzsch, *Altfranzösisches Wörterbuch*, III (1954), 1486.

93

This type of commentary which we have been discussing was followed by other types, some better, some worse. Mention must be made of the philosopher, William of Conches, whose gloss on Juvenal is still unpublished. It is said to show his predilection for natural science; for example, when he talks about the *antrum Vulcani*. Bernard Silvestris's well-known allegorical interpretation of *Aeneid* i to vi exemplifies yet another approach. Its moralising tendency became general with that wealth of later commentaries and other similar works which have been so admirably discussed by Miss Smalley in her book, *English Friars and Antiquity in the Early Fourteenth Century*.

It will be obvious from what has been said that the large majority of medieval commentaries still require thorough examination. Thanks to the enterprise of Professor Kristeller, a beginning has been made with the publication of the *Catalogus Commentariorum*. Let us hope that it will proceed more rapidly in the future.

9

LA LECTURE DES AUTEURS
CLASSIQUES À L'ÉCOLE DE CHARTRES
DURANT LA PREMIÈRE MOITIÉ
DU XIIe SIÈCLE

UN TÉMOIN PRIVILÉGIÉ:
LES 'GLOSAE SUPER MACROBIUM'
DE GUILLAUME DE CONCHES

E. JEAUNEAU

Parmi les maîtres qui ont illustré l'école capitulaire de Chartres durant la première moitié du XIIe siècle, l'un des plus significatifs pour notre colloque est assurément Guillaume de Conches. Très connu pour ses traités systématiques — *Philosophia*, *Dragmaticon* — Guillaume n'est pas moins digne de l'être pour ses commentaires d'auteurs classiques: *Glosae super Priscianum*, *Glosae super Platonem*, *Glosae super Boetium*, *Glosae super Macrobium*, auxquelles s'ajouteront sans doute — car une heureuse découverte, en ce domaine, est toujours possible — les gloses sur le *de Nuptiis* de Martianus Capella.

Aux yeux de Guillaume de Conches, commenter les auteurs classiques n'est pas une tâche moins noble que d'écrire un traité systématique tel que le *Dragmaticon*. Bien au contraire, il déclare n'avoir entrepris la rédaction du *Dragmaticon* que pour introduire à la *Lectio philosophorum*.[1] Tel est le but, tout le reste est moyen. Il s'agit de 'lire' — c'est-à-dire de comprendre et de faire comprendre — les auteurs classiques. Voilà l'occupation majeure d'un maître comme Guillaume de Conches. Il en sait la noblesse, il en mesure les difficultés: 'Antiqui multo meliores fuerunt modernis: quod in operibus

---

[1] 'Sed quoniam irrationalia sunt infinita nec ad lectionem philosophorum, propter quod hoc opus incepimus, pertinentia, de ipsis tractare postponamus' (*Dragmaticon*, lib. VI, éd. G. Gratarolus (Strasbourg, 1567), p. 235. Passage parallèle dans *Philosophia*, IV, 6; *PL*, 172, 88 B) — 'Ea quae ad philosophorum lectionem, qui hodie leguntur in scholis, pertinent expediam, cetera de illis praetermittam' (*Dragmaticon*, lib. III, éd. cit. p. 83). Cf. *op. cit*. éd. cit. pp. 5, 220, 224.

95

eorum apparet, in quorum expositione semper laborant moderni'.[1] Il n'ignore pas, certes — car son maître Bernard de Chartres le lui a appris — que, si les Anciens sont des géants, et les Modernes des nains, les nains, montés sur les épaules des géants, peuvent voir plus loin que ceux-ci.[2] Il reste que les Anciens sont d'une taille qui lui en impose: *Antiqui multo meliores fuerunt modernis*. Aussi bien, en grammaire, tout l'effort de Guillaume de Conches tend-il à restaurer, par delà les déviations des Modernes, l'usage des grands classiques latins. Son idéal, en ce domaine, pourrait se résumer dans ces quelques mots des *Gloses sur Priscien*: 'Sumus relatores et expositores ueterum, non inuentores nouorum.'[3] Et cette réflexion d'un humaniste chartrain du XIIe siècle semble préfigurer ce qu'Erasme (1467–1536) écrira plus tard: 'Nos uetera instauramus, noua non prodimus.'[4]

Guillaume de Conches admire les écrivains classiques, non seulement pour l'élégance de leur style, mais encore et surtout pour la richesse de leur pensée. De cette ferveur, les *Glosae super Macrobium* — c'est-à-dire le commentaire de Guillaume de Conches sur les *Commentarii in Somnium Scipionis* de Macrobe — nous apportent un éclatant témoignage. C'est sur cette œuvre que je voudrais insister ici. Disons d'abord que Macrobe — *ille non mediocris philosophus*, comme l'appelle Abélard[5] — était particulièrement admiré à l'école de Chartres. Jean de Salisbury, qui fut élève de Guillaume de Conches avant de devenir évêque de Chartres (1176–1180), célèbre en ces termes le premier livre des *Saturnales*: 'Siquidem conspicuus est in sententiis, in uerbis floridus, et tanta morum uenustate redundans ut in institutione conuiuii et dispensatione Socraticam uideatur dulcedinem propinare.'[6] Tandis que Jean de Salisbury admirait les

[1] *Gloses sur Macrobe* (*Somnium* II, 11, 1), MS Copenhague, Bibliothèque Royale, Gl. Kgl. s. 1910. 4to, fo. 122r, Le même texte, à quelques variantes près, se trouve dans les manuscrits suivants: Bamberg, Staatsbibliothek, Class. 40 (H.J. IV. 21), fo. 24va et Vatican, Urbin. Lat. 1140, fo. 146v.

[2] Les textes sont cités dans E. Jeauneau, 'Deux rédactions des gloses de Guillaume de Conches sur Priscien', dans *Recherches de théologie ancienne et médiévale*, XXVII (1960), 234–6; '*Nani gigantum humeris insidentes*. Essai d'interprétation de Bernard de Chartres', dans *Vivarium*, V (1967), 84–5.

[3] *Gloses sur Priscien*, MS Florence, Biblioteca Laurenziana, San Marco 310, fo. 45r*b*; MS Paris, Bibliothèque nationale, Lat. 15130, fo. 49v*b*.

[4] Erasme, Lettre à Godescalc Rosemondt (Louvain, 18 octobre 1520), dans *Opus epistolarum Des. Erasmi Roterodami denuo recognitum et auctum*, éd. P.-S. Allen et H.-M. Allen, t. IV (Oxford, 1922), Lettre 1153, lignes 185–6 (p. 367).

[5] *Theologia scholarium, PL*, 178, 1022B

[6] Jean de Salisbury, *Policraticus*, VIII, 10; éd. Cl. Webb (Oxford, 1909), II, 284; *PL*, 199, 743 A. Cette *Socratica dulcedo* est une formule qui vient directement de Macrobe, *In Somnium Scipionis*, I, 1.6, éd. J. Willis (Leipzig, 1963), p. 2, ligne 28.

Saturnales, d'autres Chartrains lisaient avec assiduité le *Commentaire* de Macrobe sur le *Songe de Scipion*. Ainsi, Hugues Métel († *c*. 1157) se plaît-il à évoquer, dans une lettre à son ancien condisciple Hugues de Chartres, le temps de sa jeunesse studieuse, celui où il méditait sur quelque belle page pythagorisante du *Commentaire* de Macrobe.[1]

Avant d'entreprendre l'examen des *Glosae super Macrobium* de Guillaume de Conches, plusieurs questions se posent. D'abord, peut-on dire, au moins approximativement, à quelle période de sa vie Guillaume les a rédigées? Selon toute vraisemblance, il faut ranger les *Glosae super Macrobium* parmi les œuvres de jeunesse et, plus précisément, avant la première rédaction des *Glosae super Platonem*. En effet, au cours de ses Gloses sur Macrobe, Guillaume renvoie souvent à ses futures Gloses sur le *Timée*.[2] Une autre difficulté, bien connue de ceux

---

[1] 'Dum enim ego cum Scipione somniarem, dum radio totum polum perquirerem, quaesiuisti, si bene memini, quid propinquius consideretur circa substantias, an qualitas, an quantitas. Lectio uero Macrobii, quae detinebat me, forte haec erat: "Cogitationi nostrae meanti nobis ad superos occurrit prima perfectio incorporalitatis in numeris" [Macrobe, *In Somnium*, I, 5.4; éd. cit. p. 15, lignes 10–11]. Tum ego, inquam: "Macrobius ab hac quaestione me liberat, cum *cogitationi nostrae meanti a nobis*, id est a substantiis, *ad superos*, id est ad accidentia, primo numeros occurrere affirmat.' Et sic per Macrobium a manibus tuis liberatus sum, et euasi per te a manibus Hugonis sophistae qui sophistica delusione gestiebat me circumuenire' (Hugues Métel, *Epistola 34*, éd. Hugues d'Estival, *Sacrae Antiquitatis Monumenta historica, dogmatica, diplomatica*, II (1731), 375). Cf. Fortia d'Urban, *Histoire et Ouvrages de Hugues Métel, né à Toul en 1080* (Paris, 1839), pp. 187–92; A. Clerval, *Les écoles de Chartres au Moyen Age* (Paris, 1895), pp. 176–7.

[2] *In Somnium*, I, 2.13: 'de daemonibus, de quibus latius in Thimaeo Platonis disseremus' (MS Bern, Burgerbibliothek 266, fo. 3 v a).

In Somnium, I, 11.7: 'qui daemones nuncupantur, de quibus in Thimaeo Platonis dicemus' (MS Bern, Burgerbibliothek 266, fo. 9 r b). Cf. MS Vatican, Urbin. Lat. 1140, fo. 70r; Vatican, Palat. Lat. 953, fo. 101 v; Copenhague, Bibliothèque Royale, Gl. Kgl. s. 1910. 4to, fo. 53 v.

In Somnium, I, 22.5: 'ile de qua satis supra diximus, et dicemus in Platone' (MS Bern, Burgerbibliothek 266, fo. 13 v b). Cf. MS Vatican, Urbin. Lat. 1140, fo. 127r; Copenhague, Bibliothèque Royale, Gl. Kgl. s. 1910. 4to, fo. 100r.

In Somnium, II, 1.22: 'Nam longum esset qualiter semitonium ex illa proportione constet ostendere, et aptius erit de his in Pla(tone) disserere' (MS Vatican, Urbin. **Lat.** 1140, fo. 131r) — 'Quare autem hoc in minoribus numeris assignari non poterit, et **de** huiusmodi aliis in Musica siue in Anima Platonis conuenientius dicemus' (MS Copenhague, Bibliothèque Royale, Gl. Kgl. s. 1910. 4to, fo. 106r).

In Somnium, II, 2.14: 'Quare sic dicatur dictum est superius, et in glosulis Platonis inuenies' (MS Copenhague, Bibliothèque Royale, Gl. Kgl. s. 1910. 4to, fo. 110r).

In Somnium, II, 2.15: 'Quid Plato uocauit fermentum [firmamentum, *Cod.*], in suo Timaeo ostendemus...Quid sit quod spatia illa hiabant, et qualiter sint impleta, hoc totum, Deo annuente (uitam), in Platone exponemus' (MS Bamberg, Staatsbibliothek, Class. 40 (H.J.IV.21), fo. 21 v a). Cf. MS Vatican, Urbin. Lat. 1140, fo. 134v; Copenhague, Bibliothèque Royale, Gl. Kgl. s. 1910. 4to, fo. 110r.

In Somnium, II, 2.20: 'Qualiter Pla(to) suppleuit interualla illa, et quid per interualla et implectionem interuallorum intellexit, in Thimaeo Pla(tonis) exponemus' (MS Vatican, Urbin. Lat. 1140, fo. 135r). Cf. MS Copenhague, Bibliothèque Royale, Gl. Kgl. s. 1910. 4to, fo. 110v.

qui se sont penchés sur les écrits de Guillaume de Conches, est celle de leurs rédactions multiples.[1] La tradition manuscrite des *Glosae super Macrobium* nous offre des rédactions différentes, au sujet desquelles des problèmes d'authenticité peuvent se poser. Mademoiselle Helen Rodnite, de Columbia University, étudie actuellement, à Paris, ces délicats problèmes. On peut fonder les plus grandes espérances sur son travail, conduit avec critique et selon une excellente méthode. Il faut même souhaiter que, sans attendre l'édition intégrale des *Glosae super Macrobium* — œuvre colossale et qui pourrait l'occuper pendant des années — Mademoiselle Rodnite puisse publier rapidement quelques uns des résultats auxquels ses recherches l'ont conduite. Selon Mademoiselle Rodnite, on peut distinguer une rédaction brève (MSS Bamberg, Staatsbibliothek, Class. 40 (H.J.IV.21) et Bern, Burgerbibliothek 266) et une rédaction longue (Munich, National-bibliothek, Clm 14557 et Vatican, Urbin. Lat. 1140). Les deux rédactions, tant la longue que la brève, peuvent être attribuées sans hésitation à Guillaume de Conches.[2]

Qu'on les lise dans la rédaction brève ou dans la rédaction longue, les *Glosae super Macrobium* sont du plus haut intérêt pour l'étude de la transmission de l'héritage classique au Moyen Age. On sait, en effet, que le *Commentaire* de Macrobe sur le *Songe de Scipion* est un coffret précieux où sont renfermés les plus riches joyaux de la mythologie et de la philosophie grecques. Guillaume de Conches a su exploiter ce trésor. C'est par le *Commentaire* de Macrobe qu'il a connu Plotin: 'Plotinus, magis quam quisquam uerborum parcus' (*In Somnium* II, 12. 7), 'Plotinus inter philosophiae professores cum Platone princeps' (*op. cit.* I, 8. 5). C'est par lui aussi qu'il a connu Porphyre, car, comme l'a établi M. Pierre Courcelle, 'le véritable maître de la pensée de Macrobe est, non pas Plotin, mais Porphyre'.[3] On pourrait allonger la liste. Ou plutôt, puisqu'il est impossible ici de l'allonger, contentons-nous de donner un exemple.

---

[1] A. Vernet, 'Un remaniement de la *Philosophia* de Guillaume de Conches', dans *Scriptorium*, I (1947), 243–59.

[2] Les manuscrits Copenhague, Bibliothèque Royale, Gl. Kgl. s. 1910. 4to, et Vatican, Palat. Lat. 953 posent de délicats problèmes d'authenticité (interpolations possibles) qu'il n'est pas question d'aborder ici. Dans le manuscrit Zwettl 363, fos. 132r–135r le texte de Guillaume de Conches s'interrompt sur Macrobe, *Somnium*, I, 2. J'ai esquissé une description sommaire de quelques uns de ces manuscrits dans l'article suivant: 'Gloses de Guillaume de Conches sur Macrobe. Note sur les manuscrits', dans *Archives d'Histoire doctrinale et littéraire du Moyen Age*, XXVII (1960), 17–28. Les travaux de Mademoiselle Helen Rodnite permettront de faire plus de lumière sur l'histoire de la tradition manuscrite des *Glosae super Macrobium*.

[3] P. Courcelle, *Les Lettres grecques en Occident, de Macrobe à Cassiodore* (Paris, 1948), p. 22.

Au livre I, chapitre 12, de son *Commentaire*, Macrobe évoque, d'après Homère (*Odyssée* XIII, 102–12), et surtout d'après le *de Antro Nympharum* de Porphyre, 'la sainte grotte obscure et charmante des Nymphes, qu'on appelle Naïades'. Cette grotte a deux entrées : 'Par l'une, ouverte au nord, descendent les humains ; l'autre s'ouvre au midi, mais c'est l'entrée des dieux, jamais homme ne prend ce chemin d'Immortels.'[1] Assurément, Guillaume de Conches n'a aucun mérite particulier à interpréter les deux portes de l'Antre des Nymphes comme étant les deux tropiques, celui du Capricorne et celui du Cancer. Il lui suffit de suivre Macrobe. Il sait, d'ailleurs, qu'Ovide, au livre II des *Métamorphoses* (vv. 1–5), décrit la demeure du Soleil et ses deux portes : *bifores ualuae*.[2] Macrobe lui apprenait aussi pourquoi le Cancer est la porte des hommes, et le Capricorne celle des dieux : c'est que la descente des âmes dans le monde de la généra-tion se fait par le Cancer, tandis que leur remontée vers la demeure d'Immortalité se fait par le signe du Capricorne. Mais Macrobe n'explique pas tout ce que Guillaume de Conches désirerait savoir. Il ne dit pas *pourquoi* la descente des âmes se fait par le Cancer, ni *pourquoi* leur remontée se fait par le Capricorne. Guillaume va pour-tant chercher à l'expliquer :

Sed quare pocius per cancrum animae dicuntur ad corpora descendere quam per capricornum ; uel per capricornum ascendere pocius quam per cancrum, tacet hoc Macrobius. Dicunt tamen magistri nostri sic. Sol causa uitae nostrae. Sed sol a cancro descendit, per capricornum ascendit. Sic ergo, sub hoc integumento, dicitur animarum descensus fieri per cancrum, ascensus uero per capricornum. Aliter tamen quidam senciunt dicentes quasdam qualitates esse in sole, quarum quae-dam est causa uitae nostrae, ut calor, quaedam uero causa est dissolucionis, ut frigiditas, unde omne mortuum est frigidum. Sed, sole existente in cancro, domina-tur feruor, quia cancer signum illud calidum est. Quia ergo omnis uita ex calore habet esse, merito dicitur per cancrum fieri animarum descensus. Item, sole manente in capricorno, dominatur frigiditas, quae est causa dissolucionis uitae : iure per capricornum animae dicuntur reuerti ad caelestia.[3]

---

[1] Homère, *Odyssée*, XIII, 102–12, traduction V. Bérard, Collection Guillaume Budé (Paris, 1953) (5e édition), p. 140. Porphyre, *De Antro Nympharum*, éd. R. Hercher (Paris, 1858) [*Aeliani de Natura Animalium*..., Coll. Firmin Didot, 2e partie, pp. 87–98] ; éd. A. Nauck (Leipzig, Teubner, 1886), pp. 53–81 ; traduction française dans F. Buffière, *Les mythes d'Homère et la pensée grecque* (Paris, 1956), pp. 595–616. M. Jean Pépin, directeur de recherche au Centre national de la Recherche scientifique, prépare une étude sur le *de Antro* de Porphyre. En attendant la parution de ce travail, on consultera : J. Pépin, 'Porphyre, exégète d'Homère', dans *Fondation Hardt pour l'étude de l'Antiquité classique*. *Entretiens*, XII (Vandœuvres-Genève, s.d.), pp. 231–72.

[2] '*Has solis*. Vnde dixit Ouidius in II Met(amorphoseon) quod "biformes ualuae cingebant tegmina solis", uolens per ualuas significare cancrum et capricornum ; quæ signa ualuae solis dicuntur, ut expositum est' (MS Bern, Burgerbibliothek 266, fo. 9v*a*).

[3] MS Bern, Burgerbibliothek 266, fo. 9v*a*–9v*b*.

Quels sont ces *Magistri nostri* à l'opinion desquels Guillaume de Conches se réfère pour interpréter et compléter Macrobe? Et où donc ces derniers avaient-ils eux-mêmes puisé leur exégèse? Nous nous heurtons ici à un obstacle majeur: notre manque d'information sur la période qui a précédé la 'renaissance' du XIIe siècle. Un peu plus loin, un problème analogue se pose. Guillaume déclare que l'Antre des Nymphes symbolise le monde: 'Et notandum quod Homerus per antrum itacense significauit mundum, in medio cuius sol est locatus a deo.'[1]

C'est exactement ce que dit Porphyre.[2] Mais c'est ce que Macrobe ne dit point, du moins en ce passage de son *Commentaire*. Guillaume aurait-il spontanément retrouvé l'exégèse porphyrienne qui, selon toute vraisemblance, était l'exégèse traditionnelle? Lui a-t-elle été transmise par une autre voie, de nous inconnue, celle de tous les commentateurs médiévaux de Macrobe qui ont frayé la voie aux *Glosae super Macrobium* du philosophe de Conches? Dans l'état actuel de nos connaissances, il me paraît difficile de répondre avec certitude à ces questions. De toute façon, par les renseignements qu'elle nous fournit, et par les problèmes qu'elle nous pose, cette page d'exégèse allégorique mérite de retenir notre attention. Maintes autres le mériteraient également.

Au demeurant, le *Commentaire du Songe de Scipion* n'a pas seulement fourni à Guillaume de Conches des exemples d'exégèse allégorique. Il lui a donné aussi une théorie très élaborée de l'exégèse allégorique des mythes. On connaît, en effet, la page fameuse dans laquelle Macrobe raconte ce qui arriva au philosophe Numénius pour avoir transgressé la loi sacrée qui commande de n'évoquer les mystères d'Eleusis que sous le manteau de l'allégorie. Les déeses éleusiniennes lui apparurent en songe sous l'aspect de prostituées, voulant signifier par là qu'en parlant ouvertement de leurs mystères, Numénius les avait littéralement prostituées.[3] Comme la Nature, la divinité aime se cacher dans les galeries souterraines des mythes: *Figurarum cuniculis operiuntur.*[4] Commentant ces derniers mots, Guillaume écrit: '*Operiuntur cuniculis*, id est integumentis in quibus latet ipsa ueritas.'[5] Nous

---

[1] MS Bern, Burgerbibliothek 266, fo. 9 v b.
[2] Porphyre, *de Antro Nympharum*, 21; éd. R. Hercher, p. 94; traduction F. Buffière, *Les Mythes d'Homère*, p. 608.
[3] Macrobe, *Somnium Scipionis*, I, 2.19; éd. J. Willis, pp. 7–8. Cf. J. Pépin, 'Saint Augustin et la fonction protreptique de l'allégorie', dans *Recherches augustiniennes*, I (Paris, 1958), 269–70 [pp. 243–86].
[4] Macrobe, *Somnium Scipionis*, I, 2.18; éd. J. Willis, p. 7, ligne 19.
[5] MS Bern, Burgerbibliothek 266, fo. 4 r a.

retrouvons ainsi la notion d'*integumentum* dont j'ai essayé de dire l'importance en un article qu'il faudrait reprendre et enrichir, puisqu'au moment où je le rédigeais, je n'avais pas encore pu étudier les *Glosae super Macrobium*.[1]

Il va sans dire que ces *Gloses*, comme les autres écrits du philosophe de Conches, renferment de nombreuses citations d'auteurs classiques. J'y ai relevé, entre autres, sept citations de Cicéron, quatre d'Horace, trois de Lucain, six d'Ovide, une de Salluste, une autre de Stace, neuf de Virgile, etc.[2] Bref, les *Glosae super Macrobium* sont un document précieux. Il faut souhaiter qu'un travailleur patient puisse les éditer. Une telle édition nous apportera des éclaircissements sur la 'renaissance' du XIIe siècle. Elle nous aidera peut-être à poser quelques jalons sur les routes qui relient cette dernière à la 'renaissance' carolingienne d'une part et, d'autre part, à la renaissance du XVe siècle.[3]

[1] 'L'usage de la notion d'*integumentum* à travers les gloses de Guillaume de Conches', dans *Archives d'Histoire doctrinale et littéraire du Moyen Age*, XXIV (1957), 35–100.

[2] Voici, à titre d'exemples, quelques unes de ces citations. Guillaume cite Salluste, *de Coniuratione Catilinae* (I, 5.4) au début de ses *Glosae super Macrobium* : 'Et Salustio in descriptione Catelinae: *Satis eloquentiae sibi inerat, sapientiae parum*' (MS Bern, Burgerbibliothek 266, fo. 1 r a). La même citation de Salluste se retrouve dans les *Glosae super Boetium* (Consol., Prosa 1, 4; éd. L. Bieler, p. 2): MSS Troyes, Bibliothèque municipale 1101, fo. 3 r a; Troyes, Bibl. mun. 1381, fo. 39 r; éd. Ch. Jourdain dans *Notices et extraits des manuscrits de la Bibliothèque impériale*, XX, 2 (Paris, 1862), p. 73. Par ailleurs, j'ai relevé dans le manuscrit du Vatican, Urbin. Lat. 1140, les citations suivantes d'Ovide: fo. 82 r (*Métamorphoses*, I, 85–6); fo. 89 r (*Métam.* I, 175); fo. 141 r (*Métam.* I, 61); fo. 148 v (*Métam.* XV, 165; I, 1); fo. 146 r (allusion). Enfin, j'ai noté plus haut (p. 99 n. 2) une réminiscence d'Ovide, *Métam.* II, 1–5.

[3] Nous trouvons, dans les *Glosae super Macrobium*, quelques jalons, posés par Guillaume de Conches lui-même, sur la route qui relie son époque aux époques précédentes. Il se réfère, en effet, aux auteurs suivants: Gerbert d'Aurillac (MSS Copenhague, Bibliothèque Royale, Gl. Kgl. s. 1910. 4to fo. 95 r; Vatican, Urbin. Lat. 1140, fos. 120 v–121 r); Guido d'Arezzo (MSS Bamberg, Staatsbibliothek, Class. 40 (H.J. IV. 21), fo. 20 r *b*; Bern, Burgerbibliothek 266, fo. 14 v *b*; Vatican, Urbin. Lat. 1140, fo. 130 r–130 v); Remi d'Auxerre (MSS Bamberg, Staatsbibliothek, Class. 40 (H.J.IV.21), fo. 157 r a; Bern, Burgerbibliothek 266, fo. 10 r a; Vatican, Urbin. Lat. 1140, fo. 72 v). Par ailleurs, les *Glosae super Macrobium* ont certainement exercé une influence sur les siècles postérieurs. On peut en donner quelques indices. Tout d'abord, il est significatif qu'on les ait recopiées au XVe siècle pour la Bibliothèque du duc d'Urbino: MS Vatican, Urbin. Lat. 1140. De plus, Jean Le Bègue (1368–1457) en donne un extrait dans son florilège (MS Paris, BN Lat. 3343, fo. 143 v. Cf. 'Gloses de Guillaume de Conches sur Macrobe. Note sur les manuscrits', dans *Archives d'Histoire doctrinale et littéraire du Moyen Age*, XXVII (1960), 28 n. 40). Par ailleurs, Miss Beryl Smalley a fait remarquer que Robert Holcot (+ 1349) mentionne un *Guilelmus* commentateur de Macrobe: 'Quicumque autem nascuntur ante septimum mensem communiter moriuntur, sicut dicit Guilelmus de mortibus, exponens Macrobium, de Somnio Scipionis' [Sap. Lect. LXXXIX, 302] (texte cité par B. Smalley, 'Robert Holcot', dans *Archivum fratrum praedicatorum*, XXVI (1956), 41). Cf. B. Smalley, *English Friars and Antiquity in the Early Fourteenth Century* (Oxford, 1960), p. 157. Le texte de Robert Holcot peut faire penser à Guillaume de

Conches, *Glosae super Macrobium* (*Somnium*, 1, 6.14): MSS Bern, Burgerbibliothek 266, fos. 7v*b*–8r*a*; Vatican, Urbin. Lat. 1140, fo. 29r–29v; *Dragmaticon*, lib. vi, éd. G. Gratarolus (Strasbourg, 1567), pp. 247–9.

Pour l'histoire de la fortune de Macrobe durant le moyen âge, on consultera: P.-M. Schedler, *Die Philosophie des Macrobius und ihr Einfluss auf die Wissenschaft des christlichen Mittelalters* (Münster, 1916); W.-H. Stahl, *Macrobius. Commentary on the Dream of Scipio* (New York, 1952); 'Dominant Traditions in Early Medieval Latin Science', dans *Isis*, L (1959), 95–124; P. Courcelle, 'La postérité chrétienne du Songe de Scipion' dans *Revue des Etudes latines*, XXXVI (1958), 205–34; H. Silvestre, 'Une adaptation du Commentaire de Macrobe sur le Songe de Scipion, dans un manuscrit de Bruxelles', dans *Archives d'histoire doctrinale et littéraire du moyen âge*, XXIX (1962), 93–101; 'Note sur la survie de Macrobe au moyen âge', dans *Classica et Mediaevalia. Revue danoise de philologie et d'histoire*, XXIV (1963), 170–80.

10

THE *OPUS DE CONSCRIBENDIS EPISTOLIS* OF ERASMUS AND THE TRADITION OF THE *ARS EPISTOLICA*

A. GERLO[1]

Antiquity was well acquainted with the epistle as an independent literary genre. The great collections left by Cicero and Pliny, Libanius and Synesius furnish ample proof of this. And alongside the genre, the theoretical treatise on the *ars epistolica* had also come into being. The περὶ ἑρμηνείας which bears the name of the orator and statesman, Demetrius of Phaleron (about 350–283 B.C.) has a section on epistolary style, and Gregory Nazianzen discusses its rules in a letter to Nicobulos (No. 51).

The composition of fictitious letters purporting to come from some celebrated mythological or historical figure was a regular exercise in the rhetorical schools of the ancient world. Successful practitioners published collections of models, and some evidence of their activities has survived. In that curious borderland where philosophical and rhetorical interests met there was a whole literature of pseudo-letters, from monarchs to philosophers, for example, or from philosophers to monarchs. And we have also the ἐπιστολιμαῖοι χαρακτῆρες which the manuscripts attribute sometimes to Libanius, sometimes to Proclus, but which almost certainly go back to the third or fourth century A.D.[2]

We know moreover that collections of model letters for administrative and diplomatic purposes also had a very long history. We hear of them in Egypt as far back as 1500 B.C. Later, the Hellenistic monarchs and the Roman emperors employed ἐπιστολογράφοι and clerks *ab epistulis* or *amanuenses* to handle their correspondence. A secretarial force of this nature required training; and their education was bound to make use of formularies and collections of model letters which are therefore inevitably as old as the chanceries themselves.[3]

---

[1] The abbreviations used in these footnotes are listed on p. 114.
[2] Schmid-Stählin, II, 2, 995–6; Pauly-Wissowa, 12. 2523.
[3] Schmid-Stählin, II, 1, 301⁸, 482–5; Pauly-Wissowa, 6. 210–11.

The Middle Ages simply carried on this tradition. At first, while literacy remained at a low ebb, elementary formulas were all that men required for the conduct of their daily business, and collections of these have survived from Merovingian and Carolingian times.[1] Then, with the spread of education, a more sophisticated approach came into fashion and the study of letter-writing emerged as a special branch of rhetoric. Here Alberic of Monte Cassino who lived at the end of the tenth and the beginning of the eleventh century was a pioneer of note. His work, the *Rationes Dictandi*, led during the fifty years which followed his death to the development of an *ars dictaminis* which flourished at Monte Cassino, the Roman Curia and the Bologna schools.

During the twelfth and thirteenth centuries we find everyone, even the most eminent authors, conscientiously following the rules which are laid down for letter-writing by the *dictatores*. A comprehensive examination of their *summae* or formularies would have a great deal to teach us about the intellectual history of the period, but the conditions for such an examination do not yet exist. We need many more modern editions of formularies such as the *Schlesisch-Böhmische Briefmuster aus der Wende des vierzehnten Jahrhunderts* which Konrad Burdach published in 1926.[2]

The tradition which the *ars dictaminis* embodied had its origins in antiquity. It drew on the τόποι and τύποι of Greek rhetoric, on Cicero's youthful *de Inventione* and on the *Rhetorica ad Herennium* which at that time was still attributed to Cicero. This restricted, but genuine, classical orientation, which we find already in the heyday of the Middle Ages, may have helped to prepare the way for the Renaissance. As Burdach has pointed out, many of the late medieval teachers of rhetoric in both Italy and Germany were 'subaltern pioneers of humanism' though the precise nature of the contribution they made remains to be assessed.

With the fourteenth century and the coming of humanism, a new element was introduced which changed the whole development of epistolary art. The rediscovery of the correspondence of Cicero and the younger Pliny between 1345 and 1419 gave birth to a genre that was wholly independent of the existing tradition. We arrive at the

---

[1] Merovingian, Carolingian, Frankish and Burgundian collections of *formulae* are known: E. de Rozières, *Recueil général des formules usitées dans l'empire des Francs du Ve au Xe siècle* (Paris, 1859–71); K. Zeumer, *Formulae merovingici et karolingi aevi. Monumenta Germaniae Historica, Legum Sectio*, v (Hanover, 1886).

[2] Berlin, Weidmannsche Buchhandlung, 1926 (*Vom Mittelalter zur Reformation*. Bd v).

great age of the *Humanistenbriefe*. Petrarch's imposing collections showed the way, and his example was soon followed by a host of other scholars: Leonardo Bruni (1369–1444), Aeneas Sylvius (1405–64), Marsilio Ficino (1433–98), Politian (1454–74), Bembo (1470–1547) and last, but not least, Erasmus.

The emergence and unparalleled success of this new genre was bound to affect the way letter-writing was taught; and it is from the late fourteenth century onwards that we find the most obvious examples of that trend towards humanism which Burdach observed among traditional teachers of rhetoric. Their *artes dictandi* may follow medieval lines, but they do so with a difference. They spare a glance for the achievements of Petrarch and his disciples. The Netherlands schoolmaster, Carolus Menniken (or Virulus), whom I shall have occasion to mention later, belonged to this confused period open to influences from both the Middle Ages and the Renaissance.

But not all the writers of the period were like Menniken uneasily balanced between the old world and the new. There were committed humanists who wanted everything they wrote—their private letters as well as the formal epistles which they composed for publication—to bear the stamp of the classics: and they felt the need for a new kind of manual modelled on the περὶ ἑρμηνείας and Quintilian's *Institutio*, just as the great humanist practitioners of the art of epistolography modelled their work on Cicero, Seneca or Pliny.

Once the need was clearly felt, attempts were made to satisfy it without much delay. The humanist manuals which then came into being fell into two categories. On the one hand, there were the anthologies containing examples of all the different kinds of letters. On the other hand, there were the treatises proper, handbooks which provided set formulas for describing or addressing the recipient, set formulas of salutation, introduction and conclusion. These anthologies and treatises made their first appearance in Italy during the second half of the fifteenth century, but soon afterwards we find them also in France, Germany and the Low Countries. They have been totally ignored in Paul van Thieghem's *la Littérature de la Renaissance*, though there are some fifteen authors who ought to have been mentioned for the Low Countries alone in the fifteenth and sixteenth centuries.

Erasmus is without question the most important of the fifteen. We have two treatises from his pen. The first one, rather short, is the *Brevissima maximeque Compendiaria Conficiendarum Epistolarum Formula*.

It was printed first in September 1520 by Schoeffer at Mainz, but without Erasmus's consent; and it was only at the end of his life that he consented to acknowledge the edition.[1] The second treatise, substantially longer, is known as the *Opus de Conscribendis Epistolis*. Erasmus had it published in 1522 by Froben at Basel; and once again publication occurred after an unauthorised and much shorter version had been issued—by Siberch at Cambridge during the previous year.[2] This *Opus* is the treatise which in the Clericus edition of 1703 is wrongly called *de Ratione Conscribendi Epistolas Liber*. Reference to it in Erasmus's lifetime was always by the title we have given, while the unauthorised Siberch edition was entitled *Libellus de Conscribendis Epistolis*.

It would be easy to devote an entire lecture to the genesis of these two treatises and to the relationship between them. The introductions, both genuine and false, to the different editions and statements in Erasmus's correspondence provide a mass of fascinating data. But such an enterprise would take us too far afield. What we need to bear in mind however is that the earlier and shorter work, the *Brevissima Formula*, contains Erasmus's original formulation of that *ars epistolica* which he practised in such a masterly way.[3] He seems to have composed it during the last decade of the fifteenth century—round about 1495 in all probability; and if we can accept his own account, given in 1536, it was written 'in the space of two days for one particular man', the man in question being his English pupil, Robert Fisher.[4]

The *Opus de Conscribendis Epistolis* is the natural successor of this

---

[1] *Bibliotheca Erasmiana, listes sommaires* (Gand, 1893), 1e série, pp. 54–5. This compendium was reprinted twenty-five times between 1520 and 1579. The preface is addressed to a fictitious character called Peter Paludanus, cf. Allen, IV, Ep. 1193, p. 456. The authorised edition of 1536 was by Platter at Basel.

[2] *Bibliotheca Erasmiana, ibid.*; Allen, I, 198. In his preface to John Fisher, Bishop of Rochester, Siberch tells us that the book was printed after a copy made by a friend a few years before of Erasmus's own manuscript. Robert Fisher, to whom the work was dedicated, was a relative of the famous bishop.

[3] Erasmus's first collection of letters was published in 1516 at Louvain by Thierry Martens: *Epistole aliquot illustrium virorum ad Erasmum et huius ad illos*. By 1522 ten sheaves had been published: *BBr*, I, 99.

[4] In the revised and enlarged 1522 edition of the *Opus de Conscribendis Epistolis*, which Froben published in Basel, the original dedication to Robert Fisher is replaced by a dedication to Nicolas Bérauld dated 25 May 1522. Erasmus states in this that he drafted the work thirty years before, that is round about 1492, while the conclusion to the 1536 authorised edition of the *Brevissima...Formula* informs us that this compendium was composed forty years earlier, that is round about 1496. But we know that Erasmus was not very exact about chronology.

initial formulation; and its final authorised version of 1522 is such a remarkable work that we may legitimately devote some time to it. Already by 1536, the year of Erasmus's death, it had been reprinted thirty times, and the reprints had appeared in Basel and Cologne, in Antwerp, in Leyden, in Cracow—not just in one place, but all over Europe. This is the record of an exceptional success. Erasmus wrote the *Opus* in Paris during the 1490s, prompted it would seem by a very practical need to earn some money. But this mundane aim did not prevent his putting into the work the fruits of his teaching experience and using it to express his growing dislike of scholastic pedagogy. This is the period when many of the pedagogic treatises which brought him fame later were initially conceived: the *de Copia Verborum ac Rerum* (1511), the *de Ratione Studii* (1511), his excellent dialogues, the *Familiarium Colloquiorum Formulae* (1518) and the paraphrase of Valla's *Elegentiae* (1529). The *Opus* is the first product of this line of thought, and it makes a vigorous attack on the medieval *formulae* for letter-writing.

The work runs to thirty-nine folio columns in the Clericus edition and has seventy-four chapters which follow each other in a somewhat haphazard sequence.[1] Erasmus deals successively with the definition of the genre, its principal characteristics, the divisions of a letter and their arrangement, and after chapter 31 he goes on to discuss the different types of letter one may be called upon to write. He breaks with the medieval tradition[2] and declares himself opposed to stereotyped artificial divisions: 'Finally there are letters which have no obvious order: these may have an order, but they are better at hiding than displaying it' (chapter 29). Having made this protest, which has wide implications since it foreshadows a freer, more natural approach to the art of writing, Erasmus goes on to consider an allied problem. Ancient rhetoric which was concerned exclusively with the making of speeches had established three broad categories: *demonstrativum, deliberativum* and *judiciale*. But once you step off the rostrum, once you start to broaden your theory of rhetoric to include forms of composition other than oratory, these three categories will not cover the ground. Erasmus realised this; and so for the subject he was

[1] *O.O.* I, 345–484.
[2] In the Middle Ages the doctrine that there should be five main divisions to every letter formed the kernel of the *ars dictaminis*. These divisions were commonly given as *salutatio, captatio benevolentiae, narratio, petitio* and *conclusio*. H. S. Herbrüggen, *Sir Thomas More, Neue Briefe mit einer Einführung in die epistolographische Tradition* (Münster, 1966), pp. xxviii–xxxv states that clear traces of this medieval tradition can be found in More's writing.

considering, the art of letter-writing, he added a fourth category, the *genus familiare*.[1]

He then proceeds to discuss letters written to persuade, to console, letters commemorating or recommending someone, declarations of love, letters on judicial matters, abuse, petitions, panegyrics, condolence, congratulation and letters written in jest. Finally he devotes a section to the *disputatoriae genus* or dialectical epistle used by scholars for transmitting or debating learned information. With this, the treatise comes to an abrupt end.

The sequence of topics does not seem to be governed by any logical plan; and the impression of haphazardness is heightened by the presence of extensive digressions where for instance Erasmus, seduced by an interest in traditional rhetoric, discourses at length on the use of the *exemplum* in persuasion or on 'the dilemma and other figures of speech'. But these are faults common to the period, and one needs to set against them on the credit side the liberal provision of illustrative passages and the more or less detailed bibliographies which complete the account of each genre. The measure of Erasmus's achievement must not be underrated.

So much then for the actual content of the *Opus de Conscribendis Epistolis*. This was Erasmus's contribution. But if we are to assess its value correctly there are two further matters which we ought to consider.

What was the attitude of Erasmus to his predecessors who wrote about the *ars epistolica* in antiquity or during the early days of humanism?

What influence did his own writings have in this particular field?

In a letter to Robert Fisher (March 1498) Erasmus wrote as follows:[2]

For what will the critics say, what will they not say, when they see that I have dared to write about a subject on which so many learned authors have written with diligent expertise? 'Do you want to take Penelope's web and weave it again?' they will say. 'For what do you see that they have not seen before you? Coming after such great authorities, what you write is bound to be unoriginal or inferior.'

These fears proved baseless as we have seen. Where other humanists had been content to make summary mention of different kinds of letters, indicating their main divisions and referring for the rest to Cicero or Quintilian, Erasmus dealt with each kind separately, giving in each case useful hints on style, structure and tone. He pro-

---

[1] *O.O.* I, 379–80.   [2] Allen, I, Ep. 71, p. 198, 3–8.

vided copious illustrations and bibliographies. And going beyond the limits normal in a handbook, he added hints on teaching and learning. He showed what lines instruction and the correction of work should follow, condemned *ex cathedra* lecturing and defended a form of tuition which by means of questions would stimulate the pupil to make active use of his knowledge. The *Opus de Conscribendis Epistolis* was a manifesto against the outdated manuals and old-fashioned methods of the day, and its originality was quickly recognised. It was a masterly attack on those inefficient teachers who, as Erasmus put it, would have been better advised to find work on a farm and to occupy themselves with oxen and donkeys.

Among his Italian predecessors, he condemns Francisco Negro and Giovanni Maria Filelfo who had both written during the second half of the fifteenth century.[1] In a letter dated November 1499 and addressed to Lord Mountjoy he says:

> But why is Franciscus Niger read by children? The directions he gives are banal. They are not derived, as was fitting, from good writers on rhetoric; and the letters he gives so far from being stylish and graceful are not even in correct Latin. As for the well-known work which circulates under the name of Marius Philelphus, this appears to me rather confused. In plain words, it is insufficiently scientific and does not live up to the claims it makes.

But in the same letter he writes more generously about Giovanni Sulpizio who had published a *de Componendis et Ornandis Epistolis* in 1489 and about Niccolò Perotti whose grammar, first published 1473 but frequently reprinted, also contained a chapter *de Componendis Epistolis*.[2]

Another victim of Erasmus's attacks was Carolus Menniken or Carolus Virulus whose name I mentioned above. A former director of the *Paedagogium Lilium*, he had published by Jan Veldener in Louvain in 1476 a work called *Epistolarum Formulae*.[3] It consisted of 337 letters which he had composed for his students as models of correct usage. They have the common fault of being conventional and impersonal in tone. As the title of the work already indicates, they are formulas and as such could not teach young men to think or express themselves in an unaffected way.

Menniken's book enjoyed some forty years of unprecedented suc-

---

[1] Francisco Negro's *Opusculum Scribendi Epistolas seu Modus Epistolandi* (Venice, 1488) was reprinted a number of times before the end of the fifteenth century. G. M. Filelfo's *Epistolarium seu de Arte Conficiendi Epistolas* was published in 1484 by Pachel and Scinzenzeler in Milan.

[2] Allen, I, Ep. 117, pp. 271–2, 29–35.   [3] *BBr*, IV, 330–2.

cess. More than fifty editions of it appeared between 1476 and 1520 in the Low Countries, Germany and France. But with the coming of the sixteenth century, scholars who were influenced by Italian human-ism began to voice objections to Menniken's Latin. They assaulted him without mercy. For instance, we find the German Heinrich Bebel, who in 1503 published his *Commentarius Epistolarum Conficien-darum...contra Epistolas Caroli*, speaking of him contemptuously as an *audaculus verborum structor*. The *Epistolarum Formulae* were printed for the last time in 1520, after which their prestige faded away altogether.

The success of the *Opus de Conscribendis Epistolis* probably contri-buted in no small measure to this decline in Menniken's fortunes. Erasmus states in that treatise that 'in Italy literature had already started to revive while in Louvain the letters of a certain Carolus were still zealously read'—*Caroli cujusdam qui multis annis moderatus est paedagogium Lilense*—and he adds disdainfully 'but today nobody would dare to look at them any more'. Again, a little further on, he writes that the young should not be introduced to the work of Carolus Virulus Lovaniensis 'cujus scripta cito gratiam exuerunt. Non quod negem in his esse, quod aliquis possit imitari, sed quod mediocribus, aut tolerabilibus tantum anteferri malim eximios'.[1] In short, Menni-ken is *mediocris* or *tolerabilis*. It seems to me that Erasmus may have been too severe with him. The style of the *Epistolarum Formulae* may verge occasionally on the precious and some of the idioms may lack the support of a Golden Age authority, but the Latin is by and large correct. Menniken, who had read Bruni and Petrarch, tried to model his style on Cicero's *Epistolae ad Familiares*, of which Jan Veldener had just published an edition, and on the *Rerum Familiarum Epistolae* of Aeneas Sylvius, which Veldener intended to publish, and which Menniken had certainly been able to consult in manuscript.[2]

In the first passage where Menniken is mentioned, Erasmus com-ments on another of his contemporaries: 'apud Hollandos orbis lumen habetur Engelbertus quidam qui suis *Epistoliis* nihil aliud docebat pueros quam inepte scribere'. The reference is undoubtedly to Engelbertus Schut of Leyden,[3] a fifteenth-century humanist,

[1] *O.O.* I, col. 352 c; 364 b.

[2] It was the publisher Pierre César in his edition of the *Epistolarum Formulae* (Paris, 1478) who first mentioned Cicero and Aeneas Sylvius as having been the models for Menni-ken's work. This information was then repeated in about twelve other editions: *BBr*, IV, 332.

[3] For the scanty information we have about his life see J. F. Foppens, *Bibliotheca Belgica* (Brussels, 1739), I, 263; *NNBW*, IX, 593–4. In 1458 the City Fathers of Leyden nomin-ated Engelbertus Schut to the headmastership of their 'grote school'. We have from his

whom Foppens calls *versificator et grammaticus*, and who must have published *Epistolia* or short model letters which have not been preserved. The validity of Erasmus's judgement on him cannot therefore be checked.

The authors whom Erasmus regards as the Grand Masters of the epistolary style all come from Italy. They are Cicero and Pliny among the ancients, and Angelo Poliziano among the moderns. He refers to them constantly, especially in the second part of his treatise where he is considering different styles, while Ovid, Seneca, Jerome, Cyprian, Augustine, Ausonius and humanists like Poggio, Valla, Bartolommeo Scala[1] and Budé receive only casual mention.

In the second chapter of the *Brevissima Formula*, where Erasmus discusses imitation, we find all three Grand Masters characterised:

It goes without question that we must follow those whose merit has been approved unanimously through many centuries. If it is true, as has been said, that Cicero, although he is the prince of Latin eloquence, has more of nature than art in his letters, and that Pliny is technically more perfect and correct, nevertheless both are excellent. But even so we should not limit our reading to them, but should read also those others who have applied themselves to the imitation of ancient excellence. In my opinion, Politian has his place among those we ought to read, because of the brilliance of his topics and the perfect care he uses in certain letters.[2]

And he goes on to say that Seneca is a model appropriate only for advanced students and not for adolescents because of his *stilus sterilis et circumcisus*.

Erasmus gives Cicero his due, but he is manifestly opposed to any kind of Ciceronian monopoly. As far as letter-writing is concerned, the younger Pliny and Politian are placed on a level with the author

pen a *Tractatus Metricus de Locis Rhetoricis* and a *de Moribus Mensae Carmen*. Erasmus tried to win his friendship 1488-9, which shows that he must have been a desirable patron (Allen, I, Ep. 28, 23-33). It is to this period that we must assign a laudatory poem in which Erasmus expresses his respect for Schut (C. Reedijk, *The poems of Desiderius Erasmus*...(Leyden, Brill, 1956), nr. 11, pp. 156-9). Schut must have rejected these overtures because in his next letter Erasmus talks about him with sarcasm: 'quod si videtur, Engelbertum istum tuum, qui, ut scribis, ita Castaliis aquis potus est ut nihil expuat, nihil emungat nisi versus accersendum tibi censeo et si qui sunt illius similes; qualium ubique non difficilis copia'.

[1] Bartolommeo Scala (1430-97), Italian man of letters, was a protégé of Cosimo de' Medici who gave him the opportunity to study law. He became Chancellor of Florence. In 1484 he formed part of an embassy to congratulate Innocent VIII for his zeal in the pontificate. Scala was jealous of Politian and had serious disputes with him about the use of Latin. We possess fourteen of his letters (*Nouvelle biographie générale*, XLIII, 446).

[2] Erasmus, *Brevissima maximeque Compendiaria Conficiendarum Epistolarum Formula* (Basel, Platter, 1536), p. 49.

of the *ad Familiares*, the *princeps latinae eloquentiae*. And it is made plain that Sallust, Quintilian, Horace, Virgil and Ovid also belong to the canon of correct authors whom it is safe to imitate. It is by taking Cicero's Latin as a basis and adding elements from other writers, including humanists like Politian, that we arrive at what may be called a personal style. We see here quite clearly the line of thought which was foreshadowed by the *de Ratione Studii* of 1512, and which was to lead six years later to Erasmus's revolt against the Cicero-mania of Bembo and his like. The *Opus de Conscribendis Epistolis* contains the germs of the *Ciceronianus*.

Erasmus knew Politian's correspondence well and must have used it often. It was published first in 1494 in twelve books which constitute, as it were, a doctrinal and polemical appendix to the famous *Miscellanea*. Politian's speciality was the short letter, and this distinguished him from the majority of his fellow humanists who tended to be prolix. The seventh book of his *Epistolae* consists entirely of short pieces, almost prose epigrams. Erasmus describes his skill as follows:

Some writers recapitulate their correspondents' letters pretty well in full and provide almost more by way of detail than the originals. If it is necessary to recapitulate, it should be done with a clever and appropriate concision. Politian showed himself a great expert in this field. Because of his solicitude for his readers, he was unwilling for them to miss anything and so produced a great many summaries in case the letters he was answering perished or happened to be dull to read.[1]

In conclusion, something must be said about the fortunes and influence of the treatise. As has been stated, it was a bestseller from the first moment it appeared; and the unauthorised *Brevissima Formula* sold nearly as well as the *Opus* itself. The latter was adopted as a textbook by the University of Cracow;[2] and summaries were written of it for the use of schools. For example, Johannes Nemius or Govertz from 's Hertogenbosch published an *Epitome ex Opere Erasmi Roterodami de Conscribendis Epistolis* (Antwerp, 1556).[3] Erasmus's book being

[1] *O.O.* I, 351 A.
[2] In a Cracow University resolution of 1538, it is determined that instead of Donatus and the *Parva Logicalia* of Petrus Hispanus, the *Modus Epistolandi* of Fr. Niger and Erasmus's *Opus de Conscribendis Epistolis* will for some years be the subject of the normal lessons and the final examinations, also the grammar of Perottus and his *Modus Epistolandi* and *Ars Metrica*, also the *Rhetoric* and *Letters* of Cicero and the *Dialectica* of Caesarius (F. Paulsen, *Geschichte des gelehrten Unterrichts* (Leipzig, 1919–21), I, 130).
[3] Joannes Nemius, otherwise known as Jan Govertzoon or Godevaarts, was born in 's Hertogenbosch at the beginning of the sixteenth century and died around 1593. His *Epitome ex Opere Erasmi Roterod. de Conscribendis Epistolis: cui quod ad scribendi artem pertinet, accessit ex Ecclesiaste, Copia Rerum, castioribus Colloquiis et aliis Erasmi scriptis. Item ex Rhetorum libris* (Antv., J. Latius, 1556, now in Bibl. Univ. Gent) is dedicated to the brothers

primarily intended for the instruction of teachers was too difficult and too elaborate for children; and in these summarised adaptations the attacks on the educational system and on pedagogic incompetence were also omitted.

Besides the thirty reprints of the *Opus* which existed in 1536, some fifty more were added before 1600 and the work was republished at regular intervals during the seventeenth century. The example of Erasmus served moreover as an inspiration both to his contemporaries and to later humanists. Large numbers of handbooks on letter-writing appeared in Italy, France, Germany and especially in the Low Countries. Here we have Vivès,[1] Macropedius,[2] Vibotius,[3] Magnus de Ramlot,[4] du Four,[5] Verepaeus,[6] Vladeraccus,[7] Gramaye[8] and finally the great Justus Lipsius himself whose *Epistolica Institutio* (1591) was reprinted eighteen times.[9] All these treatises owed a substantial debt to Erasmus. Many followed his division of the material or borrowed from him in detail. Some merely paraphrased his text, summarising his instructions and adding only a few examples of their own. The *Ars Epistolica* of Despauterius[10] quotes whole sec-

Busaeus who were well-known writers in Nimeguen: *NNBW*, VIII, 1209; *BN*, XV, 587; *BHB*, p. 166.

[1] Juan-Luis Vivès (1492–1540), *de Epistolis Conscribendis* (Antwerp, Michael Hillen, 1533).

[2] Georgius Macropedius (1475–1558), *Epistolica Studiosis Traiectinae Scholae Tyrunculis nuncupata* (Antwerp, Michael Hillen, 1554). An appendix 'de paranda copia verborum ac rerum' was added after the author's death and the work was republished under the title: *Methodus de Conscribendis Epistolis a Georgio Macropedio secundum veram artis rationem tradita* (Dillingen, Mayer, 1565). It had in all sixteen editions and reprints: *BN*, XIII, 1022.

[3] Joris Vibotius or Wybo, *Rhetoricae et Artis Epistolicae Compendium* (Antwerp, J. Verwirthagen, 1556).

[4] S. Magnus de Ramlot, *Methodus Artis Epistolicae* (Louvain, Bogard, 1563).

[5] Henri du Four (Furnius or Farnèse), born Liège *c.* 1550, died Padua 1609, was a classical scholar, teacher and moralist. He wrote a *de Imitatione Ciceronis seu de Scribendarum Epistolarum Ratione* (Antwerp, J. Lœus, 1571); *BN*, VI, col. 253.

[6] Simon Verepæus (Verrepæus or Verrept) (1522–98), *de Epistolis Latine Conscribendis* (Antwerp, A. Tilenius Brechtanus, 1571) is a work based on the best Latin writers. The model letters give the names of many relatives, friends, protectors and pupils of the author. There were a number of editions: Antwerp, Cologne, Lyons, Poland: *BN*, XXVI, col. 609.

[7] Christ. Vladeraccus (1520–1601), *Formulae Ciceronianae Epistolis Conscribendis utilissimae* (Antwerp, Plantin, 1586): *BN*, XXVI, 806; *NNBW*, IX, 1214.

[8] J.-B. de Gramaye, *Libellus Phrasium et Epistolica* (Cologne, Herardus, 1597): *BHB*, p. 166.

[9] Justus Lipsius, *Epistolica Institutio, excerpta e dictantis eius ore...* (Leyden, F. Raphelengius, 1591): *BBr*, III, 985–91.

[10] Johannes Despauterius (*c.* 1475–1520) published an *Ars Epistolica* in 1509 as an appendix to his *Syntaxis*. The separate edition of 1513 (Badius, Paris) was a revised and enlarged reprint of this. In addition to Menniken, Schut and Despauterius who have already been mentioned, the predecessors of Erasmus included Antoine Haneron from Arras. He was Rector at Louvain in 1434 and died in 1490. The date and place of publication

tions verbatim. That Despauterius who wrote in 1513 should have laid Erasmus's work under contribution might appear surprising; but a copy of Erasmus's text could have been made available to him by the good offices of the printer Josse Bade.

English letter-writing is also indebted to Erasmus though in this case his influence did not altogether displace the medieval tradition. Angel Day's *English Secretarie* (Part I, 1586; Part II, 1592) imitates Erasmus's divisions, arrangement and terminology; and in 1678 we find in F.B.'s *Clavis Grammatica* a restatement of his theories. William Fulwood's *Enimie of Idleness* (1568) is an earlier if less obvious echo.[1]

Even Shakespeare, as Rolf Soellner has proved,[2] shared in this inspiration. He borrowed a passage from Erasmus's *epistola consolatoria* as a model for the *consolatio* which Brother Lawrence addresses to Romeo after his banishment.

NOTES

The following abbreviations are used in the footnotes to this article:

Allen   P. S. Allen, H. M. Allen, H. W. Garrod, *Opus Epistolarum Des. Erasmi Roterodami* (Oxford, 1906–58), 12 vols.

BBr   *Bibliotheca Belgica*, réédition M.-Th. Lenger (Bruxelles, 1964), 5 vols.

BHB   A. Gerlo and E. Lauf, *Bibliographie de l'Humanisme belge* (Bruxelles, Presses Universitaires, 1965) (Travaux de l'Institut pour l'étude de la Renaissance et de l'Humanisme, Instrumenta Humanistica I).

BN   *Biographie nationale* publiée par l'Académie Royale des Sciences, des Lettres et des Beaux-Arts de Belgique (Bruxelles, 1866–1963), 32 vols.

NNBW   *Nieuw Nederlands Biographisch Woordenboek* (Leyden, 1911–37), 10 vols.

O.O.   D. Erasmus, *Opera Omnia*, ed. Clericus (Leyden, 1703–6), 11 vols.

of his *de Epistolis Brevibus Edendis* are not known. There is also J. Badius Ascensius, *de Epistolis Componendis Compendium* (Paris, Thielman Kerver, 1502).

[1] H. S. Herbrüggen, *Sir Thomas More*, pp. xli–xlii; J. Robertson, *The Art of Letter-Writing* (Liverpool University Press, 1942), pp. 10 ff.

[2] R. Soellner, 'Shakespeare and the "Consolatio"', *Notes and Queries* (1954), 108–9; for the passages see *O.O.* I, col. 428 and *Romeo and Juliet*, III. iii. 54–6.

11

HUMANISM AND HUMANIST LITERATURE IN THE LOW COUNTRIES BEFORE 1500

J. IJSEWIJN

The Dutch bibliographers, Bob and Maria Emilie De Graaf, introduce the first volume of their new series, *Bibliographies of Dutch Humanists* with this pessimistic statement: 'Dutch learning has neglected and still neglects the heritage of 16th-century Humanism; and this indictment is the more serious in that it is not new but was voiced already 45 years ago when Lindeboom referred to the period as a "fertile and little cultivated field of work".' We are concerned today with an earlier age, with the years before 1500. But I want to begin by emphasising that what the De Graafs say about the sixteenth century applies to that earlier age with even greater force. If there is much to be learnt even today about the contemporaries of Erasmus, there is still more to be learnt about their predecessors. Our knowledge of the period before 1500 is full of gaps that urgently demand attention.

It was a period of impressive cultural change, when the Netherlands saw the shift from scholasticism and medieval patterns in language and literature to a humanist interest in the classics and the imitation of ancient prose writers and poets. It was the lifetime of Rudolfus Agricola, a fine Latin stylist and a famous translator from the Greek. Schools of international fame flourished at Zwolle and Deventer. Aduard Abbey near Groningen had its circle of active humanists, and at the University of Louvain a great battle was fought over the new study of the classical poets. At Münster in Westphalia, at Bruges in Flanders and elsewhere, the classical theatre was resuscitated. Changes in literary taste among the educated swept away medieval Latin versification, vocabulary and style; and it was at this critical moment that young men such as Erasmus, Murmellius, the Canters, Ulsenius, Remaclus Arduenna and numerous others received their classical training and learnt to look with wondering eyes at the accomplishments of contemporary Italian scholars and poets. But these developments, which are of manifest importance, remain for all practical purposes unexplored. Histories of humanism and neo-Latin literature in old 'Belgium' traditionally begin with the sixteenth century and present at best a short survey of fifteenth-century origins by way of an introduction, as is the case, for example, with the outstanding *History of the Foundation and Rise of the Collegium Trilingue Lovaniense* by my predecessor, Professor Henry de Vocht.

It is true that much work has been done on the period by the historians of the so-called Brethren of the Common Life, that is by Hyma, Post, Lourdaux, Persoons and others. But the theory that these brethren were the founders of Northern humanism is not one which can be accepted without qualification. Many of the men who later played a leading role in the development of Netherlands humanism attended schools which were directed or influenced by the Brethren. But these men needed to look for other ideals than their schooling had provided before they rose to their full stature. They had to turn their eyes to Italy. And even in those circumstances their early education often prevented them from becoming genuine humanists. We find them abandoning their classical studies and returning to a traditional routine of theological enquiry. The history of the Brethren which has attracted so much attention is not the true history of Netherlands humanism.

Given this situation, we must now consider the tasks which require doing in the immediate future.

Our greatest and most urgent need is for sound critical editions of the fifteenth-century Latin authors. With a few exceptions, such as some minor writings by Rudolfus Agricola or the early letters and poems of Erasmus, works produced in the Netherlands before the emergence of humanism must be read today either in manuscript or in extremely rare early printed versions.[1] Among the more obvious *desiderata* are the following:

Rudolfus Agricola: We need editions of his correspondence, his poems and his principal work, the *de Inventione Dialectica.*

Cornelius Aurelius of Gouda: This interesting author has been the victim of a *damnatio memoriae* on religious grounds. I am preparing the

---

[1] Dr P. C. Boeren has just published the works of two Latin poets who were in the service of Duke Charles the Bold: *Twee Maaslandse Dichters in dienst van Karel De Stoute* (The Hague, Nijhoff, 1968). The poets in question are Bartholomaeus Tungrensis and Simon Mulart. Dr Boeren calls them 'prehumanists', but I cannot agree with him on that point. Mulart's taste and techniques seem wholly medieval, and even Bartholomaeus styles himself *versificator* and never *poeta* as the real prehumanists and humanists invariably do.

first edition of that portion of his *Marias* which has been discovered and is now available to scholars; and we have many other works of his which await publication. As far as we can judge today, Aurelius was Holland's finest Latin poet at the end of the fifteenth century, and he exercised a great influence on the young Erasmus whose friendship with him is well known.

Engelbertus Schut of Leyden: His works include an interesting *Ars Dictandi* in verse and a treatise on rhetoric in prose, which earned him the admiration of the young Erasmus. He was also praised by Stephanus Surigonus, a Milanese humanist temporarily established at Louvain. Although his versification remained medieval, he was to some degree influenced by humanist thought. He claimed that good Latin must be learnt directly from the ancient authors and had a great respect for the teachings of Quintilian.

Carolus Virulus: This man was for half a century the director of the *Pedagogium Lilii* at the University of Louvain and made this college the first, and for a long time the only, stronghold of humanism in that essentially scholastic university. Vivès still remembered him as a man of exceptional merit whose abilities were hampered by his thankless milieu. Virulus's *Epistolicae Formulae*, which cite Petrarch, Boccaccio, Salutati, Bruni and Gasparino da Barzizza, certainly deserve the attentions of an editor. Together with Schut's treatises, this work by Virulus can be regarded as the immediate forerunner of Erasmus's Latin handbooks based on Valla, Agostino Dati and other fifteenth-century Italian humanists.

Arnoldus Bostius: A Carmelite living in Ghent and Bruges, he had many friends among French, Italian, German and Dutch humanists and was known for the encouragement he gave to authors capable of composing Christian poems and treatises in correct classical Latin.

Alexander Hegius: He was the director of the Deventer School where he made use of classical authors and the works of Italian humanists, such as Tortelli, instead of the barbarous medieval grammarians. His teaching of Latin was based on the principle: 'quemadmodum is non loquitur Teutonice, qui ita loquitur quomodo nullus Teutonorum locutus est, ita nec Latine is loquitur, qui ita loquitur quomodo nullus Latinorum locutus est'.[1]

Jacobus Magdalius Gaudensis: His Christian heroical epistle, *Epistola divae Mariae Magdalenae ad Christum in Infirmitate Lazari Fratris* was written more than ten years before Eobanus Hessus's exercises in the

---

[1] *Farrago* (c. 1490), p. 13. We cite from the copy in the Royal Library at Brussels.

same genre. He has therefore a strong claim to be regarded as the first writer of humanist *Heroides Christianae*.

These are the most obvious names whose works call for attention, but one could add to them: William Hermans of Gouda, poet, historian and friend of Erasmus; Bartholomaeus Coloniensis, a wandering teacher and poet; Kempo Thessaliensis (of Texel), grammarian and poet; Carolus Fernandus and Petrus Burrus who worked in Paris and numerous others.

In some cases, the works of these humanists still await discovery. We have cited the instance of the 'lost' parts of Aurelius's *Marias*. But there is also Adam Jordaens of Louvain, once celebrated as a great humanist poet and as a correspondent of Ermolao Barbaro. Notwithstanding patient research for many years, not a single line of his poems was found until recently when Dr Persoons of Louvain came across some *Carmina et Epitaphia* in the *Chronicon Bethlehemicum*.[1] His letters remain lost.

Another important field for research would be the compilation of a full-scale study which would give a picture of the cultural relations between Italy and the Low Countries. We need to know more about Italian scholars and travellers in the North, about Netherlands students in Italy, about the importation or the printing of Italian humanist works and about exchanges of learned correspondence.

We also need to form some idea of how scholars learnt to use a correct classical Latin. There is an astonishing difference between the Latin poetry written round about 1440 and that which was written fifty years later, a difference which marks an obvious increase in men's knowledge and understanding of the classics.

Finally we need to investigate the renaissance of Greek learning; and here the relationship between Agricola's translations and those published by his heir, Erasmus, needs to be studied and resolved.

A great deal of work must be done on all these aspects of the subject before we can produce a worthwhile survey of early humanism in the Low Countries. For what we want is a survey comparable to the excellent studies of Weiss and Schirmer on early English humanism and one which will not confine itself to repeating generalisations based on unchecked traditions.[2]

---

[1] *Chronicon Bethlehemicum*, VI, 8, 35, fo. 280. Dr Persoons is publishing the *editio princeps* of this chronicle.

[2] For bibliographical information concerning Dutch and Belgian Humanism please apply to: *Seminarium Philologiae Humanisticae*, University of Louvain, Leopoldstraat 32, B-3000 Leuven, Belgium.

12

THE CHARACTER OF
HUMANIST PHILOLOGY

E. J. KENNEY

The term 'philology' is often used in connection with the scholarly activities of the humanists. It is part of the thesis of this paper that the uncritical use of the term may tend to foster misunderstanding of the thing itself and that increased caution in its application is desirable in the interests of historical clarity. My remarks are designed to reveal my ignorance in as many different fields as may be conveniently possible in the space allotted me. The justification for this approach is that it has been precisely in the course of attempts to enlighten this ignorance that I have seemed to myself to become aware of the areas in which further exploration might be profitably undertaken. What interests me, specifically, is the problem of humanist textual scholarship, and in particular the proceedings of the editors of the early printed editions of classical texts.

In his brilliant history of classical philology Wilamowitz concludes a discussion of the limitations of humanist scholarship with a trenchant and dismissive verdict from which, as with many of his verdicts, he clearly expected there to be no appeal. The humanists were unequal to philology: *Wir dürfen eben von den Humanisten keine Philologie verlangen*.[1] That was said (originally) in 1921. In 1965 Sesto Prete, writing in *Philologus* on 'Die Leistungen der Humanisten auf dem Gebiete der lateinischen Philologie', saw the achievements of humanist critics as entitling them to consideration as the legitimate predecessors of Lachmann and the modern school of critics.[2] One may, I think, entertain doubts as to the pretensions to pass such a judgement of a scholar who discusses Lachmann's position even in passing without reference to Sebastiano Timpanaro's fundamental *La Genesi del Metodo del Lachmann* (1963), which first saw the light as two articles in *Studi italiani di filologia classica* so long ago as 1959–60; but that is by the way. The important point is that a glance at the respective contexts

---

[1] U. von Wilamowitz-Moellendorff, *Geschichte der Philologie* (1959), p. 11.
[2] *Philologus*, cix (1965), 259.

of these two evaluations will show that they stem from different pre-
misses; or at all events that the words 'humanist' and 'philology' are
used with different chronological implications and on the basis of
different assumptions about the nature of philology and more particularly of textual criticism.

Any attempt to clarify the situation must start in the Middle Ages
and must do so with a backward glance into classical antiquity itself.
I will begin by venturing the observation that of conjectural criticism
in anything like its modern sense the Middle Ages knew nothing.
Such an observation cries aloud for contradiction; it could be shaken
if not refuted by one positive example to the contrary. All I can say
is that I have not so far encountered that example. The evidence
known to me suggests that in the Latin West, certainly down to the
Carolingian period and for some time after, the general attitude to the
copying and correction of classical texts was broadly speaking what
it had been in the ancient world. That is to say, in the monastic
scriptorium the ancient grammatical tradition, in however garbled
or imperfectly realised a form, was respected: the thread uniting
antiquity to the modern world, though severely stretched, was not
broken. Copyists saw it as their task to reproduce the transmitted text,
that of their exemplar; correction was limited to diorthosis and
collation, criticism to choice between existing variants. Conjecture,
so far as it played a part at all, was generated by the tradition itself,
not by the mind of the corrector. I have not so far seen a fundamental
discussion of this question as it affects Latin texts that may be set
beside the careful examination that Professor Zuntz has devoted to
the activities of Triclinius in his *An Inquiry into the Transmission of the
Plays of Euripides* (1965), in which he emphasises the vital distinction
between diorthosis and conjecture. Only one identifiable western
medieval copyist and corrector suggests himself, I think, as anything
like a possible parallel to Triclinius: Lupus of Ferrières. Professor
Billanovich sees in Lupus 'un filologo armato dello scudo laborioso
della collazione e della spada, sebbene ancora poco tagliente, della
congettura'.[1] Well, not even the authority of Billanovich can quell
my doubts; the essential distinction is, in the crucial cases, unexpectedly difficult to draw. So much seems to turn, for instance, on the
view one takes of such matters as the origin of the supplement at
Valerius Maximus III, ii, 10, where in my view it is quite inadmissible

[1] G. Billanovich, 'Dall'antica Ravenna alle biblioteche umanistiche', *Aevum*, xxx (1956),
320.

to talk in terms of proof.[1] It is not often that scholars seem to examine a medieval text-tradition with precisely this point, and this distinction, in mind. One who has is Dr H. C. Gotoff, of Harvard University. In a careful and minutely detailed study of the ninth-century MSS of Lucan he has established, it seems to me convincingly, that Lucan's Carolingian copyists did not innovate *ingenii ope*: on the contrary they seem to have been absurdly content to copy and to cross-copy gibberish with meticulous accuracy, but conjecture they would not. If one comes down to the MSS of Latin classical writers copied, with far less real care though with much more surface elegance as to the text, in the twelfth and thirteenth centuries, one finds these copies teeming with 'good' readings which editors often print in preference to those of the older MSS. Whether or not they print them editors tend to assure one that such readings are 'medieval conjectures'—a fact which true or false has no bearing whatever on whether they are right or not—but it is striking that whenever an older MS previously unknown comes to light it almost invariably offers some of these readings, which are thus shown to be traditional. Such is the case, for instance, with the *recentiores* of Seneca's *Epistles* as Mr Reynolds's excellent study shows.[2] Discoveries such as that of the Graz fragment of the Virgilian Appendix are instructive, not because they 'confirm' this or that conjecture of Heinsius or Haupt—that is not the point—but as reminders of how slender is the basis of surviving evidence from which we are too prone to generalise. Unless therefore proof positive is forthcoming—and the search for such proof is clearly a possible field of further enquiry—I am disposed to suggest that we should do well to accept, *mutatis mutandis*, the conclusions that Professor Zuntz has formulated regarding Greek texts: 'Conjectural alteration, independent of any evidence is—so far as I can see—in the Middle Ages a new departure by the scholars of the Palaeologan era, at least in poetic texts.'[3] The concluding rider is important since, as I have already said, it is with classical and literary texts that I am concerned.

By 1400 this tradition had been definitively broken; when and how and where the break occurred is very difficult to establish. The

[1] Cf. Lindsay, *Classical Philology*, IV (1909), 113–17; Schnetz, *Philologus*, LXXVIII (1922–3), 421–2; C. J. Carter, *The Manuscript Tradition of Valerius Maximus* (unpublished Cambridge Ph.D. dissertation), pp. 34–5.

[2] L. D. Reynolds, *The Medieval Tradition of Seneca's* Letters (1965); cf. Kenney, *C.R.* XVI (1966), 343.

[3] Zuntz, *An Inquiry into the Transmission of the Plays of Euripides*, p. 201.

thirteenth and fourteenth centuries saw the secularisation of the copying of texts, with the decline of the monastic scriptorium and the rise of the professional scribe; and of course the advent of what we may call the scholar. With him came a new kind of MS and a new kind of activity, vividly described by Billanovich, particularly in his classic paper 'Petrarch and the textual tradition of Livy'.[1] It would be quite improper to quarrel with Billanovich's description of Petrarch's Livy as a 'philological chef-d'œuvre',[2] so long as the description is accompanied by certain qualifications. These are in fact to be found, either implicitly or explicitly conveyed, in Billanovich's discussion, and the possible misconceptions that may arise, indeed I think have arisen, cannot be laid at his door; but they are real and must be guarded against. Two points, I think, should be made. First, however brilliant the contribution made by an individual, it could at this date, in what was essentially an anti-philological environment, have only a temporary and local effect. Thus, as Billanovich points out, the advances made by Petrarch in the textual study of Livy were absorbed anonymously into the stream of transmission, and the first editor, though a friend of Valla's and hence in touch with the Petrarchan tradition, prepared the text for printing in essential ignorance of it.[3] Secondly, it is unsound to generalise from the exceptional and well-documented case, such as that of Petrarch clearly was. The typical humanist MS is rather such a book as the Leidensis of Tacitus or the copy from which the pseudo-Virgilian *Aetna* was first printed (I restrict myself to two instances which have been recently investigated by Professor Goodyear and others):[4] in no real sense a 'philological' production, but a random hotchpotch of tradition and often wilful and occasionally violent alteration. Of course the result of such activity may be highly deceptive, what looks like a 'good' text though it is nothing of the sort. Only the sort of painstaking investigation accorded to the MSS of Iamblichus, *de Mysteriis* by Professor Sicherl can reveal such MSS for what they are.[5]

The first editor of Livy just mentioned (and also of *Aetna*) was

---

[1] *Journal of the Warburg and Courtauld Institutes*, XIV (1951), 137–208; cf. *idem, I primi umanisti e le tradizioni dei classici latini* (1953), pp. 34–40.

[2] *I primi umanisti*, p. 34.

[3] 'Petrarch and the textual tradition...', p. 180.

[4] F. R. D. Goodyear, 'The readings of the Leiden manuscript of Tacitus', *C.Q.* XV (1965), 298–322; *Incerti Auctoris Aetna* (1965), pp. 5–6, 10–11.

[5] M. Sicherl, *Die Handschriften, Ausgaben und Übersetzungen von Iamblichus de Mysteriis* (1957), p. 83.

Giovanni Andrea de' Bussi (Johannes Andreas de Buxis), Bishop of Aleria, styled by Sabbadini the hero of the *editiones principes*.[1] In the years 1469–71 he acted as midwife not only to Livy but to Apuleius, Caesar, Gellius, Lucan, Virgil, a good deal of Cicero, and the whole of Ovid. This does not sound much like editing as we know it now. Was de' Bussi more than an indefatigable corrector of the press? Certainly he was no scholar as Valla or Politian or Hermolaus Barbarus or even Merula were scholars. One would like to know more than I have hitherto been able to find out about his dealings with the printers who rushed these texts on to the market, Sweynheim and Pannartz. Of *their* motives there can be, I take it, no doubt: they were predominantly commercial, and the same was broadly speaking as true of the early printers in general as it is of publishers today.[2] If classical texts were hurried into print at this time, it was not because readers thirsting for pleasure or instruction would otherwise have gone without so much as because this new product seemed to have good marketing prospects. The provisos were that it paid to play safe, that is, to stick to the common authors, and those Latin rather than Greek; and that it was necessary to be quick off the mark. Since capital and resources were limited, editions were small and there was no incentive to spend more than the absolute minimum on fundamental editorial activity. In this hasty and competitive atmosphere purity of texts was not a prime consideration, though naturally lip-service was paid to superficial accuracy in such promotional material as might accompany the text. It suffices to read de' Bussi's prefaces, if the length of the list just rehearsed is not itself revealing enough, to discover that his editorial efforts were on his own admission of the most perfunctory description. Even when fortune threw good materials in his way the haste of the whole undertaking forbade their effective use: the Medicean Virgil was in his hands but he hardly had time to do more than glance at it. His first copy of Caesar, corrected (he says) *multa diligentia*, he lost, and as the printers (fearing obviously to lose their market) would brook no delay, he provided another, revised—the word is his own—'perfunctorily'. The text of Ovid's *Metamorphoses* he prepared as a summer vacation from Cicero; and so on. Sabbadini has examined in some detail a specimen passage of his edition of Pliny the Elder, published in 1470 (it was

[1] R. Sabbadini, *Le scoperte dei codici latini e greci ne' secoli xiv e xv* (1905), p. 122.
[2] For the general picture see L. Febvre and H.-J. Martin, *L'apparition du livre* (1958), esp. pp. 172 ff.; C. F. Bühler, *The Fifteenth-century Book* (1961), pp. 40–65; R. Hirsch, *Printing, Selling and Reading 1450–1550* (1967), p. 22.

not the *editio princeps*), and has established that all the readings in it that are due to the editor are arbitrary depravations of the text.[1] Contemporary complaints by Merula (who protested too much) show that de' Bussi's proceedings must have been remarkable only for their wholesale character.[2]

Exceptions there were. Lascaris seems to have produced his text of the Greek Anthology with exemplary fidelity, blunders and all;[3] whether he appreciated the point or not, this was in fact the most useful thing that he could possibly have done to set criticism on a stable footing for the future. But this was, I believe, a special case, and I know of no satisfactory evidence for any fundamental distinction between the methods of Greek and Latin editors as suggested by Dr Bolgar. 'The high standards of accuracy', he writes in his indispensable *Classical Heritage*, 'which had been established in the first place by the editors of the Greek texts who had risen to the challenge of an exceptionally difficult task, were rapidly adopted by their colleagues working on the easier Latin authors. The triumphs of Chalcondyles, Lascaris and Musurus were equalled by Politian, Merula and Beroaldo.'[4] Lascaris's *obscura diligentia* has already been mentioned. Of the other two Greeks Musurus is in a class by himself as a critic of the first rank, if by criticism be understood *emendatio*, divinatory criticism; but chronology forbids that he should have exerted any very substantial influence on either Politian or Beroaldus. Chalcondylas's *editio princeps* of Homer is of course in a sense one of the great books of the world, but as textual criticism it is naught; his latest biographer, Cammelli, echoes the general verdict that it reproduced the Byzantine vulgate and is not disposed to take seriously the editor's claim to have used Eustathius.[5] Politian makes an odd figure in this company, for precisely the reason that, as I shall attempt to emphasise, makes him important to our thesis: though as a scholar he out-tops all the rest of the group, as indeed he does all fifteenth-century scholars except Valla, I believe I am right in

[1] Sabbadini, *S.I.F.C.* VIII (1900), 443.
[2] See Merula's preface to his edition of the *Scriptores Rei Rusticae* (Venice, 1472; Hain 14564), reprinted by B. Botfield, *Prefaces to the First Editions of the Greek and Roman Classics and of the Sacred Scriptures* (1861), pp. 146–7; and cf. F. Gabotto and A. Badini Confalonieri, 'Vita di Giorgio Merula', *Riv. di storia, arte, archeologia della provincia di Alessandria*, II (1893), 60–1.
[3] Fr. Jacobs, *Animadversiones in Epigrammata Anthologiae Graecae*, I, i (= *Anthologia Graeca*, V, 1798), p. xciii.
[4] R. R. Bolgar, *The Classical Heritage and its Beneficiaries* (1954), p. 375.
[5] G. Cammelli, *I dotti bizantini e le origini dell'umanesimo*, III, *Demetrio Calcondila* (1954), pp. 88–92.

saying that he edited no texts with the trifling exception of the Fifth Hymn of Callimachus, and that (the *editio princeps*, in fact) *en passant* in the *Miscellanea*. As to Merula, he performed no editorial feat known to me that could conceivably be termed triumphal; his biographers make no attempt to elevate him from the second rank of scholars—'D'ingegno grande non fu' is their verdict.[1] In writing of a 'high standard of accuracy' I suspect that Dr Bolgar has allowed himself to be cozened by what Musurus (and his publisher) said about himself, for the editions tell a different tale. The Aldine Hesychius of 1514 may be confronted with its source, which is the *codex unicus*; if that MS had chanced to be lost, as happened to so many MSS at this time, Hesychian criticism, in spite of Musurus's numerous and excellent conjectures, would now be in a bad way. Geanokoplos is on the right lines when, in his *Greek Scholars in Venice*, he describes the 'ultimate objective' of Aldus as 'the preservation and diffusion of the ancient masterpieces so that his own countrymen and the Westerners could read, *easily and unhindered by innumerable difficulties*' [my italics].[2] It is precisely because the early editors of classical texts had few scruples about the methods used to further this objective that it is inappropriate to characterise their activity as 'philological' in any proper sense of the term.

Of the scholars mentioned in the preceding discussion Beroaldus was at least respectable—in Cambridge, I should explain, that is a technical term meaning that he was praised by Housman[3]—but the only one who was a great philologist was Politian. That he edited virtually nothing is immensely significant. Two things distinguish Politian among the later humanists, his natural gifts and his failure to publish, and the two things are intimately connected. He died at the early age of 40, and we cannot tell what he might have achieved if he had lived out his span. So far as the study of texts is concerned, it is, as Petrus Victorius said, the margins of his books that tell the story.[4] In those early years he was equipping himself for the real work ahead. Alone among his contemporaries, it seems, he saw the tasks confronting textual scholarship with anything approaching clarity; and alone he acted on his insight by making haste slowly.

[1] Gabotto–Badini Confalonieri, *Riv. di storia, arte, archeologia*,...III (1894), 350.
[2] D. J. Geanokoplos, *Greek Scholars in Venice* (1962), p. 155.
[3] *M. Manilii Astronomicon liber primus*, rec. A. E. Housman (1937), p. xiii.
[4] *Explicationes suarum in Catonem, Varronem, Columellam Castigationum* (1541–2), pp. 142–3 (quoted in *Mostra del Poliziano nella biblioteca Medicea Laurenziana...*, Catalogo a cura di A. Perosa (1954), pp. 27–8).

He recognised the problem as essentially one of the control of sources: the famous *subscriptiones* show his concern that the wellsprings of knowledge should not be muddied and his fear that the well-intentioned but haphazard and undocumented efforts of his predecessors might already have confused the record past disentangling. 'I have collated...in such a way as to note even the obviously corrupt readings. For this is the method I have decided on, not to add my own conjectures nor to omit anything that I have found in the old copies. If this procedure had been observed by earlier copyists, we their descendants would have had very much less to do.'[1] For all the *perizia filologica* that Billanovich rightly praises in Lovati and Mussato,[2] these words are to their address. So, slowly and patiently, Politian set about assembling and recording the facts. Yet even he, one supposes, would have quailed if he could have had any real inkling of the magnitude of the problem and the dominating rôles of time and chance. Until the epoch, long in the future, when the MSS on which our texts depend should be discovered, catalogued, and made accessible to the learned, the foundations of the whole enquiry were treacherous. Chance was on occasion kind. Politian, as is well known, had at his disposal in the famous Florentine codex of the Pandects a most potent instrument of textual philology, and there is no doubt that he was aware of its importance. Unhappily he died before he could exploit his knowledge, though the collation of the MS that he left behind him constituted for almost half a century almost the only source of information about it, since access to the original was granted sparingly if at all. It was not until 1541–2 that the Spanish scholar and bibliophile Antonius Augustinus collated the MS afresh and not until 1553 that an edition appeared in which this new knowledge was systematically used for the establishment of the text.[3] With the appearance of Torelli's work the fundamental problem was solved; but the credit in the end belongs to fortune, who provided the necessary conjunction of man and material and opportunity. Generally she has been niggardly, withholding as often as she dispenses benefits: denying the Oblongus and the Quadratus to Bentley and granting them to Havercamp.

[1] In a copy of Merula's *Scriptores Rei Rusticae* (Paris, B.N. **Inc. Rés. s. 439), quoted by Perosa, *Mostra*, p. 26; and by I. Maïer, *Les manuscrits d'Ange Politien* (Travaux d'humanisme et renaissance, LXX, 1965), p. 354 (reproduced by R. Merkelbach–H. van Thiel, *Lateinisches Leseheft zur Einführung in Paläographie und Textkritik* (1969), no. 22, p. 111).

[2] *I primi umanisti*, p. 23.

[3] F. de Zulueta, *Don Antonio Agustín* (Glasgow Univ. Publ. 51, 1939), pp. 36–44.

It has not escaped my notice that in the course of these remarks I have allowed my argument to proceed some half a century beyond the official chronological limits of our deliberations. That is not an oversight and I do not apologise for it. In this particular field the date 1500 is almost totally devoid of significance. If an era is needed, it should be 1550. By that time most classical texts were in print and it was becoming possible to assess the critical problems. There was general agreement that much remained to be done, less general agreement about methods. The search for and documentation of better sources, that is, older MSS, went on with increasing pretension to system. However, the situation was fundamentally bedevilled by the confusion which Politian foresaw but could not avert and which was the inevitable result of the *un*philological, because unhistorical, character of humanist textual scholarship. The average classical text first saw print in a state that represented what one might call a more or less random dip into the stream of tradition, at a point as far from the source as could be; and in that state it was, as it were, 'frozen' by the new medium. It is curious that a belated rigidity may be seen in some of the critical pronouncements of the sixteenth century regarding alteration to 'the text'; but the damage was now done. 'The text' was the *lectio recepta*, not the *lectio tradita*, a product of precisely that type of haphazard emendatory activity that sound critics saw was to be avoided. The historical insight that could discern the true nature of the problem was sparingly vouchsafed—even Scaliger does not seem to have grasped the full implications of the tradition of Catullus—and in any case in default of the appropriate material even the best critics could return no more than approximate and provisional answers. Through a series of such approximations and experiments during the seventeenth to the nineteenth centuries a science of historical editing slowly emerged; that it took so long must in large part be ascribed to the activities of the humanist copyists, correctors and editors who in all innocence combined to confuse the record. The problem confronting their successors was essentially that of attempting to peel back the layers of error that had accreted during the period loosely called the Revival of Learning and to arrive at the medieval *status quo ante*; then the real tasks of criticism could begin. It is rarely if ever quite as simple as that: even in the model tradition, as once it appeared to be, of Lucretius areas of uncertainty remain.[1]

---

[1] Timpanaro, *La Genesi del Metodo del Lachmann*, pp. 102-8.

In sum, the main object of these remarks is to suggest that further investigation in the field of textual scholarship between, let us say, 1350 and 1550 might be profitable, to be directed towards establishing some sort of documentation of the typical rather than the atypical; though in suggesting this emphasis I am not suggesting that we should neglect the outstanding personalities. We still lack, so far as I can discover, a monograph on Hermolaus Barbarus, to mention only one name, that of the only scholar consistently adduced by Erasmus and his correspondents in the same breath with Politian. It may be that enough fundamental research has already been done and that the principal need is for some kind of synthesis. What I am thinking of is a treatment that would, among other things, attempt: to describe and explain the character of the humanist MS of a classical text; to analyse and document the attitude of the copyist-scholar-reader to the correction of texts; to examine the editorial procedures behind the *editiones principes*; to establish the relationship, the symbiosis if you like, of the early editors and their printers; to follow, from the point of view of the constitution of the text, the transition from MS to printed book; and in particular—at least this is something that I myself find interesting—to investigate the self-assessment by the humanist textual scholars themselves of their function—what I mean by this is the evaluation and relation to the evidence of the texts themselves of those familiar, indeed stereotyped images of rescue,[1] restoration, refurbishing, renewal, removal of accretions, and the historical or unhistorical assumptions underlying them. Such a synthesis would of course call for the combined exploration of fields that at present tend to be discrete and cultivated by specialists working in isolation from each other: textual, historical, bibliographical. This is obviously a tall order, but the organisers have not forbidden speakers to cry for the moon, and to conclude this paper such a cry may serve to emphasise the keynote of the conference. Some such unified treatment of what has been called 'philology' during this period is what I have found myself desiderating, and so I have been impelled to offer this crude and ambitious specification to the better judgement of a learned audience. Perhaps it will at any rate be ready to extenuate and to say with Propertius

> audacia certe
> laus erit: in magnis et uoluisse sat est.

[1] Cf. Billanovich, *I primi umanisti*, p. 5.

PART IV

THE INFLUENCE
OF CLASSICAL
LITERATURE

13

LA SURVIE COMPARÉE DES 'CONFESSIONS' AUGUSTINIENNES ET DE LA 'CONSOLATION' BOÉCIENNE

P. COURCELLE

A un siècle et quart de distance, furent rédigés les deux derniers chefs-d'œuvre littéraires de l'Antiquité latine : les *Confessions* de saint Augustin tout à la fin du IVe siècle, la *Consolation* de Boèce vers l'an 524. Je ne ferai pas à mes auditeurs l'injure de résumer ici ces deux livres. Vous tous, j'imagine, avez lu le récit autobiographique où Augustin confesse non seulement ses péchés passés, mais la gloire de Dieu qui l'a poussé à la conversion. Quant à la *Consolation* de Boèce, elle est certes moins lue aujourd'hui ; du moins le public cultivé n'a-t-il pas oublié comment le 'dernier Romain', emprisonné par l'ostrogoth Théodoric, exprime peu avant d'être décapité son amertume de voir anéantis tous les efforts qu'il a déployés pour rénover la civilisation gréco-latine ; le personnage allégorique de Philosophie lui apparaît dans sa détresse et le console par une sorte de protreptique en cinq livres. Ces deux chefs-d'œuvre, fort différents l'un de l'autre malgré leur commun caractère autobiographique, ont été lus de siècle en siècle. Je voudrais résumer brièvement leur histoire, comparer leur fortune[1] et en tirer quelque conclusion touchant le sort de l'héritage gréco-romain, si menacé aujourd'hui.

Nous sommes assez bien renseignés sur les mouvements divers qu'ont suscités les *Confessions* dès le temps de leur publication. Ce sont surtout des mouvements hostiles. Rancunes des amis de la culture profane : car Augustin y exprime un profond mépris à l'égard des professeurs de lettres : grammairiens, rhéteurs, dialecticiens, ainsi qu'à l'égard des astrologues ; il déplore, en effet, ce que furent ses études et

---

[1] Le présent rapport peut être considéré comme une synthèse et une réflexion sur mes trois livres : *Les 'Confessions' de s. Augustin dans la tradition littéraire, antécédents et postérité* (Paris, 1963) ; *La 'Consolation de Philosophie' dans la tradition littéraire, antécédents et postérité de Boèce* (Paris, 1967) ; *Recherches sur les 'Confessions' de s. Augustin*, 2e éd. (Paris, 1968). Divers compléments sont précisés dans les notes ci-après.

son enseignement passés. Rancunes des Manichéens; car Augustin narre comment il s'est détaché de leur secte, au moment précis où celle-ci se cachait par crainte de persécutions; il montre que la théologie manichéenne contredit l'astronomie scientifique; il attaque sans cesse la foi qui avait été la sienne pendant une dizaine d'années; bref, il fait figure d'apostat aux yeux des Manichéens. Les Donatistes, eux, profitent des aveux d'Augustin sur son inconduite passée pour insinuer qu'il reste impur et qu'il joue double jeu, membre officiellement de la hiérarchie catholique mais resté en secret manichéen de cœur. Quant à Pélage et à ses disciples, ils ne peuvent tolérer les passages des *Confessions* qui touchent la prédestination et le 'péché de nature'; ils y sentent un relent de manichéisme.

Toutes ces critiques n'empêchent que les *Confessions* suscitent aussi l'admiration en d'autres milieux, d'abord, parmi les amis et les proches d'Augustin. Paulin de Nole, qui l'avait sans doute incité à les écrire, s'intéresse en particulier au livre x, sur les épreuves et les tentations du genre humain. Evodius avait partagé avec Nebridius et Alypius la vie d'Augustin lors de son séjour en Italie; il cite les lignes consacrées à leur ami commun Nebridius qui, dans l'au-delà, 'boit à la coupe de la sagesse' et se nourrit de l'Intelligence divine. Orose, qui publie en 417 ses *Histoires* à la demande d'Augustin, emprunte aux *Confessions* tel renseignement sur la persécution des enseignants chrétiens par l'empereur Julien. Paulin de Milan, qui écrit en 422 la *Vie de saint Ambroise* à la demande d'Augustin découvre dans les *Confessions* des précisions de première main sur les graves événements de Milan en 386, lorsqu'Ambroise était combattu par l'impératrice Justine et par les Ariens. Enfin, au lendemain de la mort d'Augustin, son disciple Possidius retrace la vie du maître en se fiant plus d'une fois aux *Confessions*, notamment pour décrire les années de jeunesse d'Augustin qu'il n'a pu connaître personnellement.

Du Ve au VIIIe siècle, l'ouvrage est déjà diffusé en Occident, si l'on en juge par ses imitateurs. A la vérité, les *Confessions* du gallo-romain Paulin de Pella, de l'irlandais Patrick et d'Ennode de Pavie ne se ressemblent guère. Seul saint Patrick semble avoir été touché intimement par l'ouvrage d'Augustin; les deux autres, prisonniers de leur formation littéraire, se contentent de rédiger des pastiches. Deux savants compilateurs, Prosper d'Aquitaine dans ses *Sentences* et Eugippius dans ses *Extraits*, négligent, au contraire, l'intérêt autobiographique des *Confessions*, et s'attachent uniquement aux développements de portée doctrinale: les *Sentences* empruntées aux *Confessions* sont d'ordre spirituel ou ascétique; les *Extraits* sont choisis pour leur portée métaphysique ou théologique. D'autres écrivains, comme Claudien Mamert en Gaule, Cassiodore en Italie, admirent Augustin à travers ses *Confessions* pour sa compétence intellectuelle et philosophique, les semi-pélagiens de Lérins[1] et Ferrand de Carthage pour sa psychologie de la conversion ascétique, Grégoire le Grand pour la description des mouvements du contemplatif, notamment le 'choc en retour' (*reuerberatio*) que ressent l'œil du contemplatif à l'instant même où il se croit capable d'apercevoir la divinité. Isidore de Séville, érudit de grande classe, a consciencieusement et intelligemment mis en fiches les *Confessions* pour son propre recueil de *Sentences*. Ce qu'il retient surtout, ce sont d'une part les renseignements sur la mentalité des philosophes de l'Antiquité, d'autre part — à travers le cas personnel d'Augustin — l'analyse du processus qui mène de la tentation au péché, puis du péché à la conversion. Un magnifique manuscrit du Ve ou VIe siècle, le *Sessorianus*, nous montre avec quel soin, à cette date, les *Confessions* étaient recopiées et glosées.[2]

Dans le même temps, nous ignorons tout à fait comment la *Consolation* de Boèce, ouvrage forcément clandestin à l'origine, puisque l'auteur est en résidence surveillée et traite de tyran le roi Théodoric, a pu être préservée pendant trois siècles. Ce livre ne semble pas avoir connu alors la moindre diffusion. Aucun fragment d'époque précarolingienne ne subsiste. Seul le mystérieux Virgile de Toulouse fait allusion aux échelons qui ornent la robe du personnage de Philosophie et mènent de la sagesse pratique à la théorétique. Or brusquement, à l'époque carolingienne, au moment même où les compilateurs ne s'intéressent plus aux *Confessions* que pour en extraire quelque formule de prières ou pour enrichir quelque dossier patristique, la *Consolation* est découverte et connaît aussitôt un succès éclatant. Le responsable de ce succès est l'illustre Alcuin. Il puise dans ce livre les idées fondamentales de son introduction aux bonnes études et s'y réfère aussi pour la doctrine pédagogique et politique qu'il propose à Charlemagne. Il doit à la *Consolation* l'image platonicienne de l'âme enivrée qui se laisse choir dans la matière au lieu de goûter le banquet divin que lui procurent les *rationes*; de Boèce provient aussi la doctrine d'Alcuin sur l'aide morale que fournit la philosophie et sur la valeur intrinsèque des arts et des disciplines. Il lui emprunte encore l'idée

---

[1] P. Courcelle, 'Nouveaux aspects de la culture lérinienne', dans *Revue des études latines*, t. XLVI (1968), 379–409, traitant de l'utilisation des *Confessions* par Eucher de Lyon, Faustus de Riez, Hilaire d'Arles et l'auteur de la *Vita Hilarii*.

[2] La datation au Ve siècle est préconisée par B. Bischoff, dans *C.C.* XXIII, xxxviii n. 1.

que l'étudiant doit commencer par se purifier, chercher la culture
pour elle-même et non en vue d'acquérir la gloire politique ou les
autres biens de Fortune; le maître, lui, doit posséder les qualités
pédagogiques qui étaient le propre de Boèce et savoir graduer son
enseignement selon le niveau intellectuel de ses disciples. Enfin, c'est
d'après Boèce qu'Alcuin définit à Charlemagne l'idéal platonicien du
souverain-philosophe. Son souci constant est d'interpréter la *Consolation* — malgré son aspect purement philosophique et 'laïque' — en
sens chrétien. Il l'éclaire sans cesse et la justifie par référence aux
saintes Ecritures; les disciplines ne sont légitimes à ses yeux que dans
la mesure où elles constituent une propédeutique et mènent à la
sagesse biblique; bien plus, le personnage boécien de Philosophie
n'est autre, selon Alcuin, que la Sagesse de Dieu en personne: idée
reprise et illustrée, au XIe siècle, dans la *Lettre* d'un abbé bénédictin
de Cologne sur la vraie philosophie: *Ipsa Philosophia Christus.*[1] Grâce à
Alcuin, cette figure féminine de Philosophie va, pendant trois siècles,
se dessiner en filigrane chez toutes sortes d'auteurs littéraires: Gautier
de Spire, Anselme de Besate, Hucbald de Saint-Amand, Baudri de
Bourgueil, Bernard Silvestre, Adelard de Bath,[2] Pierre de Compo-
stelle, Matthieu de Vendôme,[3] Alain de Lille, Henri de Settimello,

[1] Élie, *Epist. ad Iohannem*, éd. H. M. Rochais, dans *Mediaeval Studies*, XIII (1951), 246:
'Socrates et socratici, Plato et platonici, Tullius ac tulliani philosophari se putauerunt,
sed euanuerunt in cogitationibus suis et obscuratum est insipiens cor eorum (cf. Rom. 1.
21). Denique ipsa Philosophia Christus, Dei uirtus et Dei sapientia (cf. 1 Cor. 1. 24),
carnem nostram induit, terrigenas uisitauit semitasque suas rectissimas nos docuit, quas
qui sequuntur uere philosophantur. Ceteri "caenicas meretriculas" (cf. Boèce, *Cons. Ph.*
I, pr. 1, 25, p. 2) amplexantur, procul a "laribus Philosophiae" (*ibid.* I, pr. 3, 4, p. 5),
ieiuni et errabundi uagantur. Ecce quanti mercenarii in domo patris uestri abundant
panibus, et uos famelici oscitatis, in longinqua regione porcos pascitis, immo ipsi siliquas
porcorum comeditis (cf. *Luc.* xv, 15–16)'. Dom Rochais, 'Ipsa Philosophia Christus',
art. cit. pp. 244–7, a bien montré l'intérêt de cette *Lettre*, conservée dans le manuscrit de
Rome, Biblioteca Vittorio Emanuele, 1484, s. XI, et adressée vers l'an 1040 par Élie,
abbé bénédictin de Saint-Martin des Écossais à Cologne, à Jean, écolâtre au monastère
bénédictin de Saint-Mathias à Trèves. Mais il n'a pas noté que la mention des *scenicae
meretriculae* et celle des *lares Philosophiae* procèdent de la *Consolation* de Boèce. Le développement d'Élie a un rapport direct avec l'illustration et les gloses des manuscrits de Maihin-
gen et de Sélestat; le premier a été copié, justement à Cologne, par Froumund de Tegern-
see. Cf. P. Courcelle, *Histoire littéraire des grandes invasions germaniques*, 3e éd. (Paris, 1964),
pp. 366–9 et pls. 38–9, et *Die Tegernseer Briefsammlung (Froumund)*, éd. K. Strecker, dans
Monumenta Germaniae Historica, Epistulae selectae, III (Berlin, 1925), xi–xiii et 171.
[2] P. Courcelle, 'Adelard de Bath et la *Consolation* de Boèce', dans *Festschrift J. Quasten*
(sous presse).
[3] Matthieu de Vendôme, *Ars uersificandi* II 5, éd. E. Faral, *Les arts poétiques du XIIe et du
XIIIe siècle*, dans *Bibliothèque de l'Ecole des Hautes Etudes, sciences hist. et philol.* CCXXXVIII
(Paris, 1924), 152: 'Descriptio *Philosophiae* ministrarumque suarum...Haec igitur, nullius *artificii* picturata deliciis, quadam speciali praerogatiua quasi diuinam expirare
reuerentiam et multimodis coniecturis humanae naturae fragilitatem fastidire: frontis

tout en se transformant avec le temps et selon la pente doctrinale de chacun, tantôt en 'Théologie', tantôt en 'Nature'.

Pendant toute la période carolingienne, la *Consolation* allait être recopiée non moins souvent que les *Confessions*, et même illustrée. De magnifiques miniatures nous montrent alors Boèce patron de l'arithmétique ou de la musique ou maître en théologie. Surtout, on le représente dans sa prison, tantôt captif désespéré derrière de lourds barreaux ou gardé par des brutes barbares, tantôt reprenant espoir au moment où Dame Philosophie lui apparaît, ou encore penché sur ses tablettes, en train de rédiger son testament philosophique. Les miniaturistes décrivent volontiers aussi le personnage de Philosophie, hiératique, de taille surhumaine, avec ses livres, son sceptre, sa robe dont les galons dessinent l'échelle des disciplines. Plus tard seulement, elle deviendra une jeune et jolie femme qui se penche tendrement vers Boèce captif et qui a pour suivantes les sept disciplines libérales.[1] Par contraste, le personnage de Fortune, tel que le décrit pour la première fois Boèce, sera une folle perverse, qui se plaît à renverser les hommes de leur condition sociale en donnant le branle à sa roue. Motif iconographique tout indiqué pour garnir les rosaces des cathédrales.

Ce n'est pas tout. A côté de ces magnifiques exemplaires enluminés, d'autres, plus humbles, mais plus souvent feuilletés, sont des livres de classe garnis de nombreuses gloses. Il n'existe pas moins de douze commentaires carolingiens sur tout ou partie de la *Consolation*. Grâce à Remi d'Auxerre qui écrivit le premier commentaire complet, elle devient un ferment d'humanisme. La variété même de la *Consolation*, où se mêlent les thèmes littéraires, philosophiques, poétiques, permet à Remi d'inculquer à ses disciples toutes sortes de notions: grammaire et linguistique, rhétorique, dialectique, philo-

seueritas matronalis modestiae rigorem pollicetur; uirile supercilium nullo nutu petulantiae praenuntio luxuriat; *ardor oculorum* directo et penetrabili procedens intuitu ad partes collaterales renuit obliquari; genarum *uiuida* superficies, hypocritae *coloris* a se relegans adulterium, praedicat exercitium... Facies informata *uigore inexhausto* naturam fragilem destinat diffiteri. Eius *statura* descriptionis *ambiguae* certo termino nequaquam potest describi. *Vestes* eius, ut asserit *Boetius, tenuissimis perfectae filis subtili artificio, indissolubili materia*, ad cuius habitum et proprietates explicandas humanum languescit ingenium, mendicat facundia, humana discretio offendiculum pati profitetur. Haec siquidem dum disciplinalibus inuigilat documentis et facundi pectoris delicias inter artes alumnas et pedis sequas non cessat dispensare.' Les expressions soulignées et toute la mise en scène touchant Philosophie et ses compagnes sont issues de la prose 1 de la *Consolation*. Je dois à M. R. Bultot de connaître ce texte.

[1] J. et P. Courcelle, 'Deux nouvelles miniatures de la "*Consolation*" de Boèce', dans *Collection Latomus* (*Hommages à Marcel Renard*, 1) CI (1969) 256–9.

sophie, histoire, géographie, archéologie, mythologie, sciences exactes ou inexactes. C'est l'occasion pour Remi de révéler à ses disciples les plus grands noms de la culture antique, non sans quelques bévues mémorables; par exemple, ignorant des mœurs grecques, il prend Alcibiade pour une femme, erreur répétée pieusement de commentaire en commentaire, si bien que Villon, au XVe siècle, compte encore Alcibiade parmi les 'dames du temps jadis'.

Quant aux vues et aux expressions très hardies de Boèce touchant la préexistence de l'âme, la réminiscence, le char de l'âme, l'Ame du monde, la perpétuité du monde, Remi, suivant l'*interpretatio christiana* chère à Alcuin, les édulcore ou tente de les expliquer selon une perspective chrétienne, non sans pencher lui-même vers les erreurs érigéniennes.

Cette interprétation tendancieuse allait confirmer le succès de la *Consolation* pour sept siècles; mais, dans l'immédiat, elle suscite aussi la controverse, notamment à l'occasion du fameux Chant 9 du Livre III, qui conte l'histoire du monde en termes issus du *Timée* de Platon. Après la période ingrate du XIe siècle, le renouveau des études platoniciennes au sein de l'école de Chartres a pour effet de rendre un prestige exceptionnel à la *Consolation*. Quatre nouveaux commentaires paraissent au XIIe siècle, dont trois sont l'œuvre des meilleurs esprits de l'époque. Deux familles d'esprits se dessineront désormais de siècle en siècle: ceux qui suivent l'*interpretatio christiana*; ceux qui, se rendant compte que l'ouvrage est imprégné de platonisme, s'en réjouissent ou, au contraire, le condamnent comme dangereux.

L'intérêt pour le platonisme conduit de même, à partir de Jean de Fécamp (fin du XIe siècle), les 'spirituels' et les 'contemplatifs' à apprécier de façon neuve les *Confessions* d'Augustin. Non seulement, à cette date, Yves de Chartres, Rupert de Deutz, Philippe de Harvengt, écrivent chacun une *Vie* de saint Augustin, mais Abélard et ses disciples se couvrent du nom d'Augustin comme d'une autorité qui les convie à une formule audacieuse de compromis entre le platonisme et la théologie chrétienne du prologue johannique. Les Cisterciens et les Victorins s'attachent surtout au chapitre des *Confessions* où Augustin déclare qu'à l'instant de sa conversion, il prit conscience d'être sis dans la 'région de dissemblance' par rapport à Dieu, comme l'Enfant prodigue de la parabole était dans la 'région d'indigence'. L'expression 'région de dissemblance', issue du *Politique* de Platon fit alors fortune et l'on a pu, jusqu'à ce jour, en dénombrer quelque 142 emplois de

66 auteurs différents.[1] Le sens varie selon les contextes: dissemblance de soi-même à soi, dissemblance du non-être par rapport à l'Un, perte de la ressemblance originelle avec le Créateur, du fait du péché. D'autres penseurs, en ce XIIe siècle, s'attachent surtout à l'extase d'Ostie que décrit Augustin; d'autres enfin décrivent leur propre vie à la lumière des *Confessions*. Chez Guibert de Nogent, il s'agit seulement d'un pastiche médiocre; mais Ailred de Rievaulx, lui, exprime et interprète les événements et l'évolution de sa vie: méfaits de jeunesse, passions, amitiés, deuils, conversion monastique, à la lumière de la vie d'Augustin. Celui-ci est, à ses yeux, à la fois l'homme-type et son maître par excellence en matière de spiritualité.

Par suite de la crue de l'aristotélisme, les hommes du XIIIe siècle se détournent, semble-t-il, de la *Consolation* comme des *Confessions*. Celles-ci ne fournissent plus que des extraits parmi bien d'autres, dans les *Sommes* diverses, d'Alexandre de Halès à Thomas d'Aquin; saint Thomas s'oppose même directement à la vue optimiste d'Augustin selon laquelle les Néo-platoniciens, par la seule raison naturelle, ont pu découvrir la Trinité des personnes divines. Seul Maître Eckhart a scruté les *Confessions* avec la plus vive sympathie pour les vues stoïciennes et néo-platoniciennes sur l'immanence divine, au point qu'il se fit taxer de panthéisme.

Au XIVe et au XVe siècle, voici que les *Confessions* et la *Consolation* connaissent de pair un regain de faveur, pour des motifs très différents. Les Ermites de saint Augustin, ordre devenu puissant, utilisent et complètent les *Confessions* de manière tendancieuse, jusqu'à présenter, en Augustin, un Ermite comme eux. Pétrarque, dont le frère fut Ermite de saint Augustin, n'est pas moins imbu des *Confessions* qu'Ailred de Rievaulx deux siècles plus tôt. Il porte constamment sur lui un exemplaire de poche, mais il y apprécie surtout le culte de la personne et de l'individu Augustin. Il cherche à se représenter de la façon la plus précise la topographie du séjour milanais d'Augustin, qu'il regarde un peu comme son voisin. Les *Confessions* lui plaisent pour les descriptions psychologiques de l'amour, de l'amitié, de l'inquiétude, de la gloire, de la vie solitaire; mais il s'intéresse aux prodromes de conversion plus qu'à la conversion elle-même. Il sait gré à Augustin de préserver, dans ses *Confessions*, la

[1] R. Javelet, *Image et ressemblance au XIIe siècle, de s. Anselme à Alain de Lille*, II (Paris, 1967), 240–3 et 367; P. Courcelle, 'Complément au "Répertoire des textes relatifs à la région de dissemblance"', dans *Augustinus. Strenas Augustinianas P. Victorino Capanaga oblatas curavit edendas Iosephus Oroz-Reta*, II (Madrid, 1968), 135–40.

légitimité d'un humanisme chrétien d'où Platon et Cicéron ne sont pas exclus. Mais on découvre dans les gloses inédites de Pétrarque qu'il s'est intéressé encore à divers passages de caractère métaphysique ou religieux. Sous la même influence naît alors l'iconographie de saint Augustin, bien plus tardivement, comme vous voyez, que celle de Boèce. On cherche à représenter sa vie de bout en bout et, de ce fait, on puise dans ses *Confessions* les scènes les plus vivantes et les moins légendaires: chacun de vous a pu apprécier la qualité des fresques de San Gimignano, chef-d'œuvre de Benozzo Gozzoli qui attire tant de touristes. Il existe, sur le même sujet, bien d'autres chefs-d'œuvre non moins admirables, mais beaucoup moins connus.[1]

La *Consolation* reprend vie, elle aussi, à cette époque tardive. Elle est recopiée sur de nombreux et somptueux exemplaires à l'usage des Grands. Par exemple, Charles VIII en fit exécuter d'un coup plusieurs pour son usage personnel, magnifiquement enluminés. Certains traducteurs sont particulièrement célèbres: Jean de Meun surtout. Quinze commentaires nouveaux sur la *Consolation* voient aussi le jour. On n'oserait dire, pourtant, que l'œuvre exerce autant d'emprise qu'à l'époque carolingienne ou au XIIe siècle. Ces commentaires sont maintenant le fait de scolastiques ou de pédants qui n'ont plus guère de réactions personnelles — favorables ou hostiles — à l'égard de Boèce, mais écrivent des compilations de plus en plus longues et fastidieuses, tant en latin que dans les divers parlers vulgaires. A la fin du XVe siècle, Josse Bade d'Assche, humaniste de qualité, écrira un dernier commentaire, très bref cette fois, pour faire justice de toutes les insanités accumulées par une fausse science de l'Antiquité et par l'abus de l'*interpretatio christiana*. Lui-même considère la *Consolation* comme un chef-d'œuvre littéraire, mais met en doute sa portée philosophique. Désormais l'on préfèrera lire Platon dans le texte plutôt que d'étudier le platonisme à travers Boèce. Plusieurs éditions et traductions paraîtront encore, mais on peut dire qu'au XVIIe siècle l'ouvrage se meurt. Sans doute, l'abbé Jérôme Coignard assure qu'il porte constamment dans sa poche le chef-d'œuvre de Boèce, parce qu'une seule page de ce livre admirable affermit son cœur; mais c'est pure raillerie d'Anatole France, car au moment même où l'abbé prononce ces fières paroles, le voici qui tombe au milieu d'un

---

[1] J. et P. Courcelle, *Iconographie de s. Augustin, Les cycles du XIVe siècle* (Paris, 1965), 253 pp. et 110 pls.; *Les cycles du XVe siècle* (Paris, 1969), 369 pp. et 138 pls.; *Vita s. Augustini imaginibus adornata* (*Manuscrit de Boston, Public Library, no. 1483 s. XV, inédit*), *édition critique et commentaire iconographique* (Paris, 1964), 256 pp. et 109 pls.

bassin et accable d'invectives la lune, 'astre obscène, polisson et libidineux'.[1]

Rien de tel pour les *Confessions*. Au XVIe et au XVIIe siècle, elles reprennent vie plus que jamais. L'ancien augustin Luther les lit beaucoup plus religieusement que Pétrarque. Il réfléchit longuement sur la vie d'Augustin, qu'il divise en trois étapes: sa conversion *pleno corde*, sa confession devant les hommes, son enseignement magistral. Il y voit illustrée la doctrine de justification par la foi. Pour lui, la conversion augustinienne a consisté à considérer l'homme dans sa turpitude, avec une componction qui exclue toute idée de mérite personnel. Tandis que les 'spirituels' espagnols et François de Sales goûtent surtout ce livre pour la doctrine de contemplation amoureuse, Jansénius, dans la ligne de Luther, s'informe, à travers la vie d'Augustin, de la concupiscence et de l'impuissance humaines. *Les Confessions* fournissent encore un cadre et un style aux mémorialistes de Port-Royal: Lancelot, Hamon, Nicolas Fontaine, non moins qu'aux artistes, à commencer par le plus grand: Philippe de Champaigne.[2] Peintres et graveurs rivalisent de zèle pour représenter avec cent variantes la scène capitale aux yeux des Jansénistes: celle du jardin de Milan, la conversion d'Augustin par la Grâce.[3] Lors du fameux *Entretien* avec Pascal, Sacy recourt aux *Confessions* pour combattre la méthode apologétique de Pascal, qui veut conduire à la foi en mon-

---

[1] Anatole France, *La rotisserie de la reine Pédauque*, dans *Œuvres complètes*, VIII, 182: 'Vous avez raison, Monsieur, dit mon bon maître, on n'y voit pas bien clair et j'en éprouve quelque déplaisir...par l'envie que j'ai de lire quelques pages des *Consolations* de Boèce, dont je porte toujours un exemplaire de petit format dans la poche de mon habit, afin de l'avoir sans cesse sous la main pour l'ouvrir au moment où je tombe dans l'infortune, comme il m'arrive aujourd'hui. Car c'est une disgrâce cruelle, Monsieur, pour un homme de mon état, que d'être homicide et menacé d'être mis dans les prisons ecclésiastiques. Je sens qu'une seule page de ce livre admirable affermirait mon cœur qui s'abîme à la seule pensée de l'official. En prononçant ces mots, il se laissa choir sur l'autre bord de la vasque et si profondément qu'il trempait dans l'eau par tout le beau milieu de son corps. Mais il n'en prenait aucun souci et ne semblait point même s'en apercevoir; tirant de sa poche son Boèce, qui y était réellement, et chaussant ses lunettes, dont il ne restait plus qu'un verre, lequel était fendu en trois endroits, il se mit à chercher dans le petit livre la page la mieux appropriée à la situation. Il l'eût trouvée sans doute, et il y eût puisé des forces nouvelles, si le mauvais état de ses besicles, les larmes qui lui montaient aux yeux et la faible clarté qui tombait du ciel lui eussent permis de la chercher. Mais il dut bientôt confesser qu'il n'y voyait goutte et il s'en prit à la lune qui lui montrait sa corne aigüe au bord d'un nuage. Il l'interpella vivement et l'accabla d'invectives: "Astre obscène, polisson et libidineux, lui dit-il, tu n'es jamais las d'éclairer les turpitudes des hommes, et tu envies un rayon de ta lumière à qui cherche des maximes vertueuses!".'

[2] J. et P. Courcelle, 'Le *Tolle, lege* de Philippe de Champaigne', dans *Recherches augustiniennes*, V (1968), 3–6 et 2 pls., dont une en couleurs.

[3] J. et P. Courcelle, 'Nouvelles illustrations des *Confessions* augustiniennes', dans *Revue des études augustiniennes*, XXIII (1964), 343–4 et 14 pls.

trant d'après Montaigne l'impuissance de la raison. A travers les *Confessions*, Sacy s'est constitué tout un dossier pour atteindre Montaigne: il a relevé les passages où Augustin se reproche ses diverses lectures profanes; un de ces passages, surtout, frappa intimement Pascal, celui où, selon Augustin, l'homme 'rend hommage aux démons de bien des manières'. Pascal dut convenir que cette phrase dénonçait par avance aussi bien la lâcheté de Montaigne que la superbe d'Epictète.[1]

En ce XVIIe siècle, Bossuet et Fénelon ont tiré des *Confessions* des leçons très différentes: Bossuet, surtout sensible au jeu du libre arbitre humain et du 'coup de la Grâce'; Fénelon, sévère pour le style peu classique des *Confessions*, est heureux d'y puiser un programme scolaire, une pédagogic de la conversion et se sent attiré, comme Mme Guyon, par le silence intérieur de l'âme, lors de l'expérience d'Ostie. Même au 'siècle des lumières', les *Confessions* ne laissent indifférents ni Voltaire qui les raille, ni Rousseau qui les imite à sa manière très personnelle. Voici qu'elles deviennent, au XIXe siècle, le bréviaire des Romantiques. L'inquiétude de Pascal procédait déjà en droite ligne de l'*inquietum cor* d'Augustin.[2] Mais à partir de Chateaubriand cette inquiétude devient celle de trois générations qui se confessent à qui mieux mieux. Chateaubriand lui-même a relu Augustin pour peindre l'' 'ennui' de *René* adolescent. Musset cite expressément les *Confessions* augustiniennes dans sa *Confession d'un enfant du siècle*'; George Sand conte avec prolixité, dans l' *Histoire de ma vie*, que depuis son adolescence chez les Dames anglaises, elle reste sous l'emprise d'une toile du XVIIe siècle où était représentée la conversion d'Augustin sous le figuier; elle prétend avoir entendu elle-même retentir à ses oreilles les paroles *Tolle, lege* et être tombée dans un 'ravissement', comme ç'avait été déjà le cas de sainte Thérèse d'Avila. Bien plus, la correspondance des 'Amants de Venise' montre qu'ils ont échangé leurs vues sur Augustin et sur cet épisode de 'révélation'.[3]

La Mennais, Sainte-Beuve et Guttinguer se reconnaissent aussi dans le jeune Augustin. *Joseph Delorme*, les *Consolations*, *Volupté* se ressentent nettement des *Confessions* et Sainte-Beuve témoigne, dans le poème *A Viguier*, qu'il songea pendant un temps, pour lui-même,

[1] P. Courcelle, L''Entretien' de Pascal et Sacy, ses sources et ses énigmes (Paris, 1960).
[2] P. Courcelle, 'De s. Augustin à Pascal par Sacy,' dans Pascal présent, 2e éd. (Clermont-Ferrand, 1963), pp. 140–4.
[3] J. et P. Courcelle, 'Le Tolle, lege de George Sand', dans Revue des études augustiniennes, XII (1966), 1–7 et une pl. en couleurs.

à une conversion tout inspirée de celle d'Augustin. Il va jusqu'à comparer, dans une lettre, les larmes de son Adèle (c'est-à-dire, Mme Hugo), à celles d'Augustin gémissant sur lui-même. Plusieurs épisodes de son roman *Volupté* sont un 'à la manière des *Confessions*'. Si cette inspiration reste chez lui d'ordre uniquement littéraire, il se plaît pourtant à orienter et confirmer dans la piété son ami Guttinguer, l'aîné du cénacle romantique, libertin converti sur le tard, mais tout de bon.

Les *Confessions* ont encore exercé une influence durable sur Renan, depuis le temps où il commençait au séminaire ses propres '*Confessions*', jusqu'au temps de ses '*Souvenirs d'enfance et de jeunesse*'. Dans la '*Prière sur l'Acropole*', il reprend mot-à-mot l'exclamation d'Augustin : 'Tard je t'ai aimée, Beauté' et en fait la trame de cette 'Prière'; mais il retourne le sens de cette invocation. Augustin l'adressait au Christ. Renan, lui, se repent devant Pallas Athéné d'avoir tant tardé à découvrir la beauté du rationalisme grec.

Si l'on embrasse du regard toute cette longue histoire, on notera que la survie de ces deux chefs-d'œuvre correspond à quelques tournants de l'évolution de la culture. Par exemple, tous deux suscitent l'intérêt au XIIe siècle, qui est platonisant, mais laissent indifférents les lecteurs du siècle suivant, où l'on préfère Aristote. Toutefois, ces deux chefs-d'œuvre ont aussi chacun sa vie propre. La *Consolation*, qui a suscité tant de commentaires, fut appréciée avant tout comme un livre classique; les *Confessions*, elles, ne furent jamais lues comme un livre de classe, mais d'abord comme une histoire de l'homme ou comme un livre de prière, puis — à l'époque romantique — comme une œuvre romanesque. Les auteurs littéraires les plus hostiles au classicisme et qui ne lisent plus du tout Boèce s'attachent alors à l'individu Augustin parce qu'il est le seul homme de l'Antiquité gréco-romaine à nous laisser pénétrer si avant dans son intimité, même s'il ne prend nullement l'étalage du moi pour fin de sa description. On le lit comme on lit les *Confessions* de Rousseau; on lui attribue à tort ce que Georges Gusdorf, dans sa thèse sur *La découverte de soi*, appelle l''attitude d'immanence'. L'on pourrait ainsi conclure, non sans quelque malice, que le livre le mieux assuré de survivre est celui sur lequel les lecteurs peuvent faire le plus de contresens variés, de génération en génération, pour s'en approprier la substance.

Tout chef-d'œuvre antique mérite une étude analogue, lorsqu'il a été fréquemment recopié et relu par les générations successives.

Cette histoire du *Nachleben* doit s'attacher simultanément à l'étude de la tradition manuscrite, des gloses, des traductions, des commentaires, des citations littéraires, des réminiscences inconscientes, des imitations et de l'illustration. Bien peu de travaux existent à ce sujet. Quand ils existent — comme le livre estimable de Comparetti sur Virgile — ils sont loin d'envisager tous ces points de vue et d'aller pour chacun au fond des choses. Tel vers fameux de Virgile ou d'Horace devrait faire l'objet d'une monographie où serait réservée une place considérable à l'*interpretatio christiana*. Ainsi, pour en revenir à Augustin et Boèce, le *Sero te amaui* des *Confessions* est orchestré par Ailred de Rievaulx et Alcher de Clairvaux sous forme de gémissement sur soi-même. Jacques de Voragine le rattache directement à la componction de la scène du jardin, tandis que Louis de Grenade l'enregistre comme un remords lancinant de l'évêque d'Hippone au moment où rédige ses *Confessions*; Jean d'Avila voit là une malédiction lancée rétrospectivement sur le temps de l'aveuglement, François de Sales un élan mystique, Bérulle une résolution de réparation, Silesius une mélancolie à l'idée du temps passé hors du bercail,[1] Louis Racine un cantique d'action de grâces, Mme Guyon une plénitude succédant à une longue faim d'amour. L'*inquietum cor nostrum*, le *da quod iubes*, le *pondus meum amor meus* ont chacun une histoire particulière qu'il vaudrait la peine de conter.

De même, à travers la *Consolation* de Boèce, la maxime de Platon 'Bienheureux les états, si les philosophes étaient rois ou si les rois étaient philosophes' est reprise et commentée par Walahfrid Strabon sous Louis le Pieux, par un poète anonyme au temps de Louis le Germanique, recommandée à Charles le Chauve par Heiric d'Auxerre, à Otto II par l'auteur de la *Vie* de la reine Mathilde, à l'empereur Henri IV par Benzo d'Alba. Ce n'est pas seulement un cliché littéraire dans les dédicaces aux Grands de ce monde; la parole a stimulé la réflexion sur la forme du meilleur gouvernement; chacun s'en est inspiré dans la conjoncture présente, en revivant en quelque sorte les péripéties qui furent celles-mêmes de Boèce, comme Ailred de Rievaulx, Pétrarque ou Guttinguer ont assumé pour eux-mêmes les étapes de la vie et de la conversion d'Augustin. Tant qu'un livre suscite pareil enthousiasme, il n'est certes pas mort.

---

[1] Cf. Abbé Prévost, *Cleveland*, xv, vii, 363 et suiv. (à propos de la mort d'une jeune protestante) : '...ne respirant que la possession d'un bien qu'elle regrettait amèrement d'avoir connu trop tard'.

14

CLASSICAL INFLUENCE ON EARLY NORSE LITERATURE

U. DRONKE

For more than a hundred years Norse scholarship has been haunted by the problem of classical influence upon the vernacular literature, and the ghost has not yet been laid, nor the ancestor proved.

The conversion of the Scandinavian lands to Christianity and to literacy did not begin effectively until the end of the tenth century, but some of the vernacular poetry can be shown to be at least one hundred years earlier. So the span in time of the early Norse literature with which I am concerned reaches from the end of the ninth century to the end of the thirteenth, the close of the great creative period. The geographical span of Scandinavia open to classical influence reaches from Iceland and the Norse kingdoms of Ireland and England in the west, to Sweden and the Swedish settlements in Russia to the east. In the middle of the eleventh century there was a Norwegian bishop of Kiev and a bishop of the Greek Church established in Sweden, and three bishops of the Greek Church preaching in Iceland, much to the displeasure of the Roman See. Greek merchants, we are told by Adam of Bremen, found good harbouring in the Baltic, at the mouth of the river Oder. The Norse language was being spoken on the banks of the Volga until the thirteenth century.[1]

The possibility of classical influence through some of these early and wide-reaching contacts has excited the imagination of scholars for very good reason. The Norse vernacular is one of the richest in medieval Europe in the originality of its literary forms: no parallels are extant in other Germanic languages for the stylistic variety of the poems of the *Edda*, nor for the profusion of complex metres and the arcane intensity of diction in the poetry of the scalds, the court poets of the kings of Norway, nor indeed is there any parallel for the genre of the prose saga. Where so much is unknown, scholars seek in known fields for understanding. So, to account for the unique phenomenon

---

[1] See Magnús Már Lárússon, 'Um hina ermsku biskupa', *Skírnir*, CXXXIII (1959), 81–94 for a well-documented account of early Scandinavian connections with the Greek Church.

143

of scaldic poetry, it has been suggested that the influence of Latin hymn metres, transmitted through Irish, together with certain Irish habits of poetic style, may have inspired one brilliant Norwegian poet, the first whose name we know, Bragi Boddason, to compose in a completely new manner of metre and diction. This creative step would have been taken towards the end of the ninth century, not long after the establishment of the Norse kingdom in Ireland.[1]

Against this theory of the individual creation of a novel poetic mode stands an important consideration that is also linked with the problem of classical influence. Two of the earliest scaldic poems, one of them by Bragi himself, are 'shield poems', odes in which ornate stanzas describe scenes carved or painted on a shield, and offer static fantasias upon the heroic and mythological narratives portrayed. It was argued by Hellmut Rosenfeld in 1936[2] that this literary genre should be related to the shield-descriptions in Homer and Hesiod and their imitators, and should be linked with a cult of votive shields which may at one time (he suggests) have been common in Scandinavia, either as a native cult, or one that had travelled in ancient times from the Black Sea regions. From these regions, early Byzantine and provincial Roman influence on Scandinavian art is well attested:[3] that a literary genre so closely associated with representational art should also have been stimulated by Greco-Roman tradition is not impossible. The value of Rosenfeld's argument, however, consists not so much in establishing any specific origin for a Norse poetic genre, as in providing the background against which this poetic genre must be understood, a background of cult, involving close association with mythological themes, meticulous preservation of tradition, and a heightened, obscured, periphrastic sacral language, to which Rosenfeld compares the language of Pindar. This cannot therefore be a diction created by a single man; it is ancient and rooted in ancient, pagan religious practice: perhaps that is why it survived nowhere else in Christian Germanic Europe. Any possible metrical influence, therefore, from Irish Latin in the ninth century can only have contributed to a scaldic style of composition already highly developed.

---

[1] See G. Turville-Petre, 'Um dróttkvæði og írskan kveðskap', *Skírnir*, cxxviii (1954), 31–55.

[2] 'Nordische Schilddichtung und mittelalterliche Wappendichtung', *Zeitschrift für deutsche Philologie*, lxi (1936), 232–69.

[3] Besides Rosenfeld's references, see H. Shetelig, *Classical Impulses in Scandinavian Art from the Migration Period to the Viking Age* (Oslo, 1949).

For many Norse poems and for many aspects of Norse mythology classical origins or influence have been claimed.[1] In the general context of a study of classical influence all these claims could be re-examined with great profit, but I can pause only on one: the influence of the Sibylline Oracles upon the greatest of the Norse mythological poems, *Völuspá*, 'The Prophecy of the Sibyl'.[2] Here an awesome seeress, fostered by giants, summoned from the other world by the command of Óðinn, declares before the audience of mankind the origins and fate of the world, the encroachment of evil, the slaughter of the greatest gods by monsters, the destruction of the world by flood and fire, and its resurrection, cleansed and renewed, rising from the sea. As in the Greek Sibylline Oracles and in the rare Latin version that Professor Bischoff has discovered in two ninth-century manuscripts,[3] there is here too the conjunction of past and future—as if it were the grasp of the past and its truths that gave the sibyl confident power of insight into the future. All the narrative facts in the Norse poem are drawn from the native pagan mythology —these are not borrowed. But what has galvanised these facts into a sibylline structure? In no other Norse poem is the fate of the world and of the gods presented as a matter of urgent concern, or linked with the moral degeneration of gods and men. Is this particular Norse poem uniquely inspired by the Sibylline Oracles of the Hellenistic-Christian world, or has a mode of sibylline composition, anciently common to Greco-Roman and Germanic paganism, been fortuitously preserved only in this one poem? One thing at least is clear:

---

[1] For example, influences of a general, and perhaps popular, kind, as of Greek legends on the myth of Iðunn's apples (S. Bugge, 'Iduns Æbler', *Arkiv för nordisk filologi (ANF)*, IV (1889), 1–45), or of the legend of Daedalus on *Völundarkviða* (cf. J .de Vries, *Altnordische Literaturgeschichte* (2nd ed. 1964–7), I, 85), or of the legend of Protesilaos on *Helgakviða Hundingsbana*, II (most recently, A. Kabell, 'DgF 90 and the Danish Novel', *Scandinavica*, VI (1967), 85), or of Hellenistic astral religion on *Grímnismál* (F. R. Schroeder, *Germanentum und Hellenismus* (1924), pp. 15 ff.); as well as influences which may derive from a literary contact, as the influence of Lucian, *Assembly of the Gods* on *Lokasenna* (F. R. Schroeder, 'Das Symposium der Lokasenna', *ANF*, LXVII (1952), 1–29), or of Ovid's tale of Procne on *Atlakviða* (S. Bugge, 'Erpr og Eitill', *Christiania Videnskabsselskabs Forhandlinger* (1898), pp. 1 ff.), or of Martianus Capella on Eddic cosmology (H. Falk, 'Martianus Capella og den nordisk Mythologi', *Aarbøger for nordisk Oldkyndighed og Historie* (1891), pp. 266–300), or of Boethius, *Consolatio Philosophiae*, upon the elegiac verses of Egill Skallagrímsson (A. Bouman, *Patterns in Old English and Old Icelandic Literature* (Leiden, 1962), pp. 29 ff.).

[2] See A. C. Bang, 'Vøluspaa og de Sibyllinske Orakler', *Christiania Videnskabsselskabs Forhandlinger* (1879, no. 9), pp. 1–23; countered by V. Rydberg, *Sibyllinerne og Völuspá*, in his *Skrifter*, XII (1898), 317–434.

[3] B. Bischoff, 'Die lateinischen Übersetzungen und Bearbeitungen aus den Oracula Sibyllina', *Mittelalterliche Studien*, I (1966), 150–71, especially 164 ff.

if this poet has borrowed from an alien source, he has borrowed at the highest level of understanding, and has incomparably enriched the theme that inspired him. Comparison with classical tradition here establishes the stature of the vernacular.

Before the introduction of Christianity and clerical learning to Scandinavia, any influence from classical sources must have been upon illiterate Norsemen, and the channels by which such influence could have operated require very careful study—a study in which conjecture must base itself upon all available evidence as to the nature of the contact between the literate and illiterate worlds. With the establishment of Christianity came the reading and writing of Latin, sacred and profane; classical and Christian learning were absorbed by literate Norsemen in a society still rich and inventive in native oral tradition. In Iceland one of the first bishops, at the end of the eleventh century, struggled simultaneously against the immorality of young clerics reading Ovid and against the native custom of love-singing, in which men and women sang lascivious verses to each other.[1] The biographer adds ruefully that the bishop was not able entirely to stamp out this custom, though evidently he prevented these verses from achieving written record.

In his splendid articles on classical manuscripts in Scandinavian libraries and on the contribution of Scandinavia to the Latin literature of the Middle Ages, Paul Lehmann drew together ample evidence of the reading and translation of classical authors in medieval Scandinavia, especially historical, didactic and grammatical writings —Sallust, Lucan, Justinus, Josephus, Pliny and Isidore, Priscian and Donatus.[2] What needs now to be established is precisely what this Latin culture contributed to the formation of the original vernacular literature—in what does its creative influence consist?

In Iceland and Norway, Latin and vernacular historical writing are closely interlocked. The first writer of the history of the kings of Norway, the Icelander Sæmundr Sigfússon, wrote in Latin; he was educated in France, probably in Paris, about 1070. His works, which are now lost, were regarded as authoritative by the Icelandic historians who followed him. Around 1130 another Icelander, Ari Þorgilsson, also trained in Latin learning, wrote in Icelandic the history of Iceland and its first settlers, basing this on the oral memory of native

[1] *Jóns Saga*, ch. 13.
[2] P. Lehmann, 'Auf der Suche nach alten Texten in nordischen Bibliotheken', *Erforschung des Mittelalters*, I, 280–306; 'Skandinaviens Anteil an der lateinischen Literatur und Wissenschaft des Mittelalters', *ibid.* v, 275–393.

informants. While he owes much to his Latin training—his systematic method, the logical construction of his periodic sentences—the
vitality of the vernacular narrative that underlies his writing frequently shines out. Fifty years later the Norwegian monk Theodricus
wrote a Latin history of Norway in which he cites moral and political
sententiae from Sallust, Lucan, Ovid and Pliny, but claims that his
main source of information is the oral poetry of Icelanders. Consciously profiting from the confluence of two cultures, Theodricus
epitomises a situation that must have been common to many Norse
clerics of his time.

A more dynamic step is taken in Norse historical writing when at
the end of the twelfth century the incredible King Sverri of Norway—
a renegade priest from the Faroe Islands, who claimed to be a bastard
son of a Norwegian king—assured his own fame by hiring an Icelandic abbot and 'sitting over' him while he wrote the saga of his life.
This saga, unforgettably vivid both in its exultant, polemical speeches
and in the homely actuality of its scenes, bears unmistakable marks of
Sverri's clerical training: a persuasive style designed for the pulpit, a
superstitious imagination nurtured by hagiography, and a biblical
romanticism that inspired him to see himself as a David anointed
by God.[1]

In the thirteenth century the vernacular almost entirely takes over
the task of historical writing, and a style of narrative develops refined
from all moral and judicial comment: judgement flows through the
presentation of facts, and through the arguments that are put into
the mouths of the historical characters themselves. Some scenes have
become so polished by the imagination of successive tellers that they
stand out with a symbolic quality that irradiates the whole saga. The
finest exponent of this historical style is Snorri Sturluson. Sigurður
Nordal states categorically that Snorri knew Sallust, but does not set
out any evidence.[2] If Snorri knew Sallust, what did he learn from
him? From Snorri's use of known vernacular sources we can gauge

---

[1] The first thirty chapters of *Sverris Saga* are, in all probability, those written under
Sverri's supervision. On Sverri's learning see G. M. Gathorne-Hardy, *A Royal Impostor*
(1956), especially p. 90.

[2] S. Nordal, 'Sagalitteraturen', *Nordisk Kultur*, VIII B (1952), 221. Some scholars have
examined certain aspects of (mainly Christian) Latin influence on Norse saga-writing
(especially L. Lönnroth; see the references listed in the summary of his researches,
European Sources of Icelandic Saga-writing (Stockholm, 1965); and Jakob Benediktsson,
'Traces of Latin prose-rhythm in Old Norse', *Fifth Viking Congress*, Tórshavn, 1965).
These valuable studies are not, however, directed towards the particular problem I have
in mind, the nature of the narrative art of the native oral traditions.

the perceptive, rationalising, clarifying quality of his mind. If Snorri had studied Sallust, it seems certain that he would have learnt from Sallust's historical genius at the highest level of understanding. Thus it is, I think, an imperative task to make a comparative stylistic study of the Norse and the classical historians, to try to distinguish the intellectual and artistic stature of the native oral historical traditions upon which the influence of classical writers would work. Was this influence only the initial stimulus to writing history at all, with the occasional copying of a mannerism of style—or was it a more subtle thing, an external influence that held up a mirror to the native traditions, stimulated self-recognition, and developed in the native creative genius a power of coherence and of carrying through themes of imagination on a scale greater than oral tradition was capable of maintaining?

This problem is vital because upon it depends also our understanding of the literary development of the great tragic sagas, the family sagas. It is firmly maintained by many scholars, most recently by Walter Baetke,[1] that the Icelandic sagas had no artistic form before the influence of Christian and classical literature. Neckel stated dogmatically: 'Like all new literatures, that of Iceland also arose from the contact of ecclesiastical education and Greco-Roman tradition with the cultural heritage of the people.'[2] Was this 'cultural heritage'—*geistiger Besitz des Volkes*—formless, waiting for centuries like a bear-cub, to be licked into literary shape? Until a more thorough analysis of learned and literary influence on the family sagas is undertaken, so that the artistic character of the native traditions can emerge, we are left in doubt, in the dark.

One more problem of classical influence must be the last I mention, though it is by no means the last there is.[3] In 1220 Snorri Sturluson wrote his *Prose Edda*; for the plan of this work no source has been found, though Rudolf Meyer insisted that it must go back to some variant version of the Third Vatican Mythographer.[4] The first part

---

[1] *Über die Entstehung der Isländersagas* (Berlin, 1956).

[2] G. Neckel, 'Von der isländischen Saga' I, *Germanisch-romanische Monatsschrift* (1911), 371.

[3] I would note here two further subjects for study: (1) a comparison of Snorri's work on the art of poetry (*Skáldskaparmál*) with Latin *Artes Poeticae*: Snorri's work appears to be highly original, while that of his nephew on rhetoric (*Málskrúðsfræði*) is conventional, based mainly on Donatus; and (2) an examination of Saxo's use of the 'mixed' form of verse and prose composition in his first nine books, reflecting both classical (Martianus Capella) and native (*fornaldarsögur*) traditions; an analysis of the classical elements in his verses will also help us to achieve a clearer picture of his lost vernacular sources.

[4] R. M. Meyer, 'Snorri als mythograph', *ANF*, xxviii (1912), 109–21.

presents a euhemeristic account of the Norse gods—a variation on Euhemerism found in no other source and presumably devised by Snorri himself. It is remarkably close to the fiction that Euhemerus himself devised (which Snorri, of course, cannot have known at first hand), in that it consists of a journey to a strange land, which reveals to a human being the historical existence of the men now thought to be gods. This part of the *Edda* has a wonderful prologue, for which again no source has been found. In it Snorri accounts for the fact that wisdom could exist among the heathen. Through wickedness mankind lost knowledge of God, even of the name of God; but though they were spiritually blind, God still granted them intellectual insight, 'so that they knew all earthly matters and every phase of whatever they might see in the air and on the earth'. He describes their growing awareness of the living nature of the earth, and of the analogy between the physical construction of man and the earth: 'Boulders and stones they likened to the teeth and bones of living beings...' Snorri must have had in mind in this prologue Christian scientific speculations on the nature of the world, on microcosm and macrocosm, speculations that have their roots in Hellenistic thought.[1] At the same time he surely could not help recalling his native mythology, verses he himself quotes, that depict the creation of the cosmos from a gigantic body:

> From his flesh the earth was made,
> from his blood the sea,
> rocks from his bones, trees from his hair,
> and from his skull the sky.

Was it perhaps the confrontation of pagan myth with Christian scientific speculation that inspired his apologia for heathen wisdom, a wisdom granted by God to the heathen, though they had lost knowledge of him? Has Snorri recognised that European mythology has here come full circle?

I hope that this rapid survey may indicate in some measure what substantial and exciting literary and historical exercises remain to be undertaken, in which classical scholars can contribute profoundly to the studies of their Norse colleagues, and may in their turn receive illumination in their own field of work from a medieval literature unique in its close relationship to oral traditions.

[1] See R. Allers, 'Microcosmos', *Traditio*, II (1944), 319–407; F. Rico, *El pequeño mundo del hombre* (1970) 11–45. A. Holtsmark (*Studier i Snorris Mytologi* (1964), 11, 32) does not note what is distinctive about this part of the prologue.

15

POETIC RIVALRIES AT
THE COURT OF CHARLEMAGNE

D. SCHALLER

Very frequently in the Middle Ages it is the poetry that furnishes us with detailed information about the intimate life of an epoch, since historians, biographers and other serious writers considered it beneath their dignity to pay attention to such charming trivialities. This observation applies with particular force to the court of Charlemagne and its social and literary culture. Most of the intimate details which we learn from the poets—from the Visigoth, Theodulf of Orléans, the Anglo-Saxon, Alcuin and the Frank, Angilbert—were known to Charles's biographer, Einhard, for he was present at the court during the last decade of the eighth century. But having decided to follow an idealising classical pattern in his *Vita Caroli*, he chose for his part to build a monument to Charlemagne which was concerned with the king alone. Similarly, in that learned monument of our own day, the four volumes of the *Festschrift*, '*Karl der Große*', compiled for the occasion of the Aachen centenary (1165–1965)[1] the court poetry is treated exclusively from the point of view of how the poets represent Charles, and what their relation to him may have been. This kind of interest prevails in most of our works of scholarship, and so certain poems which reflect with great delicacy the more intimate social life of the Aachen court at the end of the eighth century have not yet been thoroughly enough examined. I should like in this brief lecture to call attention to some of these poems, pieces of rhetorical verse cast in the form of letters[2] which exemplify one aspect of the poetic activity we find in Charles's court, namely the utterance in verse of feelings of rivalry, mockery and hatred. These poems often reflect the inevitable conflicts in which the groups of scholars whom Charles collected around him came to be involved, because of their different nationalities and their different notions of erudition: groups such as the Irishmen, the Anglo-Saxons, the

[1] *Karl der Große—Lebenswerk und Nachleben*. II: *Das geistige Leben*, hg. von Bernhard Bischoff (Düsseldorf, 1965).

[2] The texts are edited by E. Dümmler in *Monumenta Germaniae historica: Poetae latini aevi Carolini*, I (Berlin, 1881). The numbers given for particular poems refer to this edition.

Lombards, the Visigoths and the Franks themselves. In this circle of friends, rivals and enemies, it was the practice for those who were sent on a mission by the king, and so were compelled to be absent from the court for a period, to compose poetic epistles as a means of keeping their memory green and of bringing their sympathies and antipathies to bear.

It is important to note the twofold function of such an epistolary poem, which we find described very clearly by Theodulf (no. 25). First, the poem is intended to circulate round the court, passing from hand to hand:

> Ludicris haec mixta iocis per ludicra currat,
> saepeque tangatur qualibet illa manu.
> Laude iocoque simul hunc illita carta revisat,
> quem tribuente celer ipse videbo deo.   (lines 9–12)

Secondly, it is intended for public recitation at some festive gathering:

> His bene patratis, mensis dapibusque remotis
> pergat laetitia plebs comitante foras.
> Hacque intus remanente sonet Theodulfica Musa,
> quae foveat reges, mulceat et proceres.   (lines 201–4)

Another text, which comes in a poem by Angilbert belonging to the same genre, gives us a better idea of what the circulation of a letter round the court actually involved. This poem (Angilbert, no. 2) is conceived after the manner of Ovid as a command to the *cartula* (that is, to the epistle itself)[1] to hasten through the different parts of the court and to deliver the poet's greetings to certain persons or groups of persons: to the king, his sons and daughters, the court clergy (*capella*) and finally those problematic boys (*pueri*) whom everybody wants to be Angilbert's illegitimate sons, Hartnit and Nithart, but whom I prefer to think of as the young scholars of the palace school. But a discussion of this problem would take us too far from our theme. From the stylistic point of view Angilbert's epistle is lofty poetry, designed to be recited in public, embellished as it is with two series of *versus intercalares* after the manner of Virgil's eighth eclogue.

The specific effect which the twofold function of circulation and recitation was likely to produce can be seen in the manner in which

---

[1] Angilbert no. 2, lines 72–3:

> Cartula, curre modo per sacra palatia David,
> atque humili cunctis caris fer voce salutem.

mockery and invective are employed in Theodulf's poem no. 25. We have here a description of a grand festival at Charles's court, consisting of a thanksgiving service on the occasion of the victory over the Avars and their submission in 795, followed by a royal audience, a ceremonial meal and the subsequent literary entertainment. Theodulf's description is based on his remembrance of similar festivities at which he had been present and is nourished by his poetic imagination.

In hierarchic sequence, beginning with the king and his family and proceeding through the higher dignitaries down to less important persons, the whole court makes its vivid appearance in the poem, which by the way is admirably composed. But in this court society there are certain individuals who arouse Theodulf's mockery or dislike. Two of them he remembers from former occasions as specially hostile to himself and his poetry, and now—in order to inflict on them an exceptional punishment—he contrives a subtle literary effect. He suggests that while his panegyric is being recited, a stout warrior called Wibod begins to feel bored and expresses his disapproval of this sort of poetry in a rather annoying manner. The king reprimands him gently, and he drags himself grudgingly off, his round belly leading the way. His departure is accompanied by the mirth of the whole assembly; for the reciter has reached the passage where the description in the poem corresponds exactly to Wibod's actual behaviour:

> Audiat hanc forsan membrosus Wibodus heros,
>   concutiat crassum terque quaterque caput.
> Et torvum adspiciens vultuque et voce minetur,
>   absentemque suis me obruat ille minis.
> Quem si forte vocat pietas gratissima regis,
>   gressu eat obliquo vel titubante genu.
> Et sua praecedat tumefactus pectora venter,
>   et pede Vulcanum, voce Iovem referat. (lines 205 ff.)

Perhaps the poor fellow did not even understand Latin well enough to realise why the others were all roaring with laughter! His goose has been quite effectively cooked. But Theodulf's other opponent is more dangerous. He is the poet's mortal enemy. At this point, good humour and hilarity are forgotten, and the verse explodes with hatred and contempt:

> Haec ita dum fiunt, dum carmina nostra leguntur,
>   stet Scotellus ibi, res sine lege furens,
> res dira, hostis atrox, hebes horror, pestis acerba...
> (lines 213–15)

And so on for three more lines, with asyndetic agglomeration of envenomed insults, accentuated by the anaphoric *res*, devaluing his enemy to the status of a 'thing'. And now Theodulf uses once again the device of synchronising his narrative with an anticipated course of events, in order to destroy his enemy. The Irish scholar stands there in helpless fury, just as the poem describes him, pounding his fists against his breast, calling frenziedly on the bystanders, endeavouring to disparage Theodulf's poetry and even disturbing the reciter—a veritable forerunner of Wagner's Beckmesser. But the recitation continues. The Irishman must learn that he is a deplorable, quarrelsome, half-educated creature, lacking depth and wisdom.

Theodulf may have reckoned to crush the Scotellus altogether by this sharp satire. But even if he did not, even if the synchronism succeeded only half as well as he hoped, the laughter was on his side, and disgrace had fallen all of a sudden and quite unexpectedly upon his enemies. We can see moreover how the effect of this poem must have been enhanced by the fact that it was handed round as a letter before being publicly declaimed, since it had this twofold function which we mentioned earlier. Beyond doubt, it was intended to circulate only among the members of the royal family and the author's immediate friends, who thus had an opportunity of acquainting themselves in advance with all its little flatteries and jokes as well as with its massive attacks. They would have knowing smiles on their faces when the evening of the recital came. The victims on the other hand would be unprepared, unsuspecting and so all the more vulnerable.

Theodulf's campaign against the Irishman has echoes in two more poems of this period. Bernhard Bischoff has discovered a set of thirty-four clumsy hexameters, addressed to Charles by a partisan of Theodulf with the intention of defaming the latter's Irish enemy.[1] It is from this text that we learn at last who that enemy was. Called originally Cadac, he wished to be known by his Christian name of Andreas; and Theodulf himself launched another attack in a second great rhetorical poem (no. 27) against this man who seems to have been disliked by almost the whole court.

This second poem (no. 27) is interesting in another connection too; for it refers to the rivalry between Theodulf and the group headed by Alcuin. Theodulf is using the letter form again, but this

---

[1] B. Bischoff, 'Theodulf und der Ire, Cadac-Andreas' in *Mittelalterliche Studien*, II (Stuttgart, 1967), 19–25, reprinted from *Historisches Jahrbuch*, LXXIV (1955).

time the intended recipient is not Charles. The letter is addressed to a man who is called now Corvus, now Corvulus, now Corvinianus. In Old High German *corvus* (a raven) would be *Hraban*; and Adolf Ebert put forward the theory that the person intended was Alcuin's young disciple Hrabanus Maurus. This theory was then rejected by Ernst Dümmler on the ground that the concluding lines show the addressee to have been an old man with white hair:

> Nunc tibi tot salve quot sunt in vertice crines
> albentes, sic tu, Corviniane, vale.

But I am afraid that Dümmler and those who agreed with him did not understand the irony which is present not only in this distich, but in the whole poem—an irony which derives from the fact that Corvinianus is a mock addressee, introduced simply for the sake of satire. The many greetings he is supposedly sent turn out in fact to be none at all; for how many white hairs has a person who can be called not only *Corvus* or *Corvulus*, but—as if to put the matter beyond all doubt— *Corvus niger* (line 79) and *Corvule niger* (line 102)? Theodulf takes obvious pleasure in frightening this very young man by an enumeration of all the dangers that threaten him from evil persons at the court, while his allies and co-disciples, Einhard and Osulf, whom no. 25 had already ridiculed because of their smallness, are called offensively *pygmaei*. That the object of Theodulf's mockery was really the young Hrabanus can be proved moreover by another line of argument. Theodulf says (no. 27, line 61) that the Irishman was preparing to smash a *Getulum caput;*

> At tamen arma minans Scottus iam proelia temptat
> Getulumque caput ense ferire volens.

According to Dümmler, *Getulum caput* is to be taken as meaning 'a Goth's head' and refers therefore to Theodulf. This view was generally accepted until S. T. Collins observed in 1951 that *Getulum* in the verse has a long *e* and a long *u* whereas *Geta*, the word for Goth, always has a short *e* whether used about Theodulf or anyone else. Collins's observation did not attract much notice, but its relevance is obvious. In fact *Gaetuli* is the name of a dark-skinned North African people who are mentioned by Virgil, Ovid and others as being neighbours of the Moors; and *Gaetuli* was used occasionally for *Mauri* by synecdoche. I have little doubt that Theodulf's *Getulum caput* in this poem means *caput Mauri* and is an allusion to the cognomen given to Hrabanus by his teacher Alcuin. And the fact that he should have transformed Hraban's name in this way comes to seem even more likely when we find him two verses later giving his own name as *Gentilupum*, a correct enough translation of Theodulf.

The rivalry between Theodulf and the Anglo-Saxon contingent at the court dated back to the previous decade as I have tried to show in another paper.[1] Theodulf has no hesitation about mocking the disciples of Alcuin, but when he comes to deal with their master, he confines himself to a gentle irony. One example will have to suffice to show the nature of this irony, and it will be convenient to take an instance where a passage in one of Theodulf's poems (no. 25) seems to be a comment on one of Alcuin's (no. 26). Alcuin praises the royal kitchener and *dapifer*, Audulf, whom he calls Menalcas, for disciplining his cooks so that Flaccus (which it will be remembered is Alcuin's name for himself) gets his warm pap or porridge (*pultes*) properly served:

> Ipse Menalca coquos nigra castiget in aula
> ut calidos habeat Flaccus per fercula pultes
>
> (Alcuin no. 26, lines 48–9)

It is interesting therefore to find the word *pultes* occurring also in Theodulf's poem just after a mention of Alcuin's name. But here the context is very different. Theodulf has been describing how *pater Albinus* takes his pleasure at the king's table, enjoying even the stronger alcoholic drinks and becoming more and more loquacious:

> quo melius doceat, melius sua fistula cantet,
> si doctrinalis pectoris antra riget
>
> (Theodulf no. 25, lines 195–6)

And then immediately after he bursts out:

> Este procul, pultes, et lactis massa coacti,
> sed pigmentati, sis prope, mensa, cibi.

The intention is clear. Theodulf does not want to see tiresome everyday foods—porridge, sour milk, curds—at the king's feast. He wants well-spiced meat. I cannot believe that after this resounding *Este procul pultes* Alcuin could have expressed his modest predilection for warm porridge in a poem written for public recitation. It must be Theodulf who is alluding to Alcuin's already existing verses and making fun of them. And perhaps his aim was not so much to satirise Alcuin's eating habits as to use the monotonous, tiresome *pultes* as a

---

[1] D. Schaller, 'Die karolingischen Figurengedichte des Cod. Bernensis 212' in *Medium Aevum Vivum: Festschrift für Walther Bulst* (Heidelberg, 1960), pp. 20–47.

symbol for Alcuin's analogous mental disposition. If so, we ought probably to take the *pigmentatus cibus* that was actually being served as a symbol for the poetry which was to be recited with it, namely Theodulf's own. Can we talk of *Speisemetaphorik* (as E. R. Curtius would call it) as a weapon in the infighting of one court poet against another? I cannot for my part conceive of a better explanation for the passages cited.[1]

---

[1] This paper is an abstract of a larger publication in the *Mittellateinisches Jahrbuch*, VI (1969) to which I must refer the reader for the philological and historical evidence for the statements made here.

16

FUNCTIONS OF CLASSICAL BORROWING IN MEDIEVAL LATIN VERSE

E. P. M. DRONKE

For a considerable body of medieval Latin verse, we today have accurate and substantial evidence of its classical echoes and classical adaptations. To have established these in detail is the achievement of a number of outstanding scholars, such as those who edited the Carolingian poets for the *Monumenta Germaniae Historica*, or again Max Manitius and Paul Lehmann. By assembling the details relevant to classical borrowing, these scholars have laid the foundations for what I believe is the next, equally important, stage of enquiry: the evaluation of this evidence, the detailed literary study of the classical elements in medieval Latin verse, distinguishing their various functions, and assessing for each poet what the classical elements contribute to his poetic intentions, to his artistry, to the fabric of his verse.

Where do we find more than simple echoes and straight assimilations? Where does the poet effect an individual transformation of his classical reading, and for what purposes? These problems have seldom been broached. I should like to indicate by one or two specific illustrations the kinds of literary problem that arise, offering first some provisional distinctions.

Classical parallels such as are presented at the foot of the page in the volumes of the *Poetae Aevi Carolini* may include, first, unconscious borrowings—elements that would form part of the poetic *koinê* of a well-read author, expressions he would use instinctively in certain situations without focusing on their classical context, because his education had made them second nature. At times such an unconscious borrowing may be scarcely distinguishable from a mere coincidence. Second, there is conscious borrowing, ranging from unassimilated adaptation of classical phrases to the most individual and sophisticated transmutations of them. Third, there is a range of explicit quotation, where the classical borrowing is meant to be seen as such by an educated audience, and is meant to modify their response to the poem. Here it can enrich the new context, by evoking the connotations of the original context, or the poet can implicitly contrast these connotations from the older context with those of his own; this itself can have a number of different artistic effects, such as pathos, irony, critical reflection, or parody.

A passage from the *Waltharius* can serve to illustrate some of these distinctions. Walter and Hiltgund have escaped from Attila's court, and the queen has just told Attila the wounding news:

> He tears his whole robe from shoulder to foot,
> and rends his sad spirit, now this way, now that.
> As the sand is racked by Aeolian storms,
> so the king is in turmoil with cares within...
> Care could not give his limbs easeful rest.
> When black night had drawn earth's colours away,
> he sank into bed, but not closing his eyes,
> lay on his right side, now on his left
> and, as if pierced by a sharp javelin,
> shuddered, tossed his head to and fro,
> then, raising himself in the bed, sat distraught.
> Useless. He rises, races about the town,
> back to his bed, reaches it, leaves it again.
> Thus Attila squandered a sleepless night.
> But the fugitive lovers, walking through friendly stillness,
> hasten to leave his baneful land behind.
>
> Day had scarce broken when, calling his elders,
> he cried 'Oh, if any would bring me that runaway,
> that Waltharius, bound like a mangy bitch—
> I'd soon clothe such a man in twice-refined gold,
> I'd load him down with gold from all sides
> and, as I live, bar his way with talents utterly!'[1]

These are the thoughts, with their swift transitions of tone and mood, that the poet expresses in a language dense with allusions and borrowings; in the ways these are used we can perceive an individual artistry at work.

Ex humeris trabeam discindit ad infima totam...The rending of one's garments is a biblical gesture,[2] but the poet's words are closest to those evoking Aeneas's grief—*umeris abscindere vestem*—when the Trojan women set fire to the ships. What is unusual, however, is the note of violence: Attila tears his whole garment from top to toe in a single, furious gesture. The next verse—*et nunc huc animum tristem, nunc dividit*

[1] *Waltharius*, 382–407 (*MGH, Poetae*, VI, i, 39–41, with parallels cited *ad loc.*).
[2] Cf. Jud. xi. 35 (Jephtha seeing his daughter), or Matt. xxvi. 65 (Caiaphas accusing Christ).

illuc—copied almost exactly from a line describing Aeneas, gains its special effect by the way that *dividit*, describing Attila's inner state, parallels the physical *discindit* of the previous line. So two widely separated citations from the *Aeneid* are brought together for a specific purpose.

Then follow two lines that are a piece of sleight-of-hand:

> Ac velut Aeolicis turbatur arena procellis,
> sic intestinis rex fluctuat undique curis.

The Aeolian storms are Virgilian in atmosphere and diction, yet these lines are directly adapted from some humorous mock-heroic verses of Venantius Fortunatus, in which the *abbé gourmand* describes what happened inside his stomach after eating too well: *non sic Aeoliis turbatur harena procellis*! I think it possible that the most sophisticated members of the poet's audience recognised the allusion and enjoyed the recognition. It is the first of a series of parodistic touches that exaggerate Attila's hectic rage till it borders on the ludicrous. A moment later, his restlessness—*nec placidam membris potuit dare cura quietem*—is expressed in almost the same words as are used of Dido in the *Aeneid*. The incongruity is deliberate—the world-conqueror, frustrated, waxes womanish. The poet heightens the effect by yet another Virgilian allusion:

> Namque ubi nox rebus iam dempserat atra colores,
> Decidit in lectum...

Virgil's image comes at the solemn moment when Aeneas and the Sibyl descend to the shades—on a path as awesome as when 'black night has taken earth's colour away'. Here Virgil's words are used for a burlesque anticlimax: when black night had taken earth's colour away, Attila sank, not into the shades, but into bed. The effect is dramatically apt: for Attila is not the hero, he is the hero's dupe.[1]

There are further Virgilian phrases in the lines that follow—expressions such as *latus...fultus, iaculo...acuto, insomnem noctem* (which is also biblical), *patribusque vocatis*. But these are not I think used for conscious effects—they are such as would come instinctively to a well-read medieval author. When Attila wanders distraught

---

[1] The function of the phrase *decidit in lectum* is perhaps not limited to the burlesque: it occurs twice in the Bible near the opening of the First Book of Maccabees (i. 6; vi. 8), once of Alexander the Great, at the moment when he knew he had to die, and once of King Antiochus, when his armies had fled. If this phrase too should be a conscious, rather than instinctive, borrowing, then the poet must mean it to be more than simply grotesque: for those aware of its original context, it would serve to heighten the sense of a pagan king's defeat.

E. P. M. DRONKE

through his city at night, the poet may well be thinking once more of Dido (*totaque vagatur | urbe furens, qualis coniecta cerva sagitta*): Attila too, though not doe-like, is as if pierced by a shaft. Yet here it is only some of the thoughts that are alike—the language is very different. One other phrase, however, seems inserted as a deliberate quotation: the escaping lovers walk *per amica silentia*. Through its associations— the Greek moment of exultation as the wooden horse is opened in Troy—the poet may even be sounding a first note of hope for the fugitives, a turning-point in their fortunes. The two experiences of night, with all their connotations, are contrasted: Attila, like Dido, finds the night a torment; Walter and Hiltgund, like the Greeks, need the night for cover and sense it as their friend.

Attila's flamboyant speech, challenging his warriors to vengeance, is in a different key and idiom from all that has gone before.[1] It is unclassical; its closest analogue, as Jakob Grimm saw, is in a very ancient Norse poem, *The Battle of the Goths and Huns*, where the Gothic king Angantýr says to his young half-brother, who is claiming his inheritance:

> As you sit
> I will measure you in silver,
> as you walk
> I will rain down gold on you,
> so that on all sides
> rings will roll. . .[2]

Here too, as in *Waltharius*, the promise of a reward is made to sound ever more like a threat (*Atque viam penitus clausissem vivo talentis*). The choice of a contrasting diction in the Latin is deliberate: Attila may have seemed comic in his rage, he seems far from comic to his men as he plans revenge. The poet needed something that would stand out from the whole tenor of his classical echoes. Against the phrases of conflict and anticlimax, with their strongly disjunctive syntax, he sets a threefold variation on the notion of reward, that mounts inexorably to a climax; against the allusions to Dido and Aeneas in their moments of anguished weakness, the picture of a barbarian prince in the fullness of his might.

These reflections on a few lines of *Waltharius* illustrate some of the possible functions of classical borrowings in medieval Latin verse— but indeed there are numerous others. It is possible, for instance, for

---

[1] Only the phrase *auro. . .recocto* is Virgilian (cf. *Aen.* viii, 624).
[2] *Hlǫðsqviða*, st. 13 (*Edda*, ed. G. Neckel, H. Kuhn (1962), p. 305).

a poet to take a classical motif and treat it in a profoundly unclassical manner: thus we have a Latin *planctus* on the death of Hector, written down in Rome in the late eleventh century,[1] a simple lyrical-dramatic dialogue, in rhymed octosyllabic couplets, with parts for Hector, Andromache and a chorus. Each couplet has the moving refrain, *heu, male te cupimus!*, that evokes both Andromache's longing and the chorus's sense of loss. It is like the *ritornello* of Italian popular lyric. The existence of such a *planctus* is to me scarcely conceivable without supposing a tradition of contemporary vernacular ballads in Italy; but even if this is supposed, the wonder of such an alchemy of classical tragic theme and popular ballad-technique is no less.

For the subtlest Latin poetry of the twelfth century it will be necessary to enlarge and refine further our concepts of classical borrowing. The Archpoet, for instance, can gain unique poetic effects by his fusion of classical with biblical expressions, or again by using classical allusion to qualify his response to contemporary events. In the poem that is often called his 'hymn' to Frederick Barbarossa (*Kaiserhymnus*),[2] he likens the rebellious Lombards, building their towers to withstand the emperor, to the giants piling Pelion on Ossa. They will be destroyed—the poet does not say by Jupiter, but by a Cyclopean thunderbolt (*fulmine digna Ciclopeo*). Indeed the Cyclopes are traditionally said to forge the bolts for Jupiter,[3] yet the emphasis here, and the choice of adjective—not a divine destroyer but a Cyclopean one—are hardly the most flattering to the emperor. If, like the Archpoet, some of his audience had the Virgilian simile of the Cyclopes at their forge (*Georg.* IV, 170 ff.) in mind, the associations at this moment could only have been those of grotesque and mindless force. When a moment later the Archpoet compares Milan to Troy—*civitas Ambrosii velud Troia stabat*—does this not suggest that the rebels belong to a world of heroes, gallant in their defeat, rather than to a world of criminals?[4] The classical allusions help to transform an official panegyric into a comment as double-edged as Andrew Mar-

---

[1] Ed. M. de Marco, *Aevum*, XXXIII (1959), 120–2; on the provenance of the MS cf. G. H. Pertz, *Archiv*, v (1824), 85.

[2] 'Salve mundi domine', ed. H. Watenphul, H. Krefeld, *Die Gedichte des Archipoeta* (1958), pp. 68 ff.

[3] Cf. Servius, *in Georg.* IV, 171; Hyginus, *Fab.* 49; Mythogr. I, 176.

[4] These observations, slight in themselves, are borne out by many unhymnlike features in the poem, that have hitherto escaped notice. Thus in st. 2 no contemporary could have heard the suggestion that at Barbarossa's trumpet enemy citadels totter (*cuius tuba titubant arces inimice*) without thinking both of Jericho and of the emperor's recent siege of

vell's Horatian Ode to Cromwell. Once more the materials for studying such a transformation are available. It is the assessment of how the classical elements work in the poetry that is still lacking. Here is the field that awaits investigation: the literary study of how the classical past is present in this poetry. Such study is naturally inseparable from a larger task: the literary criticism of the Latin poetry of the Middle Ages.

Milan, so painfully unlike that of Jericho, as the Archpoet himself later makes plain (st. 24–5). Within the compliment lurks a grim irony. So too, in st. 3–4, the lines

> *Nemo prudens ambigit* te per dei nutum
> super reges alios regem constitutum. . .
> Unde diu cogitans *quod non esset tutum*
> Cesari non reddere censum vel tributum. . .

while they accept the realities of *Machtpolitik*, can hardly be seen as rejoicing in the idea that 'justice is the interest of the stronger'. Or again, in st. 29, the recognition of the benefits of this *Machtpolitik* in the first couplet is qualified in the second by an image worthy of Goya:

> Cesaris est gloria, Cesaris est donum,
> quod iam patent omnibus vie regionum,
> dum ventis exposita corpora latronum
> surda flantis boree captant aure sonum.

The Archpoet, even within the framework of his commissioned piece, undercuts the genre of official panegyric as much as his daring and his humanity—both of which were considerable—enabled him to do.

17

SALLUST IN THE MIDDLE AGES

B. SMALLEY

Orosius and Sallust supply the twin keys to medieval historiography: *claves scientiae*. Suetonius probably comes next, of the ancient historians, followed by 'the Latin Josephus'; Livy tags along far in the rear. I have to speak of Sallust. I shall keep to *Catilinarium* and *Iugurthinum*. Limited space obliges me to cut short at about 1200. It is a good place to stop. I should guess that first-hand knowledge of Sallust declined in the thirteenth century; the subsequent classical revival in fourteenth-century Italy raises new problems.

I need give here neither proof nor illustration of Sallust's popularity in the early Middle Ages. E. Lesne has established that his presence is normal in libraries in France and the Rhineland by the late eleventh century;[1] Manitius's indices offer guidance to his use by early medieval writers;[2] Dr von den Brincken has studied his impact on world chronicles;[3] Dr Bolaffi has written a monograph on his influence through the ages.[4] This accumulated evidence may be taken for granted. I shall consider the question it raises: what did our Roman historian mean to those who read, quoted and imitated his books?

The Middle Ages knew three aspects of Sallust. The distinction is mine; it will serve the limited purpose of this paper. First comes the moralist, second the stylistic model, as studied in the arts course, and third the historian. To begin with the moralist: 'It was a peculiarity of Roman thought', writes Mr Earl, 'generally to represent political crises as moral ones.'[5] Sallust ensured that the peculiarity, if such it was, should become universal. He worked out a theory, inconsistent but persuasive, to show the logical, disastrous sequence from peace and security, bringing wealth, ambition, corruption and discord, to social and civil war. St Augustine fitted this picture of the Late Republic into the apology against the pagans which he gives in his

[1] E. Lesne, *Histoire de la propriété ecclésiastique en France*, IV (Lille, 1938), 775.
[2] M. Manitius, *Geschichte der lateinischen Literatur des Mittelalters* (Munich, 1911–31).
[3] A. D. von den Brincken, *Studien zur lateinischen Weltchronistik bis in das Zeitalter Ottos von Freising* (Düsseldorf, 1957).
[4] E. Bolaffi, *Salustio e la sua fortuna nei secoli* (Rome, 1949).
[5] D. C. Earl, *The Political Thought of Sallust* (Cambridge, 1961), p. 44.

City of God. 'For St Augustine's audience this moral history was *the* authentic history of the period.' I quote Mr Brown.[1] Orosius had more influence than had St Augustine on medieval historians, just because he thought less deeply. He passed on a cruder version of the same theme.[2] Sallust held all the cards; he could not lose. A bored class of students will wake to life as soon as one mentions 'the decline' of anything. The old Romans, before the baths of Capua softened their army, inspire no interest in themselves (apart from the joys of erudition); their story fascinates only because it ends in the dramatic landslide into self-seeking and luxury. Cato appeals not for himself, but as a relic of ancient virtue and as a foil to his contemporaries. Sallust, therefore, as a moralist, patronised by the Church Fathers, raised the pleasurable task of historiography to the highest level. His openings on the body–soul relationship, the superiority of intellectual activity to physical and the virtue of recording events for posterity, became part of the stock-in-trade. History, even pagan history, had a moral purpose. Listen to Henry of Huntingdon in the introduction to his *Historia Anglorum*, praising Homer, whom he counts as a historian and exalts above all 'the philosophers': Homer and his like present virtues and vices more vividly in their *exempla* than do philosophers in their *sententiae*. They benefit not only spiritual men, but even seculars, attracting them to good and dissuading them from evil. Henry goes on to echo Sallust on the dignity of historiography, interest in which distinguishes thoughtful men from brutish.[3] Here Sallust stands poised on the bridge between scholarship on the one hand and popular preaching on the other, a fate which overtook many ancient writers in the twelfth century, and even more in the thirteenth. To John of Salisbury, a connoisseur of Latin classics available in his time, Sallust excelled as *historicorum inter Latinos potissimus*.[4] Yet John's allusions to him in *Policraticus* show that what he prized most highly was the moral judgements, on flatterers and toadies, for example.[5]

Here we must note that Sallust, directly and through his mediators, enlarged the perspective of those who moralised on the history of the Roman State. Some modern scholars, more at home in the Renaissance than in the Middle Ages, imagine that the empire monopolised

[1] Peter Brown, *Augustine of Hippo, a biography* (London, 1967), p. 311.
[2] See *ibid.* pp. 295–6.
[3] Ed. T. Arnold (Rolls Series, 179), pp. 1–3. Henry echoes *Cat.* 1, 1 and 8.
[4] *Policraticus*, ed. C. C. I. Webb, 1 (Oxford, 1909), p. 211.
[5] *Ibid.* p. 179.

medieval thought on Rome. Professor Hans Baron writes: 'An equally profound break with the medieval mode of thought had been effected by Petrarch's youthful rediscovery of pre-imperial Rome and of the human and national forces—the *virtutes Romanae*—which in the time of the *Respublica Romana* had made Rome great, but had afterwards declined.'[1] It is true that the Roman Principate, first as *praeparatio evangelii* and then as prolonged in the Christian Roman empire, did loom larger than the Republic in medieval thought. The pathos of Roman ruins, as visible in the Middle Ages, naturally recalled the Rome of the Caesars. But readers of Sallust knew perfectly well that the Roman people had flourished and had won their most striking victories in the good old days of early Roman tradition, after shaking off the yoke of their kings. Sallust even foreshadowed the medieval *translatio imperii* in explaining the rise of Rome to greatness.[2] Livy as abridged by Florus and the sayings of philosophers reinforced Sallust; but *Sallust* is quoted by 'Ekkehart' on the origins of Rome.[3] Freculph of Lisieux praises the valour of the Roman people, the wisdom of the senate, the magnanimity of the commanders in his world chronicle.[4] St Ado of Vienne praises Scipio Africanus for his *vigor et modestia*, which made civil war impossible during his lifetime.[5] Otto of Freising's *Historia de Duabus Civitatibus* has world empire as its main subject-matter; Frederick Barbarossa's attempted revival of empire inspired Otto with new hope for the future, as he tells us in *Gesta Friderici*. And yet he sets the rise of Roman dominion against a background of merited reward for virtue. The Romans made the world their own not by strength alone, but by prudence too; Otto quotes Sallust to the effect that wars are won by intelligence, *iuxta viri prudentis sententiam*.[6] He goes on to pair the two Scipios with the Maccabees, the latter as *optimi legis Dei zelatores*, the former as *incliti Romanae Urbis ac paternarum legum defensores*.[7] Memories of the Roman Republic remained vivid enough to offer a programme to Arnald of Brescia in 1145; he stirred up the people in papal Rome, 'putting forward the examples of the ancient Romans, who made the whole world theirs through ripe counsel of the senate and the courage of

[1] *From Petrarch to Leonard Bruni* (Chicago, 1968), pp. 39–40.
[2] *Cat.* II.
[3] *Mon. Germ. Hist., Scriptores*, VI, 50, from *Cat.* VI, 'ut Salustius ait'. On the chronicle ascribed to Ekkehart see von den Brincken, *Studien zur lateinischen Weltchronistik*, pp. 187–93.
[4] *Chron.*, Pat. lat. CVI, 1110.   [5] *Chron.*, Pat. lat. CXXIII, 65.
[6] *Mon. Germ. Hist. Script. in usum schol.* ed. A. Hofmeister (1912), III, from *Cat.* II, 2.
[7] *Ibid.* p. 117.

their youths'.[1] The Republic denoted dangerous thinking in Otto's eyes, as soon as it moved from the pages of history into present action. Both historiography and politics in the Middle Ages, however, combine to prove that knowledge of and reflection on the Roman past included the Republican period. Petrarch could reinterpret, but not rediscover what Sallust had made part of the heritage of learning. I have considered this point under the heading of 'Sallust as moralist', on the grounds that reflection on Roman history depended on a moral and religious view of history as a divine revelation, embracing sacred and profane side by side.

Come down from the heights to the library shelves. Sallust was commonly listed in the section classified as *ars grammatica*.[2] Boys learned their history in ancient and medieval classrooms alike in the margin of grammar and rhetoric: history and mythology guided them to understand the allusions in literary texts and supplied a quarry of *exempla* for the orator to draw upon. Sallust alone of ancient historians survived that reduction of school texts which marked the decline of culture in the late empire in the West. He owed his survival, I suppose, to his brevity, to his pithiness, to his moralism, since the orator had taken the side of the angels, and above all to his descriptions of characters and battle scenes and to his speeches. Sallust borrowed from Thucydides the convention of putting elegant, reasoned discourses into his characters' mouths. Their form is invention, open and unconcealed. The Moorish King Bocchus harangues Sulla in Latin 'worthy of Sallust', although we read that Bocchus spoke through an interpreter (*Iug.* cix); the latter could hardly have had such choice Latin at his disposal. Moreover, the convention that a general addresses his troops on the eve of battle must surely spring from fiction. It is hardly more credible than the framework of *The Canterbury Tales*. Even allowing for the small numbers of troops involved in ancient and medieval warfare, could the general's words have encouraged more than the first few lines of his men, especially if he had to reckon with cavalry? I doubt it. Medieval writers will make him stand in *acie media loco eminenti*;[3] but does that help? The historical basis of the content of *civilian* speeches is another matter, which need not keep us now.

[1] *Ottonis et Rahewini Gesta Friderici, Mon. Germ. Hist. Script. in usum schol.* ed. G. Waitz (1912), 134.
[2] Lesne, *Histoire de la propriété ecclésiastique*, iv, 778.
[3] Henry of Huntingdon, *Historia Anglorum*, ed. cit. p. 262, on the Bishop of Orkney's speech to the troops before the Battle of the Standard, 1138.

I have looked at a number of glossed copies of *Catilinarium* and *Iugurthinum* in the Bodleian and the British Museum, simply as samples: MSS Bodl. Rawl. G. 43 and 44 (*Summary Catalogue* 14774–5), both eleventh century, the former written in S.E. France, the latter probably in Flanders or N.E. France (it belonged to St Peter's of Ghent);[1] B.M. Add. 35,109, twelfth century (French?); Arundel 234, twelfth century (Italian?); Harl. 2598 (twelfth century); 2643, late eleventh century or early twelfth century (French?); 5412 of similar date and provenance; the glossator or his exemplar shows a special interest in allusions to Gaul. The glosses are written in hands ranging from contemporary with the text to thirteenth and fourteenth century. They may have common sources, but show no verbal identity from copy to copy. All originated in teaching in the arts course. We have textual variants and lexicographical or grammatical comments. Many of the latter aim at helping students equipped with a minimum of classical Latin, or perhaps their writers were teaching grammar from their text. Thus *praeclari facinoris* (*Cat.* II, 9) has a gloss explaining that *facinus* with an adjective has a good sense, without adjective a bad one.[2] Some glosses give the gist of the matter in plain words, designed also as marginal captions. This applies to accounts of campaigns as well as to more abstract subjects: we read on *Iug.* XLIV, 4 that Postumius Albinus was to blame, not only for not moving camp, but for not setting watches.[3] We get instruction on Roman history and institutions, on the manner of electing consuls, for instance,[4] and on the purpose of laws such as the *lex Plautica*.[5] We learn that a perpetual flame 'is said to have burned in the temple of Vesta'.[6]

Speeches have first claim on the glossators' attention. Some MSS have rubricated titles: *Oratio Catonis*, etc. Almost all show marginal headings pointing to the speeches. Glossators regarded them as models, as things in themselves, irrespective of their context in the tale. That Catiline was a 'baddy', not a 'goody' makes no difference:

[1] Mlle M. Dulong kindly gave me her opinion on these two MSS.

[2] MS Rawl. G. 44, fo. 2v: Sciendum est quod quando aliquid adiectivum nomen additur huic nomini quod est facinus in bona parte accipitur. Quando autem per se ponitur, in malo.

[3] MS Rawl. G. 43, fo. 32v: Non tanto erat Albinus vituperandus nisi quod non faciebat mutari castra, sed etiam nisi quod non adducebantur vigilie.

[4] MSS Harl. 2598, fo. 6v, 5412, fo. 4v, on *Cat.* XVIII, 2. The glosses are not verbally identical, although they deal with the same subject.

[5] MS Rawl. G. 44, fo. 10v, on *Cat.* XXXI, 4: Lex plauticia dampnabat illos qui poterant probari coniurationem fecisse contra rem publicam.

[6] *Ibid.* fo. 6, on *Cat.* XV, 1.

Oratio Catilinae ad milites suos pulcherrima runs a gloss on *Cat.* xx.[1] Any chronicler needing a literary model for a speech by a general encouraging his soldiers to face heavy odds had his *Catilinarium* to hand.

So it proves if we turn from glosses to histories. Richer puts Catiline's words into the mouth of the emperor Otto II.[2] Bruno in his *de Bello Saxonico* does the same for Duke Otto addressing the Saxon rebels, and they are the heroes of his book.[3] Even more incongruously to our minds, Rahewin makes Frederick Barbarossa quote Catiline in a speech accusing the Milanese of crimes against his imperial majesty.[4] Those famous battles and sieges of *Bellum Iugurthinum* enjoyed equal popularity. Sallust does not shine as a military historian; so experts tell us. Medieval historians, not being experts on military matters either, could borrow all the more happily. Why tell in one's own halting words what an ancient author had put better? Scratch the surface of medieval battle stories and you often find either the Jugurthine or Josephus's *Jewish Wars* as a substratum.[5] The description looks more like a flight of rhetoric than narration of fact.

A third legacy of Sallust as taught in the arts course was proverbs. His sentences gained currency out of context beside those of other 'philosophers'. His definition of friendship, *Idem velle atque idem nolle ea demum firma amicitia est* (*Cat.* xx, 4), figures in *Policraticus*, where John of Salisbury learnedly ascribes it to its author: 'ut ait historicus'.[6] Peter the Venerable quotes it anonymously.[7] Walther has listed it in his *Sprichwörter*.[8] Jugurtha's crack on Rome, 'a city for sale and ready to fall, if it could find a bidder' (xxxv, 10), delighted those who had to make costly journeys *ad limina apostolorum*.[9] Sallustian phrases, such as *ea tempestate* for *eo tempore*, passed into the diction of medieval chroniclers. How far did Sallust the stylist find true disciples as distinct from mere borrowers? I'm not competent to say. Increasing use of rhythmical prose ousted ancient models. Mrs Chibnall, in her admirable edition of Ordericus Vitalis, has exposed

---

[1] MS Harl. 5412, fo. 17.

[2] *Hist.* III, 73, *Mon. Germ. Hist. Script. in usum schol.* ed. G. Waitz (1877), 112.

[3] Cap. xxv, ed. H. E. Lohmann, *Deutsches Mittelalter*, II (Leipzig, 1937), 29.

[4] *Ottonis et Rahewini Gesta Friderici*, ed. cit. 134.

[5] Rahewin in particular draws on Josephus; *ibid. passim.*

[6] *Policr.* ed. cit. I, 179.

[7] *The Letters of Peter the Venerable*, ed. Giles Constable (Harvard University Press, 1967), ep. 58, I, 183.

[8] H. Walther, *Proverbia Sententiaeque Latinitatis Medii Aevi*, II (Göttingen, 1964), p. 384, no. 11367 c; owing to a misprint the source is given as Catullus.

[9] It figures already in Freculph, *Chron.*, Pat. lat. CVI, 1061 and Ado, *Chron.*, Pat. lat. CXXIII, 66.

Orderic's stylistic dilemma, when he quoted from that keen Sallustian, William of Poitiers. William's classicising style fitted into Orderic's Church Latin so badly that he had to modify the diction of his source in his quotations.[1] But a full history of medieval historians as Latin stylists remains to be written.

So much for Sallust in the arts course, purveying speeches, characters, battles, sieges, proverbs and tricks of style. Now we turn to him 'out of school', giving private tuition on an extra-curriculum subject, as it were, tuition on the historian's craft. Much of his teaching was valuable indeed. He presented the historical monograph as a wholesome alternative to universal history or the history of a people, on the one hand, and mere biography on the other. Bruno's *de Bello Saxonico*, William of Malmesbury's *Historia Novella* and the anonymous *Gesta Stephani* (both recounting the civil wars of Stephen's reign) spring to mind as examples of deliberately chosen monographs. He also taught the historian to study geography. Orosius reinforced the lesson; but Sallust gives more detail. The action in *Iugurthinum* takes place against a setting of North African geography, known to the author from his term of office there as proconsul of *Africa Nova*. Significantly, many medieval maps of the world have come down to us as illustrations of *Iug.* xvii. No less than 60 of the surviving 200 or more MSS are equipped with a map, according to M. Destombes. The original map dates back to before the end of the Roman empire in the West. It was modified and amplified through the ages.[2] The story of Jugurtha hinges not only on physical and political geography, but also on human, that is the nature of the Numidians and Moors. Sallust contrasts them with the Romans. Their less-developed economy gave rise to customs, institutions, ways of fighting and a mentality which explained both their resistance and their final submission to Rome, when Roman armies had defeated them. This aspect of Sallust came in useful when medieval writers wanted to portray the habits of peoples whom they regarded as less civilised than themselves, the Bretons, the Welsh or the Slavs in particular. William of Poitiers makes a thoughtful comparison between Breton marriage customs and those of 'the ancient Moors'.[3] Sallust's geography must have sharpened perception and observation.

---

[1] *The Ecclesiastical History of Orderic Vitalis*, ed. and transl. M. Chibnall, ii (Oxford, 1969), xix–xx.

[2] M. Destombes, *Mappemondes A.D. 1200–1500* (Amsterdam, 1964), pp. 65–6.

[3] *Gesta Guilelmi*, ed. and transl. R. Foreville, *Classiques de l'histoire de France au moyen âge* (Paris, 1952), p. 108.

Capacity to tell a gripping story, such as Sallust possessed, is probably a native gift, and cannot be acquired at will; but he would inspire his readers to emulate him, and the born storytellers succeeded. Incidentally, to show that readers enjoyed the tale for its own sake, notice that the last chapter of *Iugurthinum* left them unsatisfied. An answer to that Middle School question, known to all teachers, 'And how did he *die*?' was supplied in verses, copied in many MSS, telling us (erroneously) that Jugurtha met his death at the foot of 'the Tarpeian rocks':

Qui cupit ignotum Iugurte noscere letum,
Torpeis rupibus pulsus ad ima ruit.[1]

An imitable and imitated trait of Sallust was his analysis of motive, informed by cynical pessimism: suspect the worst. Professor Sir Ronald Syme sees him as a link between Thucydides and Tacitus in his deliberately disillusioned attitude to men and their conduct.[2] Medieval historians could not read Thucydides and they did not read Tacitus: so they depended on Sallust. His lesson was well learnt. The anonymous apologist of the emperor Henry IV sets out his reasons for 'deposing' Pope Gregory VII. Then in Sallust's own words the author refuses to pronounce on the truth of the accusations.[3] Readers of Sallust would understand: to leave the question open really meant that the worse was the more credible. Modern historians have dwelt on the naïvety of their medieval predecessors. Naïve they often were in their views on causation; but many show an acute awareness of self-interest covered up by hypocrisy, which they revel in exposing. William of Malmesbury offers the most pessimistic interpretation of motive of any historian that I know. Mr Hugh Farmer, an expert on Malmesbury, can find no evidence that he included Sallust in his wide repertoire of ancient authors. Even if William of Malmesbury had not read his Sallust, however, the tradition of imputing bad motives derived from the common stock of ancient historiography, and so from Sallust, indirectly at least.

Here we slide down a slippery slope. Imputation of motive must always be hypothetical, and even more so descriptions of 'states of mind' and speeches offered without supporting evidence. We have two problems to deal with. We may disbelieve a medieval writer if

[1] See MSS Add. 35,109, fo. 32v; Harl. 3443, fo. 54v. There are other examples. The verses add that according to Orosius, Jugurtha died in prison.
[2] *Sallust* (Berkeley, 1964), pp. 56, 246, 254.
[3] *Vita Heinrici IV imperatoris: Mon. Germ. Hist. in usum schol.* ed. W. Eberhard (1899), 23, quoting *Cat.* XIX, 5.

he makes his characters speak in classical Latin, just as we discount his terminology when he calls feudal levies *legiones*, and just as we interpret his numbers to mean 'a great many'. But ought we therefore to reject the arguments and opinions which he ascribes to his characters as well? Historians of the ancient world admit the possibility or even probability that Thucydides may give a true picture of the state of opinion in Athens by means of his speeches. A medieval writer is more likely to be derivative when he borrows arguments as well as words from his models. But I think that we may run the risk of throwing out the baby with the bath-water, if we reject them out of hand.

To conclude, I shall consider two faithful imitators of Sallust: Richer, writing in the late tenth century, and William of Poitiers, writing probably 1073–4.[1] Both men had a good education in arts, Richer under Gerbert at Reims, William at Poitiers, a school which concentrated on profane literature in the mid-eleventh century.[2] Both happen to be our only primary sources for much of what they tell us; hence they have been critically scrutinised. M. R. Latouche has exposed Richer's faults in merciless fashion.[3] Where we can spy on Richer at work, writing up his notes from the sober Flodoard, we see that his method is to use them 'comme thèmes de développement littéraires', mainly by injecting quotations from Sallust. His own revision of an earlier draft steps up the dosage. He twists the known facts with the same end in view, putting the siege of Laon in the wrong season of the year, so as to make it more like the siege of Suthul (*Iug.* xxxvii–xxxviii). Character sketches, motives and speeches will be copied from Sallust, sometimes 'childishly'. His method does not change when he passes to a later period, where he has no contemporary source to guide him. Richer then writes up his own short notes on events, instead of Flodoard's, for the same purpose, that is rhetorical. It looks very black; but need we discredit his history altogether, even allowing for the fact that he never intended to write history in our sense of the word? M. Latouche accuses him also of inventing illnesses for his characters, because, having studied medicine, he enjoyed describing symptoms. If so, I admire Richer for extending the technique of fake speeches to fake diseases. But can we be so sure that he invented them all, when we have no means of

[1] See Chibnall, ed., *Ecclesiastical History*, 368.
[2] See Foreville, *Gesta Guilelmi*, pp. ix–x.
[3] 'Un imitateur de Salluste au Xe siècle: l'historien Richer', *Annales de l'Université de Grenoble*, vi (1929), 289–305.

checking his data? As to the speeches: when Adalbero, archbishop of Reims, persuades the French magnates to elect Hugh Capet in 987, his argument, stripped of its classical diction, was nicely calculated to contrast Hugh's resources and power with the poverty of his rival, Charles of Lorraine. Charles had taken service with a foreign king and had married beneath him. All present must have known why: because his family lands could no longer support him or provide for a wife of his own rank. Adalbero urges them to prefer the wealthy Duke Hugh, 'quem non solum rei publicae, sed et privatarum rerum tutorem invenietis'.[1] What else did feudal vassals demand of their king and overlord? Moreover, Richer has no peer among medieval writers, when he narrates his own adventures: his tale of his journey to Chartres from Reims in the spring floods of 991 shines out from his pages.[2] It gives an example, perhaps, of one born storyteller emulating another.

William of Poitiers, for his part, chose another rhetorical genre: he wrote to glorify and justify William the Conqueror's doings in Normandy and England. Orderic praises his *Gesta Guilelmi*, 'in qua Crispi Salustii stilum imitatus subtiliter et eloquenter enucleavit', and elsewhere as 'librum polito sermone et magni sensus profunditate praeclarum'.[3] Professor Foreville argues that William of Poitiers owed more to Caesar than to Sallust, both in his military terminology and in his style. Orderic knew what he was talking about nonetheless. Those pithy sayings at the end of chapters recall the Master: *Est nonnumquam haec ambitionis caecitas*, for example.[4] Orderic also tells us that William had been a soldier before he took orders as a clerk: he fought bravely for his earthly lord, 'so that he was all the better able to describe the battles he had seen through having himself some experience of the dire perils of war'.[5] The Conqueror's chaplain and former knight certainly had every opportunity to give us an eye-witness account of Norman warfare; he seems to have crossed to England only after the Hastings campaign; but he could have got first-hand information from those who fought with the invading army. Alas! the rhetorical tradition was too strong for him. William overlays his battle scenes with classical parallels and his Channel crossing scenes derive from the *Aeneid*. Professor Foreville's edition enables us to skim off the classical sources; what is left may be accu-

---

[1] IV, 12, ed. G. Waitz, *Mon. Germ. Hist. in usum schol.* (1877), 133.
[2] *Ibid.* IV, 50, 151.
[3] Chibnall, ed., *Ecclesiastical History*, pp. 258, 184.
[4] *Gesta Guilelmi*, p. 16.   [5] *Ibid.* pp. 258–9.

rate, but is often vague. Starved of original sources for the Norman Conquest, modern historians have a legitimate grievance against William of Poitiers for telling them so much less than he might have done. At least, however, they can see the Conqueror as his chaplain wished him to appear. Propaganda constitutes historical evidence of a sort. William was a brilliant propagandist and a compelling story-teller. He and Richer show that Sallust could have both a deviant and a healthy influence on his addicts.

Must we draw the conclusion that medieval historians are the more reliable as witnesses to historical facts the less they admire Sallust? To answer that question would involve comparison with other literary influences. Biblical allusions and parallels could lead their makers as far, if not further, astray from factual truth than their classical models. The history of historiography centres on its struggle to free itself from the sister disciplines of ethics and rhetoric. Sallust welded the three subjects firmly together to the detriment of history. Medieval writers could not possibly have distinguished between moralist, rhetor and historian when they read their Sallust. The emancipation of history has meant the exorcism of his spell. That task was left to later generations.

18

'MOMUS' AND THE NATURE OF HUMANISM

J. H. WHITFIELD

My first thought was to be flattered at your inviting me, who am by no means a classical scholar. My second was the more sober one, that since you wished to see me for four days, and hear me for ten minutes, you were more curious about my face than my voice. My third was to mistrust your intentions. For to me it seems that the strength of the classical tradition is that it remained fertile for so long, over so wide an arc; and that the weakness of classical scholars is that they limit themselves to tracing the pure element like an electric current passing through a conduit, with here a point and there a point, but always the same current waiting to be tapped. Instead of watching the family grow, you are content to guard the parent stem. Yet you do not need the reminder of the last essays of Brooks Otis to know you cannot only think of Virgil in terms of Homer; and if you consult the recent volume of Hugh Honour on Neo-classicism you will find that even this period, which seems at first sight the most palpable calk of classicism, is to be judged on its own merits, and in its own context. From which there follows a simple truth, *insanire illum qui nolit eum sese esse qui sit*,[1] and *insanire illos* who do not look at a period in its own essence, and for its own sake, hoping to isolate an alien element from its texture; as one who does not look a person in the face, but limits attention to his ears, on the pretext that they are his father's.

Now my quotation, and my title, will have told you that the author whom I offer to you is Alberti. He is deliberately chosen because I have the suspicion that those who wish to reduce humanism to an episode in the history of classical scholarship, or a rhetorical flourish of literary skills, avert their gaze from him, as from one who can be reduced to neither of those terms. You may remember that one of the *Intercoenales, Virtus dea*, became embedded in the editions of Lucian, and was reprinted there quite often in the late fifteenth, and early

---

[1] Leon Battista Alberti, *Intercenali inedite*, A cura di Eugenio Garin (Sansoni, 1965), Lib. x, 101 (*Templum*).

sixteenth, centuries.[1] It is a proof, you may say, that it was an excellent imitation? Instead, it was a proof that it was not an imitation. For if it had been a copy of some piece within the canon, then its similarities would have prevented its incorporation. It is in fact because it can be taken into the fold that we realise it must be other than the pieces already there. So *Virtus dea* takes its place alongside that other Albertian piece of lucianesque, the *Musca*.[2] Guarino Veronese had turned into Latin Lucian's *Fly*, and sent it to Alberti. 'Litteris igitur et Musca perlectis facti illariores: Utrum, inquam, vestrum est quispiam, qui pro nostro more velit, me dictitante, scribere?' And here the fact that Lucian's *Musca* prompted Alberti to write another one is proof that this must be a rival, not a copy. For which I may refer you to Grayson's introduction (22–3), which points out the essential identity of the Alberti of *Musca* with the Alberti of the serious works; and to the text, where you will find, *duce natura, comite solertia*,[3] some novel lessons from the fly; as also in the preface, that the theme of Lucian's influence is largely unexplored.

What is true of *Musca* and *Virtus dea* goes for all the *intercoenales*. Their model may be Lucian, their content is Alberti. They point forwards more than they look backwards. They offer to Ariosto the lesson of irony; and we may detect a hint for a contemporary of Ariosto in an observation from the *Defunctus*:

Hoc tibi persuadeas velim, in animis atque mentibus hominum ita hanc labem manasse, ita longe lateque diffusam esse ut nulla eorum meditatio, nullus discursus, nullum judicium, nulla institutio, nulla opinio mortalium sit ab imperio stultitiae libera.[4]

For here the *Praise of Folly*, that other shoot from Lucian, is provided for. It could be that Erasmus when he talks of Momus lately hurled to earth by the indignant gods was echoing Alberti: for is there anywhere, in Lucian, or another, such a fate for Momus? But we do not need prodding by Erasmus to see in *Momus* the most conspicuous instance of the wake of Lucian. *Habent sua fata libelli*: *The Praise of Folly* caught the tide of the printing press, and was open enough in its grain to catch the general ear. *Momus* was written in the 1440s, twice

[1] Cf. J. H. Whitfield, 'Leon Battista Alberti, Ariosto and Dosso Dossi', in *Italian Studies*, XXI (1966), 16–30.
[2] Cf. *Opuscoli inediti di Leon Battista Alberti: Musca, Vita S. Potiti*, A cura di Cecil Grayson (Firenze, Olschki, 1954).
[3] *Ibid.* p. 53.
[4] Leonis Baptistae Alberti, *Opera inedita et pauca separatim impressa*, Hieronymo Mancini curante (Florentiae, Sansoni, 1890), p. 194.

printed in 1520, had no real breakthrough at either time. Yet it is demonstrably the most sustained, the most inventive offshoot from Lucian before *Gulliver's Travels*, and it is on a scale which Lucian himself never attempted; while as its subtitle, *Momus, seu de Principe*, shows, it is also the halfway house between the *Monarchy* of Dante and that other *Prince*, of Machiavelli.

You will find in the notes to Martini's edition of *Momus* a small scatter of references to Lucian; and in the Proem the dual aspect of Alberti which we have seen for *Musca*:

Itaque sic deputo, nam si dabitur quispiam olim, qui cum legentes ad frugem vitae melioris instruat atque instituat, dictorum gravitate rerumque dignitate varia et eleganti, idemque una risu illectet, iocis delectet, voluptate detineat, quod apud latinos qui adhuc fecerint, nondum satis extitere: hunc profecto inter plebeios minime censendum esse.[1]

And with this new intention to write a comic tale with a serious meaning there comes a mechanism which perhaps Alberti teaches to the world, though he ascribes it to antiquity. It is to turn the gods into mere symbols of virtue and of vice (or rather, he says of both, but the slope of the terrain makes vice more visible than virtue, as it is more risible):

Hos igitur poetas imitati, cum de principe, qui veluti mens et animus universum reipublicae corpus moderatur, scribere adoriremur, deos suscepimus, quibus et cupidos et iracundos et voluptuosos, indoctos, leves suspitiososque, contra item graves, maturos, constantes, agentes, solertes, studiosos ac frugi notarem, quasi per ironiam...[2]

In the first work of European fiction of its kind, the first use in Italian letters, is it not,[3] of this word *irony*, whose incidence in Latin is I suspect as small as Alberti's observations on his departure from a prevailing gravity suggest? There is a little difficulty here, for if you employ that old cast, the pagan gods, at all, you are bound to do so in their framework, and to be carried over into something which you cannot wholly reduce to the semblance of the world you mean to satirise. It is a question of balance, which you cannot always guarantee to keep. But with that reservation, here is a comic creation which lasts, not the short space of a dialogue, but through four books and

---

[1] Leon Battista Alberti, *Momus o del Principe* (Bologna, Zanichelli, 1942), p. 5.
[2] *Ibid.* p. 6.
[3] For scruple's sake I had better quote Dante, *De vulgari eloquentia*, II, xiv, 59 (ed. P. V. Mengaldo, Padua, 1968): Nam cum ea que dicimus cuncta vel circa dextrum aliquid vel sinistrum canamus—ut quandoque persuasorie quandoque dissuasorie, quandoque gratulanter quandoque yronice, quandoque laudabiliter quandoque contemptive canere contingit—though this is only a remark in the air.

over two hundred pages, and in which all the wheels turn, from the beginning to the end, by their own motion. And if, in this short space, I can allow myself the luxury of repetition, I would stress again that there is nothing like it in the fifteenth century, and that for sheer inventiveness we shall have to wait for Swift to find its like.

Naturally, you will have guessed (what its editor said) that the best portrait is that of Jupiter. He is the Prince, of course, and since the intention is *ad optimum principem formandum*, and the procedure irony, he is the Prince as in the mad world he really is, and not the Prince as we would have him. In point of fact, he anticipates at many points that brilliant passage at the end of the *Art of War* where Machiavelli stigmatises the princes of his day.[1] This comes out in the sequence of his actions (and inactions), as in his predicament when, having called the assembly of the gods to announce his grand decision for creating a new world, he has nothing in his head to say. Against Dante's fond imagining in the *Monarchia*,

(Ubi ergo non est quod possit optari, impossibile est ibi cupiditatem esse: destructis enim obiectis, passiones esse non possunt. Sed Monarcha non habet quod possit optare, sua namque iurisdictio terminatur oceano solum)[2]

we have a different awareness:

beatissimum principem Jovem, cui relictum esset nihil quod amplius cuperet praeterquam ut perpetuis voluptatibus frueretur.[3]

I cannot, as you know, demonstrate the series of deft touches by which the fatuous character of Jupiter is brought out, often with a surprising neatness of psychological observation. Indeed I had better limit myself to one general passage which anticipates Machiavelli on the demerits of princes:

At Iuppiter, ut est vetus quidem et usitatus mos atque natura nonnullorum, ferme omnium principum, dum sese graves atque constantes haberi magis quam esse velint, illic illi quidem non quae ad virtutis cultum pertineant, sed quae ad vitii labem faciant, usurpant; quo fit, ut cum quid prodesse forsan cuipiam polliciti sunt, in ea re apud eos minimi pensi est fallere, et fallendo perfidiam, et perfidia levitatem atque inconstantiam suam explicare cognitamque reddere; cum vero molestos nocuosque se cuivis futuros indixerint, omni studio et perseverantia libidini obtemperasse, id demum ad sceptri dignitatem regnique maiestatem deputant; itaque in suscepta iracundia plus dandum pertinaciae, quam in debita gratia retribuendum fidei, statuunt.[4]

[1] Machiavelli, *Arte della guerra*, (Feltrinelli), VII, 518.
[2] Dante Alighieri, *Monarchia*, ed. G. Vinay (Sansoni, 1950), I, 62.
[3] *Momus*, II, 79.　　　　[4] *Ibid*. III, 110.

For there you will be able to test, from your classical resources, the gap from Lucian, the seriousness and the originality of Alberti's purpose. For the rest, and to keep within Alberti's purpose, which is to promote festivity and laughter, I had best refer you to that comic scene in which the courtiers (the other gods) attempt in the assembly in a few ill-chosen words to discuss the project of a brave new world. Of which the first will do for my excuse:

Tandem, rogatus, primam dixit sententiam Saturnus, voce ita supressa, verbis ita raris gestuque ita defesso, ut potius conatum loqui quam locutum diceres.[1]

[1] *Ibid.* III, 125.

19

TONI ED ECHI OVIDIANI NELLA POESIA DI GIANO PANNONIO

T. KARDOS

La sopravvivenza della letteratura antica è infinitamente ricca, se ne distinguono però nettamente due tipi d'irradiazione: l'influsso dei motivi (sia testualmente identici, sia trasformati nella concezione e nell'espressione) e l'influsso di esempi personali. Nel secondo caso viene ispirato alla creazione un poeta di una epoca posteriore da una personalità della letteratura antica in senso largo con tutti i suoi caratteri genuini. Il nostro tema però ci presenta un intreccio particolare dei due tipi d'influsso letterario, tanto per un'affinità profonda di situazioni personali, quanto per quella dei motivi poetici e questo influsso complesso induce Giano Pannonio, il maggior poeta dell'umanesimo ungherese a scrivere le sue elegie. Egli, formatosi in Italia per il lunghissimo periodo di undici anni, e tornato nella patria nel 1458 per coprire alte cariche nella cancelleria di Mattia Corvino e nella gerarchia ecclesiastica, subì una crisi profonda, ma sentì fortemente anche la vocazione di trasportare le Muse nella sua patria.[1] Questo secondo periodo della sua vita, il quale finì con la sua morte prematura nel 1472, costituisce il soggetto della nostra attuale analisi.[2]

Giano Pannonio, educato e cresciuto nell'ambiente culturale della scuola di Guarino da Verona, in una delle città più splendide dell'Italia rinascimentale, a Ferrara, durante il regno di Lionello d'Este, un ex-allievo del maestro, dovette tornare nella patria ricca sì, potente sì sotto il dominio di un monarca pure rinascimentale, cioè

---

[1] Per questo problema e per la vita di Giano Pannonio vedi la monografia di József Huszti: *Janus Pannonius* (Pécs, 1931), pp. 1–447, e specialmente pp. 200, 209, 286–96.

[2] Ad un ispirazione ovidiana di Giano Pannonio richiamò l'attenzione lo stesso Huszti, però con un accento negativo definiendola *morbosa*, quale prima manifestazione di una moda *occidentale*, pp. 203–4; egli riconosce però una certa sincerità dell'influsso ovidiano, per es. nel motivo della malattia cf. p. 199; ho risposto alla concezione di József Huszti in tono polemico nel mio saggio, *Janus Pannonius bukása* (*La tragedia di Giano Pannonio*) (Pannonia, 1935), p. 131; ho ribadito brevemente le mie tesi dopo trentadue anni nel saggio 'Petrarca e la formazione dell'umanesimo ungherese' (*Italia ed Ungheria. Dieci secoli di rapporti letterari* (Budapest, 1967), pp. 82–3; ma non ho analizzato finora dettagliatamente la dialettica di questo nesso ricco e profondo.

di Mattia Corvino, eppure per la letteratura in quel periodo ancora non abbastanza favorevole. Mattia Corvino promosse gli studi di ogni sorta, ed anch'egli ebbe una educazione umanistica sotto il segno di Pier Paolo Vergerio e del suo amico ungherese, János Vitéz. Ma non esisteva ancora un pubblico sensibile eccetto il re e pochi ecclesiastici di altissimo rango. Il monarca aveva già cominciato ad organizzare una biblioteca che più tardi diventò famosa, cioè la Biblioteca Corviniana, egli gettò le basi di una corte colta che poteva interessarsi per la letteratura, ma la quale si sviluppava solo passo a passo.[1]

Ed appunto l'applauso e la partecipazione di un pubblico sensibile alla creazione poetica, la vita letteraria palpitante furono i fattori che mancarono a Giano Pannonio. Poi, anche la sua salute era fragile, anzi da vari sintomi possiamo dedurre il fatto che egli avesse avuto la tisi, la quale era sopportabile sotto il clima mite dell'Italia, ma la quale diventava fatale nel clima più nordico dell'Ungheria e soprattutto fra le condizioni di vita di un paese feudale dove c'era continuamente la guerra, soprattutto quella contro il turco. Giano Pannonio non era avvezzato alle armi, a stare sul cavallo, a fare lunghi viaggi di giorno e di notte, a vivere sotto tende, a muoversi sotto una armatura pesante che era per lui più che pericoloso.

Così si formò nella sua mente un senso di vita elegiaco, tragico, il quale trovo il suo modello nella *Tristia* e nelle *Epistolae de Ponto* di P. Ovidio Nasone. Il poeta romano relegato dall'imperatore Augusto a Tomi, fornì l'esempio a Giano Pannonio perché questo possa esprimere i suoi dolori veramente esistenti. Giano Pannonio sentì nello stesso tempo il proprio carattere intimamente connesso con quello del poeta del secolo d'oro romano. Anche Ovidio aveva il complesso fisico debole, anch'egli non era abituato alle armi ed aveva vissuto precedentemente in un ambiente splendido, ad alto livello intellettuale, fra le condizioni della Roma augustea. Ovidio dovette lasciare quest'ambiente tanto incitativo per la creazione letteraria e andare fino ai confini del mondo conosciuto sotto un clima inospitale, freddo, in una provincia dove la vita era incerta e si trovava in continuo pericolo per la vicinanza del *barbaricum*. La sorte di Giano Pannonio, tenendo conto della sua salute precaria e del pericolo turco, poteva far intuire certe analogie. Ovidio accentuò

---

[1] Cf. i miei saggi, *La Renaissance en Hongrie*, Tirage à part de la Nouvelle Revue de Hongie (Budapest, 1939); 'Mattia Corvino, re umanista', *Rinascita* (1940), anno III, pp. 803–41 e (1941), anno IV, pp. 69–83.

nelle sue elegie ed epistole tomitane l'influsso dell'ambiente sfavorevole per la creazione, osservò la mancanza d'ispirazione, l'inaridirsi
dell'estro poetico ed i difetti dello stile. Tutto questo non era solo un
ruolo assunto, ma naturalmente conteneva certi germi della verità.
Ovidio dovette sopportare anche malattie, ma soprattutto depressioni
psichiche. Per il poeta romano l'unico filo che lo legava ancora alla
vita propriamente umana e letteraria, fu la corrispondenza con gli
amici. Tutti questi motivi: sia quelli dell'inaridirsi e del deteriora-
mento che quelli della malattia, della depressione e quello del-
l'amicizia, ritornano in Giano Pannonio.

E se Ovidio si mostra affezionato alla sua famiglia, alla moglie,
anche il poeta-vescovo umanista, Giano Pannonio scopre la famiglia
quale tema poetico: la tenera sorella e soprattuto la madre buona.
E se lo influisce potentemente, specie in questo secondo periodo, il
Petrarca delle *Epistole metriche* nella concezione della missione poetica
e nella tematica in generale del periodo ungherese, questi motivi
petrarcheschi s'intrecciano nella maggioranza dei casi con la lirica
ovidiana dello *Metamorfosi* e dell'attività tomitana del poeta.

Naturalmente si trovano differenze fondamentali nelle due sorti
umane. Giano Pannonio dovette lasciare l'Italia non per punizione.
Egli fu mandato in Italia appunto per promuovere il progresso della
sua patria, per aiutare — dopo il suo ritorno — l'amministrazione
statale, e per il culto della letteratura. La sua vita nella patria
assolutamente non era una relegazione: egli poteva vivere nella corte
fastosa, o nel suo palazzo vescovile di Pécs. L'Ungheria era un paese
viticolo, ricchissimo di frumenti, di boschi, di fiumi ricchissimi di vari
generi di pesce. C'era il sole estivo, c'era la primavera che traboccava,
c'erano gli autunni meravigliosi. L'Ungheria aveva ereditato i resti
della Pannonia romana: le rovine, le tradizioni in iscritto e le leg-
gende orali, ella possedeva una cultura cristiana di mezzo millennio.
Tutti questi fattori raddolcivano la situazione di Giano Pannonio,
sebbene qualche volta avesse sentito la desolazione. È vero che
l'urbanità del suo paese nativo abbia subito grandi ritardi, che la
struttura e la civilizzazione della società siano stati pienamente
feudali, che la borghesia sia stata ancora uno strato esiguo, che la
vita letteraria — di cui abbiamo già parlato — non si sia ancora
sviluppata. Però la società si trovava in un movimento chiaramente
visibile, ed anche Giano Pannonio doveva osservare le tendenze
progressive espresse appunto dal suo zio materno, il cancelliere János
Vitéz e dal re stesso.

Tutte queste forze motrici contradditorie lo aiutarono a creare una poesia affascinante e del tutto personale a cui gli scrittori dell'antichità e soprattutto Marziale ed Ovidio avevano dato esempi da seguire, ma l'estro poetico di Giano Pannonio fu così forte ed originale che non 'scimmiottava' mai i suoi modelli, ma li seguiva in modo proprio. Tanto il Petrarca, quanto i poeti antichi non lo legarono, al contrario, misero in moto la sua immaginazione poetica, cioè lo liberarono. E appunto così poteva egli diventare il poeta più moderno dei primi secoli della storia di un intero popolo, perciò poteva egli sorpassare tutta la letteratura posteriore e si riconnetteva propriamente con l'illuminismo ungherese e con la letteratura del Risorgimento. I poeti dei secoli successivi, quelli dei s. XVI e XVII — quali Bálint Balassi e Miklós Zrinyi — erano meno moderni di lui. Essi poetarono in lingua volgare e perciò dovevano farsi strada con grande sforzo anche per esprimersi. Giano Pannonio invece aveva ereditato dall'antichità una lingua colta, perfetta, pensieri e sentimenti quasi moderni.

Quello che più ci impressione nella sua correlazione con Ovidio è la trasformazione dei motivi prestati secondo le esigenze della società dell'Ungheria rinascimentale e secondo i gravi problemi personali del poeta moderno. Certi motivi ovidiani che si diffondono largamente su tutta la lirica elegiaca del periodo tomitano, come per esempio quello dell'influsso funesto dell'ambiente sfavorevole sullo stile delle poesie,[1] trovano appena un'eco nella lirica di Giano Pannonio. Egli scrive solo un epigramma di tale contenuto, ed è la poesia mandata in Italia al suo amico intimo, Galeotto Marzio de Narni, umanista e poeta mediocre, filosofo degno di attenzione, astronomo eccellente, nella quale egli riassume quasi tutta la teoria ovidiana sull'influsso dell'ambiente:

Haec tibi Pannonicis, epigrammata mittit, ab oris,
    inter Hyperboreas, maximus Ister aquas,
nec te mirari nimium, Galeotte, decebit,
    esse videbuntur vix mea, si qua tibi.

Scilicet ingenio multum locus addit et aufert,
    inter et est sub quo sidere carmen eat.
In Latiis, scripsi fortasse Latinius, oris,
    at nunc barbarico, barbara, in orbe crepo.

Hic Maro ponatur, fiet lyra rauca Maronis,
    huc Cicero veniat, mutus erit Cicero.

[1] Vedi *Tristia* I. I. 3, 9–10, 12; I. 10. 20–44; III. I. 1–20, 17–18; III. 14. 45–52; V. 7. 55–64; *Epistolae de Ponto*, I.6. 3–12.

Tu tamen haec tali poteris deducere lima,
vel critici ut medio nata Helicone putent.

'Ad Galeottum Narniensem', *Epigr.* i. 35[1]

Quest'epigramma introdusse senza dubbio una raccolta di poesie mandata da Giano Pannonio al suo amico, ed ebbe la funzione di caraterizzare tutta la produzione che seguiva. Ma il suo tono non è affatto tragico ed il contenuto è molto alleggerito dall'invito cortese rivolto al suo amico che questi faccia una lima definitiva dello stile nelle poesie mandate. Il momento più significativo può essere afferrato senza dubbio nell'identità della 'barbarie' dell'ambiente e in quella dello stile, come Ovidio si esprimette tante volte e in modo più intenso forse in queste righe:

Si qua videbuntur casu non dicta latine,
in qua scribebat, barbara terra fuit.

Tristia, iii. i. 17–18

L'autodifesa ovidiana si estende all'intero tono della produzione poetica di questo suo periodo di vita (e *mutatis mutandis* è valevole anche per la lirica del secondo periodo di Giano Pannonio) formulata da Ovidio nell'espressione commovente di una della *Epistole Pontine*:

Laeta fere laetus cecini, cano tristia tristis:
conveniens operi tempus utrumque suo est.
Quid nisi de vitio scribam regionis amarae?

Epistolae de Ponto, iii. 9. 35–7

Ma questo tono ovidiano, la tristezza, non viene accentuato mai da Giano Pannonio. Ed anche le descrizioni ovidiane delle regioni desolate di Ponto mancano nel poeta ungherese, perché anche egli è consapevole che nelle sue poesie non si tratti di un paese desolato, anzi al contrario: di un paese fertile e di un popolo umano, il quale soffre delle sciagure naturali, delle irruzioni dei Turchi e delle condizioni sociali del tutto feudali. Nello stesso tempo la missione del poeta nuovò, cioè il trasportare le Muse alle rive del Danubio, esclude un contegno ironico rispetto al proprio stile poetico che in verità era tutt'altro che barbaro. La mancanza dell'ispirazione poetica, un certo inaridirsi vengono anche da lui osservati e questo fenomeno corrispondeva veramente ai fatti. I versi ironici di Ovidio contro sé

[1] Tutte le citazioni derivano dall'edizione Jani Pannonii, *Poemata*, pars i, (Traiecti ad Rhenum, 1784).

stesso come se nel suo latino fossero immischiate parole getiche, anzi scrivesse poesia nella loro lingua, poi la gioia rassegnata ed un po' amara per la riconoscenza dei cittadini greci di Tomi, i quali gli avevano offerto la corona poetica,[1] mancarono completamente nelle poesie di Giano Pannonio, eccetto l'epigramma sopraccitato. Al contrario egli e orgoglioso di poter mandare ormai poesie — naturalmente belle, limate — non dall'Italia ad un amico in Pannonia, ma dalla provincia, dalla Pannonia, all'amico italiano.

> Quod legerent omnes, quondam dabat Itala tellus,
> nunc e Pannonia carmina missa legit.
> Magna quidem nobis haec gloria; sed tibi maior,
> nobilis ingenio patria facta meo.

'Laus Pannoniae', *Epigrammatum*, I. 61

La coscienza gioiosa del poeta di Mattia Corvino corrisponde ad un atto culturale significativo nella storia dell'umanesimo europeo. Quest'atto creativo è identico con quello del Petrarca espresso nell'*Africa* ed altrove: cioè il far trasmigrare le Muse nella patria del poeta. Tutti e due i poeti, il Petrarca e Giano Pannonio adoperano l'invenzione ovidiana di formulare un'epigrafe monumentale in un momento solenne o tragico per esprimere il loro merito poetico. Il tipo ovidiano suona così:

> Hic ego qui iaceo tenerorum lusor amorum
> ingenio perii Naso poeta meo.
> At tibi, qui transis, ne sit grave, quisquis amasti,
> dicere: Nasonis molliter ossa cubent.
> Hoc satis in titulo est: etenim maiora libelli
> et diuturna magis sunt monimenta mei.

Tristia, III. 3. 73–8

Il Petrarca formula il suo merito nei versi dell'*Africa* quale vaticinio in bocca di Omero, che parla del futuro poeta toscano:

> Ille diu profugas revocabit carmine Musas
> tempus in extremum, veteresque Elicone Sorores
> restituet vario quamvis agitante tumultu;
> Francisco cui nomen erit...

Africa, IX. 229–32

Giano Pannonio torna alla formulazione ovidiana di scrivere un epitaffio, il contenuto però è una variante del merito del Petrarca. E se Petrarca nelle *Epistole Metriche* per sfondo naturale del suo merito

---

[1] Vedi *Epistolae de Ponto*, I.6. 63–6; IV.13. 18–22; IV.14. 48–62.

letterario di richiamare le Muse esiliate crea la fonte, il prato erboso e l'ombra del giardino della sua casa, Giano Pannonio si colloca nella natura vergine che crede altrettanto dolce:

> At vos defuncto tumulum componite, amici,
>   roscida qua multo gramine vernat humus,
> frondosos inter saltus et amoena virentis
>   prata soli, et Dryadum concelebrata choris.
> Assidue Zephyri spirent ubi mitibus auris,
>   semper ubi argutae, suave querantur, aves.

De se aegrotante in castris, *Elegiarum*, I. 9, 109–14

La gioia della natura è vissuta da Giano Pannonio forse ancora più profondamente che il sentimento della famiglia, o quello del dolore fisico e psichico. Appunto in questo momento tragico egli sente più che mai forte l'attrattiva della vita e della natura quali fenomeni non separabili uno dall'altro:

> ...ventis irrita verba damus.
> Agnosco vicina meae confinia vitae,
>   spiritus et numero deficiente fugit.
> O caelum! o colles! et amicti gramine campi!
>   O vitrei fontes, o virides silvae!
> Ergo ego vos dulci pariter cum luce relinquam,
>   nec reliquum de me iam, nisi nomen erit?

Ivi, 94–100

Questa forma della natura è tanto lontana dal rigido Tomi, dal mare freddo e terribile di Ovidio, questa natura è completamente antropomorfa. E l'epitaffio che segue ci colpisce nella sua brevità:

> Hinc situs est Ianus, patrium qui primus ad Histrum
>   duxit laurigeras ex Helicone deas.

Ivi, 117–18

La soluzione solenne è positiva, malgrado che nei versi susseguenti ed ultimi ritorni il motivo del 'Livor' ovidiano:

> Hanc saltem titulum, Livor, permitte sepulto,
>   Invidiae non est in monumenta locus.

Ivi, 118–19

Altri motivi ovidiani i quali non ebbero nessun risalto nelle elegie ed epistole pontine, o ebbero una intonazione, un accento tutto differenti, si estendono largamente, e si approfondiscono nella poesia di Giano Pannonio, come per esempio il pianto per le sue condizioni fisiche e psichiche, o la paura per una possibile catastrofe dell'universo, in occasione dello straripamento dei fiumi che sostituisce le descrizioni di Ovidio, nelle quali questo ritrae il clima inospitale, quasi tartareo delle regioni del Ponto.[1]

In questa elegia — forse la più grandiosa tra tutte le poesie lirico-epiche di Giano Pannonio — il tono poetico è sommamente caratteristico sia per il senso di vita del rinascimento che per i miti fondamentali dei secoli XIV–XVI. Il punto di partenza anche questa volta è doppio: da una parte una epistola metrica del Petrarca (I, 10), indirizzata a Giovanni Colonna che riproduce un aquazzone terribile, dall'altra parte naturalmente la descrizione famosissima di Ovidio sul diluvio. Ma anche l'altro motivo delle *Metamorfosi* si aggiunge a questa, cioè il mito di Deucalione e Pyrrha, i quali restituiscono il genere umano dopo il diluvo (I. vv. 262–415). Il Petrarca finisce la sua epistola con il presentimento del diluvio, chiede soltanto che l'alloro di Apolline lo metta in salvo della catastrofe. Giano Pannonio oltrepassa questo punto morto ed arriva alla domanda più che rettorica: se sia vera la dottrina dei filosofi antichi sulla catastrofi universali secondo la quale avessero il fuoco e l'acqua annientato tante volte il mondo. Ma il mondo si è rifatto tante volte. Forse i mondi nuovi sapevano niente dei mondi precedenti, eppure la vita rinacque come la fenice:

> Ergo vetus veterum verax est dogma sophorum;
> saepe homines igni saepe ferire salo;
> deleri et toties, toties deleta rinasci,
> omnia Phoebeae scilicet instar avis;
> quae se morte parit, vitam cui funera reddunt,
> natalem cinere, ultima principium.

'De inundatione', *Eleg*. I. 13. 151–6

Il simbolo mitico del Rinascimento interpretato già dal Petrarca sia per la rinascita dell'antichità che per quella della vita individuale, ottiene nella fantasia di Giano Pannonio il significato del simbolo della rinascita dei mondi. E siccome lui è un vescovo egli, Deucalione nuovo, presenta quale Pyrrha nuova sua sorella per poter rinnovare tutto il genere umano:

> Surge, age, cara soror, superantem nubila Olympum,
> scandamus, celeri, dum licet, ambo fuga.
> Vel Parnasiacae, potius fastigia, Cirrhae,

---

[1] Per le sofferenze psichiche di Ovidio vedi *Tristia*, 1.4. 53, 56, 71–4; III.8. 27–34; IV.6. 41–3; *Epistolae de Ponto*, 1.11. 5–28; le regioni e il clima terribili vedi, *Tristia*, 1.1. 42; 1.2. 20–32; 1.7. 1–8; 1.10. 37–44; III.2. 1–20 *et passim*.

altior est lymphis omnibus ille locus.
Hic ego post tergum lapides, magnae ossa parentis
jactabo exstinctos et reparabo viros.
At tu femineam renovabis femina turbam
saxa pari mittens, sed leviora manu.
Sic ego Deucalion, sic tu Pyrrha altera fies,
sic erimus mundi semina prima, novi.

Ivi, 197–206

Così l'elegia della distruzione totale, o parziale (perché può essere che solo il popolo ungherese soffra per tutta l'umanità) diventa un inno di auto-esaltazione — degno di un neoplatonista[1] come egli era — anzi di esaltazione familiare. Se Ovidio, autore delle *Metamorfosi*, gli suggeriva potentemente la trasformazione continua del mondo ed una concezione dialettica della natura e degli esseri vivi, Giano Pannonio elaborava, trasformava questo pensiero in un mito prettamente rinascimentale, entro le cui cornici trovavano posto l'idea del messianismo e la somma esaltazione della personalità umana.

Quanto la bellezza della natura (in Ovidio solo sogno anelato a Tomi, ma presente nella Pannonia di Giano Pannonio) tanto la pace è un motivo forte ed accarezzato per il poeta umanista. In questo caso Ovidio protesta in modo più evidente, contro la guerra, la quale dura continuamente, e si manifesta in frecce avvelenate, in assalti inaspettati e rende impossibile lasciare le mura della città. Anche Giano Pannonio presenta la guerra negativamente, almeno nella maggioranza dei casi. La sua protesta spesso non viene a galla in modo immediato: in quanto egli si dichiara inetto alla guerra. Risponde con ironia sprezzante ai signori feudali dalla tempra marziale, i quali lo esortano a guerreggiare, dicendo che il poeta deve conservarsi per poter cantare l'eroismo — e naturalmente anche la morte eroica — di certi grandi signori. Le malattie, la febbre, la desolazione i quali lo raggiungono sotto la tenda di campo, documentano il suo aborrimento da ogni forma di guerra. Egli odia i Turchi, distruttori della vita e della civilizzazione cristiane e naturalmente si congratula con Mattia Corvino, se gli riesce una spedizione contro il nemico mortale. Pero è convinto che il popolo ungherese sia stanco delle guerre e non vuole altro che lui: pace, pace, pace.

Ecco, come un motivo ovidiano ed anche petrarchesco si tras-

---

[1] Cf. József Huszti: 'Platonista törekvések Mátyás király udvarában', *Minerva könyvtár*, 1 (Budapest, 1925); in italiano, ' Tendenze platonizzanti nella corte di Mattia Corvino', *Giornale Critico della Filosofia Italiana* (1930).

forma. Egli sente il problema in modo non molto differente da quello del poeta dell'*Italia mia*... e scrittore di tante lettere esasperate. Però la questione viene espressa in modo più categorico e occupa un posto centrale nella sua poesia dell'epoca ungherese:

> Gradive, quinti clare dominator poli,
> spargens coruscas luce sanguinea jubas,
> Junone magna genite, Saturni nepos;
> tutela coeli; summe Titanum timor;
> gaudens tropaeis; pacis ac belli arbiter;
> decorator hominum; consecrator numinum;
> Gradive, ferro tecte semper fulgido,
> vastator agrum, dissipator urbium,
> vacuator orbis; Tartari impletor trucis,
> potor cruorum; devorator corporum;
> lues virorum; mulierum execratio;
> ditator inopum; pauperator divitum;
> osor quietis; genitor obscaenae famis;
> auctor pavorum; concitor formidinum;
> jam parce fessis, quaeso, Pannonis, pater.

'Ad Martem precatio pro pace', *Epigr.* I. 8

Il motivo che oltrepassa grandemente gli esempi ovidiani è quello della salute precaria. Ovidio fu di complessione debole, ma le dure condizioni di vita del suo esilio lo avevano temprato, almeno secondo quanto egli affermava. Eppure i componenti psichici: la disperazione, l'assoggettamento, l'insuccesso delle sue suppliche lo abbattevano, gli tolsero la voglia della vita, il sapore dei cibi, il sonno, e lo popolarono di scene, di figure terribili, le quali avevano trasportavano i timori del giorno anche nella notte.[1]

La malattia di Giano Pannonio, come si restituisce dalle sue descrizioni — egli dedica cinque elegie altema — era la tisi con complicazioni dolorose, con insonnie, dolori, e così via. A questi dolori si aggiungevano i malumori: gli intrighi della corte, le gelosie, le ambizioni d'altrui, le calunnie, la mancanza di un pubblico colto che l'applaudisse. Insomma i mali fisici sfociarono in gravi disturbi psichici. Se Ovidio invidiò Niobe per esser diventata sasso, o le vittime di Medusa per non sentire più nessuna cosa, se egli sentì il proprio dolore simile a quello di Prometeo, perché anche lui rinasceva tante volte per sentire di nuovo il dolore, Giano Pannonio arrivò al desiderio della morte assoluta, di tornare definitivamente alla sua stella — secondo la teoria neoplatonica — or se soggetto ad una metempsi-

---

[1] V. *Epistolae de Ponto*, I. 2. 44–6.

cosi, egli vorrebbe diventare non più uomo, né bello, né forte, ma animale del bosco, o del mare, per non sentire più dolore.

> Quod si te cogent immitia fata reverti,
>   quidlibet esto magis, quam miserandus homo.
> Tu vel apis cultos, lege dulcia, mella, per hortos,
>   vel leve flumineus concine carmen olor.
> Vel silvis pelagove late; memor omnibus horis,
>   humana e duris corpora nata petris.

'Ad animam suam' *Eleg.* I. XII, 39–77

Lasciato solo dalla madre morta nel 1463, egli fra malattie continue, esasperato dagli intrighi di corte, trova l'unica consolazione nella creazione artistica. Egli si ritira a Pécs, dove è vescovo e vive una vita di studi in una solitudine relativa. C'erano a Pécs i canonici colti della Cattedrale e ci vigeva parzialmente anche l'Università, forse in forma di una 'scola maior'. L'ambiente di Ferrara naturalmente mancava, ma neanche in Italia esisteva un pubblico simile a quello della gioventù della scuola di Guarino da Verona. C'era nel contegno di Giano Pannonio senza dubbio un lieve tono di affettazione. Eppure l'atmosfera veramente non era propizia ad una creazione intensa. É naturale dunque che si rivolga con un epigramma ironico ed orgoglioso al suo vicario nelle cose economiche, ad un certo Vito Huendler:

> Lector et auditor cum desit, Vite, requiris
>   cur scribam: Musis et mihi, Vite, cano!

'In Vitum.' *Epigr.* I. 312

Nei *Tristia* si esprime Ovidio con frasi molto simili:

> Sed neque cui recitem quisquam est mea carmina, nec qui
>   auribus accipiat verba latina suis.
> Ipse mihi (quid enim faciam?) scribo legoque,
>   tutaque iudicio littera nostra suo est.

Trist. IV. 1, 88–92

Agli inizi della stessa elegia Ovidio ribadisce anche la sua comunione con l'ispirazione, rappresentata dalla Musa che lo esorta a scrivere e nello stesso tempo sostiene anche la parte del suo pubblico:

> Me quoque Musa levat Ponti loca iussa petentem.
> Sola comes nostrae perstitit illa fugae.

Trist. IV. 1, 19–20

L'Orfeo romano e l'Orfeo umanista in Ungheria sentono profondamente la maestà della creazione *in extremis*, nella solitudine.

C'è anche un momento rinascimentale nell'attitudine di Giano Pannonio. Vi si può osservare un certo influsso di un'epistola metrica del Petrarca, almeno nel tono dell'epigramma sopraccitato. Il

Petrarca si rovolge sdegnato contro un suo critico insensibile alla poesia (*Ad Zoilum. Epistole metriche*, II. 18). Ma il tenore dell'epistola è un'antipatia personale concepita nel poeta contro Zoilo per la sua mancanza di sensibilità: *Quid tibi cum musis?* domanda il Petrarca.

Giano Pannonio però, il cui punto di partenza è forse l'epistola petrarchesca, si avvicina sempre più ad Ovidio. Il suo epigramma non tanto è acuito contro la persona di Vito Huendler, ma molto più è concentrato sulla maestà della creazione in solitudine. Questa è la ragione della sua vita malata ed amara. Egli scrive per la corte, per gli amici presenti e lontani e per la posterità quale antesignano ed iniziatore di un'età nuova.

Questa sua coscienza eroica e tragica coincide con la fine tragica della sua vita. Egli, propugnatore di un potere centralizzato e di una burocrazia statale moderna e vero benefattore della sua città quale vescovo-signore, diventa poco a poco sempre più avverso a Mattia Corvino principe rinascimentale. Giano Pannonio è contro ogni tipo di guerra: solo quella di liberazione contro il Turco ottiene perdono nella sua mente. Il re invece è continuamente occupato di guerre conquistatrici verso occidente. Giano Pannonio impiega le sue rendite in favore della collettività e della cultura e le taglie del re con le quali raccoglie le spese delle sue guerre e delle sue costruzioni lo esasperano. Così diventa Giano Pannonio, insieme con il suo zio János Vitéz, capo della congiura del 1471 contro Mattia Corvino. Il re vince e lui, dopo una difesa accanita, fugge con i suoi tesori a Venezia. Ma, abbattuto dalla febbre e dalle calamità, muore giovanissimo il 27 marzo 1472 nel castello di Medve in Croazia. La sua salma viene nascostamente trasportata a Pécs e sepolta in una casa attigua al duomo. Qualche anno dopo il re, venuto a Pécs, viene a sapere la sorte della salma e fra lagrime ordina le esequie solenni del grande amico di altri tempi.

Il nesso letterario fra Ovidio e Giano Pannonio e un esempio bellissimo dell'influsso letterario in senso positivo, quando cioè una personalità della letteratura antica e la sua poesia, in base ad un'affinità di situazione e di natura, liberano le forze creative di un genio creatore di un'altra epoca. In questi casi le differenze — entro la cornice delle somiglianze — hanno un ruolo straordinario. Il restringersi di certi motivi, la mancanza di altri momenti e il ritorno rafforzato, intensissimo di altri motivi, seguono precisamente le forze motrici cambiate di una società nuova e di esigenze nuove, e di gioie e dolori umani, da un certo punto di vista vecchi, ma del tutto nuovi dal punto di vista della formulazione e degli accenti.

PART V

THE INFLUENCE OF
CLASSICAL IDEAS

20

LATER PLATONISM AND
ITS INFLUENCE

A. H. ARMSTRONG

In considering what are the topics which will most repay investigation in the field of the influence of later Platonism, the first thing required is a clear and well-informed understanding of what precisely we are looking for. Later Platonism had a long and complex history. Some 600 years separate Antiochus of Ascalon, who revived dogmatic teaching in the Academy in the age of Cicero, from Olympiodorus, the last pagan to hold the chair of philosophy at Alexandria, who was still teaching in A.D. 565; and in those six centuries Platonism took many and diverse forms, a number of which had considerable direct and indirect influence on medieval and renaissance thought. If we are to arrive at any sort of precision in our assessment of these influences we must not only make a distinction between the pre-Plotinian Platonism which we loosely describe as 'Middle' Platonism and the Neoplatonism of Plotinus and his successors. We must pay some attention to the differences between the various pre-Plotinian Platonists and also take into account the Neopythagoreans, a closely related but distinct group linked to the Platonists by intercrossing influences and, still more important, we must discriminate between the different kinds of Neoplatonism. Plotinus stands very much alone: none of his successors (who did not regard him with overwhelming respect) equals his power of thought and expression or reproduces his particular philosophical, ethical and religious quality. As a result of recent scholarly work Porphyry is emerging more and more clearly as a distinct philosophical personality, with his own kind of near-monistic, ultra-spiritualist Neoplatonism. The Neoplatonism of Iamblichus and his successors is something different again, though it owes a good deal in some ways to Porphyry's developments and attempted clarifications of the thought of Plotinus. The extremely rigid and elaborate system of thought developed by these latest pagan Platonists has often been too hastily dismissed and too harshly judged. An important reason for this is that our main sources for serious later

Neoplatonic philosophy are, to put it mildly, not very readable. Proclus and Damascius take a good deal of getting through and, till recently, there has been little help available for getting through them. There have been no good critical texts of a number of major works, and very little in the way of scholarly translation or commentary, apart from Dodds's great edition of the *Elements of Theology* of Proclus. But good critical editions, translations, commentaries and scholarly studies are now multiplying—the contribution of French scholars is very notable in this field—and it is becoming much easier for the determined reader to be well acquainted with later Neoplatonism. One sharp distinction which used to be generally accepted seems to be fading, the distinction between Athenian and Alexandrian Neoplatonism. In spite of the Alexandrian preoccupation with Aristotelian commentary and less hostile attitude to Christianity, there seems no sufficient reason for supposing that the philosophical beliefs of the Alexandrian Neoplatonists of the fifth and sixth centuries were different from those of their Athenian brethren.

The improved precision of our knowledge of post-Plotinian Neoplatonism should help us to determine more accurately what particular kind of Neoplatonic influence is at work in places where it is suspected or asserted in medieval or renaissance thought. A good deal of the work which needs to be done in the field of later Platonic influences consists of going over the evidence or alleged evidence in the light of our greatly increased understanding of later Platonism. A good beginning has been made in the field of patristic studies, but much careful consideration of the allegedly Platonic influences on the thought of later periods needs to be done. There seems to be room in particular for a good deal of further study of Platonic elements in Byzantine thought, especially the unconscious or unacknowledged ones. In the West the small number of available Latin translations, of course, makes questions of precise direct influences (especially of Proclus) on later medieval thought much easier to determine.

But the main influences of later Platonism on medieval thought were not of course, either in East or West, the result of direct reading of later Platonists but came through Christian, Muslim and Jewish thinkers influenced by various kinds of Platonism. In considering this indirect influence it is important, not only to use our fuller knowledge to discriminate between the different types of Platonism themselves, and to take into account the varied dogmatic preoccupations of the Christians, Muslims and Jews through whom the influences were transmitted, but to remember that thinkers and writers who could exert a widespread influence had strongly marked and distinctive mental characteristics of their own. It is important to distinguish, in so far as this is possible, the kinds of influence exerted by Plotinus and Porphyry respectively on Augustine; and it is important to remember that Augustine was a Christian and consciously, very firmly adapted his Platonism to his Christianity, even if, unconsciously, he sometimes adapted his Christianity to his Platonism. But it is also important to remember that he had a peculiar and distinctive mind of his own and that what he transmitted to future generations was not just 'Christian Platonism' but Augustinian Christian Platonism, something very different from, for instance, the Christian Platonism of Boethius or the author of the Dionysian writings. This is an obvious, and generally recognised example of a transmitter personally remodelling what he transmits. But the principle needs to be continually borne in mind, and individual peculiarities attended to even when dealing with members of small closely related groups. Among the Cappadocians (in whom we can see the persisting influence of pre-Plotinian Platonism which is important in Greek patristic thought) the Christian Platonism of Basil is different from that of his brother Gregory of Nyssa. This discrimination of the peculiarities of individual thinkers becomes particularly important when Platonic influences transmitted through Augustine, the Cappadocians, Dionysius and Maximus, Boethius and others begin to intercross and interact in the West, from the Carolingian period onwards, to produce the very complex phenomenon of medieval Platonism.

So finally here are some topics where I think that recent advances in Neoplatonic and patristic studies might help to elucidate questions about Platonic influences in medieval and renaissance thought. There are certainly many more, and I have reluctantly to leave out of account the immensely important fields of Neoplatonic influence on Muslim and Jewish thinkers and the transmission of Neoplatonic ideas through them, on which I am quite unqualified to speak.

We need, I think, a very precise study of the idea of hierarchy, which will discriminate more carefully than has often been done between different kinds of hierarchical thinking: the simple, and very widely influential, transposition of the court order of absolute monarchy to heaven or the cosmos, with God as the celestial Great King or Emperor and his descending ranks of subordinates: the various kinds of Neoplatonic hierarchical thinking, which are different from this, though they sometimes use its language, and also from each other (Plotinus does not think hierarchically in the same way that Proclus does): and the cosmic hierarchy, in which the elements and parts of the cosmos are arranged in order of excellence.

Some studies are perhaps needed which would determine more precisely than has hitherto been done how much influence, conscious, and still more important, unconscious, was exercised on theological speculation from the patristic period to the seventeenth century by the basic Neoplatonic conviction that theology is essentially a philosophical activity: that is to say, however elaborate, and indeed fantastic, a theology may be, however much it claims to be in accordance with tradition, and however much it is presented as the correct interpretation of a particular revelation, it must be able in the last resort to justify itself rationally: one holds, e.g. a particular kind of belief about the Trinity because it is reasonable to think about God in this way rather than another.[1] I am inclined to think that this persistence of a kind of rationalism within, and not only in opposition to, dogmatic theology is very largely due to Neoplatonic influence. It is a factor of considerable importance in our intellectual history.

As will be seen from what I have said already, I think we probably need a number of more precise studies to determine exactly what we mean when we speak of a particular thinker as being Platonically or Neoplatonically influenced. An important and interesting thinker on whom a good deal more work of this kind needs to be done is Eriugena. Sheldon-Williams's new critical edition[2] and valuable studies of Eriugena's Greek background provide an excellent start to the investigation whether and in what precise sense Eriugena is a Neoplatonist.

We do seem to need a great deal more precision in our talk about alleged Platonic or Neoplatonic influences on aesthetic theory and works of literature and art in the Middle Ages and Renaissance. In my occasional random excursions into this sort of thing I have come across a good deal of vague and loose thinking. It is worth remembering that neither emphasis on number and mathematical structure nor emphasis on the excellence and beauty of light is in any way exclusively Neoplatonic.

[1] This topic was suggested to me by Olivier du Roy's remarkable study of how Neoplatonic speculation affected the Trinitarian theology of Augustine, *L'Intelligence de Foi en la Trinité selon S. Augustin* (1966).
[2] With English translation and notes. Vol. I so far published, Dublin, 1968– .

BIBLIOGRAPHICAL NOTE

A list of some of the more important recent editions and translations of Neoplatonic texts and books about Neoplatonism is given here. Books are included which will do something to fill in details and justify the assertions made in the paper, and may help in the investigation of some of the topics suggested. But it must be remembered that the list is by no means complete, and will certainly be behind the times by the date of publication.

GENERAL

The Cambridge History of Later Greek and Early Mediaeval Philosophy, ed. A. H. Armstrong (Cambridge, 1967, reprinted 1970).

W. Theiler, *Forschungen zum Neuplatonismus* (Berlin, 1966).

PLOTINUS

Texts and Translations

Enneads, ed. P. Henry and H. R. Schwyzer (vols. I–II (*Vita Plotini* and *Enn*, I–V) so far published, vol. III (*Enn*. VI) still to appear). (Paris and Brussels, 1951–).

ed. P. Henry and H. R. Schwyzer (ed. minor, extensively revised: vol. I (*Enn*. I–III) so far published). (Oxford, 1964–).

with translation and notes by A. H. Armstrong (vols. I–III (Enn. I–III) so far published). (Loeb Classical Library, London and Cambridge, Mass., 1966–).

ed. R. Harder, continued by R. Beutler and W. Theiler, with German translation and notes. 5 volumes in 11. (Hamburg, 1956–)

Books on Plotinus

Entretiens Hardt V. *Les Sources de Plotin* (Vandœuvres–Genève, 1960).

J. M. Rist, *Plotinus: the Road to Reality* (Cambridge, 1967).

PORPHYRY

Entretiens Hardt XII. *Porphyre* (Vandœuvres–Genève, 1966).

Hadot, P. *Porphyre et Victorinus*. Two volumes, the second containing texts, with French translations, which are important for the reconstruction of Porphyry's metaphysics (Paris, 1968).

IAMBLICHUS

De Mysteriis, ed. E. des Places, with French translation, introduction and notes (Paris, 1966).

PROCLUS

Platonic Theology, ed. H. D. Saffrey and L. G. Westerink, with French translation, introduction and notes. Vol. I so far published (Paris, 1968–).

Opuscula, ed. H. Boese. The medieval Latin translation of Moerbeke with substantial fragments of the original Greek text (Berlin, 1960).

Commentary on the Timaeus. French translation with notes by A. J. Festugière. 5 volumes (Paris, 1966–8).

Commentary on Alcibiades I. English translation of L. G. Westerink's critical text (Amsterdam, 1954), with notes, by W. O'Neill (The Hague, 1965).

DAMASCIUS

Life of Isidoros, ed. E. Zintzen (Hildesheim, 1967).

A new critical edition of the *Dubitationes et solutiones de primis principiis* is in preparation.

21

LE COMMENTAIRE ORDONNÉ
DU MONDE DANS QUELQUES SOMMES
SCIENTIFIQUES DES XIIe
ET XIIIe SIÈCLES

S. VIARRE

Que nous parlions de 'sommes' ou 'd'encyclopédies', ce qui nous intéresse, c'est une constante de la science — peut-être au niveau de la vulgarisation — et de la psychologie humaines. Il s'agit du souci d'entasser, mais aussi de dénombrer, de classer et de coordonner les connaissances que l'homme a du monde; en un mot de l'importance de la taxinomie. Cet effort s'est exercé de façon continue depuis l'Antiquité jusqu'à nos jours comme le montrent bien les différents articles réunis dans un récent numéro des *Cahiers d'Histoire Mondiale*.[1] On a certes abouti — et le Moyen Age l'a au moins partiellement connu[2]—au classement par ordre alphabétique, classement purement matériel, ce qui n'empêche pas une encyclopédie d'avoir une logique et des déterminantes internes, ce qui laisse aussi la possibilité d'étudier les déclarations d'intention, la signification des omissions, l'agencement propre à chaque article etc. Un examen de ce genre a été entrepris pour les ouvrages d'histoire naturelle des XVIe, XVIIe et XVIIIe siècles par M. Foucault dans *Les mots et les choses*.[3] Ce que je voudrais tenter ici, c'est de suggérer quelques lignes de recherches concernant le commentaire ordonné du monde aux XIIe et XIIIe siècles dans ses différences et ses ressemblances avec celui de l'Antiquité classique. Les questions viennent à l'esprit un peu pêle-mêle: par delà Pline si souvent cité et recopié, quelle est l'influence —

---

[1] Voir *Cahiers d'Histoire Mondiale*, IX, 3 (Neufchâtel, 1966); et notamment, en ce qui concerne l'Antiquité et le Moyen Age, P. Grimal, *Encyclopédies antiques*, pp. 459 et suiv.; J. Fontaine, *Isidore de Séville et la mutation de l'encyclopédisme antique*, pp. 519 et suiv.; M. Lemoine, *L'œuvre encyclopédique de Vincent de Beauvais*, pp. 571 et suiv.; P. Michaud-Quantin, *Les petites encyclopédies du XIIIe siècle*, pp. 580 et suiv.

[2] Voir par exemple l'ordre selon lequel sont énumérés les oiseaux dans Thomas de Cantimpré, *de Naturis Rerum*, MS B.N. fonds latin 523 A, 64 et suiv.

[3] M. Foucault, *Les mots et les choses* (Paris, 1966), ch. 2, 'La prose du monde', pp. 36-7, 40-1, 42-4, 46, 52-3, 54-5; ch. 3, 'Représenter', pp. 86-7; ch. 4, 'Classer', pp. 136 et suiv., p. 154.

directe ou indirecte — de Platon et du schéma cosmologique offert par le *Timée*?[1] Quelle est celle d'Aristote, non pas sur le contenu mais sur l'organisation des encyclopédies, en dehors des commentaires à proprement parler comme ceux d'Albert le Grand?[2] Quelle est à propos de certains sujets (éléments, tremblements de terre, foudre, marées etc.) l'action des *Questions Naturelles* de Sénèque?[3] Quelle est la signification, sur le plan de la citation, de la juxtaposition d'auteurs païens à des auteurs chrétiens? Je pense par exemple à la façon dont Alexandre Neckam[4] lorsqu'il décrit certains animaux ne cite jamais Cassiodore sans le renforcer par Solin, à moins que ce ne soit le contraire.[5] Quel est le rôle moteur — toujours dans le domaine de l'agencement qui régit ces ouvrages à prétentions scientifiques — de la pure philosophie, depuis Platon jusqu'à Boèce?[6] Comment les encyclopédies tiennent-elles compte dans leur schéma d'ensemble de celui que leur propose la Genèse et de son interprétation par Basile,[7] par Ambroise[8] ou par Augustin dans le *de Genesi ad Litteram*?[9] Lui échappent-elles complètement? Je songe à la place que Barthélémy de Glanville[10] fait à l'homme avant les plantes et les animaux, ou bien aux soixante-seize *Questions Naturelles*[11] d'Adélard de Bath inspiré par la science arabe. Lui échappent-elles partiellement?—Il faut alors distinguer deux ordres de motifs: ou bien elles subissent d'autres influences (rôle de Pline pour la médecine ou la minéralogie,[12] de la doctrine des quatre éléments dans l'œuvre de Raoul de Longchamp[13]

---

[1] Sur l'influence de Platon au Moyen Age, voir E. Gilson, *La philosophie au Moyen Age*, 2e éd. (Paris, 1944), notamment pp. 581–4; T. Gregory, *Platonismo medioevale* (Rome, 1958) etc.

[2] Albert le Grand, *Opera*, ed. Borgnet (1896–9), tomes 3 à 12.

[3] Sénèque, *Quaestiones Naturales*: I *de ignibus in aere existentibus*, II *de fulminibus et tonitribus*, III *de aquis terrestribus*, IV *de nubibus*, V *de uentis*, VI *de terrae motu*, VII *de cometis*.

[4] Alexandre Neckam, *de Naturis Rerum*, dans *Rerum Britannicarum Medii Aeui Scriptores*, ed. Th. Wright (Londres, 1863).

[5] Voir S. Viarre, 'A propos de l'origine égyptienne des arts libéraux: Alexandre Neckam et Cassiodore', note 61, dans les *Actes du IVe Congrès international de Philosophie médiévale*. pp. 583–91.

[6] Il conviendrait notamment d'étudier les citations que fait Vincent de Beauvais du *de Consolatione Philosophiae* dans le *Speculum Mundi*, édition de Douai (1626).

[7] Basile, *Homélies sur l'Hexaéméron*, ed. S. Giet, *Sources chrétiennes* (Paris, 1949).

[8] Ambroise, *Hexaéméron*, *P.L.* XIX, 1, cols. 123 et suiv.

[9] Augustin, *de Genesi ad Litteram*, *C.S.E.L.* XXVIII, 1, pp. 1 et suiv.

[10] Barthélémy de Glanville, *de Proprietatibus Rerum*, édition de Francfort (1609).

[11] Adélard de Bath, *Quaestiones Naturales*, ed. M. Müller (Münster, 1934).

[12] Pline, *Nat. Hist.* XX–XXXII; XXXIII et suiv.

[13] Raoul de Longchamp, *Summa de Philosophia*: I *Prologus*, II *de yle*, III *de elementis*, IV *de igne*, V *de aere*, VI *de aqua*, VII *de terra*, manuscrit d'Edimbourg, University Library, 115, fos. 72–78v (transcription dactylographiée de A. Vernet). Le problème du rapport entre les éléments et le récit de la *Genèse* est notamment posé par Augustin, *de Genesi ad Litteram*, III, 3–4, *C.S.E.L.* pp. 65–6.

ou des sciences à la mode comme l'alchimie chez Vincent de Beau-vais;[1] ou bien elles assument un changement de proportions à cause de l'importance donnée aux développements zoologiques, botaniques ou géographiques, comme pour le *de Imagine Mundi* d'Honorius Augus-todunensis[2] ou les *Otia Imperialia* de Gervais de Tilbury,[3] ou bien surtout à cause de leur gigantisme comme le *Speculum Mundi* de Vincent de Beauvais. Pour définir une série d'enquêtes qui devraient être menées de façon coordonnée et systématique, il faudrait con-sidérer deux aspects de la démarche mentale des auteurs d'encyclo-pédies, analyser d'abord les déclarations théoriques à ce sujet, souvent situées dans des préfaces, introductions ou prologues; dé-gager ensuite l'ordre réel ou fictif, à un niveau général ou particulier, que chacun a essayé de mettre dans l'exposé de l'enchevêtrement des faits. Il va de soi que je souhaite partir d'une description méthodique et peut-être structuraliste des œuvres de façon à essayer — si c'est possible — de saisir dans les détails ou dans la répartition des masses autre chose que des classements par écoles ou des principes généraux comme ceux qu'ont présentés P. Duhem dans *Le système du monde*[4] ou E. Gilson dans son chapitre de synthèse sur *L'univers du XIIe siècle* : interprétations étymologiques et symboliques, raisonnement par ana-logie etc.,[5] sans tomber pour autant dans le piège démodé mais tou-jours efficace de la *Quellenforschung*.

En laissant de côté pour le moment le problème de l'évolution historique et des jalons importants que constituent par exemple Varron ou Isidore de Séville, je vais donc choisir de mesurer la distance qui sépare un point d'aboutissement de l''entassement' antique — je veux dire l'*Histoire Naturelle* de Pline l'Ancien — et une époque de foisonnement intense (XIIe et XIIIe siècles), située avant que ne s'isolent les sciences de la nature comme dans les ouvrages considérés par M. Foucault. Et je tâcherai dans les deux cas de déchiffrer les déclarations théoriques.

Au premier siècle après J.-C., Pline adresse sa préface à Vespasien dont il fait l'éloge et qu'il regarde comme un juge.[6] Il définit son

---

[1] Vincent de Beauvais, *Speculum Naturale*: VII *de mineralibus*, 6, 13, 18, 26, 38, 42, 54, 70, 75, 85, 95.

[2] Honorius Augustodunensis, *de Imagine Mundi* (*P.L.* CLXXII, cols. 119 et suiv.) : géographie, I, 6–36 par exemple.

[3] Gervais de Tilbury, *Otia Imperialia*, ed. G. G. Leibnitz (Hanovre, 1707), livre II.

[4] P. Duhem, *Le système du monde, histoire des doctrines cosmologiques de Platon à Copernic*, III (1915).

[5] E. Gilson, *La philosophie au Moyen Age*, pp. 318 et suiv.

[6] Pline, *Nat. Hist.*, *Plinius Secundus Vespasiano Caesari suo s.* 1–7.

sujet par le ton: le travail est peu relevé, sans discours ni dialogues, sans événements merveilleux: 'rerum natura, hoc est uita narratur, et haec sordidissima sui parte'.[1] Il insiste sur l'originalité que revêt de son temps une tentative de dénombrement complet: le chemin n'a encore été foulé ni par les Latins, ni même dans sa totalité par les Grecs.[2] Au cours de son exposé, il cite Catulle, qu'il déforme,[3] Cicéron,[4] Tite-Live etc.[5] Surtout, il marque l'ampleur de son entreprise: vingt mille faits relevés, deux mille volumes lus, cent auteurs cités, trente-six volumes écrits, avec les additions aux faits déjà connus,[6] malgré sa modestie ('nec dubitamus multa esse quae et nos praeterierint').[7] A son épître dédicatoire, il ajoute honnêtement une table des matières et une liste des auteurs cités dans chaque livre; ainsi savons-nous d'emblée que le livre II forme une cosmologie; les livres III, IV, V et VI concernent la géographie; puis vient la zoologie (VII, l'homme; VIII, les mammifères; IX, les animaux aquatiques; X, les oiseaux; XI, les insectes); la botanique (XII à XIX) mène naturellement à la médecine (XX à XXXII); et la minéralogie couronne le tout (XXXIII à XXXVII). Ce n'est donc qu'au livre II qu'il fait allusion aux fondements philosophiques de sa cosmologie: 'mundum...numen esse credi par potest' (30)[8]; et lorsqu'il répète sa référence au système stoïcien ('naturae potentia idque esse quod deum uocemus'),[9] il la présente comme une sorte de digression.[10]

Dans le premier quart du XIIe siècle,[11] Honorius Augustodunensis

---

[1] 'Meae quidem temeritati accessit hoc quoque, quod et leuioris operae hos tibi dedicaui libellos. Nam, nec ingenii sunt capaces, quod alioqui in nobis perquam mediocre erat, neque admittunt excessus aut orationes sermonesue aut casus mirabiles uel euentus uarios, iucunda dictu aut legentibus blanda, sterili materia: rerum natura, hoc est uita, narratur, et haec sordidissima sui parte, ut plurimarum rerum aut rusticis uocabulis aut externis, immo barbaris etiam cum honoris praefatione ponendis' (Pline, loc. cit. 12–13); pour la mise en œuvre, voir aussi 15.

[2] 'Praeterea iter est non trita auctoribus uia nec qua peregrinari animus expetat: nemo apud nos qui idem temptauerit, nemo apud graecos qui unus omnia ea tractauerit' (loc. cit. 14).

[3] Pline, loc. cit. 1 cite Catulle, 1, 3–4.

[4] Pline, loc. cit. 7 cite une phrase de Cicéron qui ne nous est pas parvenue par d'autres voies.

[5] Pline, loc. cit. 16 cite une phrase de Tite-Live dans les mêmes conditions.

[6] 'XX rerum dignarum cura (quoniam ut ait Domitius Piso, thesauros oportet esse, non libros), lectione uoluminum circiter II, quorum pauca admodum studiosi attingunt propter secretum materiae, ex exquisitis auctoribus centum inclusimus XXXVI uoluminibus, adiectis rebus plurimis, quas aut ignorauerant priores, aut postea inuenerat uita' (Pline, loc. cit. 17).   [7] Pline, loc. cit. 17.

[8] Pline, Nat. Hist. II, 1. 1.   [9] Pline, Nat. Hist. II, 5. 27.

[10] 'In haec diuertisse non fuerit alienum, uulgata propter adsiduam quaestionem de deo.'

[11] Pour la chronologie des encyclopédies qui servent ici d'exemples, voir tableau dans S. Viarre (La survie d'Ovide dans la littérature scientifique des XIIe et XIIIe siècles (Poitiers, 1966), p. 33). Ce tableau s'appuie dans la plupart des cas sur C. H. Haskins, Studies in the

met en tête de son *de Imagine Mundi* deux lettres (*Epistola Christiani ad Honorium Solitarium de imagine mundi* et *Epistola Honorii ad Christianum de eodem*) dont la seconde[1] constitue, elle aussi, une déclaration d'intention. Honorius définit son entreprise et ses difficultés; il va décrire ce qui fait la règle de l'univers: 'totius orbis tibi depingam formulam... quod negotium sudore plenum ipse melius nosti, quam sit laboriosum quamque periculosum'. Il justifie son titre en disant que l'image est celle qu'on voit dans un miroir de l'agencement du monde: '...nomenque ei Imago mundi indatur, eo quod dispositio totius orbis in eo quasi in speculo conspiciatur'.[2] Le miroir et l'image se trouveront d'ailleurs confondus chez Vincent de Beauvais: 'Titulus, speculum, uel imago mundi, in quo scilicet huius mundi sensibilis dispositio, et ornatus paucis uerbis describitur'.[3] Car le miroir n'est plus celui que décrit Sénèque;[4] mais celui, plus abstrait, qu'Augustin évoquait au livre XIII des *Confessions*[5] ou dans son *de Scriptura Sacra Speculum*[6] avant Crollius pour qui le livre est un miroir.[7] Honorius, sans la moindre feinte, ne se soucie ni du style ni du ton;[8] mais l'organisation de son œuvre est lumineuse, au moins lorsqu'il la résume en passant d'un livre à un autre: il esquisse une représentation visible de l'univers avant de schématiser le déroulement du temps.[9]

History of Mediaeval Science (Cambridge, 1924); G. Sarton, *Introduction to the History of Science*, 5 vols. (Baltimore, 1927 et suiv.) etc. Voir aussi dans les *Cahiers d'Histoire Mondiale*, IX, 3, pp. 453–6 le tableau de R. Collison.

[1] *P.L.* CLXXII, cols. 119–20.　　　　　[2] *P.L.* CLXXII, col. 120.

[3] Vincent de Beauvais, *Speculum Naturale, Generalis Prologus*, ch. 3 *primo de Creatore, postea de Creaturis.*　　　　　[4] Sénèque, *Quaestiones Naturales*, I, XVII.

[5] Augustin, *Confessions*, XIII, 15: 'uerbum autem tuum manet in aeternum' (Isai. 40. 9); 'quod nunc in aenigmate nubium et per speculum caeli' (1. Cor. xiii. 12) '...apparet nobis'.

[6] Augustin, *P.L.* XXXIV, col. 889, *de Scriptura Sacra Speculum*: 'omnia talia de canonicis libris colligam, atque ut facile inspici possint, in unum tanquam speculum congeram.'

[7] Voir M. Foucault, *Les mots et les choses*, p. 42.

[8] Il avoue même: 'Hic nihil autem in eo pono, nisi quod maiorum commendat traditio.'

[9] 'Priori libello globum totius mundi oculis corporis repraesentauimus, sequenti iam tempus in quo uoluitur, oculis anteponam', *P.L.* CLXXII, cols. 145–6.

Le problème de la projection de la Création dans le temps est posé par Augustin dans tous ses écrits sur la *Genèse* et notamment dans les *Confessions*, XIII, XXIV, 44: 'Et attendi, ut inuenirem, utrum septiens uel octiens uideris, quia bona sunt opera tua, cum tibi placuerunt, et in tua uisione non inueni tempora... Ad haec tu dicis mihi, quoniam tu es deus meus et dicis uoce forti in aurem interiorem seruo tuo perrumpens meam surditatem et clamans: "O homo, nempe quod Scriptura mea dicit, ego dico. Et tamen illa temporaliter dicit, uerbo autem meo tempus non accidit, quia aequali mecum aeternitate consistit. Sic ea, quae uos per spiritum meum uidetis, ego uideo, sicut ea, quae uos per spiritum meum dicitis, ego dico. Atque ita cum uos temporaliter ea uideatis, non ego temporaliter uideo, quemadmodum, cum uos temporaliter ea dicatis, non ego temporaliter dico."'

Voir aussi: Augustin, *de Doctrina Christiana*, II, XXII. 50 (*P.L.* XXXIV, col. 58) 'Ipsa

Entre 1125 et 1135, le Chartrain Guillaume de Conches place au début des quatre livres du *de Philosophia Mundi* une véritable préface. Comme Pline, mais avec plus d'abondance, il appelle à la rescousse poètes et prosateurs païens: Cicéron,[1] Térence,[2] Horace,[3] Juvénal,[4] Ovide[5] sans compter un mystérieux *Poeta* que cite aussi Vincent de Beauvais.[6] Mais il se sert en même temps de l'Ecriture, notamment du second livre d'Esdras[7] et de la seconde Epître à Timothée[8], ce qui trahit des préoccupations nouvelles (*sana doctrina*) par rapport à celles de Pline. Avant de définir la philosophie comme la véritable appréhension de l'invisible et du visible,[9] Guillaume de Conches expose son plan: 'incipientes a prima causa rerum Deo usque ad hominem continuabimus tractatum'.[10] D'où vient l'expression *prima causa rerum Deus*? De Platon, dont il a commenté le *Timée*? D'Aristote? En tout cas elle est déjà assimilée par Arnobe et peut-être par Augustin.[11] Le livre I constitue une sorte de théologie suivie

tamen ueritas connexionum non instituta, sed anidmaduersa est ab hominibus et notata, ut eam possint uel discere uel docere: nam est in rerum ratione perpetua et diuinitus instituta. Sicut enim qui narrat ordinem temporum, non eum ipse componit; et locorum situs, aut naturas animalium uel stirpium uel lapidum qui ostendit, non res ostendit ab hominibus institutas; et ille qui demonstrat sidera eorumque motus, non a se uel ab homine rem institutam demonstrat...'

1 A peu près de Cicéron, *de Inuentione*, I, I. I.
2 I *Praef.* à peu près de Térence, *Andrienne*, 755–6.
3 I *Praef.* Horace, *A.P.* 361 (*P.L.* CLXXII, cols. 41–3). III *Praef.* Horace, *Ep.* I. II, 57 (*P.L.* CLXXII, col. 75).
4 IV *Praef.* Juvénal, *Sat.* III, 47.
5 IV *Praef.* Ovide, *A.A.* III, 132 (*P.L.* CLXXII, cols. 83–5).
6 III *Praef.* (*P.L.* CLXXII, col. 75) cite:

> Iustius inuidia nihil est, quae protinus ipsum
> Auctorem rodit, excrucians animum.

cf. Vincent de Beauvais, *Speculum Morale*, III. IV. I:

> Iustius inuidia nihil est, quae primitus ipsum
> Corrodit auctorem excruciatque suum.

Il s'agit en fait de *Carmina Burana*, 13, IV. 7–8:

> Iustius inuidia nihil est, quae protinus ipsos
> Corripit auctores excruciatque suos.

(ed. A. Hilka et O. Schumann, Heidelberg, 1930). Voir à ce sujet: H. Walter, *Lateinische Sprichwörter und Sentenzen des Mittelalters in alphabetischer Anordnung* (Göttingen, 1964), no. 13310.
7 II *Praef.* cite 2 Esdras, 4. 17 (*P.L.* CLXXII, col. 57).
8 IV *Praef.* cite 2 Tim. 4. 3 (*P.L.* CLXXII, col. 83).
9 'Philosophia est eorum quae sunt et non uidentur et eorum quae sunt et uidentur uera comprehensio' (*P.L.* CLXXII, col. 43).
10 *P.L.* CLXXII, col. 43.
11 Aristote définit le premier moteur (*Métaphysique* Λ 7, 1072 b; *Physique* Θ 5); il définit aussi la notion de cause et en particulier de cause finale (*Physique* B 3, 194 b 20 τὴν πρώτην αἰτίαν; *Métaphysique*, Γ 1, 1003 a 31 τὰς πρώτας αἰτίας λαμβάνειν τοῦ ὄντος ᾗ ὄν).

d'une analyse de la création selon le récit de la Genèse. La préface du livre II précise le ton général de l'œuvre (*ariditas nostri sermonis*) et annonce un plan fondé sur la distinction des éléments: 'nunc de singulis elementorum et ornatu uniuscuiusque dicere incipiamus, a superiori, id est ab igne, incipiendo'.[1] Le livre III, avec des réminiscences de Boèce[2] et une préface à portée morale[3], concerne l'air et les phénomènes météorologiques. Quant au livre IV, il traite de la terre[4] et de son *ornatus* suivant un ordre (la terre et le monde, les limites, les arbres, la reproduction de l'homme etc.) qui exigerait un déchiffrement minutieux et attentif.

Un peu plus tard sans doute, Alexandre Neckam nous offre un *de Naturis Rerum et super Ecclesiasten*[5] dont les intentions chrétiennes sont claires, même si le *super Ecclesiasten* n'a jamais été écrit. Il souligne un but moral; un but d'édification sans recours aux artifices de la rhétorique,[6] avec insistance: 'moralem enim libet instituere tractatum'.[7] Sa culture classique — si évidente dans le corps de l'œuvre — le conduit dès le prologue du livre I à citer les échecs de Phaéton ou d'Icare;[8] mais quand il reprend l'opposition classique des ténèbres

Mais c'est chez Platon que la notion de cause première intervient dans la temporalité de la création (*Timée*, 29 a: ὁ δημιουργός...ὁ...ἄριστος τῶν αἰτιῶν). Dans son commentaire du *Timée*, Guillaume de Conches utilise l'expression *causae primae* (*in Timaeum* 46 e, dans E. Jeauneau, *Guillaume de Conches, Glosae super Platonem* (Paris, 1965), p. 251). Mais, bien avant lui, Arnobe, s'adressant à Dieu, écrit: Prima enim causa tu es (*Adu. Nat.* I, 31). Et Augustin emploie souvent ce mot de *causa* à propos de Dieu créateur du monde. Voir notamment, *Ciu. Dei*, v, 9: causa itaque rerum, quae facit nec fit, Deus est; *de Doctrina Christiana* I. v. 5 (*P.L.* XXXIV, col. 21) 'Res igitur quibus fruendum est, Pater et Filius et Spiritus Sanctus, eademque Trinitas, una quaedam summa res, communisque omnibus fruentibus ea; si tamen res et non rerum omnium causa sit, si tamen et causa.'

[1] 'Si quis tamen est cui ariditas nostri sermonis displiceat, si nostri animi occupationes cognouerit, non tantum ornatum sermonis non quaesierit, sed de illo quod agimus stupebit. Quis enim ullus reliquus locus potest esse ornatui cum oporteat quid et qualiter legamus excogitare, demum legendo exponere, in disputationibus contra falsa declamare, de aliorum inuentis iudicare, contra inuidorum detractiones linguam acuere, ut iam nobis impletum sit illud de filiis Israel, qui reaedificantes templum, in una manu gladium, in alia lapidem habebant (2 Esdr. iv. 17). Sed haec hactenus. Nunc de singulis elementorum et ornatu uniuscuiusque dicere incipiamus, a superiori, id est ab igne, incipiendo' (*Praef.* II, col. 57).

[2] '...multas uestes philosophiae abscindentes et cum panniculis arreptis totam sibi eam cessisse credentes', cf. Boèce, *de Consolatione Philosophiae* I Prosa III, 7.

[3] *P.L.* CLXXII, col. 30.

[4] 'ad caetera transeamus. Et quia de aliis elementis, et ornatu, et eorum sectantes compendia diximus, de terra et ornatu eius dicere incipiamus' (*P.L.* CLXXII, cols. 83–5).

[5] Voir R. W. Hunt, *Alexander Neckam* (Oxford, 1936) (Bibliothèque Bodléienne, MS D. Phil. c. 101), p. 78.

[6] 'Sic et materia tractatus ad morum aedificationem instituendi simplicibus uerbis expedietur, exclusis penitus ornatus rhetorici lenociniis', *de Naturis Rerum*, édition citée, pp. 1–2).

[7] *de Naturis Rerum*, p. 3.　　　　　　　　[8] *de Naturis Rerum*, p. 2.

et de la lumière, elle est christianisée.[1] Alexandre Neckam veut mettre symboliquement son lecteur aux pieds du Créateur[2] en opposant l'attitude païenne à l'attitude chrétienne avant d'invoquer Jésus-Christ dans une phrase où s'entremêlent une citation d'Homère, son interprétation stoïcienne et un verset de l'Evangile selon saint Jean.[3] Le prologue du livre II a des résonnances chrétiennes encore plus nettes : 'Eructauit cor Patris uerbum quod bonum est, immo etiam ipsa bonitas est'.[4] Le monde, dessiné par la plume de Dieu, est une écriture[5] qui représente la *potentia*, la *sapientia* et la *benignitas*[6] de son auteur.[7] L'agencement du second livre de Neckam se veut donc d'abord théologique ; et les différents aspects du monde — couleurs, beauté, ordre, utilité, plantes, lions rugissants, ânes, brebis, taureaux, grenouilles et êtres humains — ne font qu'exprimer les trois qualités du Dieu créateur :[8] 'Diuersitates igitur facierum animalium, formarum, uocum, nonne sapientiam Dei loquuntur? Adde, quia superiora corpora quodammodo accedentius potentiam et sapientiam et be-

---

[1] 'In hoc enim opusculo lectorem ad opera lucis inuitamus ut abiectis operibus tenebrarum demum aeterna luce fruatur' (*de Naturis Rerum*, p. 2).

[2] 'Decreuit itaque paruitas mea quarundam rerum naturas scripto commendare, ut proprietatibus ipsarum inuestigatis ad originem ipsarum, ad rerum uidelicet opificem, mens lectoris recurrat, ut ipsum admirans in se et in creaturis suis pedes Creatoris, iustitiam scilicet et misericordiam, spiritualiter osculetur' (*de Naturis Rerum*, p. 2).

[3] 'Auream igitur Homeri catenam aliis relinquo' (Homère, *Iliade*, VIII, 19) 'qui in libertatem proclamo de qua in Euangelio dicitur, "Si uos Filius liberauerit, uere liberi eritis"' (Jean, 8. 36) ; cette citation annonce sans doute le chapitre 1 : *Reductio Principii Johannis ad Initium Geneseos*.

[4] *de Naturis Rerum*, p. 125.

[5] 'Mundus ergo ipse, calamo Dei inscriptus, littera quaedam intelligenti repraesentans artificis potentiam cum sapientia eiusdem et benignitate. Sic autem totus mundus inscriptus est, ita totus littera est, sed intelligenti et naturas rerum inuestiganti, ad cognitionem et laudem Creatoris. Nec hoc propter figuram mundi rotundam dixerim, quamquam et in hoc perfectio conditoris eluceat, sed quia quaelibet creatura repraesentat potentiam Dei et sapientiam et benignitatem' (*de Naturis Rerum*, p. 125) ; cf. Augustin, *de Genesi ad Litteram*, I. XIX (*C.S.E.L.* p. 28).

[6] Cf. Augustin, *de Genesi ad Litteram*, I. VIII (*C.S.E.L.* p. 11).

[7] *de Naturis Rerum*, pp. 125–6, voir note suivante.

[8] 'Potentiam enim Patris loquuntur ea per quae res potens est. Substantiales autem proprietates potentem esse rem faciunt. Sapientiam autem Dei enarrant color rei, et pulchritudo, et forma, cum figura et dispositione partium et numero. Benignitatem autem artificis summi loquuntur conseruatio rei in esse et utilitas eiusdem. Non est enim uel herba communis quae multas non habeat in se utilitates. Ad haec, inspice tot auium species, quaelibet ab alia suo garritu differt. Considera diuersitates animalium, reperies quamlibet speciem suum genus soni uocalis sibi uendicare. Rugitum dant leones, rudit asinus, balatum dat ouis, mugit taurus, coaxat rana, et ita in aliis reperies quamlibet speciem animalis suo discerni sono. Nobilem creaturam attende, hominem loquor, uix aliquos expresse similes reperies. Diuersitates igitur facierum animalium, formarum, uocum, nonne sapientiam Dei loquuntur? Adde, quia superiora corpora quodammodo accedentius potentiam et sapientiam et benignitatem, sed et immensitatem et aeternitatem, Dei exprimunt quam ista inferiora.'

nignitatem, sed et immensitatem et aeternitatem, Dei exprimunt quam ista inferiora.'[1] Après quelques considérations sur la splendeur du soleil, le prologue se conclut par une comparaison du Dieu avec sa création: 'Deus uero infinito decentior est omni specie quam condidit, maior omni quantitate'[2] et par une référence à un plan partiel fondé sur les éléments et l'ordre naturel: 'Postquam autem de aere et ornatu eius tractauimus, desiderare uidetur ordo naturalis ut de aquis et ornatu ipsorum, pisces loquor, agamus'.[3]

Quant à Barthélémy de Glanville, dans son *de Proprietatibus Rerum*, il explique l'ordonnance de son œuvre de façon métaphysique,[4] d'après la distinction et l'ordre des substances.[5] Il invoque le témoignage de Denys l'Aréopagite[6] pour montrer qu'étant donné l'infériorité de l'esprit humain par rapport au Saint-Esprit, seule l'intelligence du visible peut mener analogiquement l'homme à une appréhension de l'invisible; et il confirme alors Denys l'Aropagite par un passage de *Epître aux Romains*: 'Inuisibilia enim Dei per ea quae facta sunt intellecta conspiciuntur ut dicit Apostolus.'[7] Ainsi arrive-t-il à une sorte d'allégorisme,[8] et annonce-t-il son plan: 'In quo agitur de quibusdam proprietatibus rerum naturalium, quarum alia est incorporea, alia corporea.'[9] La fin de la préface expose le sujet des

[1] Voir p. 210, note 5: *potentia, sapientia* et *benignitas*.
[2] *de Naturis Rerum*, p. 127.
[3] *de Naturis Rerum*, p. 127.
[4] 'Cum Proprietates rerum sequantur substantias, secundum ordinem substantiarum, erit ordo et distinctio proprietatum de quibus, adiutorio diuino, est praesens opusculum compilatum.'
[5] Cf. Aristote, *Métaphysique*, Z 1–3, 1028 a–1029 b; H 1, 1042 a; Λ, 1 1069 a (traduction J. Tricot 2e éd. Paris, 1948).
[6] 'Vtile mihi et forsitan aliis, qui naturas rerum et proprietates per sanctorum libros nec non et Philosophos dispersas non cognouerunt, ad intelligenda aenigmata scripturarum, quae sub symbolis et figuris proprietatum rerum naturalium et artificialium a Spiritu Sancto sunt traditae et uelatae quemadmodum ostendit beatus Dionysius in Hierarchia Angelica, circa principium dicens: non est aliter nobis possibile lucere diuinum radium, nisi uarietate sacrorum uelaminum anagogicè circumuelatum. Quoniam impossibile est animo nostro ad immaterialem coelestium hierarchiarum ascendere contemplationem, nisi ea quae secundum ipsum est, materiali manuductione utatur, etc. quasi diceret' (c'est une traduction assez libre de Denys, *de Coelesti Hierarchia*, 1, 2 et 3 (*P.G.* III, 1, col. 62).
[7] 'Non potest animus noster ad inuisibilium contemplationem ascendere nisi per uisibilium considerationem dirigatur'. 'Cf. Rom. i. 20: Inuisibilia enim ipsius, a creatura mundi, per ea quae facta sunt, intellecta, conspiciuntur.' On notera l'absence du membre de phrase 'a creatura mundi' également omis chez Augustin, *de Doctrina Christiana*, I. IV. 4 (*P.L.* XXXIV, col. 21).
[8] 'Et ideo Theologia prouidè sacris et poeticis informationibus usa est, ut et rerum uisibilium similitudinibus allegoricae locutiones et mystici intellectus transumptiones formentur et sic carnalibus et uisibilibus spiritualis et inuisibilis coaptentur.'
[9] Edition citée, p. 3.

dix-neuf livres.[1] Les trois premiers traitent de la métaphysique;[2] le quatrième des propriétés de la substance corporelle;[3] les livres cinq à sept concernent l'homme (corps et parties du corps; âges de la vie; maladies et poisons);[4] le livre huit présente le monde et les corps célestes;[5] le livre neuf, le temps;[6] le livre dix consacre le passage à l'étude de éléments;[7] de ce fait, le livre onze parle de l'air et le livre douze des oiseux;[8] le livre treize de l'eau et des poissons;[9] le livre quatorze de la terre et de ses parties; le livre quinze des provinces; le livre seize des pierres et des métaux; le livre dix-sept des herbes et des plantes; le livre dix-huit des animaux;[10] quant au livre dix-neuf, il est réservé aux accidents[11] (couleurs, saveurs etc).[12] La conclusion marque la part énorme de la compilation à la façon de Pline, mais sans oublier les Livres Saints.[13]

L'entreprise la plus importante par ses dimensions est sans doute le *Speculum Mundi* (1244) de Vincent de Beauvais dont les intentions se trouvent clairement explicitées dans un long prologue général. Il veut rassembler une somme des connaissances acquises tant par les païens[14]

[1] Il présente alors un à un ses dix-neuf livres.
[2] 'Primo igitur agitur de Deo et nominibus diuinis quae dicuntur de Deo uel quoad essentiam, uel personam, siue quoad effectum siue appropriationem. Secundo de proprietatibus Angelorum tam bonorum, quam malorum in generali et speciali. Tertio de proprietatibus Animae rationalis, quoad naturae suae simplicitatem et quoad uirium suarum diuersitatem et de huius unione et operatione in corpore, prout confert ei formam et perfectionem.'
[3] 'Quarto de proprietatibus substantiae corporeae, scilicet de Elementis et elementaribus qualitatibus ex quibus componuntur omne corpus, et de quatuor humoribus ex quibus componuntur corpore tam hominum quam brutorum.'
[4] 'Quinto de hominis corpore et singulis eius partibus de quibus sacra scriptura fecit mentionem. Sexto de aetatibus. Septimo de infirmitatibus et uenenis.'
[5] 'Octauo de mundo et corporibus caelestibus.'
[6] 'Nono de tempore et partibus temporis.'
[7] 'Decimo de materia et forma earumque proprietatibus et Elementis.'
[8] 'Vndecimo de Aere et passiones eius. Duodecimo de auibus in generali et in speciali.'
[9] 'Tertio decimo de aquis et eius differentiis et ornatu, scilicet de piscibus.'
[10] 'Quarto decimo de terra et eius partibus. Quinto decimo de prouinciis. Decimo sexto de lapidibus et metallis. Decimo septimo de herbis et plantis. Decimo octauo de animalibus.'
[11] Cf. Aristote, *Métaphysique*, Δ 30, 1025 a; E 2–3, 1026 b–1027 b.
[12] 'Decimo nono de accidentibus, scilicet de coloribus, saporibus etc.'
[13] 'In istis nouem decim libellulis rerum naturalium proprietates summatim et breuiter continentur, prout ad manus meas spicae quae effugerunt manus metentium, pertingere potuerunt. In quibus de meo pauca uel quasi nulla apposui, sed omnia quae dicentur de libris authenticis Sanctorum et Philosophorum, excipiens sub breui hoc compendio pariter compilaui, sicut per singulos titulos poterit legentium industria experiri.'
[14] Comme Pline. Voir sur sa culture païenne, E. Boutaric, *Vincent de Beauvais et la connaissance de l'Antiquité classique au XIIIe s.* dans *Rev. Quest. Hist.* XVII (1875), 1–57; A. Marigo, 'Cultura letteraria e preumanistica nelle maggiori Enciclopedie del '200: lo Speculum

que par les chrétiens.[1] Et nous avons vu de quelle façon il commente son titre.[2] Il justifie sa description du visible de la même façon que Barthélémy de Glanville qui a peut-être comme lui repris de *l'Hexaemeron* de Basile[3] la citation de *l'Epître aux Romains*.[4] En outre, cette description se subordonne à l'explication des figures et de la signification mystique de l'Ecriture avex une citation empruntée au *de Doctrina Christiana*.[5] La dépendance des arts libéraux par rapport à la science sacrée fait l'objet du chapitre 7.[6] Au chapitre 8, il passe en

e il Tresors,' dans Giornale storico della letteratura italiana, LXVIII (1916), 7–42, 289–309; L. Lieser, *Vincenz von Beauvais als Kompilator und Philosoph...im* Speculum Naturale (*Buch 23–27*), dissertation de Cologne (1927), pp. 1–37.

[1] *Generalis Prologus*, chapitre 1: 'Mihi omnium fratrum minimo plurimorum libros assidue reuoluenti ac longo tempore studiose legenti uisum est tandem (accedente etiam maiorum meorum consilio) quosdam flores pro modulo ingenii mei electos, ex omnibus fere quos legere potui, siue nostrorum, id est Catholicorum Doctorum, siue Gentilium, scilicet Philosophorum et Poetarum et ex utrisque Historicorum in unum corpus uoluminis quodam compendio et ordine summatim redigere.'

[2] Voir p. 207 n. 3.

[3] 'Nam (ut ait magnus ille Basilius) ab his qui ueritatem intelligentes ex uisibilibus inuisibilia reputant, in terra et in aere, in aquis et in caelo, et in omnibus quae cernuntur, benefactoris monimenta certissima capiuntur. Sicque domino sensibus eorum iugiter adhaerente, nec peccatis tempus datur, nec inimico locus suggerendi contraria relinquitur.' (*Generalis Prologus*, ch. 6 *Apologia de natura rerum et historia temporum.*), La traduction latine de Basile, *Hexaemeron* III fin (*P.G.* 29, 1, col. 45) dit exactement: 'Deus autem qui tanta effecit, et quo disponente pauca haec dicta sunt, tribuat nobis in omnibus suae ueritatis intelligentiam, ut per uisibilia inuisibilem cognoscatis, atque ex magnitudine, ac pulchritudine creaturarum decentem de conditore nostro opinionem concipiatis. Invisibilia enim ipsius a creatura mundi per ea quae facta sunt, intellecta conspiciuntur: sempiterna quoque eius uirtus et diuinitas (Rom. i. 20): adeo ut in terra, in aere, in caelo, in aqua, in nocte, in die, et in omnibus uisibilibus, non obscure eius qui nobis benefecit recordemur. Neque enim peccatis occasionem ullam sumus daturi, neque inimico in nostris cordibus locum relicturi, si modo per assiduam memoriam Deum in nobis inhabitantem habeamus.'

Pour quelques-unes des formules précises, voir aussi: *Eustathiana interpretatio Hexaem. lib. III* (*P.G.* 30, 2, col. 931): 'Dominus dat nobis intellectum suae ueritatis; ut ex uisibilibus inuisibilem reputetis, et ex magnitudine ac pulchritudine creaturae, decentem gloriam conditoris mens uestra percipiat, ut et in terra, et in aere, et in caelo, et in aquis, et inter diem et noctem, et in omnibus quae cernuntur benefactoris monumenta certissima capiatis. Neque enim aut peccatis tempus dabitur, aut inimico locus suggerendi contraria relinquetur, Domino uestris sensibus adhaerente.'

[4] Voir p. 211 n. 7.

[5] 'ut enim Augustinus dicit, rerum ignorantia facit obscuras figuratas locutiones, cum scilicet, ignoramus uel animantium, uel lapidum, uel herbarum naturas, aliarumue rerum quae ponuntur plerumque in Scripturis alicuius similitudinibus gratia. Numerorum quoque imperitia, multa facit in eis non intelligi mystice posita' (*de Doctrina Christiana*, II. XVI. 24, *P.L.* XXXIV, col. 47).

[6] 'Accedit ad hoc, quod omnes artes diuinae scientiae tanquam reginae famulantur; unde et illae quae liberales uocantur, plerumque in assertione ecclesiastici dogmatis assumuntur. Hinc beatus Petrus Apostolus in Epistola quadam, itinerario Clementis adiuncta, sic loquitur: Cum, inquit, et diuinis scripturis integram quis et firmam regulam susceperit ueritatis, absurdum non erit, si aliquid etiam ex eruditione ac liberalibus studiis quae forte in pueritia attigit ad assertionem ueri dogmatis conferat' (*Generalis Prologus*,

revue les désaccords entre eux des philosophes et des poètes, à propos de la nature froide ou chaude de l'air (Aristote, Avicenne, Sénèque) ou du venin du serpent (Isidore, Avicenne) tout en exposant sa propre attitude à l'égard de telles conceptions: il laisse le lecteur libre.[1] La division du *Speculum Mundi* en quatre 'tomes' ou parties conduit finalement Vincent à se référer au classement des œuvres de Platon indiqué dans la *Cité de Dieu*[2] par Augustin qui se sert sans doute d'interprétations tardives du système platonicien;[3] et il est bien évident que ce passage constitue l'un des témoignages de la tendance médiévale à résoudre les contradictions qui séparent des chrétiens les auteurs païens et singulièrement Platon.[4]

Il serait intéressant de voir comment s'organisent les trente-deux livres du *Speculum Naturale* (I le créateur et les anges; II l'œuvre du premier jour; III l'œuvre du second jour, le firmament et le ciel; IV les autres parties du monde; V l'œuvre du troisième jour et les eaux; VI la terre; VII et VIII le contenu de la terre; IX le second aspect de l'œuvre du troisième jour, les plantes et les herbes; X les autres herbes; XI les semences, les graines et les sucs; XII, XIII, XIV les arbres; XV l'œuvre du quatrième jour ('hoc est de luminaribus coeli et signis, et temporibus et huiusmodi'); XVI l'œuvre du cinquième jour, c'est-à-dire les oiseaux du ciel; XVII les poissons et les monstres marins, XVIII l'œuvre du sixième jour et les animaux terrestres, qui occupent encore les livres XIX à XXII; XXIII la création de l'homme et l'âme, dont il est aussi

ch. 7 *Apologia de Uniuersitate Scientiarum*, citant *Recognitiones Clementinae* X. XLII (*P.G.* II, cols. 1441–2).

[1] '...praesertim cum ego iam professus sim in hoc opere me non tractatoris, sed excerptoris morem gerere, ideoque non magnopere laborasse dicta Philosophorum ad concordiam redigere, sed quantum de unaquaque re quilibet eorum senserit aut scripserit recitare; lectoris arbitrio relinquendo cuius sententiae potius debeat adhaerere' (*Generalis Prologus*, ch. 8 de apologia de dictis philosophorum et poetarum).

[2] 'Si quidem et Plato (ut dicit August.) perfectiue Philosophiam laudatur, quae in tres partes ab ipso distribuitur, unam uidelicet naturalem, aliam rationalem, tertiam moralem' (*Generalis Prologus*, ch. 16 de quadrigaria diuisione totius, citant avec quelques lacunes Augustin, *Ciu. Dei*, VIII, 4).

[3] La division tripartite de l'œuvre de Platon remonte assez loin. Voir Diogène Laërce, III, 50; Cicéron, *Acad. Post.* 1. 5. 19; Albinos, introd. 3. 6 (trad. R. Le Corre dans *Revue philosophique*, LXXI (1956), 28–38; P. Louis, *L'Epitomé d'Albinos* (Paris, 1945)); Apulée, *de Platone et eius Dogmate*, 1, 3 (C. Moreschini), *Studi sul 'de dogmate Platonis' di Apuleio* (Pise, 1966), pp. 27–8); Sextus Empiricus, *Adu. math.* 7, 16 qui renvoie à Xénocrate.

[4] Augustin, *de Doctrina Christiana*, II. XL, 60–1 (*P.L.* XXXIV, col. 63) 'ab Ethnicis si quid recte dictum, in nostrum usum est conuertendum: Philosophi autem qui uocantur, si qua forte uera et fidei nostrae accommodata dixerunt, maxime Platonici, non solum formidanda non sunt, sed ab eis etiam tamquam iniustis possessoribus in usum nostrum uindicanda' (suit un développement sur ce que les païens doivent à l'Egypte ainsi que Cyprien, Lactance et Moïse).

question aux livres XXIV, XXV, XXVI, et XXVII; XXVIII le corps humain; XXIX l'univers; XXX la nature; XXXI la reproduction de l'homme...; XXXII les lieux et les temps).

Ces propos n'ont pas d'autre but que de servir d'esquisse à une sorte de préambule qui définirait un champ d'investigation et soulignerait l'unité d'une série d'enquêtes que j'aimerais entreprendre, notamment en ce qui concerne Vincent de Beauvais.

22

PETRARCH AND THE TRANSMISSION OF CLASSICAL ELEMENTS

C. N. J. MANN

Of all Petrarch's Latin works, the most widely diffused in the centuries following his death was undoubtedly the *de Remediis Utriusque Fortunae*. Its total extant manuscript tradition, if we include abridged versions, excerpts and translations into various vernaculars, exceeds two hundred manuscripts; by the end of the sixteenth century it had run to fourteen Latin and twenty-four vernacular editions, not to mention a large number of partial ones, sixteen of them prior to 1500.[1]

It is therefore through the *de Remediis* that I should like briefly to examine the extent to which Petrarch may be said to have transmitted his classical learning to the fourteenth and fifteenth centuries. I shall thus discuss his rôle less as a scholar than as a diffuser and populariser of classical material, and shall examine the work more from the point of view of its readers than from that of its author.

There are two principal ways in which the *de Remediis* might be described as a classicising work. First, it contains a mass of explicit classical material in the form of *exempla* taken from the ancient world. Of some five hundred figures mentioned by name in it, fewer than thirty-five belong to domains other than those of Greco-Roman antiquity. Being in this respect a *summa* of Petrarch's erudition, the *de Remediis* is a veritable mine of classical examples.

Second, and less evident perhaps, the work strikes a decidedly classical note in its Stoicism. Derived mainly from Seneca, but seen to some extent through Augustinian eyes, Petrarch's personal blend of Stoic and Christian attitudes is an elusive one which it would be out of place to describe here.[2] But because the framework and the contents of the *de Remediis* can certainly be interpreted as Stoic, it seems

---

[1] Most of the editions are listed in W. Fiske, *Francis Petrarch's Treatise De Remediis Utriusque Fortunae. Text and Versions* (Bibliographical Notices, III, Florence, 1888) : most of the MSS in C. N. J. Mann, *The Fortunes of Petrarch's de Remediis* (Cambridge (Ph.D. dissertation), 1967), pp. 27–102.

[2] On this question cf. K. Heitmann, *Fortuna und Virtus. Eine Studie zu Petrarcas Lebensweisheit* (Cologne, 1958).

probable that Petrarch had a part to play in that revival of Stoicism which has so far been studied only as a sixteenth-century phenomenon.

The material which is the substance of this philosophical outlook is frequently derived from classical authors and sometimes even copied word for word from them without any acknowledgement. To this extent, too, the *de Remediis* is a classicizing work. Yet it is interesting to notice that there is often a certain ambiguity, perhaps deliberate, about the argument: statements which the initiated might read in a Stoic light fit just as easily into an orthodox Christian context, an ambivalence which is perhaps in part explained by Petrarch's own insistence that his treatise was intended as much for the *vulgus*—the general reader—as for the *docti*.[1]

When one studies the diffusion of the *de Remediis* one is struck by the number of abridged versions of the text. It is evident that not every-one would have read from cover to cover a work so encyclopedic in its dimensions and its scope, and the desire for shorter manuals containing the essential fruits of Petrarch's wisdom is understandable. The value of such anthologies is thus to provide an indication of the way in which the work was read and of the material in it which was considered most important. I should therefore like to examine a few such abridged versions and to comment briefly on the interpretations of the *de Remediis* which they propose and the use they make of the two kinds of classical material—essentially *exempla* and *sententiae*—which I have already outlined.

Probably the earliest abridgement yet to have come to light is the *Flors de Patrarcha de remey de cascuna fortuna*, a Catalan compilation of the early fifteenth century.[2] Consisting of a collection of 165 maxims translated from the Latin, it reveals several features which are, as I hope to show, characteristic of such anthologies. In the first place it entirely ignores the exemplary side of the *de Remediis* and concentrates instead on its sententious content. Thus with the sole exception of a mention of Archimedes as inventor of the bombard,[3] there is no explicit classical material. Accordingly, the predominant moralising

---

[1] Cf. *de Remediis*, II, *praef.* (p. 125 in the Basle, 1554 ed. of Petrarch's *Opera*): 'neque vero te moveat fortunae nomen [...] cum his maxime qui doctrina minus fulti essent, haec necessaria praeviderim, noto illis et communi vocabulo usus sum, non inscius, [...] Communis ergo acies suum hic loquendi morem recognoscet. Docti autem, qui perrari sunt, quid intendam scient, nec vulgari cognomine turbabuntur.'

[2] Published by R. D'Alòs Moner in *Estudis Universitaris Catalans*, XXI (1936), 650–66.

[3] *Ibid.* p. 660, no. 52; cf. *de Rem.* I, 99 p. 102.

note of the *Flors* is either a neutral, proverbial one, expressed in such maxims as *occasio fa ladre*,[1] or an explicitly Christian one, clearly exemplified by the rendering of *ingratissimi mortales, bona vestra vix aliter quam perdendo cognoscitis* by *los homens mortals indiscrets anvides conexen los bens a ells donats per Nostre Senyor sino perdent aquels*.[2] Although the vast majority of the *sententiae* fit an orthodox context, however, we do find one or two maxims of a more Stoic nature, particularly concerning *virtus*,[3] and also a few quotations which Petrarch derived from classical authors such as Claudian and Cicero,[4] and which are here presented as his own. In general, however, such second-hand classical material is sparse and such Stoic maxims as appear, inconclusive. The collection as a whole represents a very unexceptional moral viewpoint.

An anthology which might be compared with the *Flors* and which in fact has thirty-eight maxims in common with it, is the *Fioretti de' rimedii contro fortuna* compiled from Giovanni da San Miniato's Italian translation of the *de Remediis*.[5] It is considerably more extensive than the *Flors*, and is divided into chapters which correspond to the divisions of the original, although the *sententiae* chosen do not always echo the contents of the individual dialogues excerpted.

Unlike the *Flors*, the *Fioretti* include quite a considerable number of classical *exempla*, and such figures as Alexander, Cato, Julius Caesar, Horatius and many others, including certain famous women, are mentioned. And it is in accord with this that there should be some stress laid upon *virtus* and other characteristics of a Stoic flavour. Further, there are quite a large number of *sententiae* of classical origin, some explicit, others presented as Petrarchan but in fact deriving ultimately from Seneca, Cicero, Claudian and Sallust, to mention but a few. But again the moral standpoint of the compiler is a rigorously Christian one and classical elements do not make for classical values; it is no doubt significant of his attitude that he should have rendered the chapter *de gratis Amoribus* as *Dell'amore vizioso*.[6]

---

[1] *Ibid.* p. 664, no. 117; cf. *de Rem.* II, 60 p. 178.

[2] *Ibid.* p. 658, no. 17; cf. *de Rem.* I, 4 p. 10.

[3] Cf. especially *ibid.* pp. 661–2, nos. 80, 83, 84, 87.

[4] Cf. *ibid.* p. 660, nos. 60 and 63.

[5] Cf. C. Stolfi (ed.), *Fioretti de' Rimedii contro fortuna* (Scelta di curiosità, LXXX, Bologna, 1867). Stolfi failed to observe that the manuscript from which he was working, the sole one of the text (Florence, Laurenziana, MS. Med. Pal. 40, *not* 49), is dated 1478, a fact which casts some doubt on his attribution of the *Fioretti* to Giovanni da San Miniato, who died fifty years earlier.

[6] *Ibid.* p. 70; cf. *de Rem.* I, 69 pp. 76–9.

I have not found any comparable anthology of disconnected *sententiae* originating from the north of Europe. In England and the Low Countries there seems to have been a preference for abridgements and adaptations of the *de Remediis* presented as works of continuous prose, often preserving the dialogue form of the original, but by virtue of their very coherence much more overtly devotional in tone than the Catalan or Italian *florilegia*. One such compilation is the late Middle English *Dialogue between Reason and Adversity*, dated by its editor to the first quarter of the fifteenth century[1] and based largely upon the opening dialogues of the second book of the *de Remediis*.

In many ways it illustrates the techniques which I have already mentioned. In the fourth and fifth dialogues, *Of unnoble cuntre* and *Of pore birþe*, for instance, it systematically omits all but two or three of the classical figures mentioned in Petrarch's *exempla* and keeps instead to the bare moral bones of the discourse.[2] And if there are certain reminiscences of quotations from Juvenal and Seneca culled from the *de Remediis*,[3] these are few and far between.

Thus this *Dialogue* illustrates admirably the way in which Petrarch is treated as a moral authority of an orthodox kind, and in which the abundance of classical material which his treatise contains is either left on one side or fitted into an unclassical context.

But it is in the Low Countries that this process can be most clearly demonstrated, even if only because it is there that the largest number of abridgements of the *de Remediis* appear to have originated. The best known, and probably the most popular in the fifteenth and early sixteenth centuries, is the *de Remediis* of Adrianus Carthusiensis,[4] which was probably compiled before 1411, and contains about one third of the original material. The abridgement was achieved by the omission of almost all explicit classical elements, and the reorientation of the work is made plain both by two new prefaces and by the substitution of *Cultor Virtutis* and *Tyro Vanitatis* for the original protagonists of Petrarch's dialogues, who were *Ratio*—Right Reason—and the four affections *Gaudium*, *Spes*, *Dolor* and *Metus*.

Even more overtly devotional in their intentions are two further works based on the *de Remediis* and emanating from the Low Coun-

[1] F. N. M. Diekstra, *A Dialogue between Reason and Adversity* (Assen, 1968); for the date, cf. pp. [10]–[11].
[2] *Ibid.* pp. 11–15.
[3] *Ibid.* p. 3, lines 9 and 22; p. 7, line 6; p. 15, line 14; p. 19, line 6. The classical sources and corresponding passages in the *de Rem.* are given in the notes.
[4] For editions and MSS cf. the two sources mentioned in n. 1, p. 217, above.

tries. The first is a fifteenth-century *Speculum Mortis* ascribed in the manuscripts to Petrarch himself, but essentially a rather clumsy collation of *sententiae* taken from the later dialogues of the second book of the *de Remediis*.[1] It is devoid of classical material, with the exception of a single Senecan maxim not derived from Petrarch, and is entirely oriented towards urging a holy life in preparation for a holy death. Its compiler's intentions are made clear by the inclusion of a lengthy passage explaining the implications of the work in terms of making a monastic profession.[2]

The other such treatise is a *Libellus de Abusu Quattuor Passionum* copied by an inmate of the Charterhouse of Zeelhem near Diest in the diocese of Liège in 1459.[3] The author explains that he compiled his work of Petrarch's *de Remediis* and several other learned sources, and that in it 'poterit quis clare perspicere de quo sive in quo vere et religiose sit gaudendum et similiter de quo sive in quo sit dolendum.'[4] The first of its two books is an extended monastic commentary on a few extracts from the *de Remediis* and *de Otio Religioso*, together with a discussion of the religious orders. Book II, however, is simply an abridgement of Petrarch's second book, with virtually no extraneous material. The criteria for abridging are the usual ones. Almost all explicit classical material is omitted, and the *de Remediis* is seen exclusively as a source of orthodox moral teaching.

I am aware that I might be accused of oversimplifying the issue by concentrating merely on *florilegia* and abridged versions. Yet a study of individual authors in the Low Countries for instance confirms the general impression which I have attempted to convey. Almost without exception, Petrarch is seen by his readers, even men such as Dirc van Herxen and the *doctor extaticus*, Denis the Carthusian, as a sound Christian moral authority whose classical learning is ignored or set aside.

This may be demonstrated by the case of Arnold Geilhoven, whom I have studied in detail elsewhere,[5] and who is probably the earliest

[1] Vienna, Nationalbibliothek, MS. Vind. Pal. s.n. 12900, fos. 42r–48r. There are at least two other manuscripts in existence.
[2] Cf. MS *cit.*, fos. 44r–44v.
[3] Paris, Mazarine, MS. 989, fos. 25r–89v, and now Cologne, Hist. Archiv, MS. w8° 9.
[4] MS *cit.*, fo. 25r.
[5] Cf. C. N. J. Mann, 'Arnold Geilhoven: an early disciple of Petrarch in the Low Countries', *Journal of the Warburg and Courtauld Institutes*, XXXII (1969), 73–108, where details concerning Dirc van Herxen and Denis the Carthusian will also be found. Cf. also C. Ypes, *Petrarca in de Nederlandse Letterkunde* (Amsterdam, 1934), pp. 1–28 and M. Dykmans, 'Les premiers rapports de Pétrarque avec les Pays Bas', *Bulletin de l'Institut historique belge de Rome*, XX (1939), 109–18.

of Petrarch's literary followers in the Low Countries after Louis Sanctus of Beeringen, the *Socrates* of the *Letters*. Geilhoven's interest in Petrarch was in fact a dual one, as is revealed by his *Vaticanus*, which he finished in 1424–5.[1] On the one hand, he uses Petrarch, and in particular the *Rerum Memorandarum Liber*, as a source of biographical and historical information about great men of the past with which to illustrate the catalogue of writers which occupies the major part of his first book. On the other hand, Petrarch, and this time the *de Remediis*, is an important source of *sententiae* for the moral vocabulary which constitutes the second book. What is striking, however, is the unexceptional and often almost proverbial character of the maxims which he borrows from the *de Remediis*. It is rare indeed that these are of classical origin, and rarer still that they preserve the Stoic quality of their source.

Geilhoven's ambiguous attitude is equally evident in another work, the *Moralizatio Currus Triumphalis*,[2] in which he shows both a historian's and a moralist's interest in a classical feature, the triumph, and draws on the *de Remediis* to illustrate both concerns, and yet leaves us with the impression that it was more for his moralising than for his erudition that he valued Petrarch as an authority.

It will be noticed that I have as yet made no mention of either Germany or France. As far as Germany is concerned, my reason is principally that the only abridged version of the *de Remediis* which I know to be of German origin is contained in the *Margarita Poetica*, a *florilegium* of largely classical material compiled by the humanist Albrecht von Eyb in 1459.[3] Here we are in a different world: Petrarch is placed in company with Cicero, Vitruvius, Valerius Maximus and others as a representative of prose style and classical wisdom. For once, and I would suggest that this occasion is an exceptional one, the *de Remediis* is presented as a classicising work and the stress is laid on its classical content. But Eyb, unlike the vast majority of his contemporaries and thus of Petrarch's public, was a humanist.

As to France, I have two reasons for having kept silent until now. First, I know of no anthology or abridged version based on the

---

[1] Cf. Paris, Mazarine, MS. 1563 and Brussels, Bibliothèque royale, MS. 1169–70 (both autograph).

[2] Cf. Brussels, Bibliothèque royale, MS. 1169–70. fos. 248r–250v. A critical edition of the text is appended to my article mentioned in n. 5, p. 221, above.

[3] Cf. M. Herrmann, *Albrecht von Eyb und die Frühzeit des deutschen Humanismus* (Berlin, 1893), pp. 174–213. I have used the Basle, 1503 ed., in which the epitome of the *de Rem.* occupies sigs. B2r–C5v.

de Remediis and emanating from France during the period with which I am concerned. Second, as I have attempted to show elsewhere,[1] I believe that it was in France and at an early date that Petrarch's Stoicism was first recognised. This was very probably partly because of the French translation which Jean Daudin made of the *de Remediis* in 1378,[2] and which he prefaced by a prologue which made the Stoic implications of the work quite plain.

On the other hand such a view was not universal in France at the time. In many ways men like Jean Gerson, who derived much of a sermon delivered to the royal court in 1389 from the *de Remediis*,[3] and Jean de Montreuil, who called Petrarch 'devotissimus catholicus ac celeberrimus philosophus moralis' and often quoted him in his letters,[4] viewed him more as a moralist than as a classical scholar and preferred to fit his moralising into the fairly traditional mould of their own thought.

As a final illustration of this point I should like to mention Pierre Flamenc, who was prior of the monastery of Saint-Benoît at Montpellier in the 1370s, then provost of the college attached to it and, from 1405, abbot of Saint-Victor at Marseilles. He is to my knowledge the first of Petrarch's French literary admirers in the period following his death.[5]

Flamenc compiled a notebook, based mainly on his reading of Petrarch's Latin works. In it he noted down a large number of classical *exempla* and a good many of the typical inventories of classical heroes who portrayed some quality or action; frequent also are explicit quotations from classical authors taken from Petrarch and so on. Yet when we come to look at Flamenc's own compositions, for the most part sermons and graduation speeches made at Montpellier, we notice how little of this material he used. Among the

[1] Cf. C. N. J. Mann, 'Petrarch's role as moralist in fifteenth-century France', *Humanism in France at the End of the Middle Ages and in the Early Renaissance*, ed. A. H. T. Levi (Manchester, 1970), pp. 6–27.

[2] Cf. L. Delisle, 'Anciennes traductions françaises du traité de Pétrarque sur les remèdes de l'une et de l'autre fortune', *Notices et extraits des MSS de la Bibliothèque Nationale*, XXXIV (1891), 273–304.

[3] Cf. C. N. J. Mann, 'La fortune de Pétrarque en France: Recherches sur le *De remediis*', *Studi francesi*, XXXVII (1969), 1–15.

[4] Cf. *Jean de Montreuil, Opera*, I, 1. *Epistolario*, ed. E. Ornato (Turin, 1963), p. 315 and *passim*.

[5] I am preparing a new study of Flamenc; in the meantime, cf. A. Germain, 'Pierre Flamenchi: étude d'après ses manuscrits autographes, entièrement inédits', *Publications de la Société archéologique de Montpellier*, VIII, no. 44 (1884), 307–76 and F. Simone, *Il Rinascimento francese* (Turin, 2nd ed. 1965), pp. 28–9, 32.

many borrowings from Petrarch which figure in these pieces, classical *exempla* are rare, and the vast majority are *sententiae* which reflect the choice of a moralist, and a stern one at that. If Flamenc borrows praise of *virtus* or *labor*—individual effort akin in Petrarch to the Stoic τόνος—it is to apply them to his scholastic context and to praise the virtues of legal studies or to warn his students against laziness.[1]

To summarize, I believe that the *de Remediis*, the work of Petrarch's maturity, is characterised both by its wealth of classical *exempla* and by *sententiae* which, by virtue of their content and frequently their classical derivation, and because of the framework in which they are set, present at least the open possibility of a Stoic interpretation.

Yet I also believe that this aspect of the most popular of Petrarch's Latin works was largely ignored in the first century and a half of its diffusion. It is rare to find authors of the late fourteenth and fifteenth centuries quoting classical *exempla* from the *de Remediis*, and far more common to find the treatise understood, presented and used in a traditional moralising context. On the other hand it is true that a number of implicit classical quotations in it reappear in the works of later authors as authentically Petrarchan *sententiae*. Whether in this way Petrarch may have played a rôle in the transmission of classical elements remains a question open to further research; on the basis of the evidence which I have outlined it seems that, until the end of the fifteenth century at least, his potential value as a source of classical material remained largely unrealised.

---

[1] Both the notebook and the speeches are contained in Marseille, Archives départementales des Bouches-du-Rhône, MS. i.h. 678. On the notebook, cf. N. Mann, 'Le recueil de Pierre Flamenc: analyse et reconstruction', shortly to appear in *Scriptorium*.

23

ASPETTI DELLA VITA CONTEMPLATIVA NEL RINASCIMENTO ITALIANO

F. SCHALK

Il riconoscimento della forza dell'impulso dall'Umanesimo conferito all'attività del pensiero è un dato comune alle numerose opere dedicate alla descrizione del movimento umanistico italiano. Sulla base delle molteplici ricerche di Kristeller, Garin e molti altri è possibile affrontare la discussione dei problemi di ordine metodico e metodologico riguardanti lo stato attuale della ricerca, quella tendenza cioè ad unire insieme intenzioni storiche ed intenzioni sistematiche. Quando, al giorno d'oggi, si parla di Rinascimento, ci si riferisce di solito ad un periodo compreso tra il 1300 ed il 1600, un'età quindi con forti differenziazioni di ordine cronologico, sociale, geografico. Se poi, come parecchi studiosi quali Ghellinck, Gilson, Haskins fanno, si vuol parlare di vari Rinascimenti, si è ugualmente costretti a considerare quello italiano non solo come l'anello finale in questa catena di Rinascimenti, ma proprio come una Rinascita avente in sè la possibilità di riorganizzare in maniera totale e nuova la vita italiana. Gli umanisti già del secolo XIII continuarono la tradizione medievale di studio dei classici latini, ma ne aumentarono il numero e abbandonarono il continuo ricorso alla teologia sviluppando una sensibilità particolarmente aperta verso la letteratura latina dapprima, verso quella greca poi: si aprì così un campo nuovo e ne uscì un nuovo programma educativo dove grammatica, retorica, storia, filosofia morale si trovarono riunite entro il concetto di *Studia humanitatis*. L'introduzione durante il secolo XV degli autori greci, il cui studio mai era stato interrotto nell'oriente bizantino, spaccò le strette barriere della tradizione scolastica del Medioevo occidentale. Alla scoperta degli autori greci tenne subito dietro il lavoro di traduzione in latino; i confini della conoscenza dello spirito antico vennero ad essere in tal modo più ampi di quanto era successo nel precedente periodo del Medioevo. Ad una conoscenza frammentaria se ne sostituì una completa, la letteratura antica gradualmente guadagnò quell'importanza che realmente le compete. A partire del secolo XV gli *Studia humanitatis* nel loro aspetto retorico e filosofico-morale vivificano tutti i campi dell'agire umano: essi diventano la forza determinante e conferiscono anche ai moduli espressivi di Pico e Ficino il tono decisivo. Un certo gruppo di uomini crea nell'attività filosofica, storiografica, politologica le premesse per cui autori diversi vengono ad incontrarsi nella stessa zona dell'antichità classica. Platonismo e Aristotelismo italiani del Rinascimento hanno più d'un legame coll'Umanesimo; come movimenti filosofici non sono però spiegabili solo sulla base dell'ascendenza umanistica. Li possiamo paragonare a ricchi fiumi che si dividono in vari bracci assumendo in Ficino, Pico, Pomponazzi e Patrizi aspetti tra loro ben diversi. Entro il punto focale della filosofia greca vennero temporaneamente a convergere tutti i raggi della vita spirituale italiana: non si insegnò più un classico in maniera scolastica, ma se ne fissarono costantemente i rapporti con altri autori antichi; il tradurre divenne fatto affascinante e gioioso: tutte le componenti di una natura di cultura umanistica ne erano, per cosí dire, eccitate e trovavano in un'imitazione non aliena da trasformazioni soggettive misure suscitatrici di creazioni personali.

A dire il vero, solo nomi di autori latini come Sant'Agostino, Cicerone e Seneca ci aiutano ad indicare il terreno da cui si sviluppano sia in poesia che in filosofia morale le linee teoriche fondamentali del primo Umanesimo italiano: la conoscenza del greco viene acquisita infatti solo in una fase successiva. Eppure già la tematica sull'*otium* e sulla *vita solitaria*, preludio a quella successiva della vita contemplativa, è dominante negli scritti del Petrarca. In testa ai *Rerum Memorandarum* (1343) c'è il capitolo *de Otio Religiosorum* (1347), il quarto libro delle *Invectivae contra medicum* (1353), ed alcuni passi del *de Remediis Utriusque Fortunae* non rappresentano momenti nettamente separati nella produzione letteraria del Petrarca, bensì devono essere considerati nella reciprocità delle loro connessioni. La funzione della vita solitaria e ritirata si rivela costante e uniforme, e non abbandona il suo orientamento di base quando si incontra con altri modi di vivere quali la *vita occupata*, la vita sociale, o anche quelle discipline opposte alla filosofia morale come la medicina; ciò nonostante da questo complesso spirituale in cui entra, tale orientamento riceve al tempo stesso una determinazione nuova. Il concetto di solitudine rappresenta nel mondo speculativo del Petrarca un punto focale: da esso si dipartono direttrici varie verso zone problematicamente differenti; in esso si fonda l'unità di pensiero insita nell'opera petrarch-esca. Negli scritti del Petrarca il fattore individuale ha assunto significato generale, il generale ha però conservato, là dove si rivela e manifesta, la pura impronta dell'individuale. Nella storia dello spirito e nella storia letteraria gli scritti del Petrarca hanno quindi carattere esemplare, non solo perchè in essi certe idee ricevono una nuova forma artistica, bensì perchè fin dall'inizio furono essi stessi una nuova e indipendente forma. L'intervento del Petrarca nello sviluppo della riflessione su *otium* e *negotium*, su vita attiva e contem-plativa, avviene su materia a lui consona già in origine, che egli non aveva bisogno per appropriarsene intimamente di estraniare del suo significato e che d'altra parte attraverso l'assimilazione ricevette una vita nuova e più ricca. Ma proprio perchè realtà ideale e realtà sociale e politica vennero confrontate l'una coll'altra come inconci-liabili opposti, il pensiero umanistico indirettamente ricevette un nuovo compito ed una ulteriore direzione di progresso. Il problema in quale reciproco rapporto si trovino vita attiva e vita contemplativa, quali possibilità abbiano di congiungersi senza che le loro specifiche qualità particolari scompaiono, questa è l'alternativa con cui si trovarono confrontati gli umanisti del Quattrocento e anche del Cinquecento. D'altro canto la sorte personale degli umanisti e la loro posizione sociale, vale a dire il rapporto coll'ambiente in cui vivevano, si erano frattanto essenzialmente mutati. Non solo il gruppo di punta (Coluccio Salutati, Gianozzo Manetti, Carlo Marsuppini, Matteo Palmieri, L.-B. Alberti, Filippo di Ser Ugolino Perruzzi), ma anche gli dei minori si trovarono condizionati dalle vicende politiche cioè dai tentativi egemonici di Milano e dalla pericolante posizione di Firenze: la politica conferì al crescente interesse degli umanisti per la vita pubblica chiarezza e forza di convinzione, ai loro principi importanza e possibilità d'utilizzazione pratica. La situazione gen-erale risvegliò forze che collaborarono alla salvezza dello stato, aspirarono ed anche ottennero una partecipazione alla sua direzione. Grande era il numero di dotti e di collezionisti di codici e anticaglie che avevano rapporti coll'Umanesimo e al tempo stesso erano pro-fondamente immersi nelle vicende storiche del loro tempo e attenti e partecipi delle sue tendenze a trasformazioni. Verso la metà del secolo il legame che congiungeva Umanesimo e potenza statale si allentò: nel 1444 fu bandito Filippo di Ser Ugolino; nei decenni successivi G. Manetti e Rinuccini furono colpiti dalla stessa sorte. Sembrò che gli umanisti fossero costretti a mettersi su di una nuova strada: quella della rassegnazione, che era poi anche quella della contemplazione? Evidentemente una libera personalità poteva salvarsi solo in quanto le si concedeva spazio d'azione fuori dello stato. Il generale estraniarsi degli umanisti da interessi politici portò a maturazione l'età dei simposi e quel profondo apprezzamento della vita contemplativa che riempie l'atmosfera di Camaldoli. Nelle fascinanti *Disputationes* del Landino non viene, è vero, negata la possibilità della vita attiva e della vita contemplativa; in genere si ha tuttavia l'impressione che volontà e intenzione restino come assorbiti dalla speculazione filosofica. Durante la prima metà del secolo però tutte le forze venivano constantemente impiegate anche nel lavoro per scopi comuni, cioè nella produzione filosofico-morale, storiografica, letteraria degli umanisti c'era continuamente anche un secondo elemento, una componente di carattere attivo, energico, diretto verso lo stato: sviluppo della letteratura umanistica e suo influsso pratico nella vita fiorentina andavano di pari passo. Per la maggior parte essi appartenevano ai ricchi strati superiori della popolazione fiorentina. Tradizioni familiari, ricchezza, attività pubblica, relazioni procurate tramite matrimoni, tutti questi fattori formavano la premessa per un'influente posizione nella società. Uomini come il Salutati, Roberto de' Rossi, Niccolò Niccoli, Leonardo Bruni, Manetti, Palmieri svilupparono un'intensa attività ed ebbero nelle mani un grande potere politico.

La situazione politica rese l'atteggiamento ideale degli umanisti aperto e ricettivo verso la Roma repubblicana (Cino Rinuccini, Leonardo Bruni). Hans Baron ha dimostrato che il dialogo tra un padovano e un veneziano di Giovanni Conversini è del 1404: l'antitesi di vita attiva e vita contemplativa si amplia e abbraccia l'opposizione tra monarchia e repubblica. La condanna dantesca di Bruto e Cassio non fa più autorità. Se prima la stima per Cicerone aveva la sua origine proprio nella supposta separazione tra attività speculativa ed impegno pratico, colla scoperta delle *Epistolae familiares* viene ora alla luce un aspetto di Cicerone nel quale i compiti dell'azione pratica e della speculazione teorica, della azione educativa e della ricerca appaiono coincidenti. In un clima politico nuovo e diverso, lo scrittore latino, anche come cittadino, viene ora valutato positivamente, come del resto successe anche a Dante.

La guerra con Milano mise in luce in così ampia maniera l'importanza della politica, da far giungere a maturazione fermenti sparsi un po' ovunque: in tal modo è possibile un crescente interesse per tutte le questioni di ordine storico-politico. Si ha quasi l'impressione che il *de Vita Solitaria* del Petrarca sia stato messo da parte e sostituito con quelle forme di vita civile cui preludeva il *de Via Associabili et Operativa* iniziato dal Salutati nel 1392. Desiderio e volontà di realizzare questa forma di Umanesimo civile raggiungono nel Bruni il loro apice divenendo una parte della stessa realtà, attesa e speranza portanti già in sè la garanzia della realizzazione. La politica doveva confermare gli ideali: è dunque ovvio che Poggio attorno al 1430 realisticamente riempia di lodi la romana res publica e la romana virtus, senza trovare un minimo di soddisfazione nel culto cesariano vivo invece nei centri dell'Italia settentrionale dominati da tiranni. Ma nella Firenze del Bruni, dell'Alberti, del Palmieri, tutta la sfera della formazione culturale dell'Individuo s'era spostata a favore di una formazione a servizio della città e degli scopi della sua politica, tanto che sembrò raggiunta l'armonia di ideali estetici ed ideali politici, il loro vicendevole intrecciarsi e reciproco completamento.

La dialettica dei concetti vita attiva e vita contemplativa si fonda su di un terreno vitale tipico e proprio del secolo XV, altrimenti resterebbe senza spiegazione il fatto che tanti scrittori s'incontrano in un medesimo scopo comune, cui in verità s'avvicinano da direzioni diverse e partendo da premesse differenti. Può succedere, ne è esempio la persona di Cosimo de' Medici, che la vita attiva porti in sè i tratti di un ideale, e che questo venga interpretato e indirizzato secondo le esigenze che il soggetto vi introduce. Quando, come spesso è il caso, non si giunge alla conciliazione degli opposti, bensì ad un loro vicendevole indistinto sovrapporsi in toni cangianti, ciò dipende dalla situazione per cui l'insieme delle opere appare in molti scrittori come un processo dialettico che si va costruendo sulla base dell'alternanza di tesi e antitesi. Ai *Libri della famiglia*, dove troviamo l'elogio della vita attiva, l'Alberti ha contrapposto il *de Tranquillitate Animae*: antitesi della *Vita civile* del Palmieri è la *Città di vita*, dove lo sviluppo della rappresentazione si muove su di uno sfondo di carattere teologico: alla sintesi si giunge tramite un superamento della realtà che viene abbandonata alle proprie spalle per giungere alla divinità. Il Landino pensa di poter raggiungere e impossessarsi della verità solo muovendosi tra forze contrastanti che si illuminino a vicenda. Dal Salutati non si sprigionò solo quella forza vivificatrice con cui il politico intervenne nella vita pubblica fiorentina: in tutto il *de Seculo et Religione* è costante la traccia che conduce al punto ascetico finale; le negazioni del mondo vengono pronunciate e ripetute capitolo per capitolo restando tanto connesse fra di esse da sembrar svilupparsi l'una dell'altra. Che nelle stesse persone gli opposti si trovino così ravvicinati dipende dal fatto che, per lo più, negli umanisti la riflessione dialettica assume forme dialogiche: le specu- lazioni teoriche dei pensatori hanno bisogno dell'interlocutore, e il colloquio, passando il filo del discorso e delle idee dall'uno all'altro dei dialoganti, si sforza di giungere a sempre maggiore nitidezza e precisione.

Quanto Leo Battista Alberti con decisione afferma nella *Famiglia* e cioè: 'L'uomo essere dalla natura costituito nel mondo spettatore et operatore delle cose', e poi anche il *de Dignitate Hominis* del Manetti (replica al *de Contemptu Mundi* di papa Innocenzo III) possono senza dubbio apparirci come chiare indicazioni per l'uomo a mettersi con fermezza sulla via dell'azione; nell'ambiente però dell'Accademia platonica si forma un nuovo rapporto tra i poli donde nasce l'opposi- zione di vita attiva e vita contemplativa. Se si richiama infatti un momento alla memoria l'ambiente ideale della *Theologia Platonica*, alla cui retta comprensione tanto hanno contribuito gli studi e le edizioni di Kristeller e Raymond Marcel, ci si presenta un'unità di concetto e visione estatica che viene indicata dalle seguenti parole del Ficino:

Quod si mens quanto alis ad contemplanda spiritualia elevatur, tanto longius discedit a corporalibus, supremus autem terminus quem attingere potest intelli- gentia, est ipsa dei substantia; sequitur ut tunc a mortalibus sensibus aliena.

Qui, al di là del mondo dei sensi, la *contemplatio* si solleva in una atmosfera mistico-platonica, in una zona sciolta da ogni legame, non più oppressa da barriere e dalla forza del tempo; e solo in tale con- testo, col compiersi dell'unificazione di attività intellettiva e situazione estatica, essa giunge a quella profondità e ricchezze che le sono vera- mente proprie: ogni tentativo di interpretazione intellettuale diventa allora inadeguato. Forse non c'è scritto quattrocentesco così intima- mente aderente alle creazioni ficiniane da poter essere considerato stringente prodotto espressivo del mondo e della sensibilità del filo- sofo fiorentino; pur tuttavia non mancano le opere dove molti sinto- matici riferimenti scoprono i rapporti che le collegano al mondo ideale ficiniano. La filosofia, inclusa quella sincretistica del Pico, il cui contenuto globale va ben oltre i confini della filosofia morale degli umanisti, poteva essere anche norma metodica ampiamente accettata.

In Firenze quelle speciale concezione della politica che ebbe nella vita attiva la sua tradizione pratica, conferì alla vita praticamente impregnata la sua importanza e il suo significato particolare: il quadro ideale era nello stesso tempo contemplazione del reale e prodotto derivato della realtà. Come il tic tac del pendolo conferisce al tempo la sua misura, così il mondo spirituale si fonda sul vicendevole connettersi ed influenzarsi di mondo dell'esperienza e mondo dell'idealità.

Negli altri stati italiani lo sviluppo dell'Umanesimo partì da premesse diverse, anche se sotto certi aspetti si trovò a percorrere la stessa strada su cui fin dall'inizio s'era messo l'umanesimo fiorentino. Decisamente su questa direzione si pose ad esempio l'Umanesimo napoletano dell'ambiente di Alfonso d'Aragona, di Alfonso il Magnanimo, il quale fin da principio ebbe lo sguardo rivolto verso l'Umanesimo fiorentino. Nel 1441 Leonardo Bruni dedicò ad Alfonso il Magnanimo la traduzione della *Politica* di Aristotele; Poggio gli inviò la traduzione della *Ciropedia*: alle corte dell'Aragonese soggiornarono umanisti come il Filelfo, il Gaza, il Barzizza. A Napoli al Panormita toccò il ruolo di mediatore; a Napoli il Valla, che per tredici anni (1435–48) fu al servizio del re Alfonso, compose tutto un gruppo di sue opere. A Napoli nacque il *de Dignitate Hominis* del Manetti, e si sa che le relazioni del Manetti con Firenze restarono anche in quegli anni molto stretti; a Napoli, ad opera di Giovanni Pontano, si formò l'Accademia Pontaniana, già anticipata dalle dotte riunioni nella Villa del Panormita. Nel mondo umanistico delle province meridionali l'Accademia Pontaniana fu un vero centro propulsore che portò avanti la tradizione umanistica e dal quale si mossero direttrici varie verso diverse sfere della problematica spirituale del tempo. Anche in questo ambiente il tema della vita contemplativa riflette sia gli elementi oggettivi che quelli personali della speculazione: tanto un capitolo del *de Voluptate* del Valla quanto il *de Morali Disciplina* del Filelfo, come anche il *de Prudentia* del Pontano riproducono quella scala di esperienze, quella graduata situazione in cui si svolge la teorica della vita contemplativa. Il Pontano nel suo trattato *de Prudentia* indubbiamente ha in mente un ordinamento di vita che ingloba sia la contemplazione che la vita attiva, e senza voler ricacciare questa nella sfera dell'utilizzazione pratica, offre quella come teoria a servizio della vita. Solamente il particolare significato di *contemplatio* svolto negli ultimi capitoli del trattato porta la contemplazione in una sfera diversa. In realtà vero è il senso di congedo dalla vita che a quest'ultima sezione conferisce il suo carattere specifico. Accanto all'esigenza di una totalità delle forze che devono giungere nello stato e nell'individuo a libera espressione, si presenta e si allinea ora il concetto di contemplatio unita alla lode dell'*otium*. La riflessione del Pontano, tramite una rievocazione delle vicende della vita trascorsa, si inserisce in quelle (nella contemplatio cioè) con un significato originario e nuovo:

Egeo vero ingenue, quo vobiscum agam, meaque pro consuetudine, nam et vos ipsi vitam, mores, studia, actionesque iam novistis meas, nunc demum ante actae vitae capio...In tranquillissimo otio constitutus coelitum mihi ipse videor sortitus vitam...Mente autem sic fruor, ut solam hanc meam ducam, soli huic inhaeream, eam unam exerceam ac colam quotidie aliquid aetate hac studiisque meis dignum contemplatus, cogitationes ipsas meas aut scriptis mandans aut cum amicis eas conferens.

Fin dagli inizi del secolo XV vita attiva e vita contemplativa hanno formato solidi punto d'avvio per molte opere e molte riflessioni; col passare del tempo, dopo ogni passo in avanti, dopo ogni scoperta, dopo ogni trasformazione della vita pubblica, quei concetti si rivestono di una problematicità che guadagna via via sempre nuova e diversa reputazione. Significa questa costante trasformazione, vicendevole ravvicinamento e reciproca conciliazione degli opposti oppure l'abisso tra di essi non si è invece unicamente andato ampliando? L'opposizione è fondata su aspetti particolari e storicamente sottoposti a mutamento, oppure si trova essa insita nella struttura stessa di questa tematica, così che il progressivo svilupparsi dei suoi metodi e dei suoi contenuti nient'altro poteva produrre se non renderla sempre più evidente?

A questo punto dobbiamo attirare l'attenzione sul fatto che le diverse teorie riguardanti la vita contemplativa sviluppate via via dagli umanisti italiani, dal Bruni al Filelfo, a Sperone Speroni, al Cardano ed a molti altri, nonostante tutte le differenze, hanno almeno una cosa in comune, e cioè esse rappresentano tentativi di chiarificazione della teoria aristotelica. Se nel Medioevo esistevano ancora legami di tradizione fra la teoria aristotelica della conoscenza e i Vittorini e San Bonaventura, essi risultano nel Quattrocento interrotti; la spiegazione del termine greco θεωρία come *meditatio*, guardare, e di Θεωρεῖν περί τινος, *intuitio*, cioè scoprire nella contemplazione, come *speculatio*, come sguardo rivolto al risultato della contemplazione, risulta possibile. La partiztione, complementare di quella già istituita da Riccardo di San Vittore, vuole indicare che la *meditatio* in certo senso avviene *sine labore cum fructu*, la *speculatio* è al tempo stesso il *fructus* del *labor* della *meditatio*, la *meditatio* ricerca di quanto deve essere trovato, la *speculatio* immediatizzazione di quanto è stato trovato. Riccardo di San Vittore invece unifica *intuitio* e *speculatio* insieme entro la *contemplatio*.

L'atteggiamento teorico (meditativo) non porta in Aristotele affatto il nome di θεωρία, ma è dal filosofo greco chiamato διανοητικόν. Al contrario la θεωρία, la contemplazione, da Aristotele considerata compimento del senso umano della vita, non è atteggiamento da osservatori, non è atteggiamento da spettatori di fronte agli avvenimenti della vita che direttamente ci toccano. Qualsiasi cosa possa accadere, il contemplante non ha mai a che fare con fatti del genere.

Destinato fin da principio al fallimento è ogni tentativo di interpretare il βίος θεωρητικός di cui parla Aristotele come un atteggiamento da spettatori verso la vita che accompagni tutta un'esistenza' come un non fare niente e quindi un darsi invece che all'azione alla contemplazione. Ad una interpretazione simile manca ogni punto di contatto con la dottrina aristotelica della θεωρία. Proprio tentativi di un'interpretazione in questa direzione hanno avuto come conseguenze tutta una catena di aberrazioni le quali hanno provocato le obiezioni più strampalate nei riguardi di Aristotele: ne esporremo due, trattandole non con intento storico, ma con intento sistematico.

Nel primo dei suoi *Six livres de la république* Bodin determina quale sia la 'fin principale de la République bien ordonnée'. Lo scopo più alto e nobile dello stato sgorga dalla 'vraie félicité', che è il senso della vita statale; identico con questi è il senso della vita individuale. Come però ha indicato Aristotele, a livello del singolo esso consiste nelle 'vertus intellectuelles et contemplatives'. Quando un popolo ha la possibilità di attuare tali virtù, 'de s'exercer', cioè 'en la contemplation des choses naturelles, humaines et divines', può dire di avere a sua disposizione anche il 'souverain bien'. Sempre secondo Bodin, tale è l'opinione anche di Aristotele, almeno là dove il filosofo non fa concessioni alla 'plus commune opinion des hommes'. In armonia con Aristotele si può in tal modo delineare il rapporto tra 'vertus contemplatives' e triplicità delle 'choses'; alle 'choses naturelles' corrisponde 'la science', la quale 'distingue il "vrai" dal "faux"', alle 'choses humaines' corrisponde 'la prudence', che decide a proposito del 'bien' e del 'mal'; alle 'choses divines' corrisponde 'la vraie religion' la quale sa discernere la 'piété' dalla 'impiété'. Chi possiede 'science, prudence et vraie religion', possiede 'la sagesse' cioè la radice della vera felicità. Soltanto la contemplazione corrisponde allora veramente e in senso completo alla dignità dell'uomo; ogni azione sia del singolo che dello stato deve essere strutturata in modo da trovarsi in armonia con esse. Ma 'contemplation' nel significato di quiete cui è riferito e tende ogni movimento della vita umana, è stata in Aristotele stesso, così afferma Bodin, celata entro 'un mot équivoque', cioè 'action de l'intellect'. Aristotele indicando 'la contemplation comme une action de l'intellect' fa scomparire la contrapposizione più importante, quella fra movimento, 'action', et quiete, 'repos'.

E chiaro che Bodin non parla della θεωρία aristotelica, anche se crede di occuparsi di essa; si è infatti visto che la parte costruttiva della θεωρία consiste proprio in un realizzare traducendo in azione, così che θεωρεῖν significa un portare a compimento lo ἐπίστασθαι mentre Bodin nella contemplazione riconosce il carattere de la quiete, 'le repos très haut', il non fare nulla.

Il non fare nulla ha però una conformazione che va descritta con precisione maggiore: si tratta di una non partecipazione alle vicende della vita pratica, e sopratutto di un abbandonarsi a disinteressati problemi speculativi. Esso comincia come vedere, 'voir la diversité des choses humaines', col proposito però di ricercare il fondamento delle cose: 'cherchant toujours les causes des effets qu'il voit'. Nelle 'choses divines' il processo ha uno svolgimento analogo; 'la contemplation' comincia coll'intravedere la 'harmonie mélodieuse de tout ce monde': in questo osservare è insito 'un plaisir admirable' come anche 'un désir perpétuel de trouver la première cause'. A questo punto c'è un arresto del processo contemplativo, 'il arreste la course de ses contemplations'. Lo speculante osserva che Dio è 'infini et incompréhensible essence'. Bodin conclude che col tramite della 'contemplation' è stato possibile dimostrare ('résoudre une démonstration') che Dio è uno, infinito, eterno.

Come si vede, la *contemplation* di Bodin è *meditatio*, fondamento di *intuitiones*, e non invece *speculatio*, vale a dire la θεωρία di Aristotele. La *contemplation* di Bodin può essere descritta come quiete in quanto essa per scopo non ha decisioni, ma cognizioni. La *meditatio* in senso cognitivo deve essere il fondamento della vita, e uomo nel senso ideale della parola è solo chi è dedito alla meditazione cognitiva. Oggetto di questa forma di meditazione può essere tutto, compreso cio che per Aristotele non può mai esser oggetto della θεωρία, e cioè la vita pratica, *les choses humaines*. Vive la vita come essa va vissuta non chi è attivo nella vita pratica, ma colui che sa contemplare tutto, tramite la meditazione cognitiva, e quindi anche la vita pratica.

Una tale concezione corrisponde a quanto in genere si pensa quando si discorre di vita contemplativa, come ad esempio dimostra la trattazione di Boll.

A questo tipo di interpretazione si deve lo sviamento della retta comprensione del significato di vita contemplativa nell'antichità.

Bodin rimprovera Aristotele di non aver trattato della *contemplatio* con serietà sufficiente; Bacon rimprovera Aristotele di aver eccessivamente gonfiato l'idea di *contemplatio*. Nel *de Dignitate et Augmentis Scientiarum* (v, 1) si legge che primo problema della filosofia morale è se si debba preferire la vita contemplativa o la vita attiva; la questione va risolta in maniera opposta all'opinione di Aristotele. Gli argomenti di Aristotele a favore della vita contemplativa risultano plausibili solo in rapporto alla dignità ed al piacere del singolo individuo, mentre la filosofia morale ha come oggetto la vita nella sua totalità. La teologia stessa, da cui poi la filosofia morale è determinata, ignora una vita puramente contemplativa, completamente rinchiusa in se stessa e che non getti raggi di luce o di calore sulla società umana. Persino la vita monastica non è puramente contemplativa; essa conosce infatti almeno alcune attività, quali ad esempio la preghiera, il sacrificio, la composizione di opere devote.

Bacon dunque non si riferisce, parlando di *contemplatio* alla *meditatio* cognitiva, come succede a Bodin, bensì ad un puro vedere, sciolto da qualsiasi forma di attività. Collegandosi al noto aneddoto nel quale Pittagora, secondo la narrazione di Giamblico, spiega il βίος θεωρηκτιός paragonandolo al comportamento degli spettatori in Olimpia, aggiunge anche: 'In hoc humanae vitae theatro Deo et Angelis solum convenit ut spectatores sint.' La vita contemplativa, la vita come puro contemplare, non può esser elevata a principio fondamentale della filosofia morale.

Si tratti però sia dell'atteggiamento positivo di Bodin verso la vita contemplativa, intesa come meditatio cognitiva, sia della posizione negativa di Bacon verso di essa in quanto pura osservazione, è chiaro che in entrambi i casi Aristotele viene inteso come se si riferisse ad una condotta valida per tutta la vita, ad un atteggiamento durevole, in poche parole ad un ideale di vita. L'atteggiamento contemplativo è di qualità tale da poter essere da un uomo assunto in funzione della vita pratica.

Secondo Aristotele invece l'attegiamento verso la vita pratica non può a fatto essere θεωρητικός: la vita stessa non puó infatti per nulla diventare oggetto di θεωρία. Se, come del resto le tradizioni ascetico-mistiche inducevano a fare, si continuò a ritenere che anche originariamente il βίος θεωρητικός dovesse essere inteso come τρόπος τοῦ βίου cioè come subordinazione a determinate regole di tutta la vita di singoli individui raccolti in una comunità, si dovette congetturare che il βίος θεωρητικός venisse concepito come modulo connettivo di tutta una vita dedita alla *meditatio*. La supposizione non corrisponde al pensiero di Aristotele. Il βίος θεωρητικός di cui egli parla non è un *tropos*, ma un' idea guida nel complesso della esistenza, con un presupposto esplicito, e cioè che solo di tempo in tempo ed in particolari momenti di grazia essa è concessa all'uomo.

Gli uomini in genere e più precisamente gli ἐλεύθεροι, i capaci di realizzare il loro essere, non un particolare strato sociale, o i filosofi o anche una scuola, afferma Aristotele, sono da considerare come coloro che vivono la vita contemplativa. Nella mente di Aristotele dunque il βίος θεωρητικός non è un ideale di vita sul tipo di una regola monastica che si presenta come fissa norma a chi voglia condurre una vita ideale. Il βίος θεωρητικός non è quella forma di vita che si conduce nell'Accademia e nel Peripato, mentre all'esterno il mondo vive la sua vita indifferente, e non è nemmeno un complesso di azioni e atteggiamenti caratterizzanti coloro che hanno deciso di dedicarsi ad essa rinunciando alla vita pubblica. Aristotele ha mostrato che ciò che ha senso in se stesso è per questo motivo il principio ordinativo della vita e della formazione culturale, in modo tale che la vita è vita in tanto che è ordinata verso la θεωρία come sua massima possibilità. Come dottrina del βίος θεωρητικός considerato la possibilità più alta e il principio fondamentale,tale dottrina si rivolge alla totalità del complesso dell'esistenza nel suo possibile ordinamento ideale.

Bruni nell'*Isagogicon moralis disciplinae* si avvicina ancora in maniera molto pronunciata all'ideale aristotelico; successivamente si compie un movimento opposto: al discorso sulla vita attiva e sulla vita contemplativa venne dato valore tipologico, la controversia sull'ideale di vita divenne al tempo stesso una contesa sulla preminenza morale dell'una o dell'altra parte contendente: quell'oggettiva unione di opposti rappresentata dal binomio vita attiva e vita contemplativa si trovò coinvolta in una problematica per la preminenza di certi valori morali. Ognuno dei due partiti volle riservare a sè l'idealità nella sua esclusività.

La controversia che dura fino a secolo XVI inoltrato, si allontana sempre di più dalla sua origine aristotelica, trovando punti d'unione con varie dottrine monastiche o mistiche. La storia dunque della dottrina della vita contemplativa nell'umanesimo è al tempo stesso storia del trasformarsi dell'interpretazione di Aristotele.

NOTA BIBLIOGRAFICA

Elenco dei principali autori che hanno trattato nel Rinascimento il tema della vita attiva e della vita contemplativa

Leon Battista Alberti, *de Iciarchia*, ed. C. Grayson, in *Opere volgari*, II (Bari, 1966).

Profugiorum ab aerumna, ed. Grayson, in *Opere volgari*, II (Bari, 1966).

I libri della famiglia, ed. Grayson, in *Opere volgari*, I (Bari, 1960).

Poggio Bracciolini, *de Varietate Fortunae* (Parigi, 1723).

de Infelicitate Principum (Parigi, 1474).

de Miseria Humanae Conditionis, in *Opera* (Basilea, 1538).

Leonardo Bruni, *de Studiis et Litteris*, ed. H. Baron, *Leonardo Bruni Aretino. Humanistisch-philosophische Schriften* (Leipzig e Berlin, 1928).

Ysagogicon moralis disciplinae, ibid.

Giannantonio Campano, *de Gerendo Magistratu*, in *Opera* (Venezia, 1459).

Pandolfo Collenuccio, *Apologhi*, in *Operette morali, poesie latine e volgari*, ed. A. Saviotti (Bari, 1929).

Agostino Dati, *Isagoras de ordine discendi*, in *Opera* (Venezia, 1516).

Oratio tertia de laudibus philosophiae, ibid.

Francesco Filelfo, *Epistola a Bartolomeo Francazano*, in *Epistolae* (Basilea, 1506), lib. I, ep. 36.

Galateo, *de Educatione*, ed. S. Grande (Lecce, 1868).

Cristoforo Landino, *Quaestiones camaldulenses* (Firenze, 1480 circa).

'de Nobilitate Animae', *Annali delle università toscane*, n.s. I (1916).

de Vera Nobilitate, ed. A. M. Bandini, *Specimen literaturae florentinae*..., II, 106–9.

Matteo Palmieri, *Della vita civile*, ed. S. Battaglia (Bologna, 1944).

Città di vita, ed. M. Rooke (Northampton–Paris, 1927).

Francesco Patrizi, *de Regno et Regis Institutione* (Parigi, 1512).

de Institutione Rei Publicae (Parigi, 1494).

Bartolomeo Platina, *de Optimo Cive*, ed. S. Battaglia (Bologna, 1944).

de Falso et Vero Bono (Parigi, 1530).

Francesco Petrarca, *de Vita Solitaria*, ed. G. Martellotti, in Petrarca, *Prose* (Milano–Napoli, 1955).

Secretum, ed. E. Carrara, *ibid.*

Fam. III, 12 e X, 5, ed. V. Rossi, vol. I, 129–31 e vol. II, 310–18.

Enea Silvio Piccolomini, *de Liberorum Educatione*, ed. J. St. Nelson (Washington, 1940).

Angelo Poliziano, *Lamia, Le selve e la strega. Prolusioni nello studio fiorentino*, ed. I. Del Lungo (Firenze, 1925).

Giovanni Pontano, *Charon*, ed. C. Previtera (Firenze, 1943).

de Principe (Venezia, 1501) e passim da altre opere.

Alamanno Rinuccini, *Dialogus de libertate*, ed. F. Adorno, Atti dell'Accademia toscana di scienze elettere 'La Colombaria' (1958).

Coluccio Salutati, *de Nobilitate Legum et Medicinae*, ed. E. Garin (Firenze, 1947).

Sperone Speroni, *Sopra le virtù discorso primo e secondo*, in *Opere*, III (Venezia, 1740), 394–402.

Della vita attiva, ibid. V, 417–18.

Lorenzo Valla, *de Voluptate (de Vero Bono)*, in *Opera* (Basilea, 1540), 896–999; *Scritti filosofici e religiosi*, ed. G. Radetti (Firenze, 1953).

Pier Paolo Vergerio, *de Ingenuis Moribus*, ed. A. Gnesotto, Atti e Memorie della R. Acc. di sc. lett. ed arti in Padova (1918).

24

THE CONFORMITY OF GREEK AND THE VERNACULAR

THE HISTORY OF A RENAISSANCE THEORY OF LANGUAGES

J. B. TRAPP

My subject is one on which, as far as I know, almost no serious work has been done.[1] A few scattered references[2] and one recent article[3] on one of the Italian upholders of the theory I shall outline, are all that exist. What follows belongs to comparative philology *avant la lettre*. Its interest for the modern student is less in its value, or lack of it, as linguistic theory—though far too little, in spite of Arno Borst's vast *Turmbau von Babel*,[4] has been written on renaissance theories of language. The use to which the supposed conformity was put in the practice of vernacular prose and verse during the late fifteenth and the sixteenth centuries in particular constitutes its claim on our attention. The rôle of Greek as a third contestant in what has usually been seen as a straight battle between Latin and the vernacular has not received its due.

At a certain point in linguistic self-consciousness practically every nation in Europe has entertained the notion that its vernacular had a special relationship with Greek. There were two chief ways in which, it was felt, the credibility of such a relationship might be established. First, if it could be shown that Greek colonists (or merchants) had settled in (or visited) one's country, it could be postulated that the Greeks had left their mark on one's language. The way was then

---

[1] What follows will eventually, I hope, be fleshed out into a book. For the moment, I attempt no more than an indication of the ground to be covered, giving only the most summary of footnote references.

[2] Bruno Migliorini, *Storia della lingua italiana*, 4th ed. (Florence, 1963), pp. 363, 459; and, especially, Carlo Dionisotti, *Gli umanisti e il volgare fra '400 e '500* (*Bibliotechina del Saggiatore*, xxix, Florence, 1968), pp. 1 ff., 38 ff. I owe thanks to Professor Dionisotti for much help.

[3] Tristano Bolelli, 'Ascanio Persio linguista e il suo *Discorso* (1592)', in *L'Italia dialettale*, xxx (n.s. vii) (1967), 1–28.

[4] *Der Turmbau von Babel. Geschichte der Meinungen über Ursprung und Vielfalt der Sprachen und Völker*, esp. vols. iii and iv (Stuttgart, 1960–3).

open for the thoroughgoing application of the second method of proof: the detection of similarities in word, phrase, structure and spirit. Once the 'conformity' of one's own language with Greek was proved to one's satisfaction it could be, and was, exploited in various ways. It could serve the down-to-earth pedagogical purpose of helping one to learn the Greek language. It could be used to justify linguistic and literary borrowing, which would be the less reprehensible if it were done from a cognate tongue, especially a classical one, rather than from what could now be seen to be a more distant relative, that is to say the Latin language. Lastly and most importantly, the kinship could, as it were, help the younger language to manhood. It would give to the vernacular a rich and sententious brevity superior to the watery diffuseness which results from the imitation of Latin, especially the Ciceronian variety. Congruity between the vernacular and the Greek could also be used to hasten the independence of the vernacular in another and more general way: by infiltrating behind Latin, the European learned language for fifteen hundred years, the hypothesis could be employed to break the hold of Latin and its prestige. If one's own vernacular was in close conformity with a classical tongue more truly civilised and more ancient yet than Latin, this would mean that the vernacular, enriched by the correspondences, was at least the equal of Latin, and even its superior.

A full account of the development, implications and applications of this curious linguistic hypothesis would involve us in a great many fields, some of them little explored: translation and imitation of Greek originals, for example; medieval and renaissance views of the validity of analogy[1] and anomaly as philological principles; the history of what E. R. Curtius has called 'etymology as a category of thought';[2] methods of teaching the classical languages; the history of dialect study and the use of 'rustic' words in poetry. The following pages cannot compass all these: they attempt no more than to present, by means of a small number of examples, a summary of how and by whom the notion was worked out and applied.

Early Italian humanist thought about language, as about other things, was anxious to throw the bridge back to the glories of Rome,

---

[1] Cf. E. Weber, *Die Bedeutung der Analogie für die Beschäftigung H. Estiennes mit der Vulgärsprache* (*Marburger Beiträge zur roman. Philologie*, xxv, Marburg, 1939).

[2] *Europäisches Literatur und lateinisches Mittelalter*, 4th ed. (Bern, 1963), pp. 486–90.

beside which the Greeks were as nothing. The single, massy strength of the Latin language was what appealed to Lorenzo Valla, about 1430: the variety of Greek, with its four dialects plus the κοινή, was an index of the giddiness and lack of stability of those who spoke and wrote it.[1] But as the century goes on and interest in and knowledge of Greek language and literature grow, a different voice is heard. In 1496 Aldus Manutius observes—more or less neutrally—that the variety and copiousness of Greek is imitated in the Italian vernacular, with its various dialects.[2] Aldus does not pursue the matter in favour of Italian, as does Raffaele Maffei ten years later.[3] Maffei argues for the similarity of Greek and Italian, pointing out a few rather haphazard resemblances in the sounds of words, as well as making the indisputable point that Greek colonisation of southern Italy has left its mark on southern dialects. A little later Baldassare Castiglione, in the *Courtier*,[4] makes the comparison an argument for eclecticism in the *volgare* against the purity of Tuscan. (It is worth observing that one of the later and most thoroughgoing Italian advocates of the 'conformity' hypothesis, Ascanio Persio, was republished in 1874, when the *questione della lingua* was once more in the foreground.[5])

By early in the sixteenth century, too, the beginnings of the 'conformity' hypothesis were apparent in France—in Jean Lemaire de Belges, for example.[6] In 1529 Guillaume Budé, the foremost Hellenist in France, is making some play with the correspondences.[7] He goes further than any of the Italians in the seeking of precise analogies, but he does not attempt to pursue the matter to practical lengths for the enrichment and exaltation of the vernacular. Nor does he invoke the example of the five Greek dialects. The sort of thing that impressed Budé was that both Greek and French possess an aorist, which Latin does not, and that both can indicate (as Latin and Italian cannot) whether something was done earlier today, or yesterday, or years ago. Vocabulary, too, shows consonances, he feels: μωκᾶσθαι/*mocquer;* πιεῖν/*boire:* δειπνεῖν/*diner:* γάρ/*car:* φελλός, cork, gives *pantophelli,* i.e. *pantofles;* ὁ χιτών is *ocheton.* Budé was, of course, aware that a good many Greek-looking words come into French via Latin.

---

[1] Preface to *De Elegantiis linguae latinae* (*Opera omnia* (Basel, 1540), i, 4).
[2] Preface to *Thesaurus cornucopiae et horti Adonidis* (Venice, 1496).
[3] *Commentarii* (Rome, 1506), fo. 435; see Dionisotti, *Umanisti e volgare*, pp. 38 ff.
[4] (Venice, 1528), Book i (*Opere*, ed. C. Cordié (Milan–Naples, 1960), p. 60).
[5] Ed. by F. Fiorentini (Naples, 1874).
[6] *Les Illustrations de Gaule et singularitez de Troie* (Paris, 1510–13).
[7] *Commentarii linguae græcae* (Paris, 1529; ed. Paris, 1548), pp. 211 ff.

Budé is concerned with scholarly likenesses: etymologies and the like. The poets of the Pléiade, a little later, with their use of Greek words and Greek forms, linguistic and poetic, take firmer steps in the direction of the practical application of the 'conformity' hypothesis, their assumption being that French will bear these better and more easily than it will bear Latin. Du Bellay,[1] for example, believes in the 'conformity' and, in the *Suravertissement* to the *Odes* of 1550, Ronsard comes down firmly for it.[2]

Just about this time, also in France, there appear the first theoretical treatises which attempt to explore, in a systematic way, the conformity of Greek and the vernacular. Not all are of equal sanity: some go so far as to assert that the Gauls were, in fact, *prisci Graeci* and the relationship is that way round. The main impulse is associated especially with Henri Estienne,[3] *le Grand*, compiler of the *Thesaurus linguae graecae*. Lesser names are Joachim Perion,[4] Jean Picard,[5] a certain Blasset,[6] and Léon Trippault.[7] The attempt to establish conformity lasts well into the seventeenth century and is still employed by Claude Lancelot,[8] of Port-Royal, in somewhat the same way as by Estienne, as an aid in the teaching of Greek. (As late as the nineteenth century, too, such eminent scholars as Emile Egger[9] and Emile Littré[10] are still asserting, though on less definite grounds, a special affinity between Old French and Homeric Greek.) Two Italians, Ascanio Persio[11] and Angelo Monosini,[12] at the end of the sixteenth century and the beginning of the seventeenth, wrote

---

[1] *Defence et illustration de la langue française* (Paris, 1529), Bk. II, cap. 9.

[2] *Les Quatre premiers livres des Odes* (Paris, 1550). On Ronsard and the Pléiade, see esp. I. Silver, *Ronsard and the Hellenic Renaissance*, I (St Louis, 1961).

[3] *Traité de la conformité du langage français avec le grec* [n.p., ?1566]; (Paris, 1569); ed. L. Feugère (Paris, 1853). Feugère's introd. to his ed., with L. Clément, *H. E. et son œuvre française* (Paris, 1898) are still the best works on this aspect of Estienne.

[4] *Dialogorum de linguae Gallicae origine, eiusque cum Graeca cognatione libri IV* (Paris, 1555).

[5] *De prisca Celtopaedia libri V* (Paris, 1556).

[6] H. Omont, 'Un helléniste du XVIe s.: *Excellence de l'affinité de la langue grecque avec la française*, par Blasset', in *Revue des études grecques*, XXX (1917), 158 ff.

[7] *Celt'hellénisme ou Etymologie des mots français tirez du grec. Preuves en général de la descente de notre langue* (Orléans, 1581).

[8] E.g. *Le Jardin des racines grecques* (Paris, 1664); still in use in French schools in the late nineteenth century.

[9] 'Revue des traductions françaises d'Homère', in *Mémoires de littérature ancienne* (1862), pp. 164–217.

[10] 'La poésie homérique et l'ancienne poésie française', in *Revue des deux mondes* (1 July 1847), pp. 109–61. On Egger and Littré in this connection see I. Silver, *Ronsard and the Hellenic Renaissance in France*, I (St Louis, 1961), 2–3.

[11] *Trattato della conformità della lingua italiana con la greca* (Bologna, 1592; Venice, 1592).

[12] *Floris italianae linguae libri IX* (Venice, 1604).

treatises on Greek and Italian in emulation of Estienne's *Treatise on the conformity of the French language with the Greek*, which was first published in 1566 and reprinted in 1569.[1] Spaniards[2] and Flemings,[3] from the sixteenth to the eighteenth centuries, asserted a similar kinship between their language and Greek. The gravity of Leibniz[4] and the fantasy of Klopstock[5] in their attempts to exploit the kinship between Greek and German, in which both of them believed, are also part of the story. English versions I leave for a little later.

All these attempts are associated to a greater or less degree with a phase of linguistic chauvinism and purism. Estienne wants French to capitalise on the supposed affinity, which he defends on etymological, syntactical and historical grounds, for various reasons. French will thus be freed, he feels, from the dominance of Latin and that degenerate (linguistically and morally) modern descendant, Italian; what borrowing is done will be done from a close relative; French will, by alliance with its close kindred classical tongue, become strong enough to stand on its own; and finally, Frenchmen will, by exploiting the kinship, be more easily enabled to learn Greek itself.

Estienne comes down heavily on the side of brevity, in which he finds Greek much superior to Latin: like most of his contemporaries he admired sententiousness. He runs through the similarities that he finds, one after the other, taking turns of phrase, constructions and the parts of speech in order, insisting sometimes on etymology, sometimes on structure as the means of establishing the analogy. French and Greek, for example, possess the definite article, as Latin does not; and the partitive genitive: French and Greek can distinguish between 'φαγεῖν ἀρτόν', 'φαγεῖν τὸν ἀρτόν', and 'φαγεῖν τοῦ ἀρτοῦ', where Latin can only say *panem edere*. French and Greek can use infinitives as nouns; τὸ φαγεῖν/*le manger*. There is no time here to go into Estienne's hundreds of particular correspondences. Again and again, too, he insists on the conformity of *esprit* between the two languages: the gaiety and lightness that both Greek and French can oppose to

---

[1] See above, p. 242 n. 3.

[2] E.g. Juan de Valdes, *Diálogo de la lengua*, composed 1535–6; Diego Matute de Peñafiel Contreras, *Prosapia de Cristo* (Baça, 1614); Bernardo Aldrete, *Del Origen y principio de la lengua castellana...* (Rome, 1606).

[3] E.g. Hadrianus Junius, *Animadversorum libri VI* (Basel, 1556); Willem Otto Reisz, *Belga graecissans* (Rotterdam, 1730).

[4] E.g. *Unvorgreifliche Gedanken, betreffend die Ausübung und Verbesserung der teutschen Sprache* (c. 1697), posthumously published in *Collectanea etymologica* (1717); *Nouveaux Essais* (1703–4), posthumously pub., Livre III.

[5] *Grammatische Gespräche, III, Der Wohlklang* (1793); *Werke*, ed. Back–Spindler, XIII (Leipzig, 1830), 61 ff.

the heaviness and stolidity of Latin; and he insists on the necessity, in translation, of matching *phrasis*.

This last had been the burden of the only English example I have time for. In about 1533 Sir Thomas Elyot, in the preface to his translation of Isocrates's *Ad Nicoclem*[1] asserts that

the forme of speakyng, used of the Grekes, called in greeke, and also in latine, *Phrasis*, much nere approcheth to that, whiche at this daie we use: than the order of the latine tongue: I mean in the sentences and not in the wordes: which I doubte not shall be affirmed by them who sufficiently instructed in all the said thre tunges, shall with a good iudgement reade this worke.

Elyot's idea of a close structural relationship between English and Greek had been stated a few years earlier, in 1528, by William Tyndale, though Tyndale is more specific about Hebrew–English resemblances.[2] It has, I believe, important consequences in England for the translation of the Bible especially and for English prose in general. I must omit the theory and practice of Sir John Cheke[3] and Sir Thomas Smith[4] and I cannot here do more than register a conviction of the significance of the belief in 'conformity' in the development of the anti-Ciceronian and the aphoristic styles.

Space is wanting, too, to trace and differentiate the history and implications of the notion of a 'conformity' between Greek and the vernacular in the many different hands in which it found itself during the Renaissance. I have merely tried, at an early stage of my work on it, to emphasise its importance for the practice of contemporary vernacular verse and prose by using as great a variety of its applications as I could. Its interest for the historian of literature and language constitutes its claim on our attention: its exemplary value for the mechanics of classical influence in the Renaissance is, I believe, considerable.

---

[1] *The Doctrynal of Princes* (London, ? 1533). See also James Wortham in *Huntington Library Quarterly*, XI (1947–8), 219–40; Elisabeth Holmes, in *Review of English Studies*, XII (1961), 352–63; and the works cited therein.

[2] Preface to *The Obedience of a Christian Man* ([Antwerp], 1528); ed. H. Walter, *Doctrinal Treatises...* (Cambridge, Parker Society, 1848), pp. 148–9.

[3] In his trans. of Matthew: Cambridge, Corpus Christi Coll., MS. Misc. D [James, 104] (ed. by Jas. Goodwin, Cambridge, 1843, is inaccurate and misleading); and his share of *De pronunciatione linguae graecae*, letters written in 1542 (Basel, 1555). *De recta et emendata linguae anglicanae scriptione dialogus* (Paris, 1568); cf. William Camden, *Britannia* (London, 1607), p. 21.

PART VI

CLASSICAL THEMES COMMON TO
LITERATURE AND ART
AND CLASSICAL INFLUENCES
IN ARCHITECTURE

25

PERSONIFICATION

E. H. GOMBRICH

In standing before this learned audience I really feel like Ignorance personified. I have never worked in the fields of which you are masters. But perhaps it is not entirely unfitting that Ignorance should be asked to open the proceedings of this Conference[1] for if I understand its purpose we have really come together to discuss that perennial Socratic or Petrarchian theme, our own ignorance. We have not been invited to tell each other what we know but what we would like to know. It is said that one fool can ask more questions than seven wise men can answer, and in the presence of so many wise men I willingly accepted the assignment of that fool. For quite honestly I do not owe the honour of heading the list of speakers to any contribution I have made or can make to the study of classical influences between 500 and 1500. I owe it, I suppose, to the undeniable fact that I happen to be the only holder of a University Chair specifically devoted to the History of the Classical Tradition. The title is somehow bound up with the Directorship of the Warburg Institute which was dedicated by Aby Warburg to the untranslatable question *Was bedeutet das Nachleben der Antike?*—what is the significance of the classical heritage for Western civilisation?[2] The very form of a question into which Warburg cast his theme may serve to remind you of the fact that he was not simply an advocate of classical education or classical studies. What really concerned him was the value of this tradition for human civilisation, which he conceived of as a precarious and most vulnerable achievement. What elements we derive from ancient civilisation have helped or hindered Western man in achieving psychological poise and rationality and keeping the powers of passion and of unreason at bay? Warburg's final answer was, I believe, that the classical heritage remained both a danger and a boon to our culture. The symbols we derive from antiquity may provoke a regression to that pagan mentality to which they owe their origins, but they may also help us to achieve what he

[1] This was the first paper of the first day of the Conference.
[2] Cf. now my book *Aby Warburg, An Intellectual Biography* (London, 1970).

called orientation, in other words they can serve as instruments of enlightenment.

Now if there is one element in the classical tradition which allows us to probe this view it is the habit of Personification. I need not enlarge on the ubiquity of this habit in the period under discussion for it is as familiar to historians of literature as it is to historians of art.[1] In fact, it seems to me sometimes that it is too familiar; we tend to take it for granted rather than to ask questions about this extraordinary predominantly feminine population which greets us from the porches of cathedrals, crowds around our public monuments, marks our coins and our banknotes, and turns up in our cartoons and our posters; these females variously attired, of course, came to life on the medieval stage, they greeted the Prince on his entry into a city, they were invoked in innumerable speeches, they quarrelled or embraced in endless epics where they struggled for the soul of the hero or set the action going, and when the medieval versifier went out on one fine spring morning and lay down on a grassy bank, one of these ladies rarely failed to appear to him in his sleep and to explain her own nature to him in any number of lines.

Confronted with such a baffling problem the line of least resistance in scholarship seems to me the suggestion that we should now go and make a survey of all personifications in our period and put their names and attributes on punched cards for computerisation. I do not want to spoil the pleasure of anyone who might propose such an enterprise, but I am not sure how much we would ultimately profit by it. Much more, in my view, can be gained by tracing the derivation and proliferation of individual personifications in the way the late Rosemond Tuve attempted in her masterly *Notes on the Virtues and Vices*.[2]

But even here, I feel, we might have profited more if we were a little clearer in our mind what the whole mode of personification is really about. I know that some of the most eminent students of our subject and our period have devoted some telling pages to the problem of personification in medieval literature; the chapters in C. S. Lewis, *Allegory of Love*[3] and of course the pages on the personal meta-

[1] Jacob Burckhardt's lecture of 1887, 'Die Allegorie in den Künsten', *Gesamtausgabe*, ed. Emil Dürr (Stuttgart, 1933), pp. 419–38.
[2] In *Journal of the the Warburg and Courtauld Institutes*, XXVI (1963), 264–303, II, XXVII, 42–72; see also the same author's book, *Allegorical Imagery. Some medieval books and their posterity* (Princeton, N.J. 1966).
[3] (Oxford, 1936), especially chapter II.

phor in Ernst Robert Curtius's book on *European Literature in the Latin Middle Ages*[1] would have to form the starting point of any future investigation. Both these authors have dwelt on the derivation of these personifications from classical antiquity, their link with classical mythology and what might be called their ambiguous origin in the twilight zone between the gods of Olympus and the abstractions of language.

To understand these antecedents we would have to ask our colleagues in Classics who have meditated about the strange disposition of Greek thought to turn concepts into gods and gods into concepts.[2] It is rarely possible to say at any particular point whether we are confronted with an abstraction or a divinity, not to say a demon. What is Nike or Kairos, the Tyche of a city or the Liberality of a Prince? St Augustine, as I have learned from Professor Perosa, made fun of the pagans who erected temples to such entities as Febris, only to serve Poliziano with a personification he could use in a poem.[3]

Personification has indeed been called by Professor T. B. L. Webster a Mode of Greek Thought,[4] and this mode, in its turn, has been linked with the peculiarity of the Greek language, matched, I believe by the Latin language, of forming abstract feminine nouns which are indistinguishable from the designation of female divinities. Max Mueller termed mythopoeic thought a disease of language, and it is indeed tempting to see in this habit one of the snares which language prepared for the unwary. In that case the belief in the literal existence of a personification would be a special case of the literal interpretation of the metaphors of language. When victory settles on the prow of the conqueror's ship she can be conceived of as a beneficent sprite or as a figure of speech.

I am sure that this description of the origins of personification is correct, as far as it goes, but I still think it leaves many questions unanswered. The first of these seems to me the most obvious one, but alas, I am not competent to discuss it: if it is true that personification

[1] (London, 1953), pp. 131–3.
[2] The standard article is L. Deubner's entry *Personifikationen* in W. H. Roscher, *Lexikon der griechischen und römischen Mythologie* (Leipzig, 1902–9), supplemented by F. Stössl's entry under the same heading in Pauly-Wissowa's *Real-Encyclopädie der Classichen Altertumswissenschaft*, xxxvii (1937). See also Roger Hinks, *Myth and Allegory in Ancient Art*, Studies of the Warburg Institute, 6 (London, 1939).
[3] Alessandro Perosa, 'Febris: a poetic myth created by Poliziano', *J. Warburg and Courtauld Inst.* ix (1946), 74–95.
[4] T. B. L. Webster, 'Personification as a Mode of Greek Thought', *J. Warburg and Courtauld Inst.* xvii (1954), 10–21.

can be explained psychologically through the structure of language one would like to know how far the habit is indeed shared among language communities other than the classical ones.

It was this I had mainly in mind when I asked at the outset whether we do not take personification a little too much for granted. Is it a more or less universal feature or is it confined to the classical tradition? If it is not, how far is it tied up with Indo-European languages? Clearly not totally, for we all remember some of the most telling and most lasting coinages from the Hebrew Psalms, such as the beautiful verse which the Vulgate renders as *iustitia et pax osculatae sunt*.[1] Could this be an echo of a Greek or Persian conceit, or is there an independent tradition of this kind in Semitic languages and literature?

The point of method which prompts me to raise this question is indeed a rather worrying one. Is it at all possible to study the classical tradition if one studies it in isolation? May not the distinctive features which give it its character escape us if we neglect looking out of the window at other traditions? The charge is frequently made nowadays against the humanist outlook that it is parochial and, as the jargon has it, Europocentric. I do not want to accept this charge, for I do think we have a perfect right to study our own tradition, first because it happens to be our own, and secondly also because it is the heritage of the Greco-Roman world which has, for good or ill, conquered and transformed the civilisation of the entire globe. But so much, I think, we can learn from this criticism, that we should never neglect comparative studies in order to find out what is distinctive in our Western modes of thought. I am lucky enough not to have to go far if I want to know how things were ordered in ancient India, for my son is a Sanskritist. I have learned from him that Sanskrit can form similar abstractions which can be and are personified. Take these charming lines of a petitioner which I quote in the translation by Daniel Ingalls from Vidyakara's *Treasury* dating from our early Middle Ages:

> Lady Speech, lend pure accent to my tongue.
> O Heart, be calm. Dignity, stand aloof.
> Shame, turn aside your face awhile
> And let Desire come forth;
> That I, foul sinner, may tell the rich man
> My humble sentence 'Give'.[2]

[1] LXXXIV, 11; for the influence see Samuel C. Chew, *The Virtues Reconciled* (Toronto, 1947), chapter II.
[2] Daniel H. H. Ingalls, *Sanskrit Pœtry, from Vidyakara's 'Treasury'* (Harvard University Press, Cambridge, Mass. 1968), no. 1477.

There exists a most interesting Sanskrit play dating from the late eleventh century A.D. which its first English editor called *The Moon of Intellect*.[1] Here Love and Passion, Hypocrisy, Avarice, Anger, Reason, Devotion, Religion and Tranquillity all make their appearance as in a medieval mystery play, and the question must inevitably arise in the mind of the Western reader whether this work, which appears to be almost totally isolated in Indian literature, may owe something to foreign influence. I do not think that this question has ever been investigated nor could I find a comparative study of the 'bounteous Immortals' in the Zend Avesta which include Good Mind, Truth or Righteousness, Rightmindedness and other *hypostases*.[2] It seems to me strange that nobody has made a cross-cultural study of this subject, but my hunch is that even within the Indo-European family the classical tradition of personification stands out. In the West these beings have not only a higher birthrate, but also a higher expectation of life. They become more fully assimilated to the immortals than they generally appear to be in the East.

Inevitably, then, our question concerning classical influences involves questions concerning the nature of the classical heritage itself. Curtius has drawn attention without much comment to the way in which classical authors draw up a kind of kinship system for Gods and personifications alike. For Homer, as he reminds us, Flight is the companion of Panic and Panic the son of Ares while Infatuation figures as the eldest daughter of Zeus, whose daughter in Hesiod is none other than Justice. Thus the personifications are drawn into the network of systematic rationalisation which characterises the development of the Olympian religion. I doubt if there is a parallel to this momentous development elsewhere. It involved, of course, the fusion of local deities and the assignment to the god of those definite roles with which a later tradition has made us familiar. It is in this tradition that the gods themselves become interchangeable with what we call abstractions, Eros becomes a mere token for love and Ares for war.

---

[1] *The Prabod'h Chandro'daya* or *The Moon of Intellect*, translated by J. Taylor (London, 1812). For a bibliography of later editions and translations see M. Schuyler in the *Journal of the American Oriental Society*, xxv (1904), 194–6. For the date see J. W. Boissevain, *Het indische Tooneelstuk Prabodhacandrodaya*, Proefschrift (Leiden, 1905), and Jai Dev., *The Prabodhacandrodaye of Kṛṣnamiśra, A critical edition of the text with an introduction and an essay on the development of allegorical literature in Sanskrit* (unpublished London Ph.D thesis, 1952).

[2] These are the terms used by R. C. Zaehner, *The Dawn and Twilight of Zoroastrianism* (London, 1961), p. 45. For a discussion of their status see Jacques Duchesne-Guillemin, *Symbols and Values in Zoroastrianism* (New York, 1966), pp. 25–39.

This was one of the ways in which Greek rationalism dissolved and sterilised the gods and prepared them for their survival within the Christian tradition. I do not think this particular development has a parallel in Eastern thought where the question whether the demons and the divinities of mythology really exist is bypassed in favour of other problems which may be more profound but do not permit this characteristic creation of a twilight zone between mythology and metaphor.

Be that as it may, the Greek way with the gods appears to me to have had another lasting influence on the Western heritage of personifications. I believe that it may be in this process of rationalisation that the most characteristic feature of this tradition is rooted, their characterisation by 'attributes'.

The images of Gods both in East and West are nearly always marked by distinctive features which permit easy identification. In the West, at least, these so-called attributes can usually be interpreted as minimal allusions to the rôle of the divinity; Zeus holds the thunderbolt and Athene is characterised by the Gorgoneion on her shield, the trophy of her victory over the monster.

But at some time in the history of Greek thought these attributes of the images were given a more rational or moral interpretation. Rudolf Pfeiffer, in a brilliant paper on 'The Image of the Delian Apollo and Apollinine Ethics',[1] has reconstructed a poem by Callimachus which must have offered such an interpretation in dialogue form. Thus Apollo is asked why he carries the bow in his left hand but holds the Graces in his right and made to reply that he uses the left because he is slow to punish mortals but the right 'always disposed to distribute pleasant things'. Pfeiffer connects this rationalisation of an ancient image with the Stoic movement and points out how frequently this form of dialogue was to be imitated later on. If you invert the procedure you have indeed the normal way of constructing an allegorical personification in which the nature of a concept is made visible by the attribute the figure displays, be it the tongues on the garment of Virgil's Fama or the forelock of Kairos whose bald hindhead will elude our grasp.

It is in this way, as we all know, that an image or a concept can be explicated by means of attributes and it is really a matter of taste or tact how far the poet or artist wishes to go in piling up these specifi-

---

[1] R. Pfeiffer, 'The Image of the Delian Apollo and Appollinine Ethics', *J. Warburg and Courtauld Inst.* xv (1952), 232–7.

cations, how many attributes he wants to give Prudence to match her definition.

We need not perhaps wonder at the fact that this technique survived in the Christian era, particularly as we know that the dependence of Christian poets and artists on classical models went so far as even to include representations of Nature divinities such as Sun, Moon, the Earth and Mount Bethlehem in biblical illustrations.[1] And yet we may ask whether there were not additional factors present to secure not only the survival but the proliferation of personification in our period.

Among the questions I should like to broach is first that of the Platonic tradition with its hierarchy of beings, its habit of hypostasis. In the Neoplatonic universe, I think, the personification of Justice or of Divine Wisdom can easily be conceived as a denizen of the intelligible world. The fact that the image approximates a definition and allows us to see the nature of the abstraction may have helped this process of assimilation. This, at least, is what I suggested in a paper I called *Icones Symbolicae*,[2] and though I am no longer quite happy with all the sections of that paper I should be grateful for critical reaction to my assertion that the picture of Justice can somehow be conceived as a kind of portrait or likeness of the Platonic idea of the concept.

When I wrote my paper I did not yet know Battista Fiera's little dialogue *De Iusticia Pingenda* which was published by Wardrop in 1957.[3] I would not want to overrate the evidence offered by this slight and half-humorous piece in which Mantegna complains of the conflicting advice he was given by philosophers whom he had asked how he should represent Justice. The dialogue is probably intended to echo the hunt for Justice in Plato's Republic rather than to tell us about the relation of artists to humanists; and yet it fits in with my interpretation that we are told that the learned scholastic theologian, the Carmelite Battista Mantovano, insisted that Justice cannot be depicted at all because she is identical with the will of God. The Dialogue thus points to the dangers and absurdities of attempting to

---

[1] Ferdinand Piper, *Mythologie und Symbolik der christlichen Kunst* (Weimar, 1847), is still worth consulting. A more modern survey is Raimond van Marle, *Iconographie de l'Art Profane au Moyen Age et à la Renaissance*, 2 (The Hague, 1932), and the entry 'Allegorie' by J. Held in O. Schmitt, *Reallexikon zur deutschen Kunstgeschichte* (Stuttgart, 1937).

[2] *J. Warburg and Courtauld Inst.* XI, 163–92.

[3] The Lion and Unicorn Press, London. The first edition dates from 1515, but the dialogue is set in Rome in 1489.

portray the virtue; throughout our period art always had a difficult stand *vis-à-vis* the intellectuals.

True, there were alternative ways of justifying these images before the court of reason. One of these has recently been rediscovered and explored—I mean the tradition of the Art of Memory so brilliantly elucidated by my colleague Frances Yates.[1] This tradition certainly created a climate that was favourable for the translation of abstract ideas into complex and striking images. And just as, in Ridewall's curious descriptions of the moralised gods known as the *Fulgentius Metaforalis*,[2] the appearance of these abstractions is distilled into little *versus memoriales*, so, I would surmise, the definition of an abstract concept could be fixed in the minds of the student by means of a painted definition.

And yet I do not think that we should overemphasise these rationalisations at the expense of what I would call the psychological problem of personification. Those who have emphasised that our languages which endow nouns with genders will tend naturally to personification are of course right.[3] In these language communities at least the disposition is always there. The real questions seem to me rather what part we should assign to this disposition and how it interacts with the tradition I have sketched. The natural dwelling place of personifications, if I may personify them in this way, is in the house of art. Art in our period is certainly conventional rather than spontaneous. It relies on precedence and this precedence points back to antiquity. If we ask what it was that led to the marriage between poetry and personification the true answer lies hardly on the purely intellectual plane. It lies less in the invention of suitable defining attributes than in the attractions of psychological and physiognomic characterisation. In describing Envy in her cave Ovid could make us visualise the evil hag who is Envy personified.

To be sure she has a serpent as her attribute but the character and feeling tone of such a creation extends far beyond the features which can be distinctly enumerated. Artistic characterisation differs from rational definition in that it creates symbols rather than signs.[4] What

---

[1] Frances Yates, *The Art of Memory* (London, 1966).

[2] Hans Liebeschütz, *Fulgentius Metaforalis*, Studien der Bibliothek Warburg, 4 (Leipzig, 1926). Beryl Smalley, *The English Friars and Antiquity in the early Fourteenth Century* (Oxford, 1960).

[3] For a survey of theories see I. Fodor, 'The Origin of Grammatical Gender', *Lingua*, VIII (1959), 1–41 and 186–214.

[4] Cf. my paper 'The use of Art for the Study of Symbols', *The American Psychologist*, XX (1965).

I mean is that the artistic personification is inexhaustible to rational analysis. It is to this that it owes what might be called its vitality or simply its vividness. While we are under its spell we are unlikely to ask whether such a creature really exists or is merely a figment of the artist's imagination. And thus the arts of poetry, of painting and sculpture, of drama and even of rhetoric aided by tradition can continue the functions of mythopoeic thought. Potentially personifications can always come to life again.

But what is potential and what actual in such psychological situations? Students of the ancient world could at least agree on a rough and ready rule of thumb by which to distinguish divinities from mere abstractions—the presence or absence of a cult. With the establishment of Christianity, of course, this simple criterion disappears, but the problem remains. How can we tell in any particular instance how a personification was seen and experienced by its creator and by his public? Should we consider the possibility of an unofficial mythology continuing into the Christian era and permitting a belief in such entities as *Natura* and *Sapientia*, Time or Death? Or is belief here too crude a category? Huizinga has suggested in an important chapter on our subject[1] that perhaps the marriage of St Francis to Poverty should be seen under the aspect of *homo ludens*, what children call pretending, and such pretending certainly extends beyond the realm of art. Don't we all pretend every year that Christmas personified will arrive in a sledge pulled by reindeers, or at least that our children believe that he will? What will a future historian make of our beliefs when he examines our Christmas cards? And what, to return more closely to the core of our problem, would be the conclusions of a visitor from Mars whose data are confined to our language habits but who could not know where figures of speech end and figures of thought begin?

Warburg certainly believed that in these matters one could and should take language at its word. One of the boldest and most imaginative passages in his paper on 'Francesco Sassettis letztwillige Verfügung' (1907)[2] attempts a psychological interpretation of the mentality of the Florentine merchant through an analysis of his last will and testament. Sassetti twice refers to Fortuna personified. 'I do not know', he writes, 'where Fortuna will take us in these dangerous and upsetting affairs, may it please God to grant us the favour of

---

[1] Johan Huizinga, *Homo Ludens* (Haarlem, 1938), chapter VIII.
[2] A. Warburg, *Gesammelte Schriften* (Leipzig, 1932), I, 127–63.

reaching the haven of Salvation', and again in commending their country palace to his sons, he adds 'However, if Fortuna should harass you, you will have to be content to sell it'. Warburg had no doubt that these words were meant to be taken literally. He speaks of Sassetti not shirking the fight with the pagan goddess who stands tangibly before his eyes, as an embodiment of the hostile world, 'an uncanny storm demon that may seize and wreck the frail ship of his life'. With that skill of forming historical associations that character-ised Warburg he linked this passage in Sassetti's will with the *impresa* of another Florentine merchant, Giovanni Rucellai, who had a figure of Fortuna with the bulging sail on his crest and who testified to his interest in the goddess by entering in his *Zibaldone* a letter by Ficino about the power of Fortuna and its limits.

I must refer you to Warburg's text for the rich and subtle way in which he uses this analysis as evidence in the psychological diagnosis of these Florentine merchants. It is a diagnosis which created a pro-found impression even on such men as Max Weber.[1] But needless to say our admiration for the boldness and profundity of Warburg's question does not commit us to accepting his answer. Is it true that in referring to Fortuna Francesco Sassetti was betraying a pagan outlook? Was such a turn of phrase felt to be at all unchristian? Did Sassetti or Giovanni Rucellai believe in the bodily existence of the goddess Fortuna?[2] Maybe they did believe in her when they did not think about it, though surely they would have denied any such belief if asked at pistol point.

But though it is true that Warburg's specific interpretation is open to criticism, I would not have referred to it in conclusion if I did not think that he asked the right kind of question. For complex and elu-sive as the real answer may prove to be, I think that if we gave up the search we would surrender the beleaguered fortress of the humanities to the enemy. What makes it worth while to busy ourselves with the period between 500 and 1500 is not, after all, that it provides material for the academic industry, but that people of flesh and blood lived at that time whom we would like to understand. If we give up this ambition we are left with the empty husk of forms and formulas.

[1] As we know from Warburg's correspondence.

[2] For the background see Howard R. Patch, *The Goddess Fortuna in Mediaeval Literature* (Cambridge, Mass. 1927). Professor Robert Browning has kindly drawn my attention to the letter of a Byzantine tenth-century scholar who was in two minds about the status of Fortuna. He has published a summary in *Byzantion*, XXIV (1954), 417, and the full text in ΕΠΕΤΗΡΙΣ ΤΗΣ ΕΤΑΙΡΕΙΑΣ ΒΥΖΑΝΤΙΝΩΝ ΣΠΟΥΔΩΝ XXVIII (1957), 192–3.

They would not be worth preserving in our libraries and museums if they did not point to a living experience. But we have no right to assume that they always point in the same direction; it is a false dichotomy to assert that those words and symbols which do not immediately reflect or express the inner life are mere empty conventions. Cultural conventions, in their turn, react back on their users, they are handed down by tradition as the potential instruments of the mind which may sometimes determine not only what can be said but also what can be thought or felt. I believe that the degree of this determination is at present being hotly debated in linguistics. I do not know whether it would be wise or foolish for the cultural historian to join this debate, but after all, I am always entitled to remind you of my rôle as the herald of Ignorance whose castle you are assembled to assail.

26

CRITICISM AND PRAISE OF THE PANTHEON IN THE MIDDLE AGES AND THE RENAISSANCE[1]

T. BUDDENSIEG

In the introduction to the third book of his treatise devoted to ancient architecture and published in 1540, Sebastiano Serlio praises the Pantheon as *la meglio intesa Architettura di tutte l'altre che io ho vedute, e che si veggono*.[2] This notion of the Pantheon as the most perfect example of architecture, and therefore the standard by which architectural excellence could be measured, was a product of the Renaissance. It remained valid until it was challenged by the discovery of the Greek temple and the Gothic cathedral in the late eighteenth century. The Middle Ages described the Pantheon either as the Christian church of Santa Maria Rotonda or, in speaking of the pagan Pantheon, as a 'house of devils'. In fact, only about a hundred years after the transformation of the pagan temple into a church in 614, the Venerable Bede relates this important and often recorded event as follows: Pope Boniface IV obtained from the Emperor Phocas the

templum Romae quod Pantheon vocabatur ab antiquis, quasi simulacrum esset omnium deorum: in quo ipse eliminata omni spurcitia, fecit ecclesiam sanctae Dei genetricis, atque omnium martyrum Christi; ut exclusa multitudine daemonum, multitudo ibi sanctorum memoriam haberet.[3]

This passage or a slightly different version in the *Chronica* was copied in most of the medieval world chronicles. We find it in the Regensburg Kaiserchronik, Gottfried of Viterbo and Martin of Troppau, to

[1] This paper is part of a more detailed study of the post-antique history of the Pantheon in Rome in my unpublished *Habilitationsschrift, Studien zum Nachleben antiker Architektur und Skulptur in Rom* (Berlin, Free University, 1965). Cf. my short note 'Das Pantheon in der Renaissance' in *Sitzungsberichte der Berliner Kunstgeschichtlichen Gesellschaft*, N.F., Heft XIII (1964–5), 3 ff. Michel Evans and J. B. Trapp from the Warburg Institute and Dr R. R. Bolgar of King's College, Cambridge, were kind enough to look through my English text.

[2] *Il terzo libro di Sebastiano Serlio*, cited after the edition of Venice, 1566, fos. 50 ff. Compare also Pietro Aretino, *Lettere sull'arte*, a cura di E. Camesasca, 1 (Milano, 1957), 49 f.

[3] *Venerabilis Bedae Historiam ecclesiasticam gentis anglorum*, ed. C. Plummer, 1 (Oxford, 1896), 88 (Lib. II, Cap. 4).

mention only a few.[1] The transformation of the pagan temple into a Christian church, the expulsion of the demons and devils was universally understood as a symbol of the victory of light over darkness, of truth over heresy, of the true God over the false gods.

In this specific instance it seems to me rather interesting to see how the horror and disgust inspired by pagan superstition generated an apparent distaste for the Pantheon, or at least produced a complete lack of interest in it as an architectural achievement. The *Legenda Aurea* describes the construction of the temple as an example of the *superbia* of the pagans, since the ground-plan was laid out with such dimensions that the dome could be finished only with the help of the devil.[2] In the *Mirabilia Urbis Romae* it was Cybele who showed Agrippa the building in a dream and asked him to build it in return for her help against the Persians.[3] All the different medieval stories about the Pantheon are united in the belief that it owed its existence to sinister forces of demons and not to the *ratio* or the genius of an architect.

This *Verteufelung* of the Pantheon is apparent in a beautiful description of it by Hermann of Fritzlar from about 1350. He tells vividly how Boniface destroyed the idols and how seventy-two demons fled in horror out of the broken statues. Then

der Romer apgot, der Tuvel, nam den Tynaphel obene von der Kirchen...Disen furte her von sente Peters munster...und das loch an der Kirchen, do der Tynaphel uffe stunt, daz stet noch offen, unde enmac nimant vorbuwen.[4] [The Romans' false God, the Devil, took the pine cone away from the top of the church...carried it in front of St Peter's...and the hole in the church where the pine cone was still remains open and nobody wants to close it.]

Hermann then concludes his story with what to my knowledge is a unique piece of architectural analysis of an ancient building in the Middle Ages:

Wanne, die Kirche ist gar groz und envhat nirgen kein sule in ir. [Ah, the church is very large and there is no column in it anywhere.]

[1] *Kaiserchronik*, ed. E. Schröder, *MGH*, D. Chron. I (1892), 171 ff.; Gottfried of Viterbo, *Pantheon*, ed. Waitz, *MGH*, ss. XXII (1872), 195 f.; Martin of Troppau, *Chron. pontif. et imperat.* ed. Weiland, *MGH*, ss. XXII (1872), 445.

[2] *Legenda Aurea*, ed. Graesse (Breslau, 1890, 3rd ed.), CLXII, 157. Arturo Graf, *Roma nella memoria e nelle immaginazioni del medio evo*, I (Torino, 1882), 180 f. The story told by Jacobus de Voragine is still referred to by Vasari in his account of the construction of the cupola of S. Maria Reparata, cf. *le Vite*, ed. Milanesi, II, 337 ff. Cf. also G. Baglione, *le Vite de' pittori ed architetti*, etc. (Roma, 1642), pp. 80 f.

[3] *Mirabilia*, ed. Valentini–Zucchetti in *Codice topografico della città di Roma*, III (Roma, 1946), 34 f.

[4] Franz Pfeiffer, *Deutsche Mystiker des 14. Jahrhunderts*, I (Leipzig, 1845), 230 f.

The eyes of Hermann of Fritzlar were so accustomed to Gothic architecture that his amazement at the enormous vault takes the form of a negative statement: the familiar dense row of pillars supporting the vault in Gothic cathedrals was miraculously lacking, and the many columns in the sidechapels of the Pantheon, structurally and virtually very different, were ignored.

It will not come as a surprise that the radical change in the attitude towards the Pantheon was due to Petrarch. A sentence of his *de Remediis Utriusque Fortunae* initiates the reappraisal of the Pantheon of Agrippa. Speaking of the transitoriness of human buildings and the vanity of glory sought through the erection of enormous edifices, Petrarch points to the decaying Rome as a monumental 'proof' of his thesis. Only the famous Pantheon of Agrippa was saved from destruction because of 'Maria, quae antiquissimam illam domum sui nominis virtute sustentat'.[1]

This means in my opinion the complete reversal of the medieval conception of the Pantheon, which involved together with the expulsion of the demons and the destruction of the idols, the literal annihilation of the pagan temple in the Christian church. Now Petrarch praises the Virgin for preserving the venerable temple which implies that Petrarch is probably the first since late antiquity to consider a pagan building worth preserving. Petrarch's pupil Fazio degli Uberti in his *Dittamondo* goes even one step further. He conceives the dedication of the temple to Mary as the peaceful and harmonious translation of power from Cybele, the mother of all gods to Mary, the mother of God.[2] Flavio Biondo is to my knowledge the first to speak of the Pantheon as Rome's most beautiful building and as the *insignis ecclesia, ceteras facile superans*. This characterisation of *Santa Maria Rotonda* as 'surpassing easily all the other churches in Rome' is a surprising and at the same time devastating critique of all of the church architecture in Rome up to Flavio's own time.[3]

The first attempts to draw or paint the Pantheon are found in two

[1] Francesco Petrarca, *de Remediis Utriusque Fortunae*, I, 118, in *Opera Omnia* (Basel, 1554), p. 42. Other references by Petrarch to the Pantheon are discussed by G. Billanovich, 'Un nuovo esempio delle scoperte e delle letture del Petrarca, I', 'Eusebio–Girolamo–Pseudo–Prospero', *Schriften und Vorträge des Petrarca Instituts Köln*, III (1954), 19, 48; and P. P. Trompeo and G. Martellotti, 'Cartaginesi a Roma' in *Nuova Antologia*, 16.12 (1943), 261. I owe these two references to the kindness of Professor Billanovich.

[2] Fazio degli Uberti, *Il Dittamondo*, a cura di G. Corsi. *Scrittori d'Italia*, 206–7 (Bari, 1952), I, 104 f. (II, ch. 6, vv.52 ff.): 'Il Panteon dentro dal grembo mio / allor fu fatto in nome d'una dia / la qual si disse madre d'ogni dio. / Di questa cosi bella profezia / non m'accorsi io allora, ma or ne godo, / Ché veggio che s'intese di Maria.'

[3] Flavio Biondo, *Roma instaurata* (1446), III, 62 ff., ed. Valentini–Zucchetti, IV, 315 f.

manuscripts of the thirteenth century. I reproduce here the remarkable and unique one in the University Library in Cambridge (Pl. 1)
It is in the Commentary on the Apocalypse by the Minorite Alexander, a north German manuscript of about 1250.[1] The illuminator
depicts the moment at which Pope Boniface dedicates the Temple to
the Virgin. Devils escape from the tabernacles and try to make their
way through the hole in the vault while the Romans look on in
amazement.

I should like to draw your attention to the remarkable skill of the
painter in conveying the main features of the Pantheon by means of
Gothic, completely un-antique forms: the circular structure, the
opening in the vault and the porch.

I am leaving out representations of the Pantheon by Cimabue in
Assisi, Taddeo Gaddi in Pisa, Masolino in Castiglione d'Olona and
others, but I shall discuss briefly the Pantheon painted by Benozzo
Gozzoli in the *Campo Santo* in Pisa of about 1470.[2] In his picture of
Babilonia (Pl. 2) he designs a beautiful ideal town composed of ancient
Roman, contemporary Florentine and invented buildings in Florentine style. In this composition Gozzoli seems to have proudly
confronted the highest achievement of ancient architecture, the Pantheon, with actual or possible Florentine buildings, indicating the
basic affinity or even identity of ancient and renaissance architecture.
Gozzoli was able to construct a stylistically homogeneous city out of
buildings which are separated by one and a half millennia simply by
looking at the Pantheon with Florentine eyes, eyes which had been
trained to admire ancient architecture mainly through the achievements of Brunelleschi.

In the map of Rome by Alessandro Strozzi from 1474[3] the Pantheon appears with all the necessary details, and even a piece of the
inscription, whereas all the other churches—with the exception of
St Peter's—are drawn without any specific features. Strozzi thus
follows completely the view expressed by Biondo that the Pantheon

---

[1] Cambridge, University Library, MS Mm. V, 31, fo. 74. The text is edited now by Alois
Wachtel, *Alexander Minorita, Expositio in Apocalypsim: MGH, Quellen zur Geistesgeschichte
des Mittelalters*, 1 (Weimar, 1955), 257. Cf. also T. Buddensieg, 'Raffaels Grab', in
Munuscula discipulorum. Festschrift für Hans Kauffmann (Berlin, 1968), p. 57, fig. 40.

[2] P. Sanpaolesi, M. Bucci, L. Bartolini, *Camposanto monumentale di Pisa* (Pisa, 1960),
pp. 115 ff.; A. Chastel, *Italienische Renaissance. Die Ausbildung der grossen Kunstzentren in der
Zeit von 1460 bis 1500* (München, 1965), fig. 173. Cf. also Berenson, *I disegn idei pittori
fiorentini*, III (Milano, 1961), fig. 49, Nr. 559 E.

[3] A. P. Frutaz, *Le piante di Roma* (Roma, 1962), Nr. LXXXIX, pl. 159; G. Scaglia, 'The
Origin of an Archaeological Plan of Rome by Alessandro Strozzi', *Journal of the Warburg
and Courtauld Institutes*, XXVII (1964), 137 ff.

is not only the most beautiful building, but also by far the most beautiful church in Rome.

In the so-called map of Mantua[1] the weight given to the Pantheon in the context of the city of Rome is different. It is not a demonstration of the superiority of the ancient monuments in comparison with all post-antique architecture, but a deliberate attempt to place the buildings of Pope Sixtus IV on the same level in size, form and conspicuousness as the ancient buildings: the rather modest cupola of Sta Maria del Popolo has grown to an almost Pantheon-like size.

After surveying the literary tradition and the general approach to the Rotonda I shall now in the last part of my paper examine a few architectural drawings of the Pantheon. The earliest known drawing of the interior is by Francesco di Giorgio Martini, now in Turin, datable to about 1486 (Pl. 3c).[2] This drawing has been, I think, utterly neglected and partly misunderstood, because the mistakes in the rendering of the building seem to be so apparent. But I hope to show you, if only briefly, that Francesco's drawing is a carefully considered interpretation of the Pantheon and as such is a precious document for the renaissance conception of ancient architecture.

What strikes us when we compare the Pantheon of Agrippa[3] and the Rotonda of Francesco di Giorgio is the obvious difference in their proportions. A detailed analysis of the measurements shows that Francesco was not merely careless or simply wrong. As you all know, the proportions of the Pantheon are very simple: it is as high as it is wide and the cupola is as high as the cylinder. In the drawing, the cylinder is as high as it is wide. The width of the building is to its height as $3:4\cdot6$. That is almost exactly the proportion which Francesco in his architectural treatise declares to be that of 'correct' architecture.[4] Thus the differences between Francesco's Rotonda and

[1] Frutaz, *Le piante di Roma*, Nr. XCVII, pls. 168 ff.
[2] R. Lanciani, 'Il Pantheon e le terme di Agrippa', in *Notizie degli scavi* (August, 1882), p. 4. C. v. Stegmann and H. v. Geymüller, *Die Architektur der Renaissance in Toscana*, XI (München, 1908), 18, fig. 55, Francesco di Giorgio Martini, *Trattati di architettura*, a cura di C. Maltese I (Milano, 1967), pl. 147, pp. 280 f.
[3] Recent treatments of the Pantheon are by E. Nash, *Bildlexicon zur Topographie des antiken Rom*, II (Tübingen, 1962), 170 ff.; W. L. MacDonald, *The Architecture of the Roman Empire* (New Haven and London, 1965), (review by F. Rakob, in *Gnomon*, XL (1968), 185 ff.); H. Kähler, 'Das Pantheon in Rom' in *Meilensteine der abendländischen Kunst*, ed. by E. Steingräber (München, 1965), pp. 47 ff.; M. Gosebruch, 'Vom Pantheon etc.', in *Römische Quartalschrift*, (1966), pp. 147 ff.; H. Burns, 'A Peruzzi Drawing in Ferrara', in *Mitteilungen des Kunsthistorischen Instituts in Florenz*, XII (1966), 245 ff.
[4] *Trattati*, ed. Maltese, II, 395 ff. For an excellent discussion of Francesco's *trattato* see S. Browning Onians, *Style and Decorum in sixteenth-century Italian Architecture* (Ph.D. thesis, London, 1968), pp. 358 ff.

the Pantheon correspond to those between 'correct' and 'erroneous' architecture, and so imply nothing less than a severe criticism of the most famous of ancient buildings. But Francesco criticizes not only the general proportions of the Pantheon but also the basic structure of its composition. He divides the attic into two parts, mainly, I think, to avoid the arch of the apse cutting into the marble pilasters of the attic, and by the same operation he places the windows in the continuous upper part of the attic.

Francesco finally changes the number and the rhythm of the pilasters in the attic and the coffering in the dome. The guiding principle is a severely imposed vertical relationship of all architectural members, a feature which is lacking in the Pantheon. Francesco's building seems to stand up. It gives the impression of an almost Gothic rigidity and delicacy, the inner and the outer structure are in perfect harmony. All that is completely absent from the Pantheon.

Again Francesco follows the rules of what he considers to be good architecture, where the solid elements have to stand above solid elements, and the empty spaces above empty spaces.[1]

This short analysis of Francesco's study of the Pantheon reveals, as I have already said, the very critical attitude of this great renaissance architect towards the Pantheon. He is faithful, or almost exclusively so, to its ornamental vocabulary, but uses this in a highly un-antique, probably traditional Gothic way.[2]

This result provides a useful insight into renaissance attitudes towards antique architecture. Whereas humanist and antiquarian enthusiasm about ancient buildings, the search for their correct names and the historical memories connected with them, was undoubtedly an important part of the renaissance outlook, nevertheless when it came down to the question of actually making use of these masterpieces in the work of the renaissance architects themselves, there was suddenly a wide gulf between ancient and modern times, at least in the Quattrocento.

Francesco di Giorgio was by no means exceptional in his criticism of

---

[1] *Trattati*, ed. Maltese, II. 412: 'Una generalissima regula da essare deservata senza eccezione...E questa è che tutti li vacui debbano essare sopra li vacui: vani sopra vani e pieni sopra pieni, stipite sopra stipite, colonna sopra colonna, e generalmente ogni posamento et ogni simile sia per retta linea dell'asse almeno sopra il suo simile.' These rules were not followed in the Pantheon. Hence the 'mistakes' corrected by Francesco.

[2] H. Millon, in *The Art Bulletin*, XL (1958), 258.

the Pantheon. Vasari criticises the porch to the sacristy of Santo Spirito in Florence in the following remarkable story:[1] he points out that the coffers of the barrel-vault do not follow the rhythm of the columns in the wall. Andrea da Sansovino, the alleged architect of the porch, defending his work against this criticism, cited the Pantheon, because there too the bands between the coffers are not related to the pilasters and columns below. Vasari then blames Sansovino for his 'ignorance', because 'many artists, including Michelangelo', had realised that the Pantheon was built by three different architects, the first and the best being responsible for the lower parts up to the first cornice, the second for the upper parts without relating the coffers to the lower structure. The third architect had built the porch. This *Baugeschichte* according to Vasari 'prevents the knowing architects of today from committing such mistakes'.

This interesting argument shows the surprising interest of renaissance artists in art history, even wrong art history, and the impact of art-historical reasoning on artists. But it also shows that the conflict between the architectural practice in an ancient building like the Pantheon and that of the Renaissance as revealed in Francesco's 'corrected' version of the same building was a general concern of 'learned' artists of the Renaissance. It shows furthermore that artists like Michelangelo,[2] Vasari, and the 'elder friends' of Sansovino tried to solve this problem by using an art-historical trick, splitting the Pantheon into the unrelated contributions of three different unequally accomplished architects, which meant getting around a problem by means of *Baugeschichte* or emphasis on *Eigenhändigkeit*. In Andrea Sansovino's reaction, on the other hand, we find, as earlier in Alberti's letter to Matteo de'Pasti (1454),[3] the opposite notion of the Pantheon as an indisputable reference-point and cornerstone of sheer excellence, sanctioning even unconventional architectural procedure.

The most radical critique of the Pantheon comes from another great architect of the Renaissance, from Antonio da Sangallo the younger, preserved in a group of mostly unpublished drawings in the

---

[1] Vasari, *Le Vite de' più eccellenti pittori etc.*, ed. Milanesi, IV, 511 ff.

[2] Cipriano Cipriani, a priest of the Pantheon in the time of Urban VIII, transmitted the following remark of Michelangelo about the Pantheon in Bibl. Vaticana, Cod. Barb. lat. 4309, fol. 11 v: 'Della bellezza a finezza dei capitelli Michelangelo Buonarota si maravigliava anzi diceva, che dal primo cornicione in giù era disegno angelico, e non humano.' That means that Michelangelo admired only the work of the 'first' architect of the Pantheon. Cf. C. Fea, *Miscellanea filologica e antiquaria*, II (2nd ed. Roma, 1836), 241. G. Kleiner, *Die Begegnungen Michelangelos mit der Antike* (Berlin, 1950), p. 12.

[3] C. Grayson, *Alberti and the Tempio Malatestiano* facs. ed. (New York, 1957).

Uffizi.[1] He changes the position of the columns of the porch because they are 'erroneously' related to the niches at the entrance wall (Pl. 3 a).[2] Antonio connects porch and rotunda with a continuous row of pilasters all around the building. In the interior he changes completely the elevation, again connecting the coffered dome, the attic and the cylinder by a unified system of continuous vertical axes, the lack of which he calls *una cosa perniciosissima*.[3] In Antonio's final proposal of an ideal and 'correct' Rotonda the Pantheon of Agrippa is destroyed (Pl. 3b);[4] and he again is like Francesco di Giorgio close to Gothic architectural practice in composing the building out of a simple multiplication of small and equal units.

At the same time Antonio transformed the Rotonda into a new building which comes surprisingly close to his final plans for St Peter's, on which he worked in the same years. It seems interesting to recall Michelangelo's devastating criticism of Antonio's plans for St Peter's, because it is valid also for the Pantheon *Sangallensis*. Michelangelo says that Antonio deviated from the *Buon modo antico* and fell back into the old Gothic errors.[5] Michelangelo's supremely clear-sighted criticism sums up the arguments I have been presenting in this paper: a 'corrected' Pantheon meant inevitably a basically 'Gothic' Pantheon. One could either surpass it as Bramante and Michelangelo tried to do,[6] or one could simply accept and admire it for what it is, as Alberti, Andrea Sansovino and Raphael did.

In his famous drawing of the interior of the Pantheon in the Uffizi Raphael achieved something very simple (Pl. 4).[7] He draws what he sees and he is able to draw that because he admires what he sees.

---

[1] The drawings are done probably *c.* 1535, when Antonio was working for St Peter's and S. Maria sopra Minerva.

[2] Uffizi A. 874 and A. 1061 v, in A. Bartoli, *I monumenti antichi di Roma nei disegni degli Uffizi*, III (Firenze, 1910), fig. 414 and fig. 450; cf. also Uffizi A. 1241 and A. 1339 v.

[3] Uffizi A. 306. Bartoli, *I monumenti antichi*, fig. 415. Cf. also A. 1241 and A. 874 r and v.

[4] Uffizi A. 190, A. 3990, perhaps also A. 841 and A. 814.

[5] Vasari, *Vite*, ed. Milanesi, v, 467. Vasari, *Vita di Michelanglo*, ed. P. Barocchi, 1 (1962), 83, III, 1448 ff.

[6] One should look at Michelangelo's design for S. Giovanni dei Fiorentini in Rome in connection with his criticism of the Pantheon. Cf. J. S. Ackerman, *The Architecture of Michelangelo* (London, 1961), I, 103 ff., II, 117 ff.; D. Gioseffi in *Michelangelo architetto*, ed. P. Portoghesi and B. Zevi (Turino, 1964), pp. 653 ff.

[7] It seems to be more and more doubtful that the 'invention' of the Pantheon drawing can be attributed to Raphael instead of Ghirlandaio. But there seems to be reasonable ground to give the drawing Uffizi no. A. 164 to Raphael himself. All the relevant copies of this drawing should be carefully examined. Cf. W. Lotz, 'Das Raumbild in der italienischen Architektur der Renaissance', *Mitteilungen des Kunsthistorischen Instituts in Florenz*, VII (1956), 218 ff.

Raphael was not interested at all in 'correct' relationships of members, or objective measurements or structural and constructional problems. What he produced was a neat statement of his personal impression looking at the shining surface of a small part of the Pantheon's interior, and easily transmitted the illusion of the whole immense building surrounding the beholder. Raphael's admiration for the Pantheon took literally the form of identification with it: he decided to be buried not in the Vatican, but in the Pantheon.[1]

[1] Cf. T. Buddensieg, 'Raffaels Grab', *loc. cit.* pp. 45 ff.

27

QUATTROCENTO ARCHITECTURE AND THE ANTIQUE: SOME PROBLEMS

HOWARD BURNS

There are no systematic studies of 'Quattrocento Architecture and the Antique',[1] and here I am not going to touch upon all the questions which such a study would involve. Instead, nearly all the problems which I shall discuss derive from a consideration of the limitations and difficulties involved in the basic and most obvious approach to the question of establishing the influence of the Antique on Quattrocento architecture, namely the search for the use of antique motifs in Quattrocento buildings.

The identification of architectural sources is of great interest in that an architect defines his preferences through his choice of motifs, and also constantly reveals himself by the ways in which he adapts, emends, or misunderstands the motifs which he borrows. But the value of the study of sources rests upon the sureness with which they are identified. If an architect's style is accounted for in terms of derivation from earlier works, which in fact he either did not know, or did not imitate, the whole character of his architecture will be misrepresented.

Questions of this sort are of particular importance when one considers the Quattrocento: whether an architect is in fact borrowing from the Antique, or from the Trecento, will have bearing not only on an assessment of his originality, but on the whole phenomenon of Quattrocento architecture.

[1] [For reasons of space the notes accompanying this paper have had to be very substantially restricted. The material touched on here will, however, be published in expanded form elsewhere.] See, however: E. Panofsky, *Renaissance and Renascences in Western Art* (Stockholm, 1960); R. Krautheimer, with T. Krautheimer-Hess, *Lorenzo Ghiberti* (Princeton, 1956); L. B. Alberti, *L'Architettura*, ed. G. Orlandi (Milan, 1966); J. R. Spencer, *Filarete's Treatise on Architecture* (Yale, 1965) (reviewed by P. Tigler, *Art Bulletin*, XLIX (1967), 352–60); Francesco di Giorgio Martini, *Trattati...*, ed. Corrado Maltese (Milan, 1967); Axel Boëthius, *The Golden House of Nero* (Ann Arbor, 1960); H. Saalman, 'Early Renaissance Theory and Practice in Antonio Filarete's *Trattato di Architettura*', *Art Bulletin*, XLI (1959), 89–106; R. Wittkower, *Architectural Principles in the Age of Humanism* (London, 1962). I have not yet been able to consult John Onians, *Style and decorum in Italian sixteenth-century architectural theory and practice: their sources in antiquity and in the fifteenth century* (London University Ph.D. thesis, Warburg Institute, 1968).

In approaching the question of the sources of early Quattrocento architecture one must begin by recognising that even if Brunelleschi and his contemporaries had wanted to ignore all the architecture between the Arch of Constantine and their own time, they could hardly have done so, as they had always lived surrounded by post-antique buildings, and their patrons constantly required buildings conforming to traditional local types. It is also to be borne in mind that architects (in any period) are potentially open to visual suggestions from any source whatever, so that an architect's ideas are not by any means solely derived from buildings, but in this period may come from frescoes, paintings, coins, reliefs, ivories, manuscript illustrations, mosaics, and so on. All of these may carry renderings of buildings, all of them may have been produced at any time from that very day back to antiquity, and any of them, even the most recent (as also the most recent buildings) may contain motifs which derive from the antique. It is easy to underestimate the richness and complexity of the architectural tradition stemming from antiquity and the abundance of sources available to Quattrocento architects, just as, on the other hand, it is easy to underestimate the ability of people to ignore things right in front of their noses, if they are not interested in them.

Something of the complexity of the position of the renaissance artist in relation to the antique has been expressed by the adoption of the useful terms Survival and Revival.[1] These categories are not adequate in themselves to give a full account of the Quattrocento's relationship to the antique. While some motifs do apparently survive throughout the Middle Ages, others were revived in the Quattrocento on the basis of antique versions, or of pre-Renaissance revivals, or on the basis of a combination of both. Survival and Revival in the Quattrocento are thus closely linked: even corrupt versions, embodied in tradition, of antique motifs, were important as they made easier the assimilation of the pure antique form. And perhaps even more important was the way in which the antique deposit in medieval tradition often did much to determine the Quattrocento interpretation of the antique, not only by influencing the way in which artists looked at ancient architecture, but in some cases by providing the direct sources of the new style. Something of the sort certainly

[1] André Chastel, Introduction to the section 'The Renaissance and Antiquity', in *Studies in Western Art*, ii (Princeton, 1963); also James S. Ackerman, 'Sources of the Renaissance Villa', pp. 6–18 in the same volume.

happened in Lombardy and in Venice, but the obvious, incontrovertible case is that of Brunelleschi and the Florentine Baptistery. Here a Romanesque work was accepted as a true antiquity, and its decorative language preferred to that of the monuments of Rome. My earlier point, that of the relationship between Survival and Revival, can be illustrated by a Romanesque capital recently found in the excavations in the nave of the Duomo in Florence.[1] It is remarkably similar to the half-column capitals used by Michelozzo on the lantern of the Duomo. The fact that Michelozzo may have taken the type straight from the antique, and not known a version of it from the demolished Santa Reparata, does not alter the force of the example: antique motifs may be imitated from post-antique versions of them, or may be taken straight from the antique, or a knowledge of the post-antique version may have led to the antique original being observed and imitated.

Not only Romanesque, but also Trecento architecture (and painted architecture) contained survivals and revivals of the antique which were influential in the Quattrocento. The lack of information as to what architects thought in the second half of the Trecento should not lead us to characterise the whole period as 'Gothic', and hence to overlook the possibility that the architectural revival of antiquity of the Quattrocento may be just as indebted to the period preceding it as is the 'revival of antiquity' of the humanists. Coluccio Salutati (born in 1331) describes the Baptistery at the turn of the century as 'templum non graeco non tusco more factum, sed plane romano' and his words open up the strong possibility that the architects of his generation were capable of making equal, or more refined, stylistic distinctions.[2] It may even be that, like Michelozzo in the next century, they deliberately gave their works now a 'Tuscan', now a 'Roman' flavour. In any case, the appearance of the round arch and what can only be termed *all'antica* detail in prominent buildings of the second half of the Trecento (Orsanmichele, the Bigallo Loggia, and the Loggia dei Lanzi) suggests a deliberate preference for at least some aspects of the 'Roman manner'.[3] And these works can be

[1] G. Morozzi, 'Indagini sulla prima cattedrale fiorentina', *Commentari*, XIX (1968), 3–17.
[2] Quoted by E. H. Gombrich, 'From the Revival of Letters to the Reform of the Arts: Niccolò Niccoli and Filippo Brunelleschi', *Essays in the History of Art Presented to Rudolf Wittkower* (London, 1967), pp. 78–9 and note 54.
[3] Thus Orcagna's tabernacle in Orsanmichele, despite its surface intricacies, is fundamentally classical in design. It is classical in its round arch, the proportions of column, capital and base, the entablature above the columns and the pedestals below them, while the detail, despite the Gothic twist given to it, is clearly *all'antica* in type.

regarded as the middle portion of a continuous *all'antica* Trecento tradition, which runs from Giotto to the Porta della Mandorla, the architectural backgrounds of Ghiberti's North Door, and the portal of the sacristy of Santa Trinita.

Donatello, moreover, can be seen as a Quattrocento continuer of a Trecento tradition of architectural decoration (itself strongly influenced by the antique) which he, as it were, purifies by direct consultation of the tradition's own ultimate antique sources, while retaining its richness and profusion of motifs. Donatello's knowledge of the antique, and the expressive power which he obtains from unexpected, usually unprecedented combinations, syntheses, and juxtapositions of *all'antica* elements, has of course no true parallel in the Trecento.[1] Nevertheless, if one looks at Orcagna's tabernacle in Orsanmichele (Pl. 5*a*), the effect is very similar to that achieved by Donatello in the entablature of the Annunciation tabernacle, or in the Cantoria: there is the same bizarre density of decoration, the liking for the shell motif, and even the motif which Orcagna uses to decorate the panels between the pedestals is echoed by Donatello in the Old Sacristy in the little screens in front of the altar (Pls. 5*b* and 7*a*).

Donatello's Cantoria thus conceals behind its overwhelmingly *all'antica* manner a reminiscence of the decorative style of the Orcagna tabernacle. But instances are also to be found where a work which (to us) is conservative in style, in fact was conceived as an innovatory essay in the *modo antico*. Such buildings are easy to overlook and dismiss as uninteresting. This is largely because our criteria for identifying an antique manner differ greatly from those of the Quattrocento so that, for instance, a feature like the round arch, which in the Cinquecento and even more today is simply taken for granted, for Filarete (and doubtless for his contemporaries) was one of the hallmarks of the 'ancient manner of building'.[2] And even in antique architecture there can be found motifs with a 'Gothic' aspect, so that a Quattrocento artist may be imitating a genuine antiquity, when he seems to us to be following medieval tradition.[3]

---

[1] On Donatello and the antique see H. W. Janson, 'Donatello and the Antique', in *Donatello e il suo Tempo. Atti dell' VIII Convegno Internazionale di Studi sul Rinascimento* (Florence, 1968), pp. 77–96.

[2] J. R. Spencer, *Filarete's Treatise*, facsimile vol. fos. 59v–60r, and P. Tigler, *Die Architekturtheorie des Filarete* (Berlin, 1963), p. 90.

[3] Cf. M. Trachtenberg, 'An antique model for Donatello's marble David', *Art Bulletin*, L (1968), 268–9.

1   Pope Boniface dedicates the Pantheon to the Virgin. North German, c. 1250

2 Benozzo Gozzoli, *Babilonia*

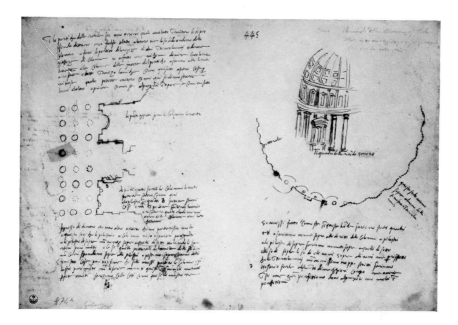

a

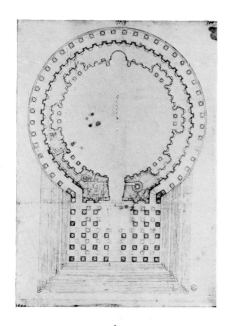

b

c

3   The Pantheon: *a* and *b*, Antonio da Sangallo the Younger;
c, Francesco di Giorgio

4 Raphael, *The Pantheon*

5a   Orcagna's tabernacle (detail), Orsanmichele, Florence

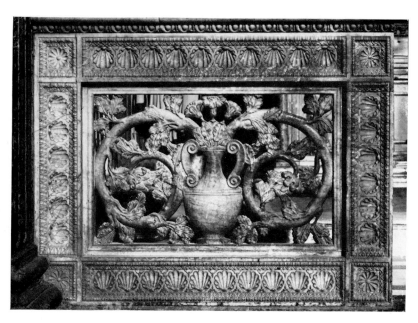

5b   Screen from the Old Sacristy, San Lorenzo, Florence

6a   Portal, Palazzo Medici, Florence

6b   Portal, Palazza Gondi, Florence

6c   Sarcophagus of the Apostles,
Grotte Vaticane, Rome

7 *a*   Old Sacristy, San Lorenzo, Florence

7 *b*   Baptistery, Padua

8*a* Giotto, Capital from *Ascension of*
the Evangelist

8*b* Capital from the Old Sacristy,
San Lorenzo, Florence

8*c* Giuliano da Sangallo, the Ionic Order after Alberti

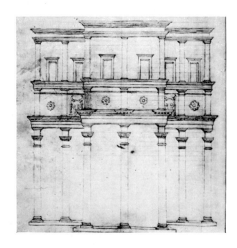

8*d* Francesco di Giorgio, 'faccia
del champitolio'

9a   Taddeo Gaddi, *Presentation of the Virgin* (detail)

9b   Nave, San Lorenzo, Florence

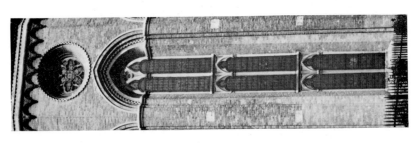

10. *a*, Window of Apse, SS. Giovanni e Paolo, Venice; *b*, Pazzi Chapel,
Santa Croce, Florence; *c*, Sarcophagus (detail), Camposanto, Pisa;
d, Masaccio, *Madonna and Child* (detail of the throne)

11 *a*   Detail from Cod. 6, fo. 83v, Royal Library,
Copenhagen

11 *b*   Brunelleschi, Aedicule at base of the Cupola,
Duomo, Florence (detail)

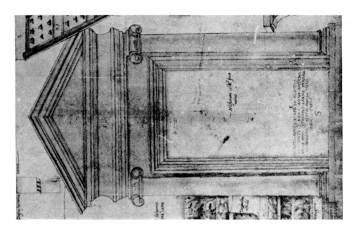

c

b

a

12.   *a*, Agnolo Gaddi, *The Making of the Cross* (detail); *b*, Donatello, Portal, Old Sacristy, San Lorenzo, Florence; *c*, Giuliano da Sangallo, an antique portal 'near the Torre de' Conti'

The Palazzo Medici, begun in 1444, is a good example of a building whose intended *all'antica* character is no longer very obvious. It seems medieval enough: its rustication and general proportions recall Palazzo Vecchio, its biforate windows, as Professor Gombrich has observed, are only modernisations, that is antiquisations, of a common medieval type.[1] And even its massive, *all'antica* cornice is close to the massive cornices which crown Orsanmichele and the Loggia dei Lanzi, while the modillions which support its projection are Trecento rather than truly antique in their profile.

But what did Michelozzo and Cosimo and their contemporaries think about the palace? Some indication is given by what Flavio Biondo says about it. Biondo, as he himself does not fail to point out, was unusually well qualified to say whether a building was comparable to the works of the ancients, as he almost certainly knew more about Roman topography than anyone then alive, with the possible exception of Alberti. He writes:

Quid quod privatae aedes suae [Cosimo's] recens in via lata extructae, Romanorum olim principum et quidem primariorum operibus comparandae sunt: quin ego ipse, qui Romam meis instauravi scriptis, affirmare non dubito nullius extare privati aedificii principum in urbe Romana reliquias, quae maiorem illis aedibus prae se ferant operis magnificentiam.[2]

The fact that in the sentence before Biondo speaks of the marble columns in San Lorenzo (Pl. 9*b*), whereas in reality they are of *pietra serena*, only emphasises his identification of the major works in the new style with the great works of the ancients. In both cases the buildings made an impression on him which called forth a comparison with the monuments of ancient Rome—in the case of Palazzo Medici explicit, in the case of San Lorenzo, by the use of an image and marble columns—which whether based on a lapse of memory, or merely on literary conventions of architectural eulogy, serves to call to mind antique magnificence.

Flavio Biondo was not an architect, but he does belong to the small number of humanists who, through their writings and their intimacy with the great, had enormous influence in forming contemporary ideas about antiquity. And if Biondo thought that the palace was comparable to the edifices of ancient Rome, Cosimo

[1] E. H. Gombrich, *From the Revival of Letters*, p. 80.
[2] *Italia Illustrata*, the section on Florence (p. 305 of the 1559 Basle edition of Biondo's works).

almost certainly thought so too.[1] But to return to the original point. As an artist Michelozzo would probably have had a richer set of visual criteria for what was or what was not *all'antica* in architecture than would Biondo. One of these criteria (probably shared with Biondo) would have been the use of the round arch—the change from pointed to round would have been for Michelozzo no trifling alteration, but one which altered the whole style of the building. Again, if Michelozzo had seen antique representations of rusticated buildings with round-topped windows, like that on Lateran Sarcophagus 174 (Pl. 6*c*), he could justifiably have considered his design as a very close reproduction of an ancient Roman palace.[2] Finally, the door of the palace (Pl. 6*a*), where the voussoirs are contained within an archivolt and are not keyed into the horizontal courses, may to us seem more medieval (it occurs for instance on Palazzo Vecchio) and less antique than the solution where such a keying in takes place. It must have seemed so to Giuliano da Sangallo when he designed the portals of Palazzo Gondi about 1490 (Pl. 6*b*). All the same, the Palazzo Medici portal solution does have antique precedents, especially in Roman bridges like the Ponte Amato on the Via Prenestina, and Michelozzo may well have been consciously imitating such an antique type.

So far I have only discussed borrowings from the antique in which the motif remains largely unchanged in the process. Such (apart from Donatello's practice of creating new types by unprecedented combinations of genuine antique motifs) is usually the case with capitals, and decorative detail. But the larger and more complex the antique scheme which a Quattrocento architect examined, the more likely he was to alter and misinterpret it when he consigned it to his memory or his sketchbook, and the process of alteration would continue if he then sought to imitate the building in his own work.

Francesco di Giorgio's drawings, although they all probably belong to the last quarter of the century, provide many instances of the importance of subjective factors in the Quattrocento's approach to the antique. His on-the-spot drawings from the antique in the Uffizi

---

[1] Cosimo of course also knew Rome and had probably been guided round the monuments by Poggio (see Krautheimer, *Ghiberti*, pp. 320–1).

[2] On the sarcophagus, now in the Grotte Vaticane, see *Repertorium der Christlich-Antiken Sarkophage*, 1, *Rom und Ostia* (Wiesbaden, 1967), no. 677, pp. 274–6.

Benozzo Gozzoli implied his acceptance of the Palazzo Medici as an antique type by placing it in his *Babilonia* fresco (Pl.2) in the Camposanto in Pisa. See also E. H. Gombrich, 'Apollonio di Giovanni', in *Norm and Form* (London, 1966), p. 14, and figs. 22 and 23.

are extremely summary: plans are in no sense surveyed, only the main measurements are given. These rough drawings then served as the basis for the collection (and presumably other, lost collections) of neat drawings of ancient buildings at the end of the Turin codex. Once Francesco had copied the rough sketch (rationalising and elaborating it in the process) he would, rather like a Quattrocento accountant when he had made a fair copy of a page of accounts, draw a line or a cross through the on-the-spot sketch, or in some cases write *fatto*, 'done', over it.[1] In at least one case it is possible to trace three stages in this progressive transformation of an ancient building through successive drawings and copies: the initial sketch in the Uffizi, its *in pulito* version in Turin, and finally a project by Francesco in one of his architectural treatises.[2]

Francesco's methods in themselves would account for many of the discrepancies between the buildings he drew and what he eventually made of them. But further investigation is needed to establish the extent to which his alterations were conscious 'criticisms' of the antique. Dr Buddensieg has already discussed a case where the alteration seems to be at least in part conscious.[3] I want to mention here a case where Francesco's alteration, whether deliberate or not, derives from his incomplete understanding of Vitruvius, of which there are many other instances, most notably his inability to give the correct names to Doric and Ionic capitals.[4]

In his Turin codex Francesco draws a Doric building in Rome (Pl. 8*d*). Though the order is clearly Doric, Francesco does not read the abacus as part of the capital at all, but, probably misled by its height, makes it into an entablature block between capital proper and architrave.[5] He has not understood the Doric frieze, and has rationalised this feature by lengthening the triglyphs so that they become little pilasters in an attic above the main entablature. All these changes may have come about unconsciously, or they may have

---

[1] The word 'fatto' is written on UA 322v (R. Papini, *Francesco di Giorgio Architetto* (Florence, 1946), fig. 43). So many drawings carry cancellations that there is no need to list them individually (see, for instance, Papini, fig. 28).

[2] Compare UA 335 (Papini, fig. 20) with Maltese, I, pl. 166, and finally Maltese, II, pl. 201.

[3] See Tilmann Buddensieg's contribution to the present volume.

[4] Francesco discusses and illustrates Doric and Ionic capitals on fo. 33r of the Nazionale MS (Maltese, II, 378 and pl. 219). It is clear that Francesco considered the difference between Doric and Ionic to be exclusively one of proportion and not a combination of proportion with specific forms.

[5] Maltese, I, pl. 150. The building is almost certainly the Tabularium, as Promis suggested.

been a conscious rationalisation and improvement of a monument which Francesco found illogical and unsatisfactory.

And here it should be added that Vitruvius in the fifteenth century offered limitless possibilities for misunderstanding.[1] Erroneous interpretations of his text *may* have had an enormous influence on Quattrocento buildings, though unless documentary evidence emerges to demonstrate it, as it has done, for instance, in the case of Alberti's Sant'Andrea, it is unlikely that study of the buildings themselves would ever reveal it.[2]

I now want to mention the main limitation to any approach which seeks to trace antique influence on Quattrocento architecture exclusively through the identification of borrowings from the antique. This is that the most important aspect of antique influence never becomes visually explicit, as it is simply the compendium of ideas about the nature of good architecture which Quattrocento architects partly read into, partly derived from, the antique, and from what they could understand, or misunderstand, of Vitruvius.

Even a cursory reading of the architectural treatises of Alberti and Francesco di Giorgio bears this out. The imitation of the antique for these writers is above all the imitation of antique principles, not antique forms. The embodiment of these principles is the true criterion for design in the manner of the ancients, not the use of the orders, as became the case in the Cinquecento. The orders in fact were only really understood in the Quattrocento, it would seem, by Alberti, and, possibly under his influence, by Giuliano da Sangallo. But neither of these architects used them 'correctly', and Alberti attaches none of the importance to their correct use, which is attributed to them in the next century.

Given this situation, two points can be noted: the first is that, contrary to all appearances, an architect may have studied antiquity intensively, seeking to understand the principles underlying ancient works and then to realise them in his own buildings. But unless there is literary evidence to show that he did this, the antique influence is likely to remain hidden. A mere examination, for instance, of the Madonna del Calcinaio at Cortona, or the Convent of Santa Chiara in Urbino, would hardly lead to the conclusion that Francesco di Giorgio had, as he puts it 'collected many various and worthy edi-

[1] See Alberti's complaints about the difficulties of understanding Vitruvius (*De re aed.* VI, 1). See also R. Krautheimer, 'Alberti and Vitruvius', in *Studies in Western Art*, II, 42–52.
[2] R. Krautheimer, 'Alberti's Templum Etruscum', *Münchner Jb. der bildenden Kunst*, XII (1961), 65–72.

fices, investigating with no little effort, as best I could, in Rome and elsewhere'.[1] It is only a knowledge of his drawings and manuscripts which enables one to see that in fact in his buildings he is seeking to realise what he believed to be the fundamental characteristics of ancient architecture, or at least of good ancient architecture.[2]

The second point is this: that as an interpretation of the basic architectural principles of antiquity depended on the ideas which were brought to the study of Vitruvius and the monuments, it is necessary, before one can understand the architectural aesthetic of the Quattrocento, to examine the whole intellectual climate within which architects sought to understand and imitate the antique. Wittkower has made a start with this in his *Architectural Principles*, but a very great deal remains to be done.

In the light of what I have said so far I want to turn to Brunelleschi, who in his own time and ever since has been rightly regarded as the founder of a new architectural style, based on that of antiquity.[3] And there is no doubt that in his use of the round arch, of columns and pilasters of fixed proportions, of an order made up of entablature, capital, column and base, of standardised detail, of articulated and (in his later works) modelled wall surfaces, of interior vistas and of centralised compositions, Brunelleschi is the true reviver of much of the spirit of ancient architecture.

It has been observed, however, that the undeniably antique spirit of Brunelleschi's architecture is not accompanied by an equally antique letter.[4] Brunelleschi, it is clear, drew heavily on post-antique sources. But I want to go beyond this generally accepted view and to argue not only that Brunelleschi preferred to express his new style through a selection of motifs and compositional schemes (all of which he transformed and set in new contexts) drawn from Florentine tradition and (it is hard to escape the conclusion) from the Veneto, but also that there is not a single major work of Brunelleschi for which a plausible and specific post-antique source (or sources) cannot be suggested.[5]

[1] Maltese, I, 275.   [2] See Maltese, I, 48.
[3] J. R. Spencer, *Filarete's Treatise*, facsimile vol., fo. 59r; Giovanni Rucellai, *Il Zibaldone Quaresimale*, ed. A. Perosa (1960), p. 61 (and cf. p. 55).
[4] P. Fontana, 'Il Brunelleschi e l'architettura classica', *Archivio Storico dell'Arte*, VI (1893), 256 ff.; P. Fontana, 'Il Brunelleschi', *Atti del X Congresso Internazionale di Storia dell'Arte* (Rome, 1922), pp. 171 f.; H. Saalman, 'Filippo Brunelleschi: Capital Studies', *Art Bulletin*, XL (1958), 114-15.
[5] Professor Howard Saalman has often expressed to me his view that Brunelleschi must have been in the Veneto, and that his works contain no specific motifs derived directly from the antique. C. v. Fabriczy, *Filippo Brunelleschi* (Stuttgart, 1892), pp. 136-7, already suggested the Veneto as the source for the balustrades used inside the Duomo cupola.

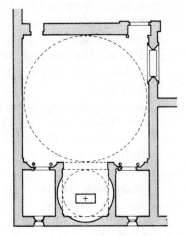

1   Plan, Old Sacristy, San Lorenzo, Florence (after Sanpaolesi)

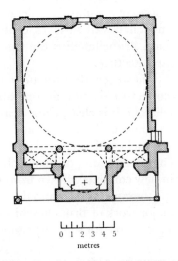

0 1 2 3 4 5
metres

2   Plan, Baptistery, Padua (after Guiotto)

278

The Old Sacristy in San Lorenzo (Pl. 7a, Figs. 1 and 4), built between 1421 and 1428, admittedly, in plan at least, has parallels with certain Roman tombs. But I think there can be little doubt as to its immediate source. The Baptistery of Padua Cathedral (Pl. 7b, Figs. 2 and 3) would have been known to many Florentine visitors and residents of the city, not least because of its dedication to San Giovanni. Like the Old Sacristy, in plan it consists of a large square, with a smaller square attached to it. Both squares are surmounted by domes, and both domes rest on pendentives. In both buildings a cylindrical drum on the outside conceals the curvature of the dome. In the interior of both, round-topped windows appear in similar positions.[1]

The Paduan Baptistery in its basic structure is thus very close indeed to the Old Sacristy. It does of course lack the articulation of its interior wall surfaces with pilasters and entablature, which is one of the most striking and original features of Brunelleschi's style. A precedent, however, for this too can be found in Padua, and was doubtless known to Brunelleschi: the treatment of the end wall of the Arena chapel is the same as that of the corresponding part of the Old Sacristy, as regards its general scheme, save that in Giotto's work the two arches are not quite concentric.

Saalman has noted the independence of the capital type which Brunelleschi adopted in the Old Sacristy (Pl. 8b) and continued to use throughout his career, from the usual antique Corinthian capital.[2] Despite the fact that he must often have seen the antique type, he preferred to use a simplified and rationalised version of it. This, it would appear, he did not invent, as it is more or less identical to capitals painted by Giotto in the Peruzzi Chapel in Santa Croce (Pl. 8a).[3]

---

[1] M. Guiotto, 'Il Battistero di Padova', *Palladio*, VII (1943); M. Checchi, L. Gaudenzio, L. Grossato, *Padova* (Venice, 1961), pp. 575–82. The measurements of the two buildings correspond so closely (they are both squares of about 11·5 m.) as to suggest that the Florentine structure is not simply influenced by the Paduan Baptistery, but is actually a replica of it, perhaps produced at the specific request of the patron. (It is also true, however, that 11·50 m. is approximately equal to the round figure of 20 *braccia*.) Giovanni d'Averardo's part in the creation of the Sacristy was clearly more than financial. This is implied by Antonio Manetti, *Vita di Filippo di Ser Brunellesco*, ed. E. Toesca (Florence, 1927), pp. 62–3, and demonstrated, as regards the iconography of the Sacristy, by H. Kauffman, *Donatello* (Berlin, 1935), pp. 85–6. There is a record of Giovanni's appointment as ambassador to Padua and Venice in 1404 (B. Dami, *Giovanni Bicci dei Medici* (Florence, 1899), p. 28). On Florentines in Padua see R. Cessi, 'Gli Alberti di Firenze in Padova. Per la storia dei Fiorentini a Padova', *Archivio Storico Italiano*, ser. 5, XL (1907), 233–84, and especially p. 238.

[2] H. Saalman, 'Capital Studies', p. 115.

[3] The capitals appear in the *Ascension of the Evangelist*. The capital of Brunelleschian type published by M. Gosebruch, *Römisches Jb. f. Kunstgeschichte*, VIII (1958), p. 78, fig. 40, as being about 1200, in fact almost certainly should be dated about 1449.

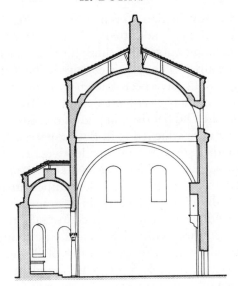

3 Section, Baptistery, Padua (after Guiotto)

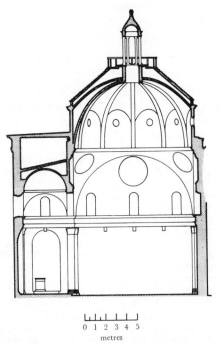

0 1 2 3 4 5
metres

4 Section, Old Sacristy, San Lorenzo, Florence (after Sanpaolesi)

If one turns to other buildings by Brunelleschi, the same picture emerges: repeated borrowings from the Veneto, from Trecento painting and architecture, from the Tuscan Romanesque, but not from the antique. San Lorenzo in plan recalls Santa Croce and Santa Trinita. Its nave (Pl. 9 b) recalls the church of the Apostoli in Florence, and even more the various representations of the Temple in Jerusalem in Trecento frescoes of the Presentation, in Santa Croce.[1] The earliest of these is by Taddeo Gaddi in the Baroncelli Chapel (Pl. 9 a): here not only are there columns carrying round arches, but even entablature blocks placed between capital and arch, as in San Lorenzo and Santo Spirito. The Pazzi Chapel is an adaptation of the Old Sacristy scheme to the chapter-house plan which appears already in Florence in the Spanish Chapel at Santa Maria Novella. The windows and wall panels (Pl. 10 b) may well be modernisations of a Gothic motif, occurring for instance on the apse of SS. Giovanni e Paolo in Venice (Pl. 10 a).

Brunelleschi's later works have been seen as showing a much stronger and more explicit influence of the antique. The more plastic and monumental handling of the later works may derive from an increasing interest in this aspect of ancient architecture, but once more, strikingly close medieval parallels can also be found for Brunelleschi's later compositions. The continuous in-and-out movement of the semicircular chapels of Santo Spirito is paralleled by that in the north wing of the atrium of San Marco in Venice where, incidentally, there is also a parallel for the decoration of the pendentives of the Pazzi Chapel with *tondi* containing the Evangelists.

The placing of paired half-columns between deep semicircular niches on the exedrae at the base of the Florentine cupola (Pl. 11 b), has parallels in the Veneto, for instance on the apse of the cathedral at Murano, and in the atrium of San Marco. Admittedly in these cases the columns do not carry a straight entablature, as in Brunelleschi's structure. An almost exact parallel, however, is to be found in an illumination in a Byzantine manuscript in Copenhagen (Pl. 11 a).[2] It would be far-fetched to suggest that this very image was Brunelleschi's source, but as Byzantine architectural backgrounds are almost always constantly repeated types, it would not be unreasonable to suggest that Brunelleschi knew another version of it. The case anyway once more emphasises the range of possible sources available to architects.

[1] The temple appears twice in the Baroncelli Chapel and once in the Rinuccini Chapel.
[2] Royal Library, Copenhagen, Cod. 6, fo. 83 v. See Kurt Weitzmann, *Die Byzantinische Buchmalerei des 9 und 10 Jahrhunderts* (Berlin, 1935), p. 26 and fig. 198.

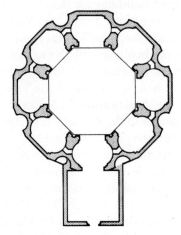

5 Plan, Santa Maria degli Angioli, Florence (after Giuliano da Sangallo)

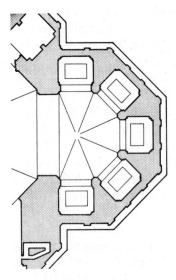

6 Transept, Duomo, Florence

I want finally to consider Santa Maria degli Angioli, Brunelleschi's unfinished octagonal church (Fig. 5), which is always regarded as the most completely antique of his works, while the so-called temple of Minerva Medica in Rome, or similar centralised ancient buildings, is usually cited as its source.[1] Brunelleschi may well have known the temple of Minerva Medica, and it may have increased his awareness of the possibilities of a polygonal structure with chapels attached to each of its sides. But a precise non-antique source for Brunelleschi's design exists, which he undoubtedly knew very well indeed, and which is much closer to the Angioli than is the temple of Minerva Medica. For the terminations of the crossing arms of the Duomo in Florence are half-octagons, with chapels attached to their sides (Fig. 6). If one imagines the octagon as being completed, the resulting structure, apart from the modelling of the chapel walls, is identical in plan to the Angioli. It is true of course that in the Duomo there are only half, not whole octagons, but it would be absurd to maintain that Brunelleschi was incapable of the conceptual agility necessary to imagine the completed octagon. And already in the Trecento free-standing octagonal structures, close to the Duomo transepts, appear in fresco backgrounds.[2]

An examination of Brunelleschi's sources does not call in question the generic antique inspiration of much of what is new in his architecture. But it does raise the problem of why he did not imitate the antique more literally, and of what he thought of those of his contemporaries who did, as well as the question of his attitude towards the architecture of the Trecento and the Veneto. It is much more likely than not that Brunelleschi went to Rome and studied its monuments on one or more occasions. Manetti's account, though it may be wrong in placing the famous visit immediately after the competition for the Baptistery gates, has in its detail a ring of truth about it.[3] And it is almost inconceivable that Brunelleschi, even with his extreme independence of mind, should have thought of himself as doing something other than reviving the 'ancient manner of

[1] L. H. Heydenreich, 'Spätwerke Brunelleschis', Jb. der preuszischen Kunstsammlungen, 52 (1931), 6–7. W. and E. Paatz, Die Kirchen von Florenz, III (Frankfurt am Main, 1952), however mention the Duomo as a source.

[2] For instance in Santa Croce in the Baroncelli Chapel (the Meeting with St Anne) and in the Road to Calvary in the Sacristy.

[3] Manetti, Vita, pp. 22–3, is clearly anachronistic, and influenced by Alberti (see Saalman, 'Capital Studies', pp. 114–15) whereas the passage on p. 21 on the use of strips of parchment does not sound like an invention.

building'.[1] But this he must have conceived as lying in general principles, so that he felt no need to copy ancient plans or details literally,
but instead moulded his new style out of generic *all'antica* principles,
combined with specific motifs taken from the Tuscan Romanesque,
from the Trecento and the Veneto. And consciously or unconsciously,
apart from the Baptistery (in any case a subjective, not an objective,
antiquity) he undoubtedly avoided direct quotation from the antique.

Brunelleschi's approach was not shared by his contemporaries.
Michelozzo, though he employed a Brunelleschian vocabulary on
occasion, designed in both a Trecento and in a completely *all'antica*
style.[2] Masaccio on at least one occasion quotes a specific antique
architectural motif: the recessed columns of the throne of the *Pisa
Madonna* (Pl. 10*d*) are accurately quoted from a Pisan sarcophagus (Pl. 10*c*), now in the Camposanto.[3] Donatello already in the
St Louis niche and in the Siena Baptistery relief brings a range of
all'antica detail into play, which has no parallel in Brunelleschi's
work. Manetti's account of Brunelleschi's hostility to the portals
added by Donatello in the Old Sacristy is well known (Pls. 7*a* and
12*b*), and whether Manetti's account is true or not (there seems no
reason to doubt it) their dainty, slightly clumsy, slightly quaint monu-
mentality is certainly out of keeping with Brunelleschi's approach to
wall design.[4] The portals conflict not only with Brunelleschi's archi-

---

[1] Within Brunelleschi's own lifetime, flat-topped doors and windows are referred to in the
Innocenti and Annunziata documents as *all'anticha*. (For the information about the
Annunziata I am indebted to Miss Louisa Bulman; for the Innocenti, see M. C. Mendes
Atanásio and G. Dallai, 'Nuove indagini sullo Spedale degli Innocenti a Firenze',
Commentari, XVII (1966), doc. XIV, p. 101.)

[2] See H. Saalman, 'The Palazzo Comunale in Montepulciano', *Zeitschrift f. Kunstgeschichte*, XXVIII (1965), 5–9.

[3] Masaccio thus anticipates Codussi, Raphael, Peruzzi, Michelangelo, and Vignola in his
use of the recessed column. For a characterisation of the architecture of the throne:
Eve Borsook, 'A note on Masaccio in Pisa', *Burlington Magazine*, CIII (1961), 212. The
panel was painted in Pisa (Martin Davies, *The Earlier Italian Schools* (London, National
Gallery, 2nd ed. 1961), pp. 348–51) and the rosettes which decorate the lower part of
the throne may well derive from Bonannus's bronze doors of Pisa Cathedral.

On the sarcophagus in the Camposanto: R. Papini, *Catalogo delle cose d'arte e di antichità d'Italia. Pisa.* Ser. I, fasc. II, part II (Rome, n.d.), p. 28; E. Carli and P. E. Arias,
Il Camposanto di Pisa (Rome, 1957), p. 58. It was originally in the church of S. Michele in
Borgo: Paolo Lasinio, *Raccolta di Sarcofagi...del Campo Santo di Pisa* (Pisa, 1814),
pp. 7–8, and tav. XXI; Alessandro da Morrona, *Pisa Illustrata*, III (Pisa, 1793), 178–9.

[4] There are strong justifications for the solution chosen by Donatello. The Old Sacristy is
not the Pazzi Chapel: it is much more of a single-viewpoint composition, not unsuited
to the application of modestly three-dimensional monumental elements on the principal
wall. On the portals see Manetti, *Vita*, pp. 65–6; Janson, *The sculpture of Donatello*
(Princeton, 1957), pp. 138–40; and Margrit Lisner, 'Zur frühen Bildhauerarchitektur
Donatellos', *Müncher Jb. der bildenden Kunst*, IX–X (1958/9), 81–3. Janson's attribution of
the portals to Michelozzo is unconvincing.

tectural aesthetic, but also with his practice of avoiding direct citation of the antique. Donatello must have chosen this form on the
basis of its antique character: columned and pedimented portals
frequently appear on sarcophagi, where they often frame doors with
relief panels.[1] And it is possible that the Old Sacristy portals are the
earliest renaissance architectural work to reproduce a specific Roman
monument: an almost identical pedimented portal, with freestanding
Ionic columns, is drawn by Giuliano da Sangallo (Pl. 12 c), whose
note indicates that it was in or near the hemicycle of Trajan's Forum.[2]
It is also worth observing that even if Donatello did go to Trajan's
Forum for the scheme for the portals, all the same they do have a
Trecento precedent, in the portal of a church (Pl. 12 a) represented
by Agnolo Gaddi in Santa Croce.[3] So Brunelleschi might well have
added to his other objections to the portals that in feeling, if not in
finish, they were *retardataire*, merely stuck against the wall in medieval
fashion, and not related to the general scheme.

What I have said so far touches upon a number of problems connected chiefly with the early Renaissance: the question of the influence of the Trecento; the need for an exploration of the intellectual
habits with which architects approached the antique; and the need
to be wary of excluding the possibility that an architect was influenced
by a conception of the antique (or even by specific antique motifs)
when his work seems basically traditional to us, and, on the other
hand, of excluding the possibility that beneath an impeccably
all'antica exterior there may not be a Trecento tradition. The remarks
about the Palazzo Medici, and about the very different approaches
of Brunelleschi and Donatello to tradition on the one hand, and the
antique on the other, however inadequate, at least indicate some of
the possible complexities of the relation of early Quattrocento artists
to the architectural past.

I now want to conclude by asking how it came about that the idea
of ancient architecture as a set of principles, rather than as a set of

[1] Freestanding columns appear also in the portal of the sacristy at Santa Trinita, and
freestanding Ionic columns, carrying a heavy entablature, frame the entrance to the
chapel of S. Zeno in S. Prassede in Rome (the arch above this portal is also reminiscent
of the Old Sacristy arrangement).

[2] Vatican Library, Cod. Barb. 4424, fo. 38v (published by C. Huelsen, *Il libro di Giuliano
da Sangallo*, Leipzig, 1910). T. Ashby, *Papers of the British School at Rome*, II (1904),
no. 65 b, a drawing independent of Giuliano's, as well as the fact that Francesco da
Sangallo added the measurements on Giuliano's drawing, tell against Huelsen's view
(*op. cit.*, text vol., p. 55) that the drawing is imaginative reconstruction, rather than a
record of an actual monument.

[3] In *The Making of the Cross* in the Cappella Maggiore.

rules as to the form of capitals, bases, and the rest, came to be over-
shadowed by the attention given to the orders. The idea of antique
architecture as a set of principles, rather than precedents, is implicit
in Brunelleschi's buildings, and explicit in the architectural theory
of Francesco di Giorgio and Alberti. Nevertheless it is Alberti who
constructed the foundations for the sixteenth-century approach, even
if other factors were involved, which cannot be discussed here. It was
he who first undertook the systematic study of the ancient monuments, and of Vitruvius, and of each in the light of the other. He is
the first to achieve a reasonably good understanding of the ancient
orders, even if he did not consider that they need be followed precisely in modern works.

Alberti in fact brought the techniques of humanist scholarship to
the study of ancient architecture, and he explicitly states, in a highly
important passage, that the architect should imitate the humanist
scholar by consulting and recording as many ancient works as he
could.[1] Alberti's injunction ultimately gave a new, systematic character to the sketchbooks in which artists had already begun recording
ancient buildings and ancient architectural details.[2] But little is
known about the developments which bridge the gap between Alberti
(he died in 1472; his book was first published in 1485) and the two
most revolutionary achievements of the early sixteenth century in the
field of the recovery of a sound understanding of ancient architecture:
Bramante's Tempietto, where the Doric order is used correctly for
the first time, and Fra Giocondo's brilliant edition of Vitruvius
of 1511.

Just one fact is clear about this period, namely the importance of
Giuliano da Sangallo as the direct follower of Alberti. He studied the
antique intensively; he took over, just as Alberti had done, whole
antique compositional schemes and used them in his own designs and
buildings.[3] Unfortunately it is not known with any exactness when
Giuliano started making detailed measured drawings of ancient archi-

---

[1] *De re aed.* ix, 10 (*ed. cit.* pp. 855–7). The architect's sketchbook would thus become analogous in scope and content to the humanist's notebook: see R. Sabbadini, *Il metodo degli
umanisti* (Florence, 1922), pp. 29–30; R. R. Bolgar, *The Classical Heritage and its Beneficiaries* (Cambridge, 1958), pp. 269–73.

[2] Giuliano da Sangallo's books of drawings in Siena and the Vatican in fact bridge the gap
between the old and the new type of architectural sketchbook. The Codex Coner
(Ashby's publication of it is cited in note 2, p. 285 above) is a good example of the
new Cinquecento type.

[3] H. Saalman, 'The authorship of the Pazzi Palace, *Art Bulletin*, xlvi (1964), 388–94,
esp. p. 392, calls attention to the Albertian character of Giuliano's approach.

tectural detail.[1] It is tempting and not implausible to suggest that the change in the character of Giuliano's drawings from the antique coincides with the printing of the first edition of Alberti's *De re aedificatoria* in 1485. A letter has recently been published which indicates that Lorenzo de' Medici's interest in the book was so great that he had it read to him, fascicule by fascicule, as it came off the press.[2] He would hardly have failed to bring it about that his leading architect was fully acquainted with the work, though it is unlikely that Giuliano would have needed it brought to his attention. And in fact a drawing in Giuliano's small parchment sketchbook in Siena (Pl. 8*c*), whose significance appears to have been overlooked, definitely establishes Giuliano's knowledge of Alberti's text.[3] For it is simply a graphic presentation of the Albertian description of the Ionic order.[4]

All this raises the problem of a possible influence of Giuliano on Bramante and the possibility that it was above all Giuliano who was responsible for Bramante's coming to understand the ancient system of the orders. But this question cannot in the present state of knowledge be satisfactorily answered, and as it carries one beyond the frontier of 1500 I will simply state it and stop.

[1] The question (full of uncertainties) of the dating of Giuliano's drawings is discussed by Huelsen, *Il libro di Giuliano da Sangallo*, text vol., pp xxv–xxviii.

[2] Mario Martelli, 'I pensieri architettonici del Magnifico', *Commentari*, XVII (1966), 107.

[3] Siena, Biblioteca Comunale, Cod. s. IV. 8, fo. 35 (published by R. Falb, Siena, 1902).

[4] Alberti describes the Ionic base in VII, 7 (*ed. cit.* pp. 570–3) and the Ionic capital in VII, 8 (pp. 576–83).

INDEX

Figures in heavy type indicate that the topic in question is discussed at some length. Figures in italics indicate that a reference is given. Where the reference is to a modern book or article, the name of the author follows in brackets. With a few exceptions such as Petrarch, names of writers after the sixth century A.D. are given in the form used in their country of origin, but where this might lead to difficulties, cross-references have been provided.

INDEX

Sallust (*cont.*)
166, by John of Salisbury, 170, by
Otto von Freising, 167, by Peter the
Venerable, 170, by Petrarch, 219, by
Richer, 170, 173, 173 n. 3, by Snorri
Sturluson, 15, 147, 148, in the arts
course, **168–71**, in popular proverbs,
170, 171
Salutati, Coluccio (1330–1406): describes
Baptistery at Florence, 271; echoes
Ausonius, 71, *71 n. 8*, mentions him,
71, *71 n. 7*, owns MS of his works, 71,
71 n. 6; ideal of an active life, 229;
political activity, 227, 228
de Nobilitate Legum, 237; *de Seculo et Reli-
gione, 71 n. 8*, 229
Sanctus, Louis friend of Petrarch ('Soc
rates,' Ludwig van Kempen, 1304–61),
222
Sand, George (1804–76), 140, *140 n. 3*
(J & P. Courcelle)
Sandys, J. E., *8*, 14
Sangallo, Antonio da, the Younger, archi-
tect (1485–1546): drawings of the
Pantheon, 265, *266 n. 1 to 4* (A. Bartoli),
Pls. 3 a and b
Sangallo, Francesco da, 285 n. 2
Sangallo, Giuliano da, architect (1445–
1516): conception of the Doric and
Ionic orders, 276, 287, 287 n. 4, Pl. 8 c;
debt to Alberti, 286, 287, 287 n. 4, Pl.
8 c; drawings, 286, 286 n. 2, 287, 287 n. 1
(Huelsen), Fig. 5 (282); Pls. 8 c and 12 c;
Palazzo Gondi, Florence, 274, Pl. 6 b;
Palazzo Pazzi, *286 n. 3* (H. Saalman)
Sanpaolesi, P., Fig. 1 (278), Fig. 4 (280)
Sanskrit Literature: its use of personification,
250, 251; *The Moon of Intellect*, 251,
251 n. 1 (J. W. Boissevain, Jai Dev,
M. Schuyler); Vidayakara's *Treasury*,
250, *250 n. 2* (D. H. Ingalls)
Sansovino, Andrea de', sculptor (1460–
1529), 74, 265, 265 n. 1
Sassetti, Francesco (1421–90), 255, *255 n. 2*
(A. Warburg), 256
Satirists: commentaries on the ancient, 12,
83–94; their appeal for the Middle
Ages, 85
Saturn, Throne of, 73, 74, 74 n. 1
Saxo Grammaticus, historian of Denmark
(1150–*c.* 1216), debt to Martianus
Capella, 147
Saxons, 85, 86, 92, 170
Scala, Bartolommeo, Florentine humanist
(1430–97), 111 n. 1

Scaliger, Joseph Justus (1540–1609), *Glossae
Scaligeri* (attributed to Isidore of
Seville), 91
Scandinavia: classical influences, 144,
144 n. 3 (H. Shetelig), 145; libraries,
medieval, 146, 146 n. 2 (P. Lehmann),
modern, 39
Scandinavian vernaculars, 147
Schalk, F., 21, 22
Schaller, D., 17; publications, *156 n. 1*,
157 n. 2
Schirmer, W. F., 118
Schoeffer, John, publisher of Mainz, 106
Scholarship, classical: history of, 24, **119–
28**; impact of New Testament studies
on, *11 n. 2* (L. D. Reynolds, N. G.
Wilson)
Scholia, see Commentaries
Schut, Englebert (*fl.* 1489), 110, 111, 113
n. 10, 117; relations with Erasmus,
110 n. 3; *Ars Dictandi*, 117
Science: Arabic influence on, 204, 214;
Christian speculation on, 149; encyclo-
pedists on, 149; history of, 21, 25
Scipio Africanus (234–183 B.C.), 167
Scotti peregrini: **45–8**; influence on later
commentators, 83; quarrels, 151,
153–4, *154 n. 1* (B. Bischoff)
Script: Anglo-Saxon, 47; Caroline, 58;
Gothic, 58, 63; humanist, 41, Niccoli's,
63, Petrarch's 70, *70 n. 4* (A. Petrucci);
Irish, 47, 48; pre-Carolingian, 58
Scriptoria: Brescia, 59; decline of monastic
scriptoria, 122
Sculpture: influence of classical models, 10;
personification in, 248; throne of
Saturn, 73, 74
Sedulius Scottus, grammarian and poet
(d. *c.* 859), 45, 48, 49
Semi-Pelagians, 133, *133 n. 1* (P. Cour-
celle)
Seneca the Elder, L(?) Annaeus (*c.* 55 B.C.–
A.D. 37), *Declamationes* owned by For-
zetta, 78
Seneca the Younger, L. Annaeus (*c.* 5 B.C.–
A.D.65): influence on letter-writing,
105, 111; role in the development of
humanism, 226; used by Adrianus
Carthusiensis, 221, by Petrarch, 219;
works: in Vienna Staatsbibl. MS lat.
3134, 79, 80, *80 n. 1* (S. Endlicher),
owned by Forzetta, 78
Epistolae: codex Querinianus, 9, 58
(A. Beltrami), 59, 60, *65* (C. Villa);
textual tradition, 53, 121; used by

316

INDEX

Seneca the Younger (*cont.*)
twelfth-cent. writers, 53 (Dechanet, L. D. Reynolds)
Quaestiones Naturales: used by encyclopedists, 204, by Vincent de Beauvais, 214
Sententiae: in Petrarch's de Remediis, 217–19, 221, 222, 224; *see also* Proverbs
Ser Ugolino Peruzzi, Filippo de, Florentine scholar and MS collector (fifteenth century), 227
Serlio, Sebastiano, architect (1475–1552), 259, *259 n. 2*
Servius, M. Honoratus (*fl.* fourth/fifth cent.): commentary on Virgil, 11, 163 n. 3; its influence 12; sought by Forzetta, 75
Sextus Empiricus (*fl. c.* 190), 214 n. 3
Shakespeare, William: debt to Erasmus, 114, *114 n. 2* (R. Soellner)
Sheldon-Williams, I. P., *200*
Shield-motif, 144, *144 n. 3* (H. Rosenfeld, H. Shetelig)
Siberch (John Lair of Sieburg, publisher *fl.* 1520–53), 106
Sibylline Oracles, 145, *145 n. 2* and *3* (A. C. Bang, B. Bischoff, V. Rydberg)
Siena: Giuliano da Sangallo's drawings at, 286 n. 2, 287 n. 3, Pl. 8c
Silesius, Angelus, German poet (Johann Scheffler, 1624–77), 142
Simone de Bidiniano (*fl.* thirteenth cent.), 54, 55
Sixtus IV (Pope 1471–84), 263
Smalley, B., 19, 94, 254 n. 2; publications, *12 n. 1, 101 n. 3*
Smith, Sir Thomas, lawyer and humanist (1513–77), *244 n. 3* (W. Camden)
Snorri Sturluson (1179–1241): his Art of Poetry, 148 n. 3; influence of Sallust on, 15, 147, *147 n. 2* (J. Benediktsson, S. Nordal), 148; *Prose Edda* 148, 149, *149 n. 1* (R. Allers, F. Rico, A. Holtsmark); *see also* Olaf Kritaskald, his nephew
Solinus, C. Julius (*fl.* 260), used by Neckam, 204
Solitude, Petrarch on, 226, 228
Spain, libraries, 39
Spalato, *see* Split
Spanish Language, its conformity with Greek, 243, *243 n. 2* (B. Aldrete, D. Matute, J. de Valdes)
Speculatio, 232–3; in Francis Bacon, 235; in Bodin, 234
Speroni, Sperone, Italian man of letters (1500–88), 232, *238*

Split, MS of Juvenal at, 38
Stadter, P. A. *33, 66*
Statius, P. Papinius (*c.* 45–96): school author, 55; work owned by Forzetta, 77; *Thebais*, 49
Stephanus, *see* Estienne
Stockholm, library, 39
Stoicism: co-exists with Christianity in Petrarch, 21, 217, *217 n. 2* (K. Heitmann), 218; in the abridgements of de Remediis, 219, 222; Stoic interpretation of Apollo's attributes, *252 n. 1* (R. Pfeiffer), of Homer's catena aurea, 210
Strasbourg, library, 35
Strozzi, Alessandro (*fl.* 1474), 262, *262 n. 3* (A. P. Frutaz, G. Scaglia)
Style: in ecclesiastical Latin, 46; influence of classical Latin, 16; in letter-writing, 107–11; medieval historians as stylists, 170, 171
Suetonius (C. Suetonius Tranquillus, *c.* 69–140), 35 n. 1; influence on medieval historians, 165; Paris MS lat 5802 of his works contains poems by Ausonius, 67, *67 n. 6* (E. Pellegrin); used by Heiric and John of Salisbury, 55
Sulla, L. Cornelius (138–78 B.C.), 168
Sulpicia (late first cent. B.C.), 38
Sulpizio, Giovanni, grammarian and rhetorician (*fl.* 1475), *109*
Surigonus, Stephanus, taught at Louvain and Oxford (fifteenth cent.), 117
Suthul, 173
Sverri (king of Norway, 1184–1202), 147, *147 n. 1* (G. M. Gathorne-Hardy)
Sweden: Greeks in, 143; libraries, 39
Sweeney, R. D., 2–4, 4 n. 1, 23
Sweynheim and Pannartz (printers, *fl.* 1465–71), 123
Switzerland: libraries, medieval, 34, 34 n. 1, modern, 39
Syme, Sir Ronald, 172, *172 n. 2*
Symon de Parma (fourteenth cent.), 75

Tacitus, C. Cornelius (35–120), 172, supposed twelfth-cent. citation, 51; Leidensis MS, 122, *122 n. 4* (F. R. D. Goodyear)
Tarpeian Rock, 172
Teichoskopia, 49
Terence (P. Terentius Afer, *c.* 195–159 B.C.): cited by Guillaume de Conches, 208, *208 n. 2*; commentary by Donatus, 11

317

DATE DUE

JE-6'72			
AG 12'72			
JY 28'89			
APR 0 4 2007			
DEC 1 3 2006			
GAYLORD			PRINTED IN U.S.A.